THE FOCAL EASY GUIDE TO

DISCREET COMBUSTION 3

The Focal Easy Guide Series

Focal Easy Guides are the best choice to get you started with new software, whatever your level. Refreshingly simple, they do *not* attempt to cover everything, focusing solely on the essentials needed to get immediate results.

Ideal if you need to learn a new software package quickly, the Focal Easy Guides offer an effective, time-saving introduction to the key tools, not hundreds of pages of confusing reference material. The emphasis is on quickly getting to grips with the software in a practical and accessible way to achieve professional results.

Highly illustrated in color, explanations are short and to the point. Written by professionals in a user-friendly style, the guides assume some computer knowledge and an understanding of the general concepts in the area covered, ensuring they aren't patronizing!

Series editor: Rick Young (www.digitalproduction.net)

Director and Founding Member of the UK Final Cut User Group, Apple Solutions Expert and freelance television director/editor, Rick has worked for the BBC, Sky, ITN, CNBC and Reuters. Also a Final Cut Pro Consultant and author of the best-selling *The Easy Guide to Final Cut Pro*.

Titles in the series:

The Easy Guide to Final Cut Pro 3, **Rick Young**

The Focal Easy Guide to Final Cut Pro 4, **Rick Young**

The Focal Easy Guide to Final Cut Express, **Rick Young**

The Focal Easy Guide to Maya 5, **Jason Patnode**

The Focal Easy Guide to Discreet combustion 3, **Gary M. Davis**

The Focal Easy Guide to Premiere Pro, **Tim Kolb**

The Focal Easy Guide to Flash MX 2004, **Birgitta Hosea**

The Focal Easy Guide to DVD Studio Pro 2, Rick Young

THE FOCAL EASY GUIDE TO DISCREET COMBUSTION 3

For new users and professionals

GARY M. DAVIS

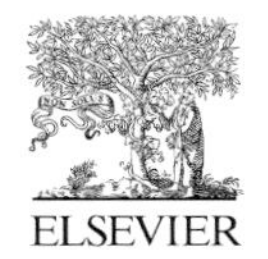

AMSTERDAM • BOSTON • HEIDELBERG • LONDON • NEW YORK • OXFORD
PARIS • SAN DIEGO • SAN FRANCISCO • SINGAPORE • SYDNEY • TOKYO
Focal Press is an imprint of Elsevier

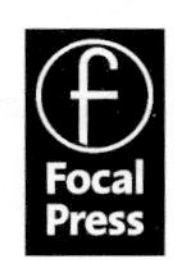

Focal Press
An imprint of Elsevier
Linacre House, Jordan Hill, Oxford OX2 8DP
30 Corporate Drive, Burlington, MA 01803

First published 2004
Reprinted 2005

British Library Cataloguing in Publication Data
A catalogue record for this book is available from the British Library

Library of Congress Cataloguing in Publication Data
A catalogue record for this book is available from the Library of Congress

ISBN 0 240 51955 8

Typeset by Newgen Imaging Systems (P) Ltd, Chennai, India
Printed and bound in Italy

Contents

About this Book

Since I began using and teaching combustion, I have had the privilege of instructing many artists from varied disciplines in the graphics community. While doing so, I have noticed and kept extensive records of the common learning hurdles that come up again and again to new users. At all times, these learning hurdles and workflow issues have been my primary focus for this book.

No volume or manual could be the entire resource for an application, and I realized this going into this project. Accepting this from the outset, I wrote this Easy Guide with a strong emphasis on the real world, everyday use of combustion and a concentration of getting the beginner over the initial, common stumbling blocks. At its heart, this book is all about workflow . . . the 'art' is entirely up to you.

This book assumes a small level of familiarity with computer graphics from you, the reader. This is, certainly, not to say one needs to be an accomplished animator prior to reading this book. On the contrary, combustion is an excellent tool for users wishing to make the transition from creating static pictures to moving images. It is, however, advantageous if you have at least a basic knowledge of working with an application such as Photoshop, Paint Shop Pro, Illustrator, Freehand and/or CorelDraw. Again, it is not required, but it can help.

In addition to my notes from teaching combustion in a classroom environment, I have pulled from my experience of actually using combustion on many different types of production tasks. This information has been gathered and edited down to become the Easy Guide in your hands. Great effort was put forth to make this the resource I wish I had when learning this phenomenally powerful application. I sincerely hope you enjoy this book and it gets you that much closer to creating spectacular images with Discreet combustion.

Gary M. Davis
Visual Effects Artist
Discreet Training Specialist
http://www.visualZ.com

Platforms

This book was created using combustion 3 for the Windows platform. Because combustion uses the 'Discreet Artist' interface, the only visual way the Macintosh and Windows versions differ from one another is the menu bar at the very top of the screen. The screen captures and projects provided should look and function identically on the Macintosh platform.

All keyboard and mouse conventions will be the same except for the three exceptions listed below. On the right is the Macintosh equivalent to the Windows function listed on the left (and used throughout this book).

PC	Macintosh
ALT key	Option key
Control key	Command key
Right mouse click	Control key + mouse click

About the Footage

While many of the lessons in this book are generic to any combustion project or piece of video or imagery, several clips have been provided for you to use while reading along with the book itself. In addition to my own work, I am providing images from a few great sources. I would like to recognize, thank and encourage you to visit these fine vendors in stock imagery:

www.MarlinStudios.com
www.DigitalJuice.com

Chroma Key sequence used with permission of Haxan Films and Clutch (from the 'Spacegrass' music video) © 2003 Haxan Films.

It should be noted that the footage made available for this book has been *extremely* compressed to reduce download time. In many cases, the original clips have been resized, shortened in length, and/or cropped to make them smaller. The quality of the files obtained for the lessons in this book is *not* representative of the fine material that these vendors typically provide end users. It should also be noted that combustion, like any application, runs slower with compressed footage. The more it is compressed, the more the application has to work at first decoding the files to use them. Working in combustion with uncompressed files will be faster than working with highly compressed ones such as these.

To download the files associated with this book, you will need to go to the Focal Press website: www.focalpress.com/companions/0240519558.
The total size of the download is approximately 56 megabytes.

Note: Since the footage is downloaded and is not on a read-only CDROM, I recommend making a second copy of the footage and project files so that if anything accidentally gets overwritten or deleted, you have a backup.

About the Author

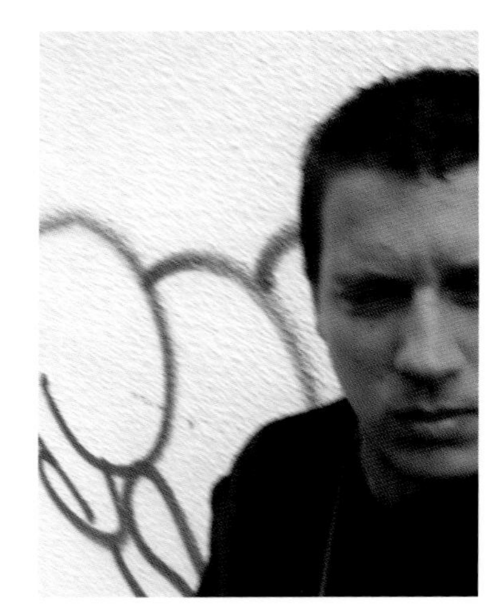

Gary M. Davis has an extensive background in broadcast design and motion-based simulator ride content creation. He has studied sculpture, photography, painting and graphic design and in 1992 received a BFA in computer animation. He then began a three-year partnership that kept him touring and doing video performance work for various recording artists including Moby, the Prodigy, Dee Lite, 808 State and Meat Beat Manifesto.

The next six years he spent developing motion-based simulator rides and leading the design team that eventually obtained over a dozen patents for the acquisition and delivery of cylindrical and hemispherical, stereoscopic digitally projected theaters.

In 1999, Gary went out on his own after becoming one of Discreet's certified Training Specialists for 3ds max and in 2000 he additionally obtained certification as a combustion DTS. Past networks that have featured his work include ABC, Fox, MTV, USA and The Sci-Fi Channel. Gary has also performed production work for Compaq, Budweiser, Lockheed, Haxan Films, Disney and Universal Studios, among others.

Gary now owns and operates visualZ, LLC, an Orlando, Florida-based consulting and training firm. In addition to contract production work and private software training, he is also a regular instructor for the Oregon3D training center and demo artist for Discreet and others at many industry trade shows. Gary has written for numerous magazines and has been a contributing author to the official Discreet Courseware and Mastering 3D Studio MAX r3.

The *Easy Guide to Discreet combustion 3* is his first solo book.

A Few Thanks . . .

First and foremost, obvious thanks go out to everyone at Discreet. You all create my bread and butter and I really appreciate you making work translate into play for me every day. A special thanks to the entire training and trade show teams, especially Roger Cusson, Diane Duffey, Shawn Hendriks and Angus Mackay. Additionally, I can't possibly say enough about combustion's development team. . . especially Josee Belhumeur. You are my friend and colleague and without you this project would have been entirely different for me. Endless thanks go out to you and your group for this wonderful gift you have given me as an artist.

I would also like to sincerely thank you, the reader, and all of my past students and production clients. I am humbled and grateful that you invest your resources in me. You are a constant reminder that using, demoing and teaching software are three extremely different things. I continue to strive to be the best I can be at all three of these disciplines largely because of you all.

Focal Press has been a real pleasure to work with and I would like to especially thank Marie Hooper for her guidance, patience, humor, and support throughout the entire process.

Everyone at the Oregon3D training center gets a big, virtual hug and my gratitude for letting me continue to visit and instruct on your behalf. Extra thanks to Mark Noland and your beautiful family for the continued hospitality towards me during my visits to this incredible training facility.

To my family and friends. . . thank you for keeping me sane and not allowing me to completely lose it to the digital realm. This goes especially for Red and Jean Resener, my closest cohorts. You repeatedly remind me that getting out, eating a good steak, having a tall drink and shaking my ass can often be far more important than making pixels change colors. I owe you both more than you know for this grounding to reality.

Lastly, to Toni. . . I sincerely appreciate your unending patience and support of my digital addiction. You complete me. You are my sweetie pie, my very own fairy princess.

PREFERENCES, UI AND KEY TERMS

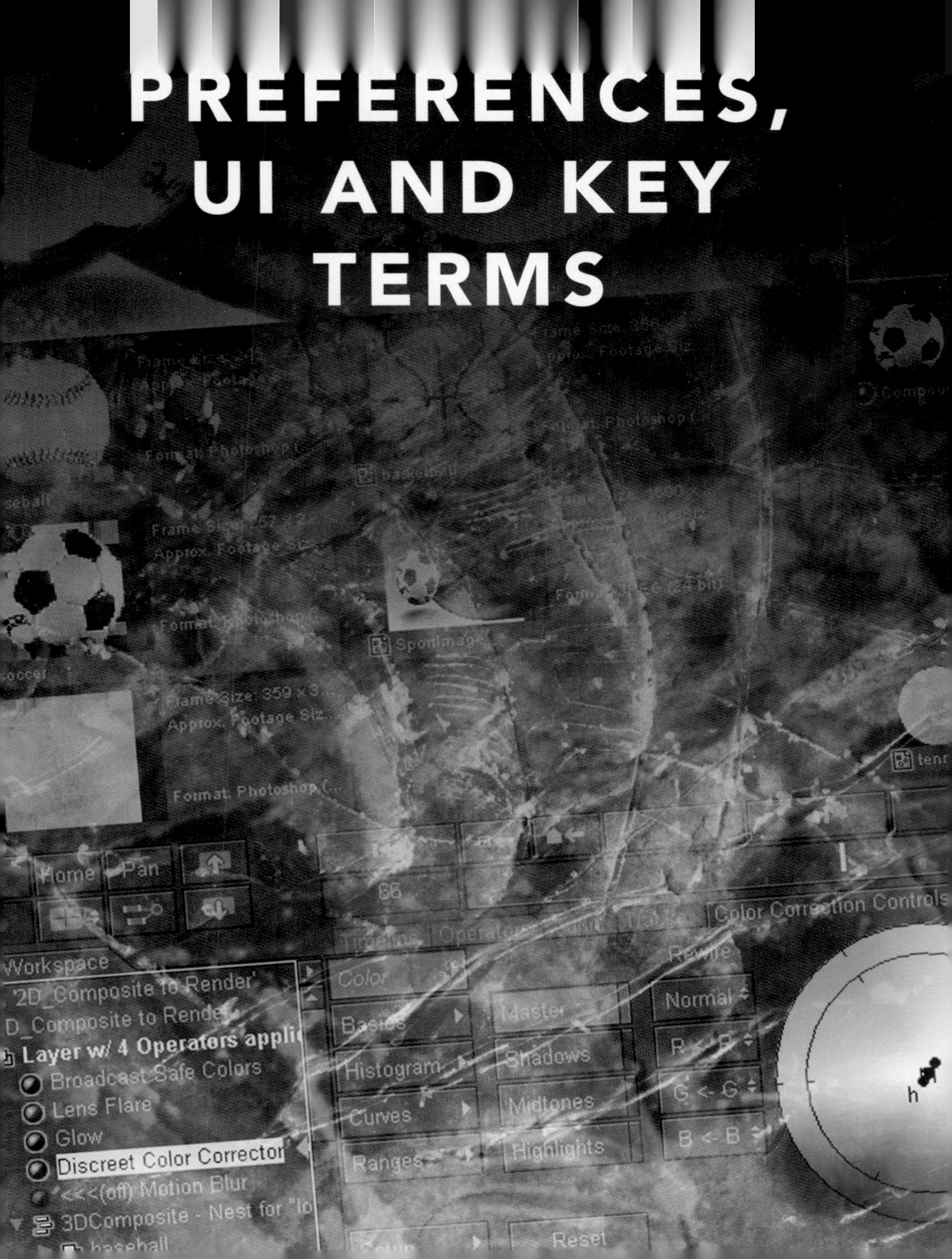

And So it Begins . . .

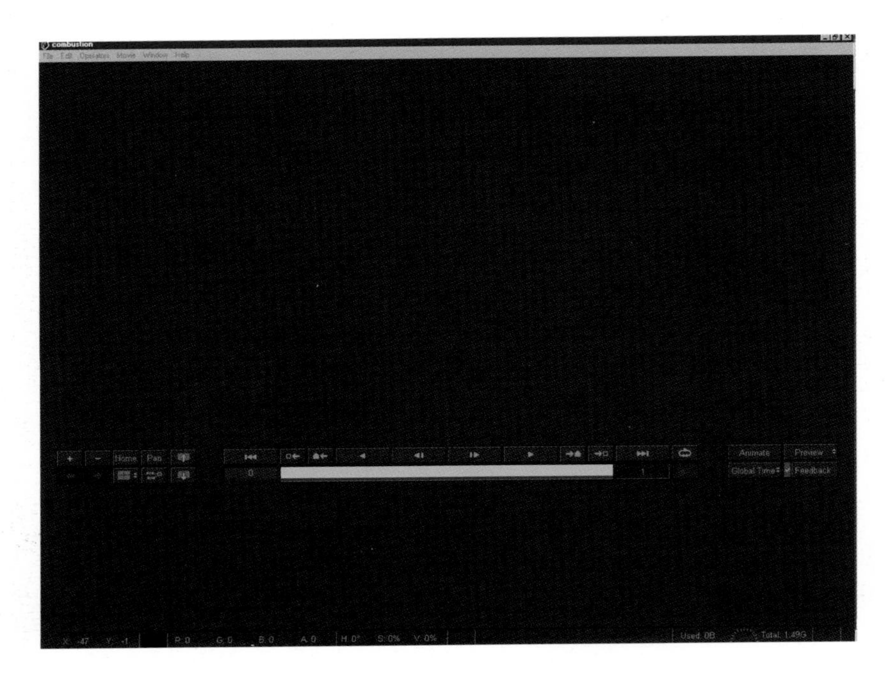

. . . with a blank slate. The Discreet combustion user interface can, admittedly, be a bit intimidating at first. This is because it is so visually different than many graphics applications you may have used in the past.

Because the interface is so barren at times and yet at other moments seemingly convoluted with sliders, it can get confusing at first. Perhaps the most important thing to understand about combustion's entire user interface (UI) is the fact that the user controls what and how images and tools are seen and edited, and only the controls relevant to the current operation are present at any given time.

At first, you will often and undoubtedly think tools or controls for something should have been somewhere and they are not. This is probably because you have not 'asked' combustion to display the tools relevant to the item you wish to edit. What may at first seem complicated will make life a lot easier as you become comfortable with combustion. We will identify several ways to control this process in a moment, but before we dive into combustion, let's first prepare our computer system.

Quick Visit to the Preferences

The default settings for all of the preferences should be fine at first. While only some points regarding the preferences will be mentioned here, others will be addressed elsewhere in this book. A few should, nevertheless, be addressed now, at the very beginning. As you progress, you will learn how to change your user preferences to accommodate different workflows and project needs.

> **Note:** At any time, if you ever feel you need to completely 'reset combustion', you can find and delete the file named *Host.ini* that pertains to combustion. This is similar to a reinstall of the application and deleting this file will reset all the user preferences. You should only do this action as needed.

Open the user preferences from the File pull-down menu. You can also bring up the user preferences using hotkeys of Ctrl + ; (Control and semicolon keys).

> **Note:** For the purposes of this book, the style of hierarchical menus and commands will be often listed in a manner that is 'vague to specific'. For example, to select Preferences from the File menu, it may be indicated as such: File > Preferences.

Figure 1.1 shows the user preferences panel that can be accessed at any time while working in combustion. The categories of preferences are on the left while the specifics of a highlighted category are detailed on the right.

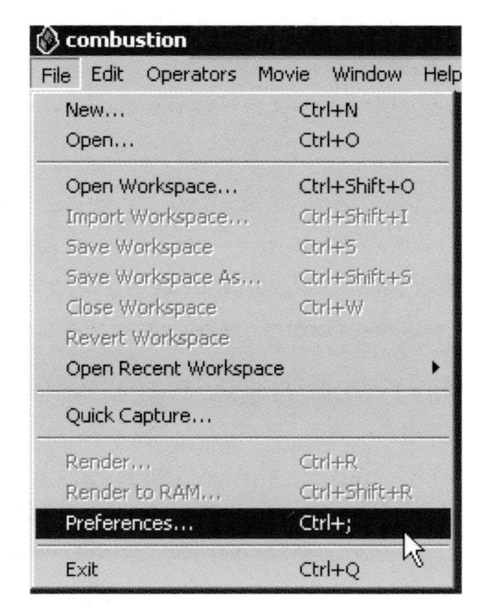

General – Several common parameters such as multiprocessing, monitor setups and different memory options can be addressed here. Many of these settings can help you optimize combustion to perform differently on different hardware setups.

If you are using a multiprocessor computer or one that supports Hyper-threading, you

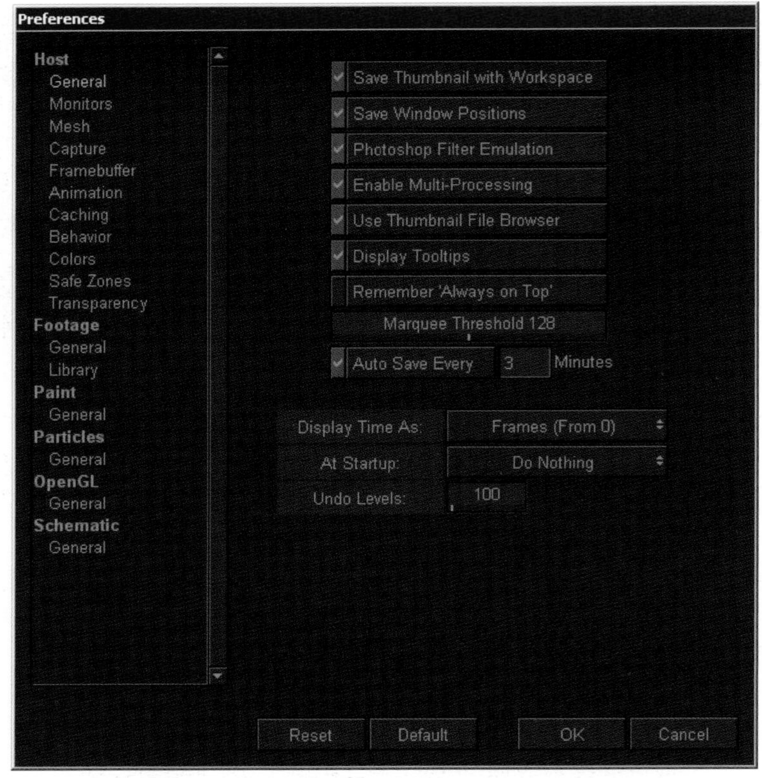

Figure 1.1

should make sure you have Enable Multi-Processing (Enable Multi-Processing) checked to utilize all processors.

The Use Thumbnail File Browser (Use Thumbnail File Browser) option is suggested, and will be explained in greater detail in Chapter 2. You can, however, turn off the Thumbnail Browser here, should you choose to at any time.

Tool tips (Display Tooltips) are the pop-ups that will help you to learn the different tools within combustion. When enabled, text will appear if you hover your cursor over many tools. Figure 1.2 shows a tool tip for the paint toolset.

Auto Save (Auto Save Every 3 Minutes) can also be especially helpful when starting out in combustion for the first few times. When enabled, combustion creates

a backup file of the current Workspace file for you and saves to this file at a set interval.
A combustion Workspace file named *FILENAME.CWS* will have a backup name of *FILENAME_BAK.CWS*. Enabling this option can dramatically lower the worry about frequently saving your work.

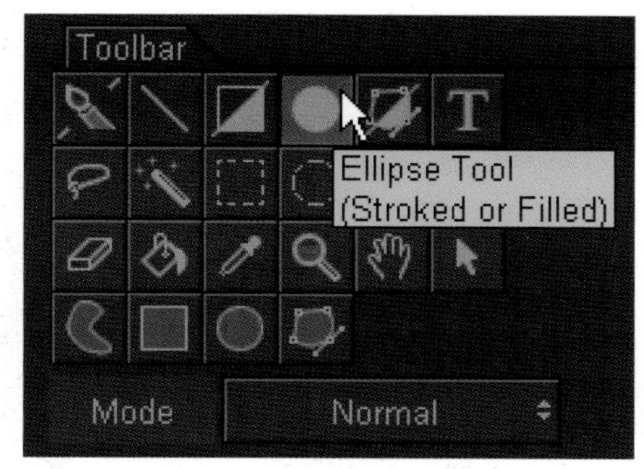

Figure 1.2

Monitors – Figure 1.3 shows where you define how the combustion interface is displayed on multiple (up to four) computer monitors. Here, you can also enable 'floating' for various menus within the combustion application itself. Many menus

Preferences

Host
General
Monitors
Mesh
Capture
Framebuffer
Animation
Caching
Behavior
Colors
Safe Zones
Transparency
Footage
General
Library
Paint
General
Particles
General
OpenGL
General
Schematic
General

Monitor Setup

Monitors: 2
Current: 1 2
Left: 0 Width: 1280
Top: 0 Height: 1024
Menu Height: 236

	Float	Palette Setup	
Views		1	2
Frame Controls		1	2
Info		1	2
Filmstrip		1	2
Toolbar	On	1	2
Workspace	On	1	2
Operators	On	1	2
Timeline	On	1	2
Tracker	On	1	2
Audio	On	1	2
Operator Controls		1	2

Reset Default OK Cancel

Figure 1.3

in combustion can overlap by default; floating some of them gives you the option of putting them in a different location than the default (docked) location.

Changing the number of monitors at the top of this dialog requires you to exit combustion and relaunch the application, but the other options here take effect immediately after you click OK to exit the preferences.

In Figure 1.4, a custom, two-monitor layout can be seen. Also notice how the Workspace panel can be seen floating just over the viewport displaying the basketball footage. This was accomplished by using the Monitor preferences seen in Figure 1.3. Floating the Workspace panel can often be a good idea for new users, because in doing so, you will be able to see both the Workspace panel and the Toolbar simultaneously.

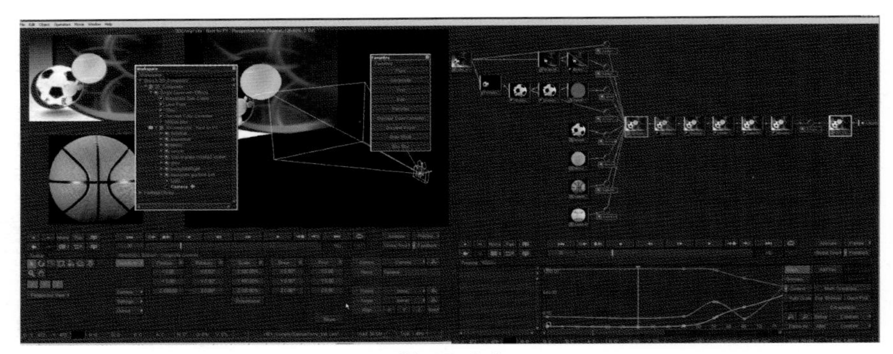

Figure 1.4

The 'Menu Height' setting of the monitor preferences changes height (in pixels) of separation between the viewports and the rest of the lower portion of the UI. You should try changing the Menu Height if you, for example, work primarily on DV footage and on a computer monitor set to 1600 × 1200 resolution. Different Menu Height settings will accommodate different aspect ratio images and viewport layouts dramatically.

Caching – Sets the maximum computer system memory (RAM) that you allow combustion to recognize. You can set the value as a percentage (%) of system memory or a specific file size in Mbytes (megabytes) of RAM (Maximum Cache Usage: 1747.88 MBytes). The default allows you to run other applications at the same time as combustion. If you plan on working primarily or exclusively with combustion, you may want to increase this preference slightly. It is not recommended to use 100%. While this will enable combustion to access to all system memory, it will cause any other applications running to take a dramatic performance hit.

Colors – It might seem odd to mention such a cosmetic thing, but people often feel very strongly about the look of their work environment and often like to adjust it to their specific needs.

In Figure 1.5, there are two different UI color versions of the exact same project. The darker image on the left is the 'Charcoal' color scheme and the lighter one on the right is the 'Platinum' color scheme.

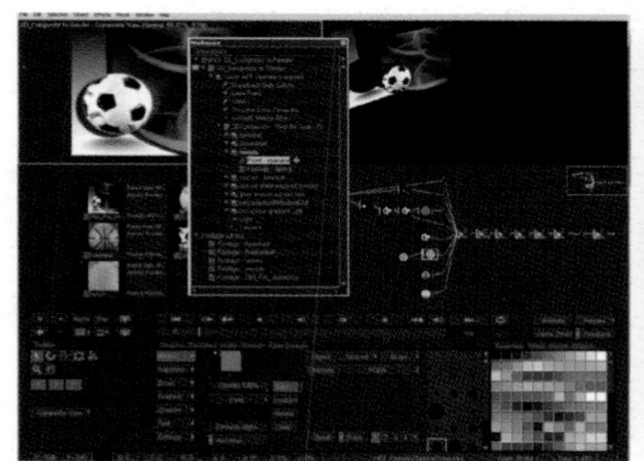
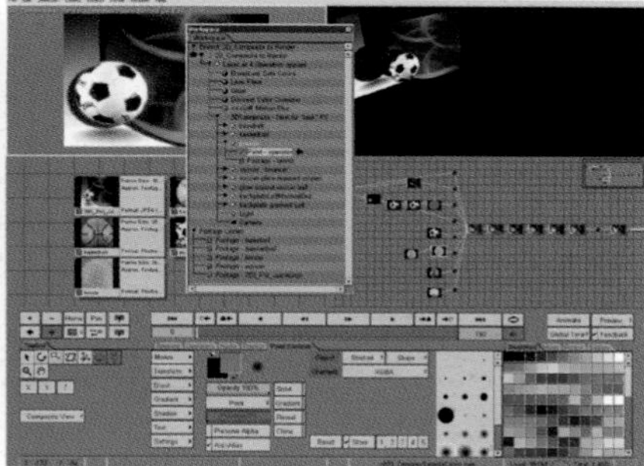

Figure 1.5

As a user, you can experiment with these color preferences to determine which is more comfortable for your particular taste. Remember that these are just two presets. You may create your own unique and individual color scheme at any time using the color pods seen in Figure 1.6.

Pen Colors			
Screen Background		Text Edit Button	
Window Background		Slider Button	
Button Fill		Label	
Button Highlight		Dark Text	
Button Frame		Medium Text	
Shine Border		Light Text	
Shadow Border		Highlight Color	

Figure 1.6

Tip: Many users like the dark interface because it is easier on the eyes when staring at a monitor for several hours at a time.

Major Project Components

Listed below are several key terms that you may have used or heard previously; however, here they are described as specifically defined in combustion. For example, while you may have worked with layer-based applications in the past, combustion has a very specific meaning for the term 'layer' which may be slightly different than in other software.

Please take a moment to familiarize yourself with these critical definitions and concepts within Discreet combustion. These will all be discussed in depth throughout this book, but familiarizing yourself with these definitions as soon as possible will ease the learning curve tremendously. Admittedly, even the simple (?) definitions below are somewhat involved. This cursory overview, if nothing else, is meant to expose you to the major terms of the application. Don't be alarmed if the next page or two have you scratching your head, just let it sink in a bit and, perhaps, come back to them after you have worked in combustion for a short amount of time. Now here we go . . .

Footage is the most basic element in combustion; that is, there is nothing more base level than footage. It all starts here. Individual pieces of footage can be very different in format, resolution, frame rate and bit depth, yet all work together in the same Workspace.

Operators are the numerous effects you can apply to footage such as blurs, paint, keyers, particles and color correctors (to name a very few). Third-party plugins are listed and accessed as operators along with the rest of the built-in effects that are included with combustion. Operators are the functions that change the look of your footage in a series of events occurring to your source footage. No amount of time or writing could cover the vast array of 'looks' you can achieve with all the operators, primarily because their effects are so varied and also because even the order in which they are applied can drastically change the final look of a project. The results from combining various operators are, quite literally, infinite.

Layers are the primary building blocks of a composite. Layers can simply be the output of a single piece of footage brought into a composite, or they can be the end result of a series of several operators applied, in sequence, to a piece of footage. Layers, not footage, define transfer mode and can hold spatial transformations such as position, rotation and scale. For example, you cannot move footage. Instead, you move the layer that is made out of a piece of footage. You might consider a layer as a container of effects applied to one piece of footage.

Composites are the end result of one or more layers and are where you typically combine the numerous elements of your projects. A composite can either be flat and two-dimensional, or can literally be a 'porthole' into a true 3D environment complete with a camera and lights. A composite can have its own resolution, duration and frame rate that are independent of the layers within. Composites can be considered a window of a defined size/resolution that allow you to see your layers. Strangely enough, a composite is considered an operator itself, primarily because, within the Workspace, the output of an entire composite can become the single input to another operator or layer. This is called a *nested* composite and is an extremely powerful feature.

An **Edit** operator is similar to a Composite operator, in that it is like a window (with its own resolution) that views several elements together as one. The primary difference is that instead of stacking layers on top of each other as a composite does, the elements in an Edit operator are ordered end to end, or 'head to tail'. This process is exactly the same as other non-linear editing applications you may have used such as Avid, Premiere or Final Cut Pro.

Workspace defines the entire project at hand at any given time. A Workspace file saved by combustion has the file extension of CWS, which stands for combustion workspace. Although there can be only *one* Workspace file open at any given time, this Workspace can contain any number and combination of footage clips, operators, layers, branches and composites. To combine elements from different CWS files, you can *import* a Workspace into another and then save this with a new name to reflect the change. You still only have one CWS file open, but have brought the contents of another into the current file. The imported Workspace and all of its branches will become a new branch in the current Workspace, and either remain a separate branch or be available for use in the composite that was already present prior to the import. Phew, that sure is a mouthful and a lot to grasp, but for now just remember that there is only ever one Workspace open at a time. The big picture, if you will.

Note: 'Workspace' and 'Workspace panel' are not the same thing. The Workspace panel is detailed in Chapter 2.

Tip: With combustion 3, you can now launch more than one combustion session from the desktop. This allows you to build and merge elements between CWS project files using concurrently running combustion(s). Be advised that launching multiple sessions of combustion can be extremely taxing on a computer system.

Branches are defined as the individual chains or sequences of data that result when operators are strung together and applied to a single piece of footage. For example, if you have a JPG image that gets color corrected and then blurred, a branch would be created that is the entire series of the three events, starting with the source footage.

In the list below, a few random example branches are listed as might be found in a combustion project.

Footage > Operator
Footage > Operator > Operator > Operator > (etc.)
Footage > Operator > Layer > Composite
Footage > Edit
Footage > Operator > Edit > Composite . . .
Etc.

Note: An 'invalid branch' can exist if you have an operator (or series of operators) in the Workspace but it has no incoming or outgoing pixel information.

Remember that when considering the endless possibilities allowed, you must also appreciate that composites and edits are also really just special operators. This allows for branches of the Process Tree to stem in an infinite number of directions. The **Schematic View** is a graphical representation of this Process Tree.

Figure 1.7 shows a brief introduction to combustion's Schematic View. Seen here is a simple representation of the example just mentioned. This shows the resulting chain of events (or 'nodes') is a branch in the Workspace.

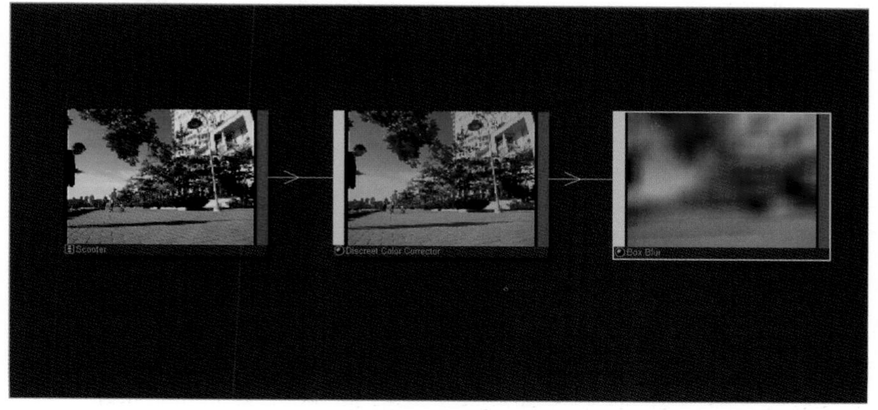

Figure 1.7

> **Note:** The Schematic will be discussed in greater detail in Chapter 5.

The last several paragraphs were, admittedly, a lot to take in this early on. Do not be alarmed if you are overwhelmed by the onslaught of terminology presented this early in the book.

Main Interface Explained Graphically

1. From the File menu, select Open Workspace. The **Thumbnail Browser** will appear.
2. Using the navigation portion on the left-hand side, navigate to the location of the project files and open the project file named *ch01_ComplexComp.cws*. This file was designed to present you with a lot of information at the outset. It is meant to be a rather complex project for a first look at many features.

Figure 1.8 shows a typical project in combustion.

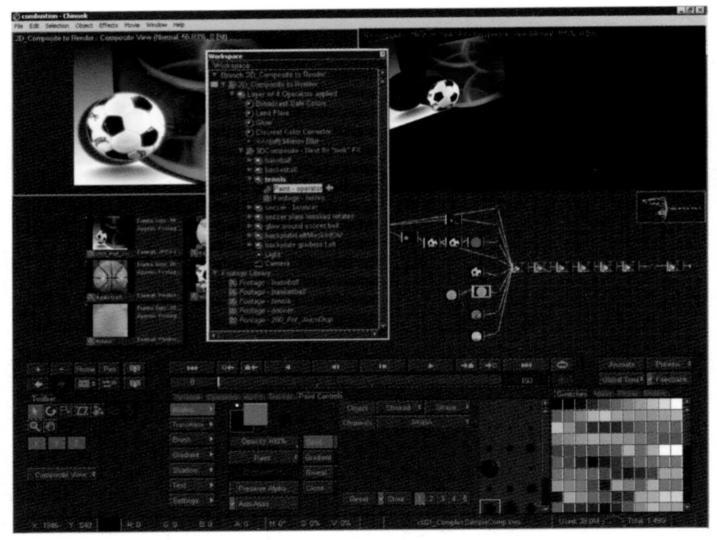

Figure 1.8

Outlined below are brief descriptions and highlights of each area.

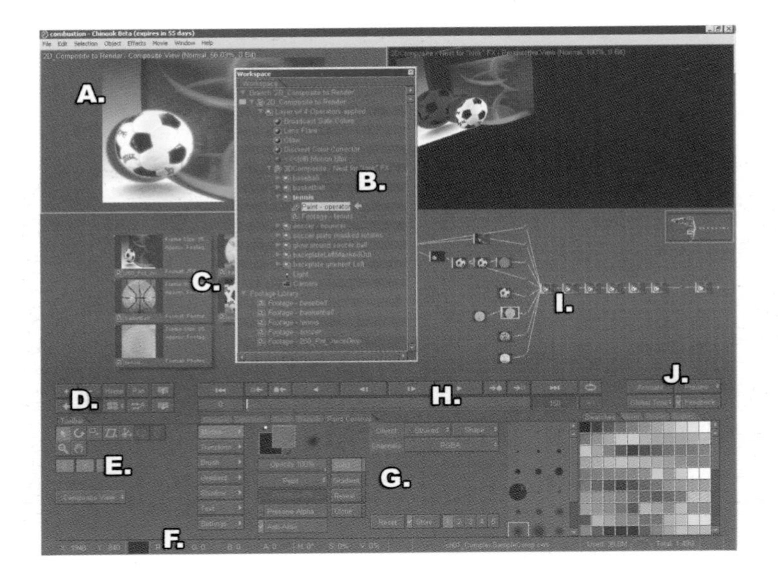

- **A** Viewports
- **B** The Workspace panel (currently floating)
- **C** The Footage Library (seen in a viewport)
- **D** Viewport Controls
- **E** Toolbar Palette
- **F** Info Bar
- **G** Operator/Footage Controls (depending)
- **H** Playback Controls
- **I** Schematic View
- **J** Animate button, Time, Feedback and Display options.

A. Viewports – In the example, there are four equal-sized viewports at the top of the combustion UI. The 'active viewport' is identified by the white outline around it. You can make a viewport the active viewport simply by clicking on it. The text in the upper left of each viewport will always provide valuable information about what that particular viewport is displaying. In Figure 1.9, you can see that the viewport is showing a composite view in Normal View Mode, is zoomed to 64.17% and is using 8-bit color. Additional clarification and detailed information about viewports will be addressed in Chapter 2.

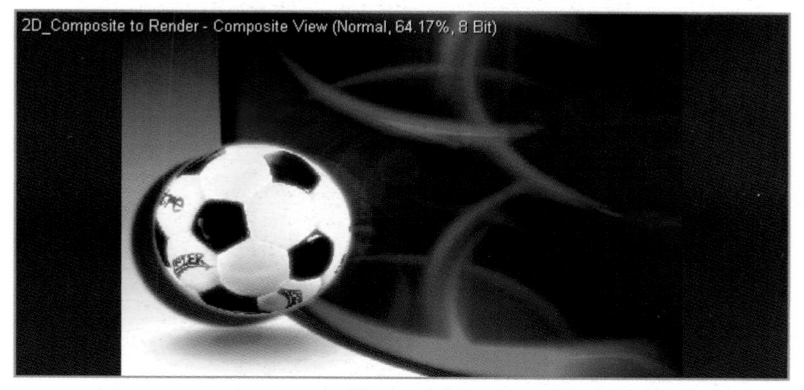

Figure 1.9

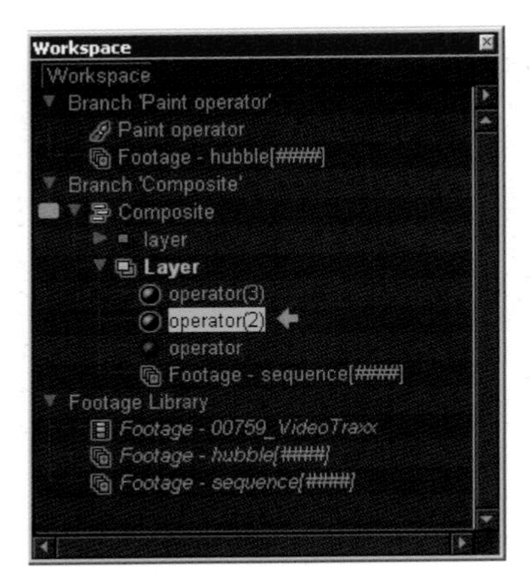

B. The Workspace Panel – Seen in 'floating' mode as set by the user preferences. Your Workspace panel tab may currently be tucked behind the Toolbar in area E. The Workspace panel is one location where you might organize footage, layers, and composites, rename items or turn on and off operators or layers, for example. At any time when working in combustion, you can also scroll down to the bottom of the Workspace panel and open a 'text-only' version of the **Footage Library.** The Footage Library is like a bin of all clips that are available within combustion's current Workspace.

C. The Footage Library – Seen here graphically in a viewport. Here, the Footage Library can be seen in a thumbnail mode rather than the text-based version available at the bottom of the Workspace panel. With few exceptions, anywhere you see a thumbnail representation of an element you can scrub the contents as if it were a VCR by clicking and dragging on the upper portion of the thumbnail. Your cursor will change to a horizontal arrow when ready to scrub the icon.

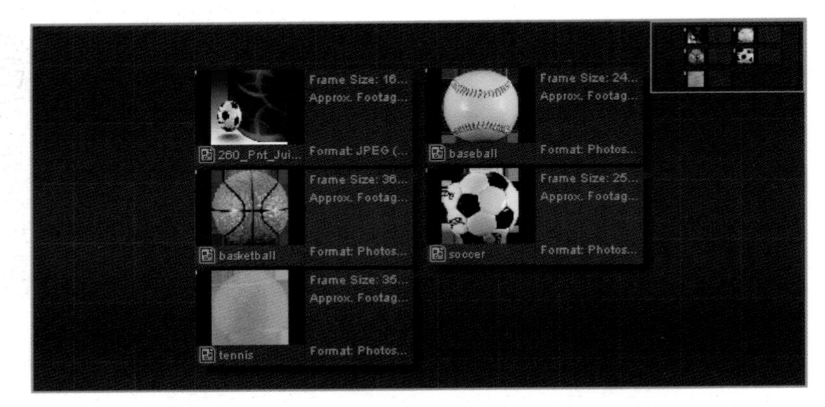

> **Note:** At any time, you can toggle the active viewport to the Footage Library by hitting Shift + F12. The same hotkey combination takes you back out.

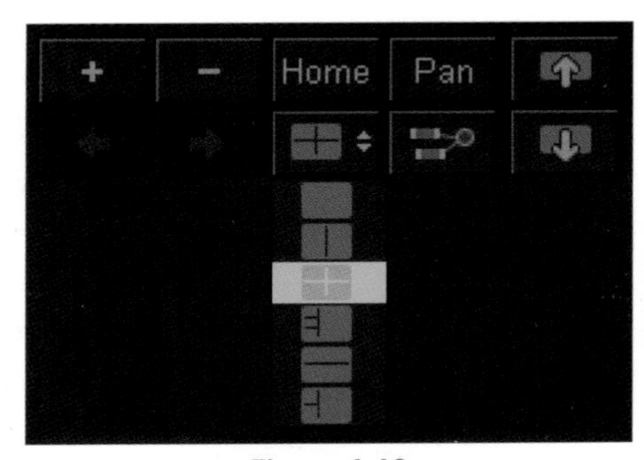

Figure 1.10

D. Viewport Controls – These controls will always be present when working in combustion. This is where you can zoom (+ - Home) and pan (Pan) viewports as well as switch between different viewport layouts using the drop-down menu seen in Figure 1.10. Here, there are also controls for enabling a Schematic View ( ) and icons ( ) controlling what gets displayed in area G.

Note: The Home and Pan buttons are 'scrub buttons' that allow you to click and drag directly on them.

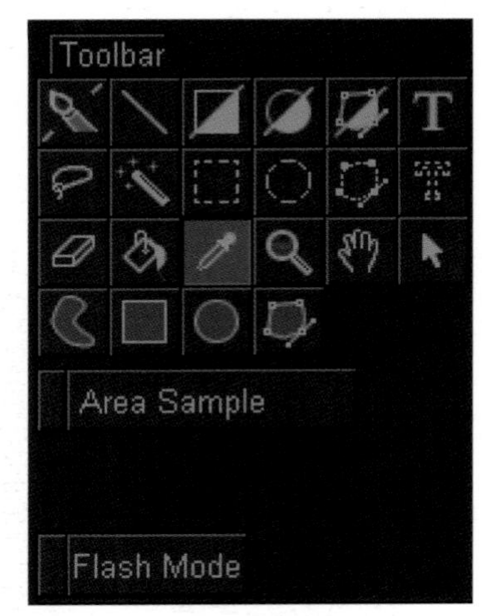

Figure 1.11

E. The Toolbar – This will constantly change depending on the contents of the Active Viewport or the currently selected item. For example, selecting the Paint operator or the Discreet Keyer operator will show vastly different toolsets. Figure 1.11 shows the Paint operator's Toolbar.

Tip: Using the default settings, the Toolbar and the Workspace panel can only be seen one at a time. Because the contents of one change depending on the other, this often confuses new users. For this reason, it is often a good idea to float either the Workspace panel or the Toolbar in the user preferences while initially learning combustion.

F. Info Palette – Along the bottom of the combustion UI is a thin strip of useful information. From left to right: X/Y coordinate information pertaining to the cursor location, the color of the pixel the cursor is over, an Error Alert indicator, the name of the project, or Workspace (*.CWS file) you have open, and the ever-looming Cache Meter.

> **Note:** Version 3 of combustion has the Cache Meter off by default. You can enable this by right clicking on the Info Palette.

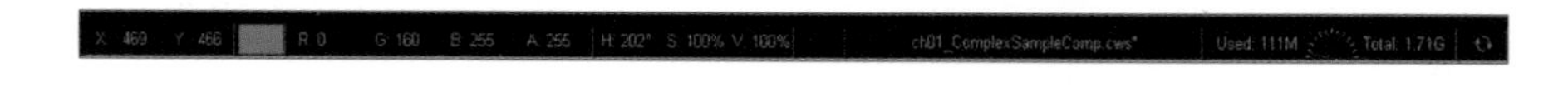

- ✔ Position
- ✔ Color Plot
- ✔ Color Values
- ✔ Error Alert
- ✔ Tool Feedback
- ✔ Cache Meter
- ✔ Progress Indicator

You can access the different Info Palette options by right clicking anywhere on this strip at the bottom of the UI.

At the far right of the Info Palette are the Cache Meter and Progress Indicator (Used: 143M Total: 1.49G). These allow you to see how much memory is available to combustion and how much is currently in use.

> **Tip:** Since the Cache Meter is something often accessed while working in any project, you might as well leave the rest of the Info Palette options enabled. They will take up no more interface real estate and may provide valuable information from time to time.

The left half of the Info Palette Bar always provides data about the current location of your cursor (X 293 Y 312 R 255 G 70 B 0 A 255 H 17° S 100% V 100%). This is provided as position data and is always represented in pixel dimensions and never spatial measurements such as inches or centimeters. The X/Y coordinates onscreen are relative to your image so that the upper left-hand corner of a graphic is always 0,0. There is a color swatch and numerical values in red, green, blue (R,G,B) and percentages of hue, saturation, and value (H,S,V).

If you notice an Error Alert (⚠) in the Info Palette, this probably indicates an error of some kind has occurred in combustion. For example, an OpenGL error for your particular graphics card or a bit depth error may cause this icon to appear. By double clicking on this icon, you will get details specific to the error that has occurred.

The very center of the Info Bar is where combustion lists the name of the Workspace (*.CWS) file that is open. Remember, although you might have 20 branches doing completely different and unrelated tasks, you can only have one Workspace open at a time. When you are using a tool such as Rotate, this file name will change temporarily to indicate Tool Feedback (such as degrees of rotation).

> **Note:** If there is an asterisk to the left of the name of the current Workspace, this indicates that changes have been made since your last save.

G. Operator Controls – Currently showing the controls for a Paint operator. The contents displayed here (area G) will change dramatically depending on what is selected in the project. For example, if a paint operator is selected, you can work and edit with hundreds of different controls. Conversely, if a Box Blur operator is selected, there are only two settings to edit.

You should take notice that when using the default, single monitor UI, the controls for accessing the Timeline, Operators panel, the Tracker and the Operator Controls are all available as small tabs between the Playback Controls (H) in this area. Figure 1.12 shows these five tabs in their default, docked state. With the exception of the Operator Controls, you can optionally float any of these tabs panels from within the user preferences.

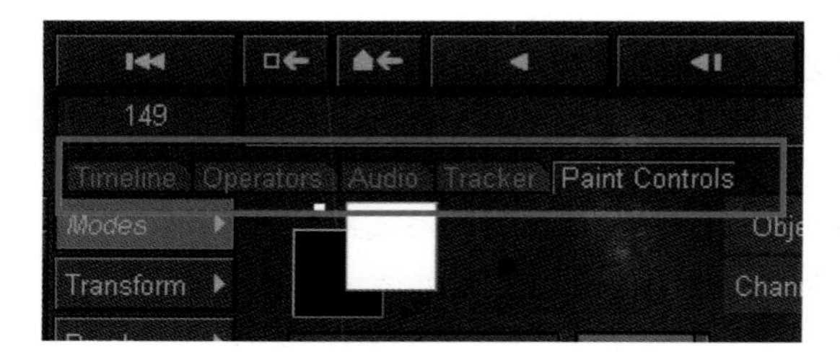

Figure 1.12

H. Playback Controls – For controlling and navigating in time. These are primarily like VCR buttons *for the active viewport.*

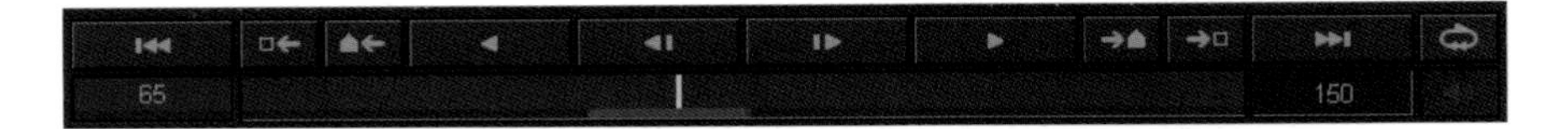

You can also get information here about where you are in time (frame number or SMPTE time code), what has been cached and where your Timeline in and out points are set.

I. Schematic View – Seen here in a viewport. This is the icon or node-based representation of the Workspace at hand.

J. Animate, Global/Local Time, Feedback and Display Quality – These controls will always be available when working in combustion.

Animate Button – This gem is always a click away and is the easiest way to create keyframes of animation. When enabled (red), changes in almost any value in combustion are being recorded and keyframes are being created on the current frame. You do not need to have the Timeline visible to use this feature.

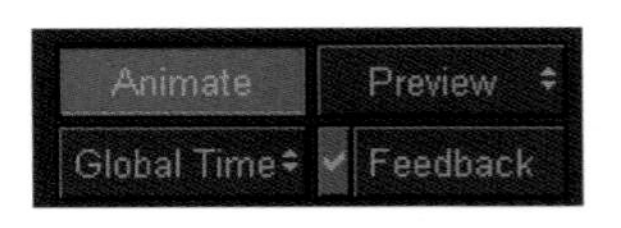

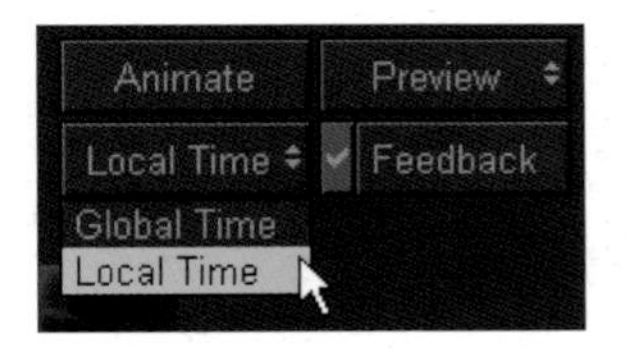

Global and Local Time – This setting changes how the Playback Controls display time. This setting also affects the response of the 'Frame All' button in the Timeline. Global Time always shows the time of the top-level operator or composite in the current branch and Local Time changes to show the duration of the current selection.

> **Tip:** While initially learning combustion, leave this set to Global Time. This will leave the time controls showing the duration of your project at any given moment.

Display Quality – This provides four preset settings for viewport resolution. This is for working only and does not affect the quality of the final rendering. These settings are very important to understand and are possibly the easiest way to speed up the entire workflow in combustion. The specifics of each setting are detailed in the next chapter.

Feedback – This is a toggle that can be enabled to let the viewports update while you are making a change in value somewhere in combustion. With Feedback disabled, the screen redraw will happen after you commit the value change (or release the mouse button, for example).

Data Entry Conventions

When you are working in combustion, you are often presented with data entry fields for use in changing various numerical values. There are three distinct ways of using these fields including keyboard entry, sliders and the calculator. To quickly go over these three methods of entering data, please follow this brief exercise:

1. Open the Workspace named *ch01_DataEntry.cws.*
2. Select the layer named 'layer' in the Workspace panel by clicking on the name (do not click on the icon left of the name). The layer should become highlighted when selected, as seen in Figure 1.13.

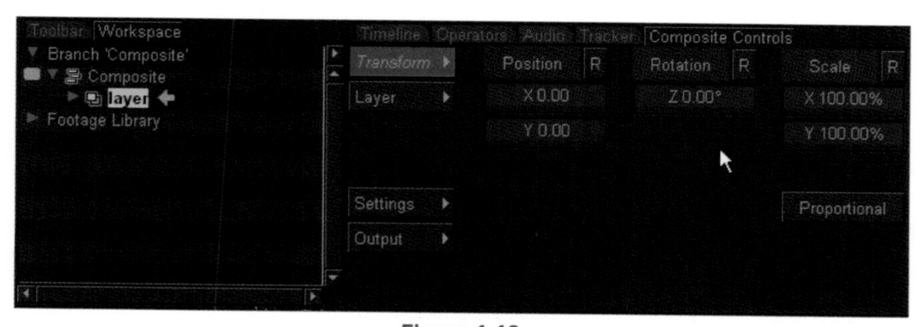

Figure 1.13

3. Switch to the Transform category of the Composite Controls.
4. To enter data with the **keyboard**, click ONCE in the Transform > Rotation data entry field. It should change color and you should also notice a blinking cursor, as seen in Figure 1.14 on page 20.

You can now enter a value using the keyboard. Often, depending on the value being edited, negative numbers are allowed (as is the case with layer rotation). To exit the field, either hit enter on the keyboard or click anywhere outside of the data entry field to accept the change.

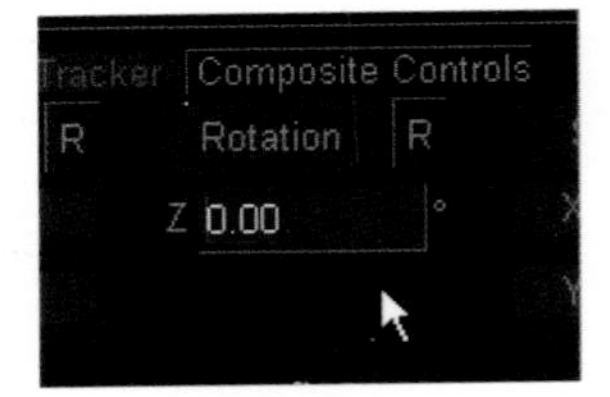

Figure 1.14

5 To use a data entry field as a **slider**, just click and drag your mouse on the data entry field. Positive values will be to the right and negative to the left. When Feedback is enabled (area J), this is the most visually interactive way of manipulating data. If, while using the slider input method, you hold down the Shift key, you will increase the rate of data entry. Conversely, if you hold down the Control key, it slows down the input rate.

6 To access the **calculator** input, simply double click on the data entry field. You should see a simple calculator appear as seen in Figure 1.15. Here, you can enter simple values or use simple math functions. For example, if a particular value was set to 36 prior to accessing the calculator, you could quickly double click to access the calculator, enter '/2' (without the quotes) and upon clicking OK to exit, the value will be changed to 18.

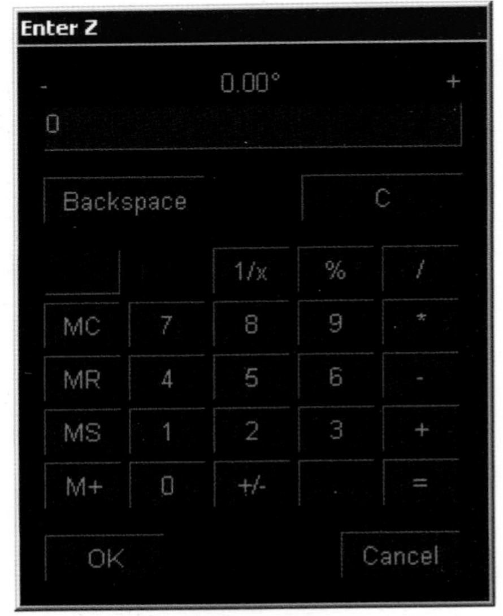

Figure 1.15

The small '**R**' button next to any data entry field (Figure 1.16) stands for reset, and is a quick way to reset *that particular field* to its default value. You will see this throughout combustion. This reset feature is not animatable and will only reset the value to its default value. Additionally, any keyframes will be deleted for that value and you will, in effect, be starting over for that particular data entry value. Use the reset with caution and only when you need a clean slate for that particular item.

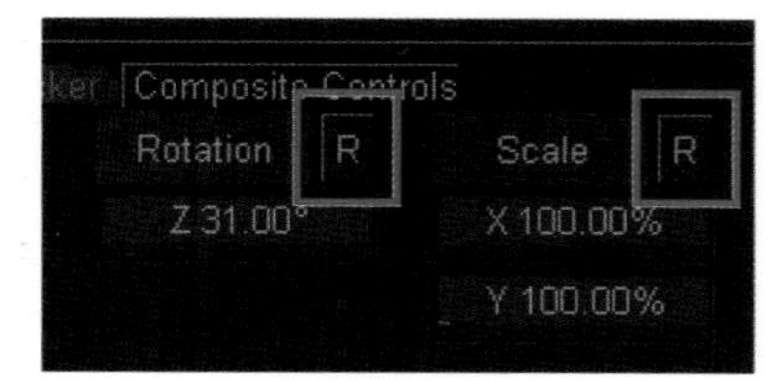

Figure 1.16

Reset buttons such as the one shown in Figure 1.17 also appear throughout combustion. However, unlike the small 'R' buttons next to specific entries a Reset button resets the entire category, not just one value. In this example, all the transformations would be reset.

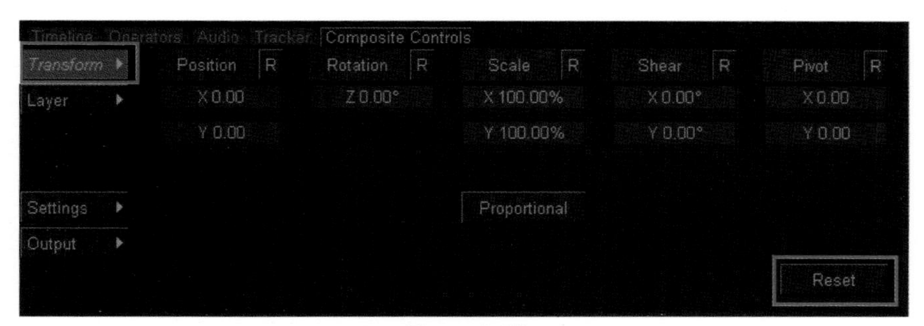

Figure 1.17

You may also come across a **Reset All** button, as seen in Figure 1.18. This example is from the Discreet Color Corrector operator, which has several categories of functions. Using the Reset All button clears all the settings from all of the operators' categories, not just the one visible.

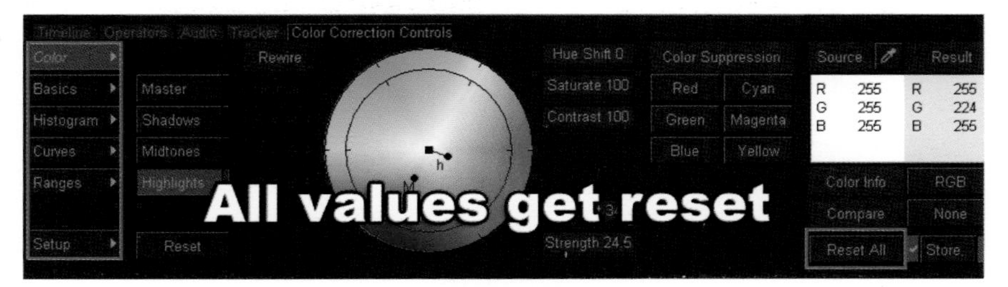

Figure 1.18

In addition to data entry fields, you may see **drop-down list** menus throughout combustion that indicate choices to be made from several available options. An example of this you have seen is the Display Quality rollout (area J). If you have a scroll wheel on your mouse, you can hover your cursor over the rollout in question and merely roll the mouse scroll wheel to flip through the changes.

Anywhere you see a small icon of a finger pointing ( ), it is a Pick button for that item. Enabling the Pick icon allows you to make a selection based on an item or area you click in a viewport.

These different ways of entering data provide you convenient access to change values in a manner most appropriate for your specific needs at that moment. Remember, these will all be available throughout combustion, not just for layer transformations and footage controls.

CHAPTER 2

WORKFLOW BASICS, FOOTAGE AND VIEWPORTS

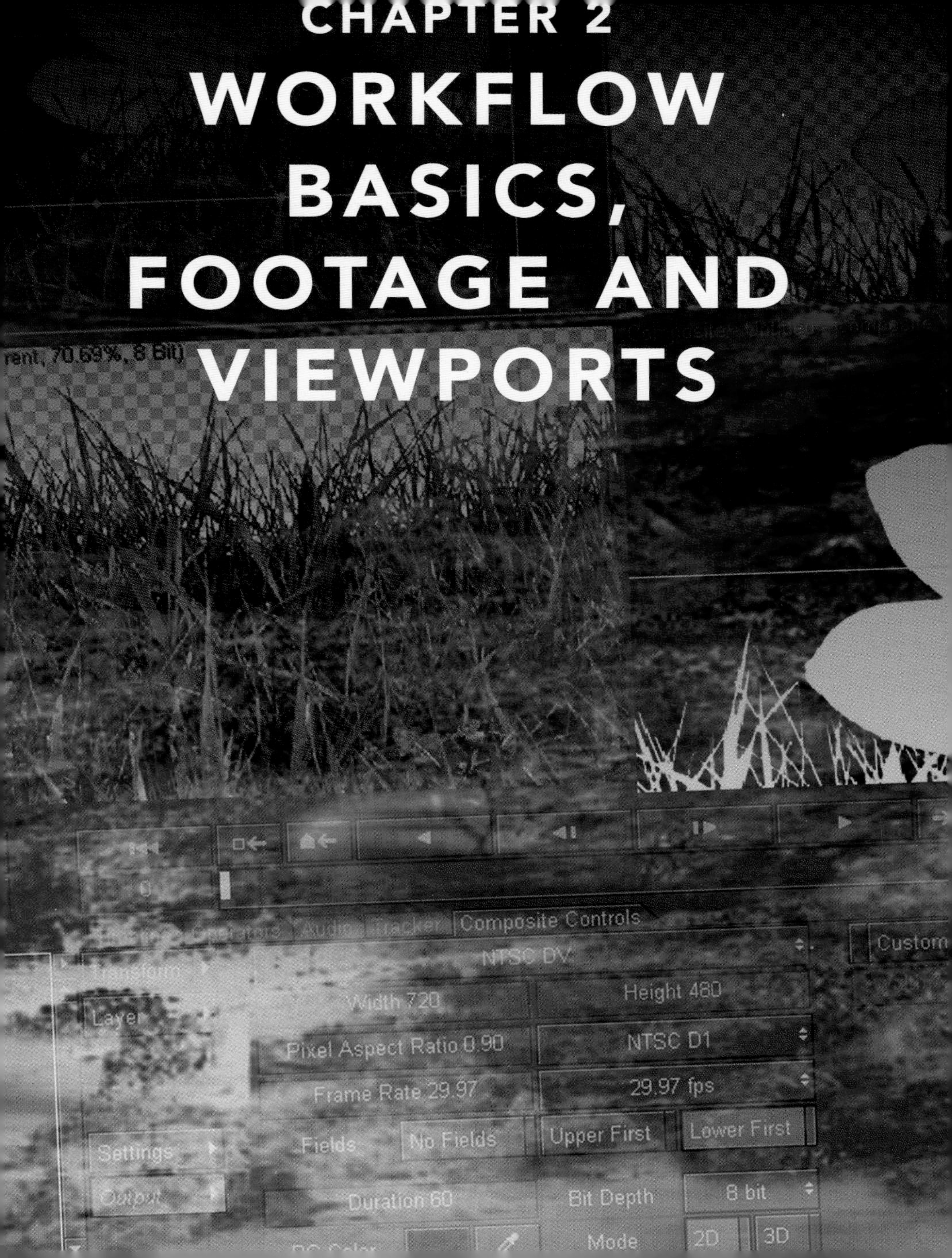

to combustion that should be understood at the outset. These are really worth learning early on, so that working on explicit features in combustion will be that much easier.

RAM Cache and Caching

At its core, combustion processes nearly all aspects of the application on the CPU(s) of the host computer; however, it stores this information in memory (RAM) *as it works*, or in real time. This storing of data to memory is referred to as RAM caching. This method of caching is how combustion achieves real-time playback at full frame rates, even on modest laptop computers. The frames are processed, then stored in RAM and played back at full frame rate.

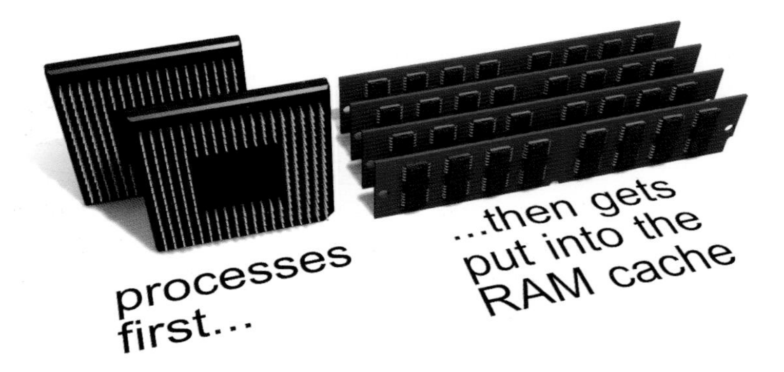
processes first...
...then gets put into the RAM cache

When combustion has used up all the memory that you have allocated in the preferences, it begins to overwrite data in the RAM cache and adds the new data, remaining 'full' at that point. Out with the old and in with the new, as it were. The more memory you have in your computer, the more you can cache and play back at full frame rate.

People have often commented, 'Gee, combustion needs a lot of memory'. To this, I typically respond, 'it doesn't waste memory, it takes full advantage of it'. These are two very different things and it is important to understand and appreciate the difference between the two.

Even when at rest, combustion has cached the frame where you are currently resting the playback controls. When you start playback of a Workspace, combustion begins to store even more data into RAM. It does this by caching *every* output in the Workspace, not just a 'flattened' version of what is visible in the current viewport. Because of this, it might be totally feasible to require hundreds of megabytes of memory just to cache 60 frames of video resolution material. A few basic examples of when this might occur are:

- Many layers all being cached in the Workspace.
- You have one layer, but a series of several operators have been applied to it, thus requiring more memory.
- You have a number of completely disjointed branches that are all being cached, but you are only currently looking at one.
- You might have many layers of high-resolution HD material in a lower resolution D1 composite. Combustion is attempting to cache all the information outside of the visible frame.

OK, so how much is enough memory to adequately run combustion? Ahhh, one of those eternal questions. Quite seriously, too much is never enough, especially when you consider how quickly you can fill it using a RAM cache. It is not uncommon to actively use 2 gigabytes of memory when working in combustion. The good news is that memory gets cheaper every day. At the time of writing, 2 gigs of RAM can be obtained from around US$300 and up. The minimum recommended is 256, but you realistically should have at least 512 megabytes of system RAM to work productively.

Note: If you exit combustion, anything stored in the cache is lost and must be recached. To save any images you have cached, you must render using the techniques described in Chapter 14.

The Cache Meter

At any time when working in combustion, you will, undoubtedly, get used to glancing down to the lower right portion of the UI at the Cache Meter. Seen in Figure 2.1, the Cache Meter

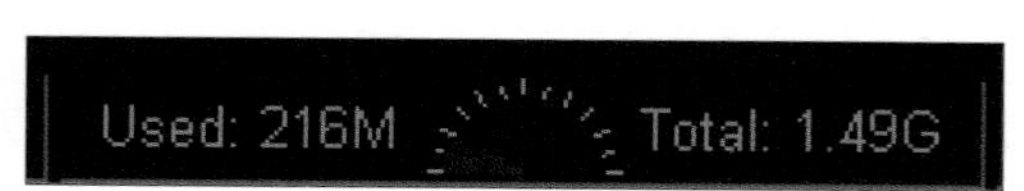

Figure 2.1

can be thought of in a similar fashion as a fuel gauge on an automobile. It shows how much is used and how much is available.

Note: If the Cache Meter is not currently visible, you can turn it on by right clicking on the Info Bar at the bottom of the UI and enabling it.

To read the Cache Meter: on the left is how much memory you are currently using and on the right is how much has been made available to combustion in the user preferences. The number on the left will change while you are working in combustion. It is a good idea to keep an eye on this value to be aware of how your system is handling a particular project. Depending on your workflow, you may be surprised at what uses little resources and what demands a lot.

You can also see what has been cached and what remains to be cached for the current viewport by looking for the ever-growing bar under the Playback controls. This is a new feature to combustion 3 and simply shows what has been cached. This bar will dynamically update itself.

If you want to flush the cache so you can concentrate on a completely different portion of your project, at any time you can right click on the Cache Meter and 'flush the cache'. Flushing the cache purges the system memory of anything previously/temporarily stored in RAM.

Note: Flushing the cache also reloads all the footage. For example, if you edit an image in Photoshop and resave it, you can flush the cache to reload it in combustion.

Display Quality and Caching

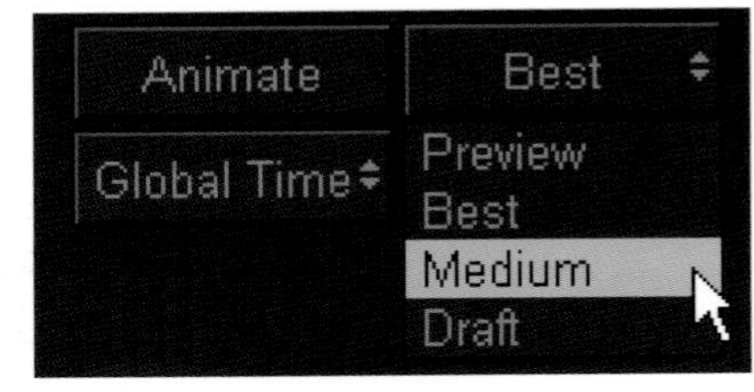

Figure 2.2

The Display Quality setting is one variable that changes the way combustion caches all material in the current Workspace. Changing the

Display Quality setting is the fastest and also easiest way to reduce the amount of RAM required to cache Workspaces. Figure 2.2 shows the Display Quality drop-down menu (this is area J from Chapter 1).

Note: Switching from one display quality setting to another does not flush the cache.

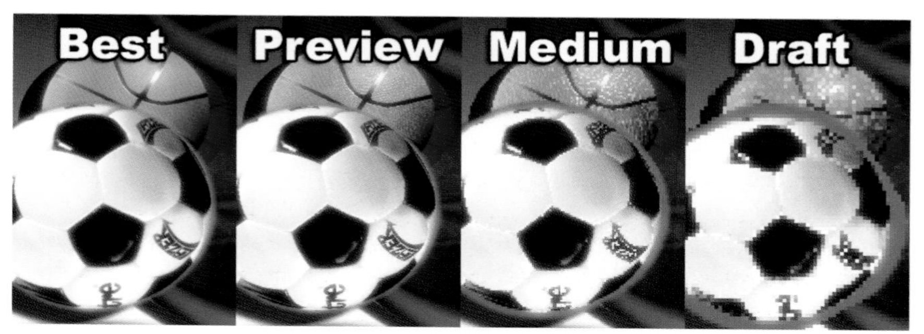

Figure 2.3

Preview – This is an exact representation of how your project looks at full resolution, except that the antialiasing and super-sampling options available in a 3D composite will be ignored. These two features are made available in Best, but require extra rendering time that you might not want to waste while building a project.

Best – The highest quality that elements can be represented. While you may certainly want to render your work with the 'Best' setting, it is often a good idea to build your project using one or all of the other three. This can dramatically increase your productivity. A common workflow is to work/cache at another setting, stop playback, then switch temporarily to Best just to spot check a few frames (perhaps a chroma key edge you have been working on). Then, when complete, you switch back to Medium, for example, to continue working with lower overhead.

Medium – The Medium setting forces clips to be viewed and cached at half resolution *or* the resolution of any footage with a defined proxy (which will be explained later in this chapter). Medium display quality will cache about twice as fast and require approximately half as much RAM as Preview. Medium is often adequate for most working circumstances and it effectively doubles the speed of the workflow in combustion.

Draft – The Draft setting processes and displays clips at one-quarter resolution, or half the resolution of any defined proxies. Working in draft will be four times faster than Preview and require one-quarter the resources to cache the same material, albeit at a cost in visual quality. For the testing of animation timing only, Draft works great because you are not bothering to cache all the miniscule image information. This allows you to quickly see gross movement, color and timing play back in real time.

Tip: Remember, you can switch between the different display quality settings at any time, even while playing back. The setting in Figure 2.3 is not tied to render quality. For example, you can work for several hours completely in Draft, and then when you are ready to output your work, you render the project with the 'Best' setting.

File Menu Options

As simple as they sound, many of the options in the File menu are one of the most notorious causes for confusion among combustion users. Figure 2.4 shows the File drop-down menu and, at first, you must be wondering what all the fuss is about.

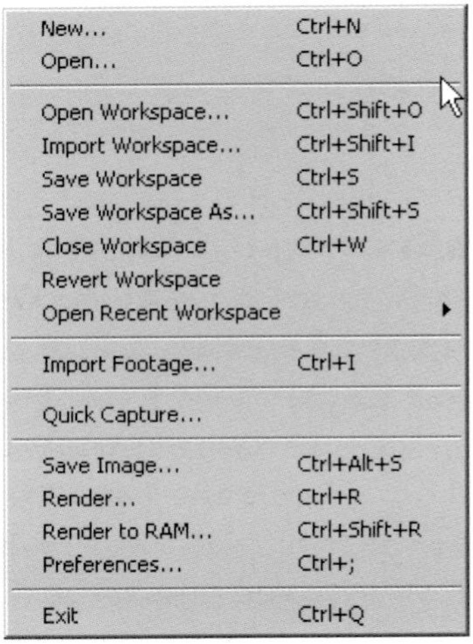

New...	Ctrl+N
Open...	Ctrl+O
Open Workspace...	Ctrl+Shift+O
Import Workspace...	Ctrl+Shift+I
Save Workspace	Ctrl+S
Save Workspace As...	Ctrl+Shift+S
Close Workspace	Ctrl+W
Revert Workspace	
Open Recent Workspace	▸
Import Footage...	Ctrl+I
Quick Capture...	
Save Image...	Ctrl+Alt+S
Render...	Ctrl+R
Render to RAM...	Ctrl+Shift+R
Preferences...	Ctrl+;
Exit	Ctrl+Q

Figure 2.4

New – This presents you with the dialog to create a new branch of some kind in the current Workspace. In Figure 2.5, the left side shows how this dialog may load and the image on the right shows the New > Type rollout expanded. Depending on the type selected, different creation parameters will be available below and a different kind of branch will be created when you click OK to confirm.

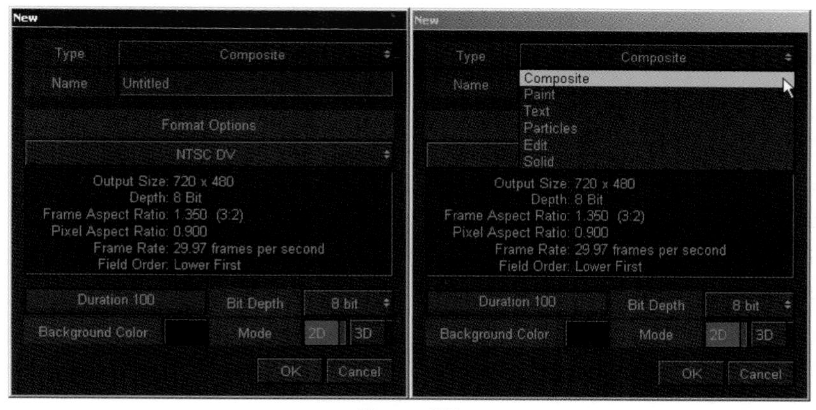

Figure 2.5

This chart briefly outlines the different types for File > New:

Composite	An empty 2D or 3D composite will be created
Paint	A solid with a Paint operator applied to it will be created
Text	A solid with a Text operator applied to it will be created
Particle	A solid with a Particle operator applied to it will be created
Edit	A blank Edit operator will be created
Solid	A solid without any operators will be created

Open – This option is for bringing in one or more pieces of footage off the computer system or network drives. You will be presented with the Thumbnail Browser to select the clip(s) and then provided with several different choices of how to bring the footage into the Workspace. This is often confused with Import Footage, which is detailed below. Opening a piece of footage into an operator creates a branch of that type. For example, if you open a still into a 2D composite, the result is a composite branch that contains a single layer. You can open multiple files at the same time, but all the parameters of the resulting branch will use the parameters for the first clip. For example, if I open three images of different sizes into a composite as layers, the first clip chosen will dictate the resolution, frame rate (and so on) of the new composite. This is typically a time-saving feature but you can, however, go and change the parameters of the composite at any time.

Open Workspace – This is only for opening a pre-existing combustion (*.CWS) project file. You will be presented with the Thumbnail Browser; however, you will only be able to browse and open CWS files. New users often get this confused with File > Open. If you open another Workspace, the current Workspace must be closed. There can only be one open at a time.

Import Workspace – This option allows you to merge the contents of one (*.CWS) project into another. The entire contents of the imported Workspace will be brought in as a separate branch, but you will still only have one Workspace open. This Workspace will have the name of the starting project, not the imported Workspace.

Import Footage – This option will only be available if you have a Composite, layer or an Edit operator selected in the Workspace. If you have an operator selected (such as a blur, for example), this option to import footage will not appear in the File menu choices. By choosing to import footage, you will then be presented with the Import Footage Thumbnail Browser. This allows the Workspace to reference one or more pieces of footage off the hard drive or network.

Quick Capture – This is a utility that allows you to digitize footage into combustion directly off video hardware devices. If you have a DirectShow or QuickTime capture device installed in your computer system through FireWire, Quick Capture allows a basic interface for capturing footage that is playing back on video equipment directly to disk and/or into the current Workspace. Figure 2.6 shows the simple interface to the Quick Capture Utility.

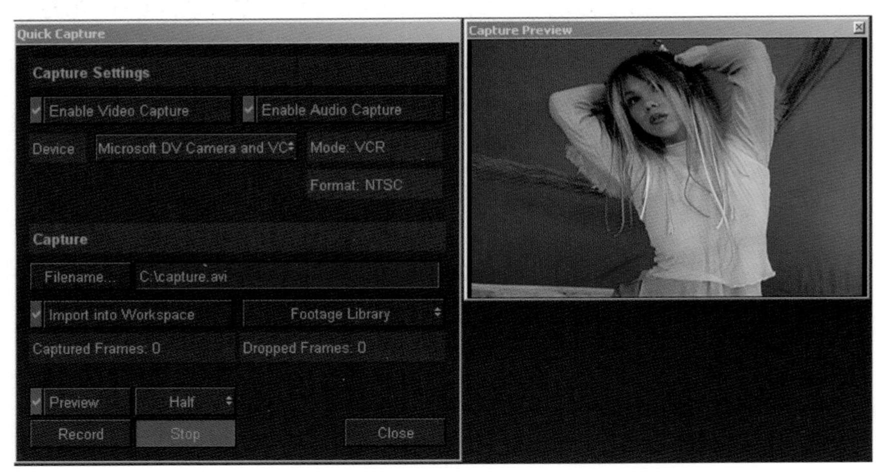

Figure 2.6

> **Note:** To use a DV device with DirectShow Quick Capture, you must first disable the DV framebuffer in the user preferences. This is because the hardware can only be used for one or the other at any given time.

The Thumbnail Browser

There are several ways to bring footage into combustion, but the most versatile is via the Thumbnail Browser seen in Figure 2.7.

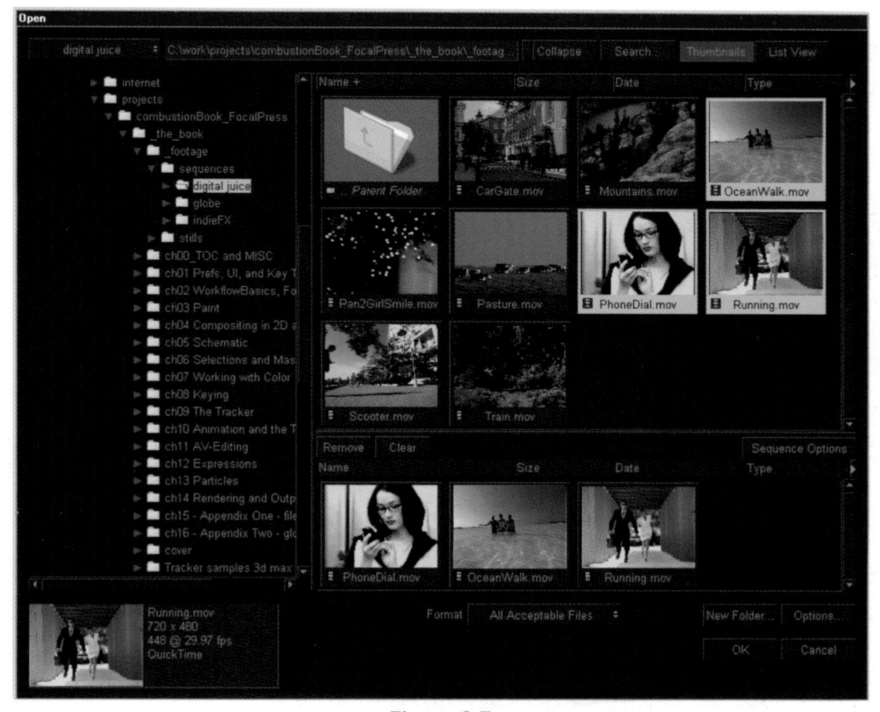

Figure 2.7

Collapse – When enabled, this feature recognizes numerically sequential files such as File000.tga, File001.tga (etc.) and treats them much in the same way as a QuickTime or AVI file by opening them as one clip. Try browsing to the . . . *Footage\Sequences\Globe* directory and turning collapse on and off. This will show you how numbered sequences can be treated as individual files or as one long clip.

Sequence Options – This is only pertinent for collapsed image sequences, and can only be accessed if a collapsed image sequence is selected in the lower 'loader' portion of the browser (not the main thumbnail area). This allows you, for example, to load only a portion of a collapsed series of frames.

Thumbnail vs List View – Thumbnails can be scrubbed by dragging on the upper third of the thumbnail. Sequences are slightly faster to navigate across your network because combustion is doing less work to list text directories. The List view is a text-only account of a directory and the files within. List view, while not as dynamic, is often quicker to use because thumbnails are not required.

Options – The thumbnail cache detailed here is on the hard drive and does not encroach on the memory cache of combustion. If you have the space, I recommend making the cache larger to accommodate more thumbnails. Directories with cached thumbnails will open faster the next time you return to get footage from this location.

Working with Footage

To actually begin working on a project you need some form of image to work on. Any piece of footage in combustion can be broken down into one of three basic categories. Footage can be a solid, a still image, or a series of images that make up a sequence of video or animation.

Solids can be thought of as a simple card of color. A solid is a full frame of color that does not exist on the hard drive. Instead, it is created and manipulated internally by combustion. You can create a new solid in a number of ways, but the easiest is from the File menu.

Solids are often transparent (0% opacity) and are merely invisible 'placeholder' sources on which you might, for example, apply a particle operator. In this case, the renderable particles are created on an invisible plate, which can be moved around independently as its own layer in a composite. All the particles applied to this solid would be visible, but the solid would never be rendered if it was set to be transparent.

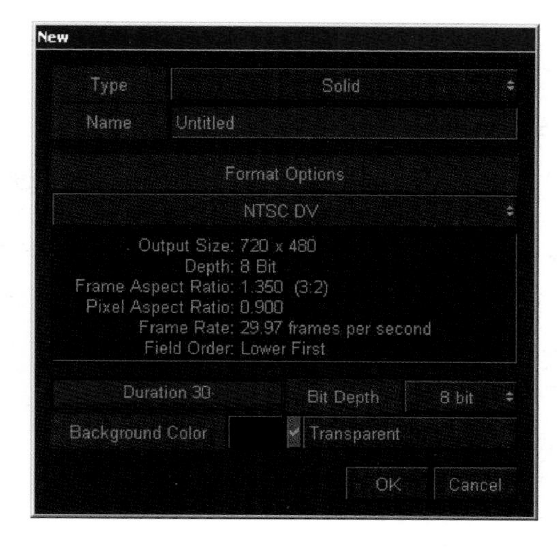

Still Images are simply pictures on your hard drive such as a JPG or TGA file. You can obtain still images from a variety of sources such as stock image libraries, scanners and digital photography.

Image Sequences can be broken down into two forms: sequentially numbered frames, or single image files that contain multiple frames. Formats vary widely, including QuickTime MOV, Windows AVI, and numerically sequential image series such as *File000.TGA, File001.TGA*, etc. Discreet combustion caches numerical-frame image sequences slightly faster than single files with multiple frames such as MOV or AVI. This is primarily because image sequences do not need to be 'read into' like a single file containing numerous frames. The final result is the same, but just something to be aware of when working with different formats of media such as MOV and AVI.

Footage Controls (Source and Output Settings)

There are several factors or variables that should be considered when discussing any particular piece of footage. Characteristics such as resolution and frame rate can be found in the Footage Controls and are broken down into two categories, Source and Output.

To access the Footage Controls:

1. Open the Workspace named *ch02_Footage.cws.*
2. Expand the Workspace panel to expose the contents of the Footage Library. Here, you will find four clips that represent the different kinds of footage available in combustion: a solid, a still image, and one of each type of image sequence (as outlined above).

3 Select the footage of the Sequential PNG series. Notice the naming convention of (####) within combustion for numbered frames. This collapsed sequence allows the rest of combustion to treat all these individual PNG files as one long sequence, much like an MOV.

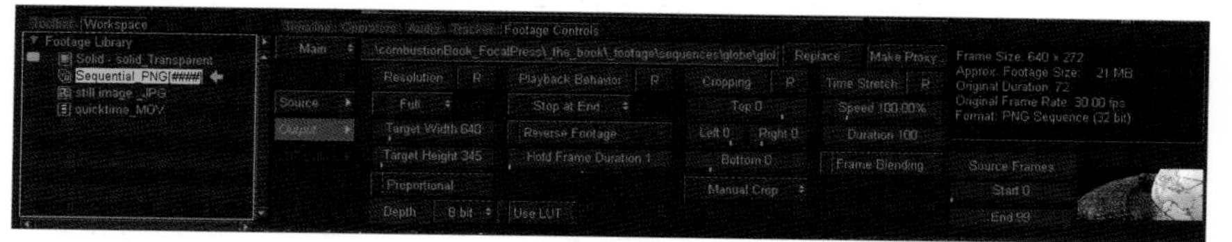

Figure 2.8

Figure 2.8 shows the Footage Controls tab as it appears. Here, the Source and Output categories are now visible for that particular piece of footage.

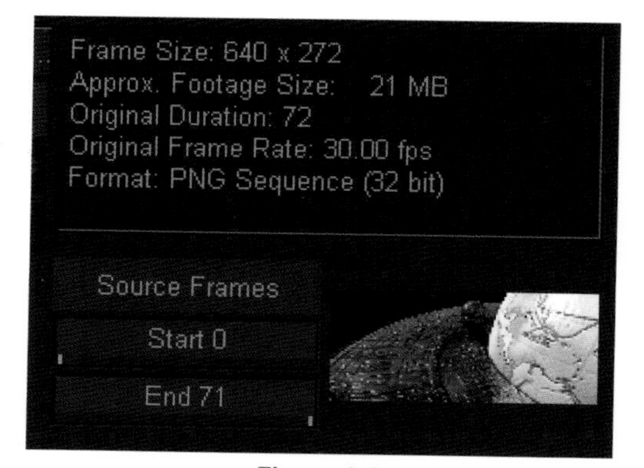

Figure 2.9

Figure 2.9 shows the information and thumbnail that can be seen at all times when accessing the Footage Controls (whether or not you are in the Source or Output category). Here, you can always get basic information about your raw footage.

Footage Controls > Source

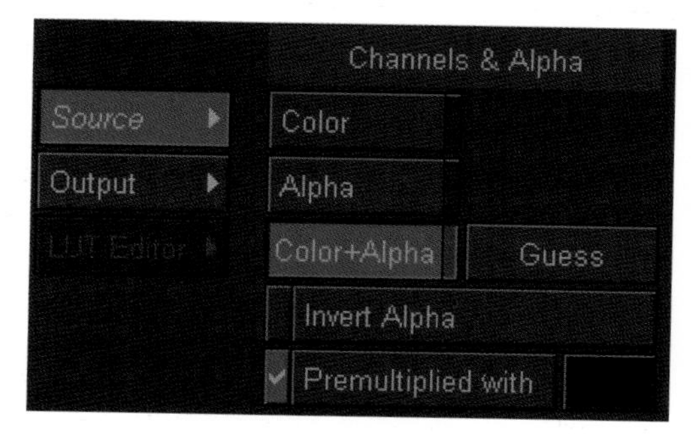

Channels & Alpha – This is where you can tell combustion to utilize an embedded alpha channel in a footage clip, if one exists.

Color – Enables only the RGB channels in the source.

Alpha – Makes the footage act as a grayscale image based on the alpha channel of the source footage.

Color+Alpha – Allows the full RGBA channels to work together to help composite your image(s) over other elements.

The checkbox for **Premultiplied with** (Premultiplied with) should only be enabled if your footage has a premultiplied alpha channel. Animation applications often render images with a premultiplied alpha channel, which can aid compositing over other images. The color swatch is provided for you to tell combustion what color the footage was premultiplied with in another application. If you ever see a white or black fringe around CG footage, this is often the culprit.

The **Invert Alpha** checkbox (Invert Alpha) enables you to flip the alpha channel so that areas of transparency are now opaque and vice versa. Quite often, different graphics applications use black as opaque. Discreet combustion allows you to flip/negate the alpha channel at the footage level to accommodate such inconsistencies.

Field Separation – This is where you can specify field dominance, if any, that your footage contains. For example, NTSC formats are almost always lower field dominant when going to broadcast. If your footage is showing fields in the viewport, you may want to change this setting to match your incoming footage.

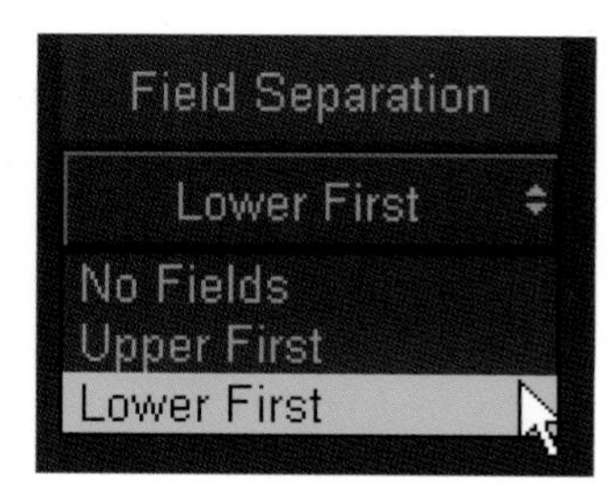

3:2 Pulldown – This is for changing the phase of field rendered footage that was created with the Telecine process. This is often the case when, for example, film shot at 24 fps is digitized to 30 fps on video equipment. Using 3:2 Pulldown allows you to work at the native frame rate of 24 fps. The Guess 3:2 Phase

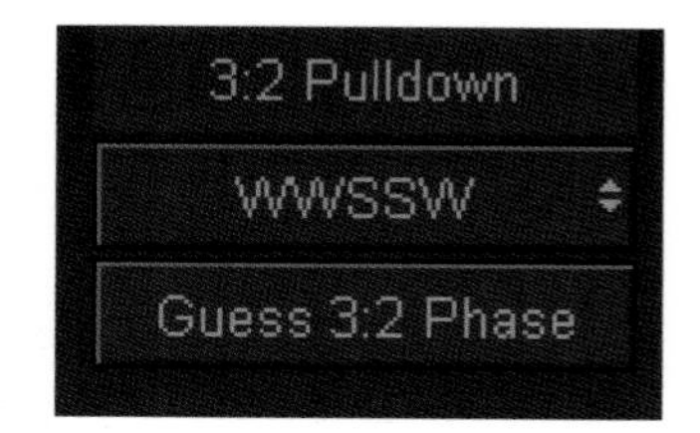

button forces combustion to briefly analyze the footage and guess the appropriate order of interpretation.

Frame Rate ( ) – This sets the frames per second of a particular clip. Typically, the 'From File' setting is fine, but you should check to verify this is correct if you are using sources of several different frame rates.

Pixel Aspect Ratio ( ) – This is a setting used by video equipment to allow images that contain pixels that are not square (1.0 pixel aspect). For example, an NTSC D1 clip that is 720×486 with a 0.9 pixel aspect looks correct on a video monitor that has a 4×3 image aspect ratio.

a 4:3 image × by a 1.0 pixel aspect = 1.333 image aspect
$(720 \div 486) \times (0.9 \text{ pixel aspect}) = 1.333$ image aspect ratio

> **Note:** You should be aware if you are mixing footage of different pixel aspects. For example, a scanned image and miniDV footage do not have a common pixel aspect ratio. You can verify your individual footage settings here.

Footage Controls > Output

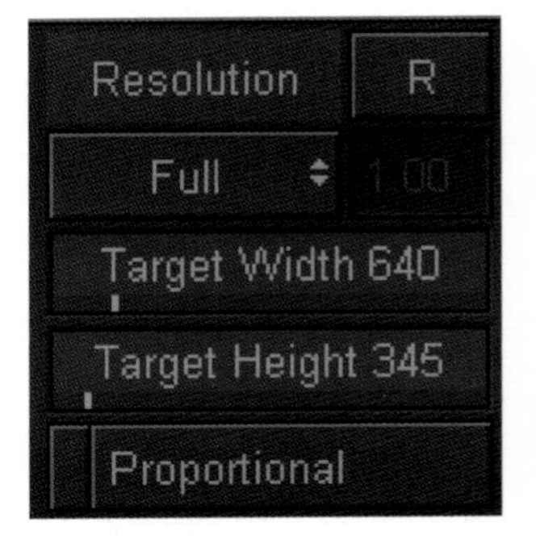

Resolution in combustion refers to the pixel dimension of an image. This is always expressed in width and height. Nowhere in combustion will you see spatial measurement such as inches, centimeters, or dots per inch (DPI) representing resolution. Since combustion was primarily designed for film and video, the spatial measurements of this type are largely irrelevant. Think for a moment if you play the same DVD on a small and large screen TV set. They both are displaying the same source image (which has the same number of pixels), but one is spatially larger as you watch it. It is all about the pixels in combustion.

Bit Depth – This controls the range of color available to the source footage. Here, you can also enable *Look Up Tables* (LUTs). You can typically leave this setting alone and let combustion read the bit depth from the source files.

Playback Behavior – Here, you can opt to reverse the raw footage to play it backwards. This is also where you can control how the footage acts when it reaches its last frame.

Stop at End	The default. This simply plays a clip through and stops when finished.
Ping-Pong	Plays the footage forwards completely, and then plays backwards completely, and then forwards . . . etc.
Loop	Plays the clip in its entirety and then starts back again on the first frame. This forces continuous playback in one direction.
Hold Last Frame	Plays the clip through, and then holds the last frame as a still image for a user-defined duration (in frames).

> **Note:** Playback Behavior is disabled for still images, as can be seen if you select either the solid or the still image in the *ch02_Footage.cws* project.

Cropping – Here, you control the size in pixels of how each edge of a clip is cropped. This crop can optionally be automated and/or animated. Cropping off unnecessary portions of an image at the footage level is an excellent way to save system resources.

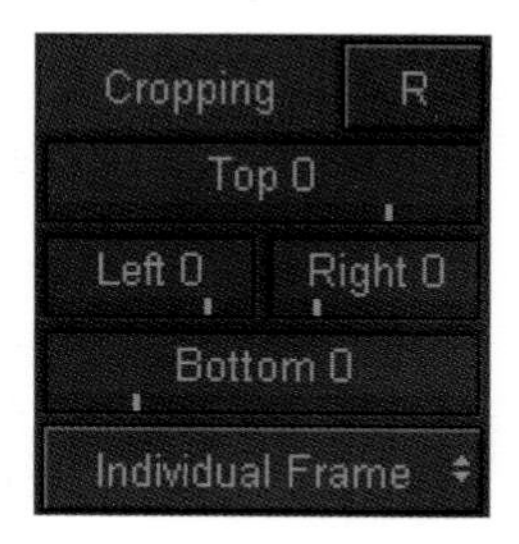

Time Stretch – This allows for linear retiming of your sequences based on either a percentage in speed or an absolute frame count. Frame Blending can be enabled to help transition from frames, should you choose to slow footage below 100%. Time Stretch is also disabled for still images and solids.

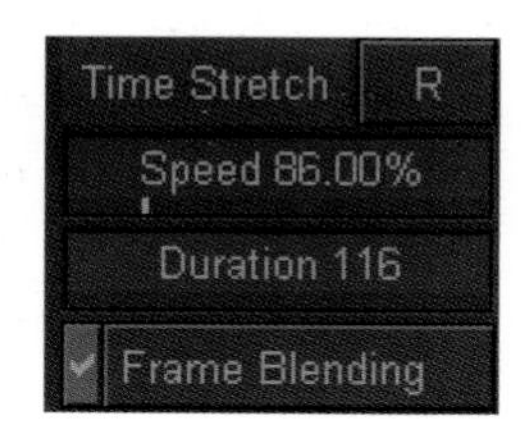

Source Frames – For still images, this is where you can control the duration of the image. For image sequences, it allows you to define the start and end

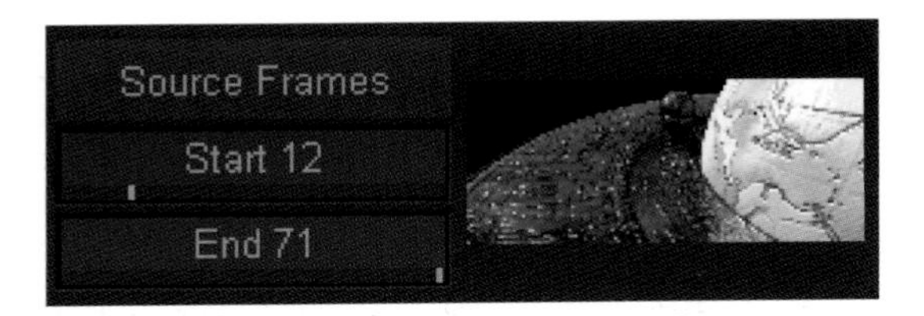

frame that combustion will use for that footage. The thumbnail updates dynamically as you change the start frame.

Working with Proxies

In addition to the Viewport Quality settings (Draft/Medium/Preview/Best), you can control the interpreted resolution of clips at the footage level using proxies. Unlike display quality, which is global to all elements in a composite, proxies are defined *per footage clip*. Proxies are merely lower resolution stand-ins for your source footage that allow better feedback and require less memory to cache. At any time, you can go to the Footage Controls for any clip and make a proxy. One example of when you might want to work with proxies is if you have extremely high-resolution footage and you're running low on system resources.

To create a proxy for a piece of footage:

1. Open the Workspace named *ch02_SimpleCompsite.cws.*
2. In the Workspace panel, expand the layer named *globe* to reveal the footage node.
3. Select the footage that is an image sequence named *globe(####).*

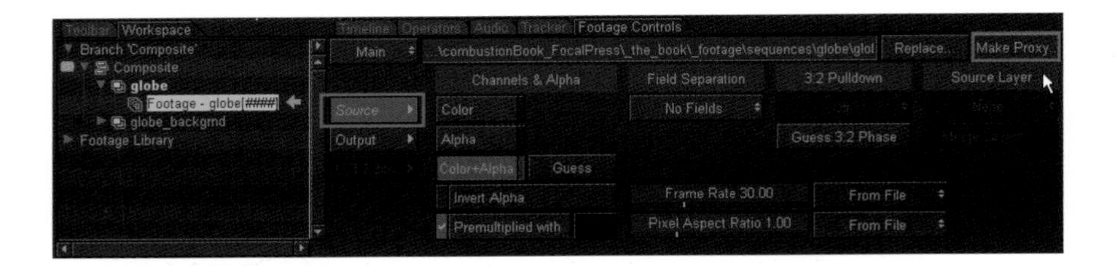

4. In the Footage Controls click on the Make Proxy button, visible just below the time indicator. The dialog seen in Figure 2.10 will appear.

5 Select an output format and resolution for your proxy. There are presets available for generating half, third, quarter and eighth resolution proxies, or you can define your own resolution.

Figure 2.10

6 Click process and the proxy file(s) will be rendered to your hard drive.

7 To switch between the rendered proxy and the original, full-resolution footage, simply switch the footage toggle from Proxy back to Main.

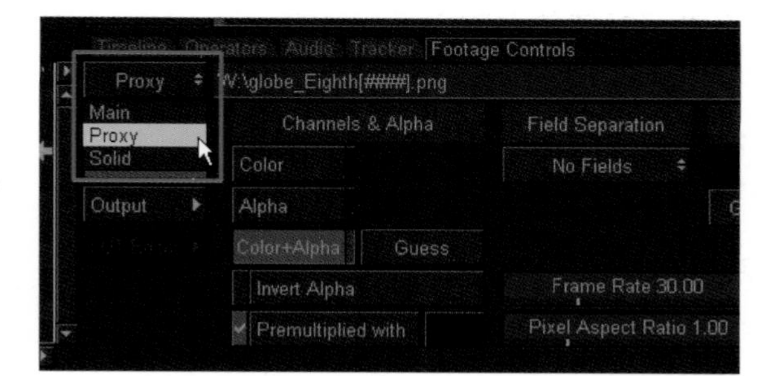

Missing Footage

Often when you move a combustion project from one computer to another, you might get the Replace Footage dialog seen in Figure 2.11. This is because the current project cannot find the source material where it 'thinks' it resides on your computer. The application will initially look for footage using the exact same path as was indicated in the original CWS file. Second, it will look recursively in directories or folders below the folder in which the CWS project file resides. This second method is how the materials for this book are arranged to help ensure no footage files will be missing when a project is opened.

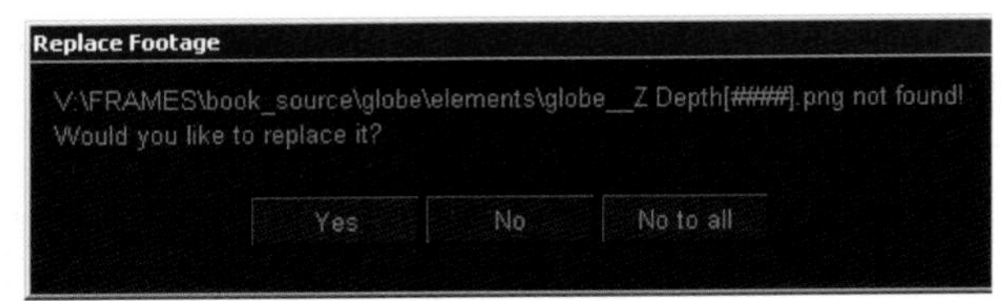

Figure 2.11

Selecting 'Yes' in the Replace Footage dialog will open the Thumbnail Browser and let you navigate to the location of the missing footage.

Tip: If you open a *.CWS Workspace and the footage is missing, it is often faster to select 'No to All' when first presented with the Replace Footage dialog. If you select 'Yes', you will have to (re)navigate to the location of the footage *each time* additional footage is missing. Instead, if you pick 'No to All', and then immediately go to the Footage Library in the Workspace panel, you can use the Replace feature (Figure 2.12) in the Source category for each missing piece of footage. Doing this will often save time because the Thumbnail Browser will then remember the location of the last directory used.

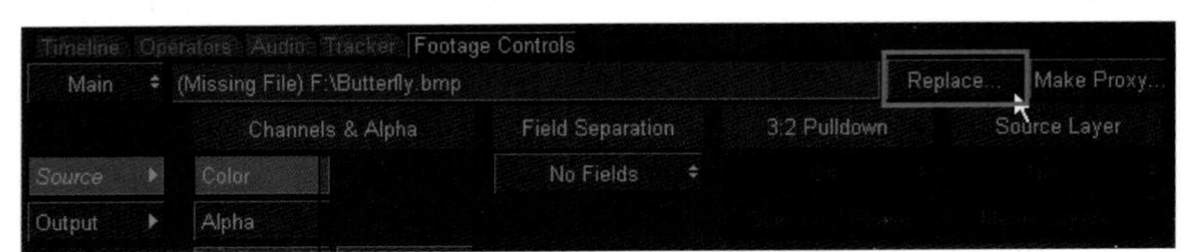

Figure 2.12

Tip: The Replace (footage) button is also a quick way to swap out source footage so you can, for example, try different versions of a project.

The Workspace Panel

The Workspace panel is a text-based, hierarchical listing of the entire project at hand. Figure 2.13 shows a typical Workspace panel that has been expanded. Conversely, the Schematic View, which is detailed in Chapter 5, is a graphical or flowchart representation of the entire Workspace. Changes made to one are reflected in the other and vice versa. While there are many valid arguments why folks prefer one method to the other, the Workspace panel is one place that you can access *every single item* in any given project, down to the very first/last brush stroke (you can optionally set the Timeline to do this as well). This is not to downplay the power and grace of the Schematic, for one is the Yin to the other's Yang. They both definitely have their advantages.

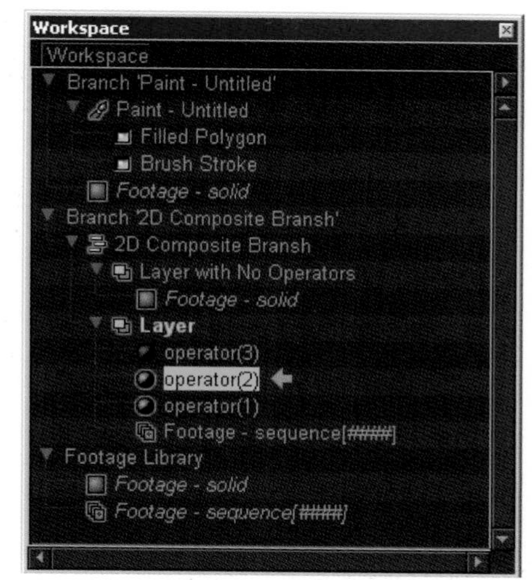

Figure 2.13

Workspace Panel 'vs' the Toolbar

Quite often, depending on what is selected in the Workspace panel, different tools will be available in the Toolbar. This is often one of the most confusing elements to new users of combustion, but once understood, it becomes one of the most powerful features of the application. This is because you will never have to hunt down menu elements. To reiterate an important tip . . . floating the Workspace panel in the user preferences can often be a good idea for new users, because in doing so, you will be able to see both the Workspace panel and the Toolbar simultaneously.

If you do, in fact, decide to float the Workspace panel, you may often have to move it about the screen to avoid conflicts with other elements of the UI. You can reposition the floating Workspace panel by clicking and dragging on the bar that displays the name 'Workspace' at the top of the Workspace panel. If, after floating the Workspace panel, you happen to accidentally close it, you can open a new one by going to *Windows* > *Palettes* > *Show Workspace* from the top menu Toolbar (or tap F3).

Selecting Items – To select anything in combustion, you click on the text name of the item, not the icon to the left of the name. Clicking on the icon will, instead, toggle the item on or off. When the icon is yellow, the item is on and when grayed, it is turned off. Committing this to memory as soon as possible will save you hours of frustration, believe me. In Figure 2.13, the item named *operator(2)* is selected and *operator(3)* is turned off.

Turning an item off instead of selecting it is an extremely common mistake made by many new users. Make sure you get used to making Workspace selections by clicking on the *names*. Based on my experiences from the classroom, I cannot reiterate this enough. As simple as this rule is, for some strange reason the vast majority of new users want to click on the icon and not the name of the item to select it. Thus, they invariably end up hunting around for some time looking for something that they think is selected, when in fact it is merely turned off. If there is an arrow to the *right* of an element's name, then it is selected.

Note: You cannot animate this on/off of elements in the Workspace panel. This toggle is merely there to turn off elements while you want to concentrate on specific operators, layers, paint objects, and so on.

Creating Multiple Selections – To select multiple items, you can either use a lasso method around multiple items or you can Control + click on names to allow a 'skip' in the sequence. If you hold down the Shift key, you can select the first and last items in a list and the named objects in between will be added to the selection as well. These three methods are common to many applications you may have used.

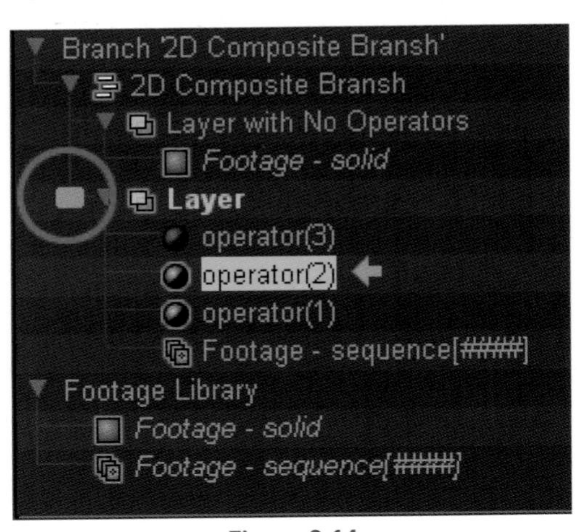

Figure 2.14

In Figure 2.14, the icon that looks like a TV monitor identifies what is being displayed in the *current* viewport at the top of the UI.

Remember, a thin white border around a viewport identifies it as the active viewport. This TV icon will always be to the left of an item listed in the Workspace panel and it will move about depending on what you are working on at any given time. Looking for this icon should become second nature.

In Figure 2.15, the icon of an arrow pointing *left* identifies what is currently selected; therefore, the parameters currently being displayed in the Operator Controls area in the lower/main portion of the UI pertain to this item. The user controls this by selecting the item in the Workspace panel. When you select something, its controls appear at the bottom of the UI. This icon will also clarify things immensely.

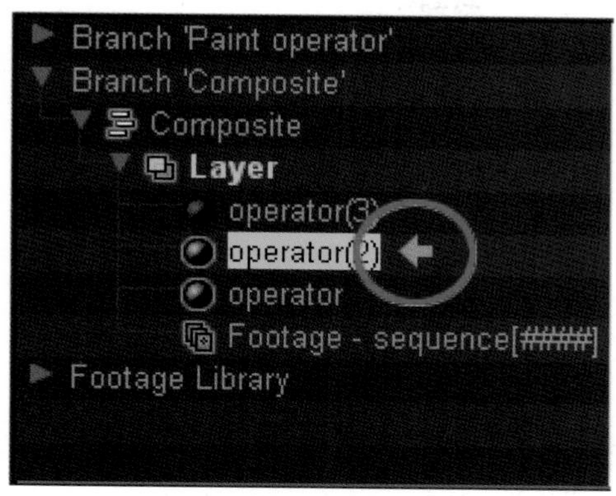

Figure 2.15

Many items in the Workspace panel may show a small gray triangle to the left of the item's name. If the triangle is pointing right, this indicates that there is more to this element that can be exposed by clicking on this triangle. If the triangle is pointing down, that item has been fully expanded. You can see examples of both of these options in Figure 2.16.

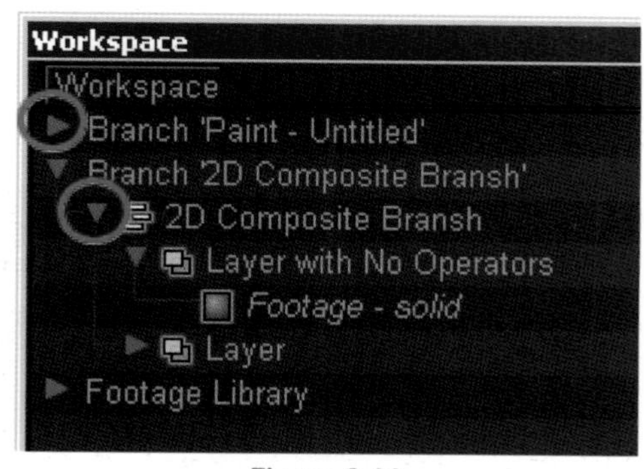

Figure 2.16

Items with their names in *italics* are duplicated or 'instanced' somewhere else in the Workspace. Instances are like copies, except changes made to one also happen to the other. Instancing is a great way to conserve the memory (RAM) of your computer system. When you create a duplicate in the Workspace an instance is created. Duplicates (instances) are not the same as items created by a copy/paste process, since the footage is not accessed a second time. Instancing is visualized and explained further in Chapter 5.

Renaming elements can typically be accomplished at any time by clicking on the name of a selected item and entering the new name. It can often be faster to right click on an item's name and selecting 'rename' from the drop-down menu, as seen in Figure 2.17. This action selects and renames in one process.

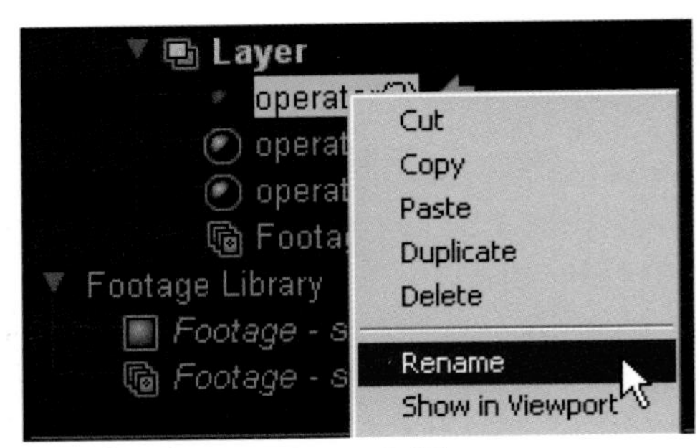

Figure 2.17

Naming and renaming items as you work is critical and can be especially helpful when learning. Believe me, it will save you time to rename things for organization and clarity as you work, especially if you share Workspace files with other users. This is, perhaps, one of the biggest tips I can suggest in this entire book.

Deleting items from the Workspace can be easily accomplished by first selecting them and then tapping the delete key on the keyboard.

Warning: If you have a saved *.CWS open and delete everything in it, the project is still open, as indicated by the file name at the center of the Info Bar. The UI will be completely blank, but the project is still open. To save at this point would overwrite your current project name with an empty Workspace. As a precaution, you must either select *File > Close Workspace* or select *File > Open Workspace* to work on another saved CWS file.

Footage Library – This can be thought of as combustion's bin of raw image resources at hand. The Footage Library is always available at the bottom of the Workspace panel. Regardless of the number of branches and various operators you may use, only footage will be listed in the Footage Library.

Working with Viewports

One of the best, unsung, features of combustion is the ability to play back and utilize multiple viewports simultaneously. If you are not used to an application that can do this, it is easy to overlook or not even be aware of this ability. You can assign the output of any part of any branch in the Workspace to any viewport at any time. Viewports are also where you can enable the Schematic View and the thumbnail-based Footage Library. Controlling the layout of the viewports, being able to identify what is happening in the viewports and knowing how to control this assignment are vital to working in combustion.

Let's begin by opening the Workspace named *ch02_Viewports.cws*.

Viewport Layouts – Discreet combustion now allows up to six different viewport configurations for your projects. Try switching between them and think for a moment about some advantages that each might present. When you are done, leave the layout as the equal 'four up' ( ) configuration seen in Figure 2.18.

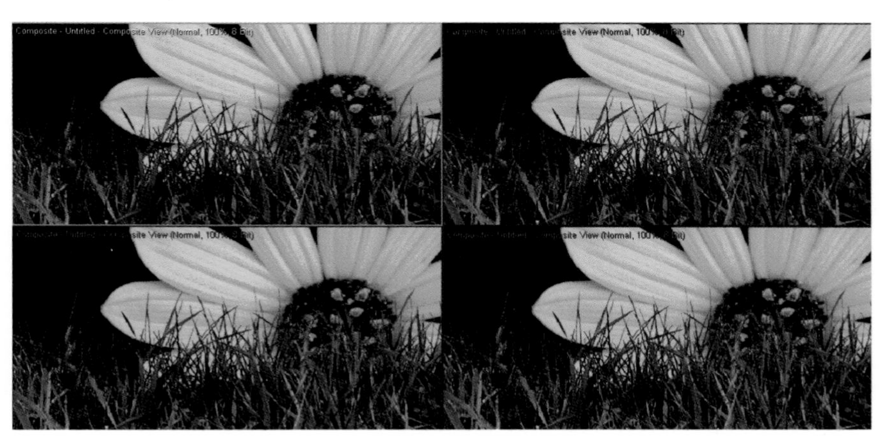

Figure 2.18

Assigning Viewport Contents – If I have a single golden rule for learning combustion, it is this . . . When you are ever in doubt of what you are *ever* looking at or editing, stop and do these two things:

1. Make any viewport the active viewport by clicking on it. The active viewport can be identified at any time by the thin white outline surrounding it.

2 In the Workspace panel, *double* click on the name (not the icon) of the item you wish to send to the active viewport. This can be any item including an operator, piece of footage, paint object, composite, etc.

By double clicking on an item in the Workspace panel, you quickly send the output of that node to the active viewport and you also put the controls for that item at the bottom of the combustion UI. This means you are looking at and editing the same thing at the same time. Many times people get confused at first because they are often inadvertently looking at and editing two different things. Referring back to these two steps at any time will hopefully save you hours of frustration. It is, indeed, extremely powerful to be able to look at and edit two different things at the same time, but this is, perhaps, the number one point of confusion for new users. If you get nothing else out of this book, just remember these two steps and what they do.

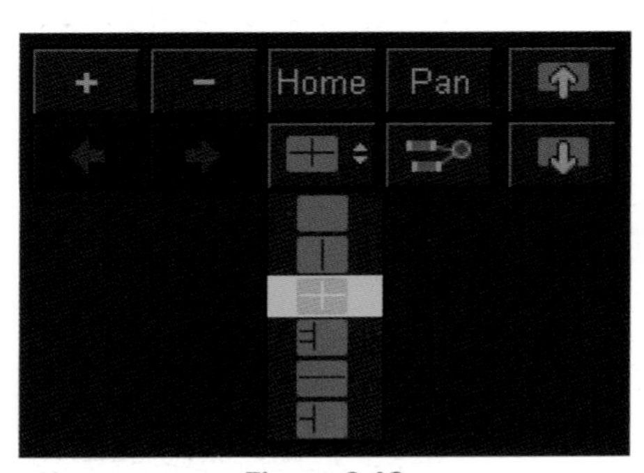

Figure 2.19

Viewport Controls – These controls will always be present when working in combustion. This is where you can zoom (+, –, Home) and pan (Pan) viewports as well as switch between different viewport layouts using the drop-down menu seen in Figure 2.19.

Note: The drop-down menu in Figure 2.19 leaves the selected choice as the icon after you use it. There are now six viewport layouts, but this drop-down is often (mistakenly) read as seven, because the active one is always left at the top.

Tip: Remember, the zoom and pan icons are 'scrub' buttons. This means you can click and drag on them for interactivity of each.

The up arrow icon ( ) is for sending the current selected item in the Workspace panel to the active viewport and the down arrow icon ( ) makes the controls of the item in the active viewport available. In Figure 2.18, the viewport layout is a four-up layout, meaning there are four viewports in which to work.

There are actually quite a few available methods of getting around and navigating within the viewports themselves.

1. Zooming can be accomplished by switching to the Toolbar and enabling the magnifying glass icon ( ). By enabling this tool, you can interactively zoom in and out of your viewports by dragging the mouse up and down. When the magnifying glass icon is selected, you also have the Toolbar Zoom Factor options seen in Figure 2.20. The hotkey for zoom is the Z key.

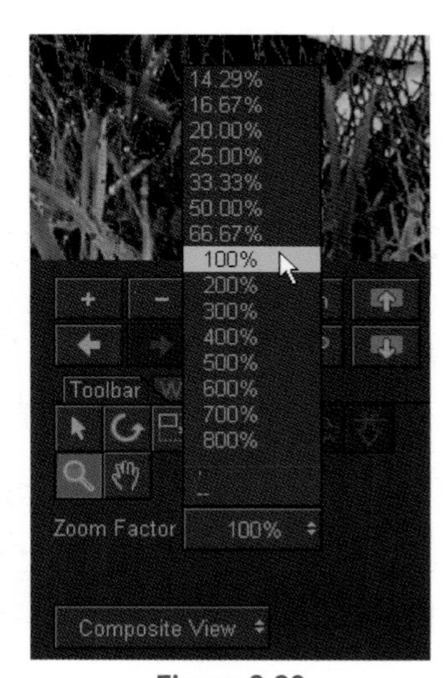

Figure 2.20

2. The + and − icons seen in Figure 2.21 will step the active viewport through the zoom levels listed in Figure 2.20. The hotkeys for these are Control + and Control −.

3. The Home button seen here has a three-state cycle. Clicking this once will set the active viewport to 100% zoom. Clicking a second time will zoom the viewport up or down as needed to fit the entire output in the viewport. A third click will take you back to the original zoom level prior to this three-state cycle. The hotkey for this button is the = key.

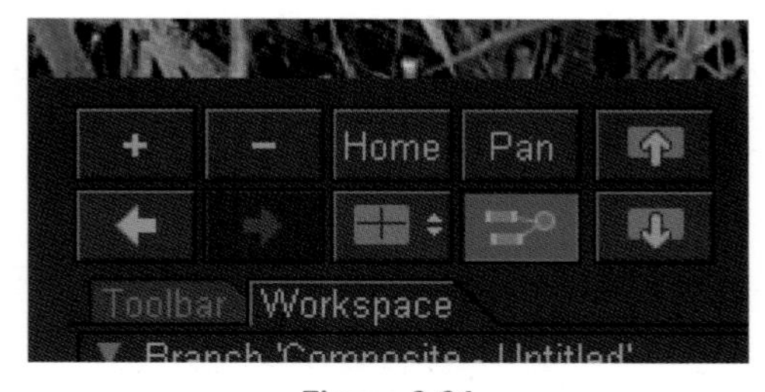

Figure 2.21

Tip: For variable zoom, you can actually click and drag right on the magnify tool or the Home button without even going to the viewports to drag the mouse.

4 The Pan button ( ) and the hand icon in the Toolbar ( ) do the same thing. Selecting either of these will allow you to drag the viewport to drag the contents in any direction. The hotkey for panning is enabled by *holding down* the spacebar while dragging the mouse in the viewport. (Warning – *Tapping* the spacebar once is a stop/start of playback for the active viewport, it does not activate the pan tool.)

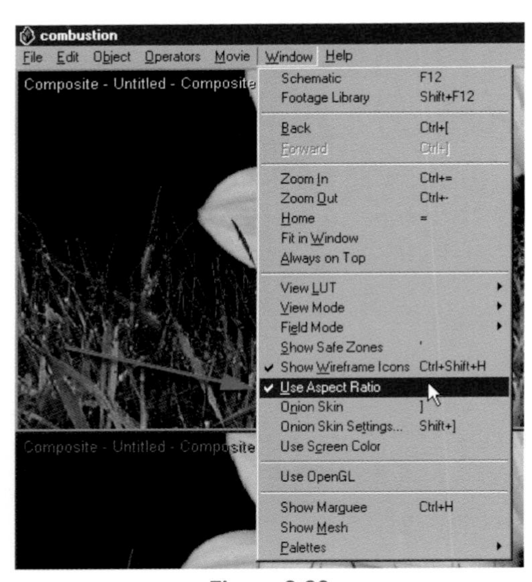

Figure 2.22

Pixel Aspect Ratio – If your project uses pixels that are not square (the pixel aspect ratio is not 1.0), then you can enable the 'Use Aspect Ratio' option *per viewport* to display images such as D1 or anamorphic footage correctly. If footage appears squashed vertically or horizontally, you might need to enable this option from the Window menu (Figure 2.22) or by right clicking on any given viewport and selecting Use Aspect Ratio. Enabling this option will let you view non-square footage and composites correctly on your computer monitor, should you so choose.

Playback Controls – These are just like VCR buttons for the active viewport. While you can have up to four viewports showing at any given time, there will only ever be one set of Playback Controls, as seen in Figure 2.23. You can make these controls active for any given viewport by first making a view the active viewport (simply by clicking on it).

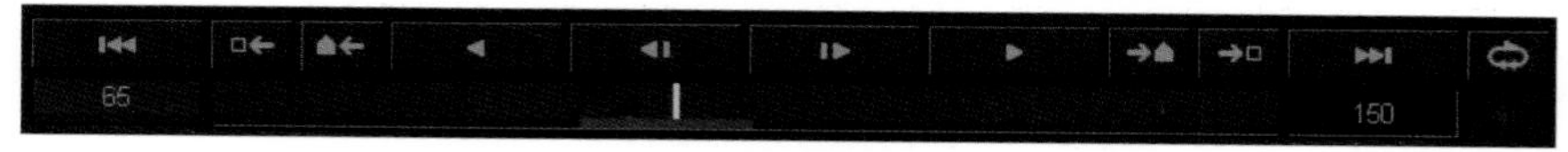

Figure 2.23

The following chart will help you navigate the Workspace using the Transport Controls. Learning these particular hotkeys can dramatically speed up your workflow when building projects.

Button	Function	Hotkey
	Go to Start	Home
	Go to End	End
	Previous Keyframe	Shift + Page Up
	Next Keyframe	Shift + Page Down
	Previous Marker	
	Next Marker	
	Play Backward	Shift + Space/Shift + Enter
	Play Forward	Space/Enter
	Previous Frame	Page Up
	Next Frame	Page Down
	Go to Frame . . .	/

Play Mode – To the right of the Playback Controls is a three-cycle icon that controls settings for play once ( ), loop play ( ), or ping-pong ( ). For most purposes, you can leave this on loop so that the viewports will continue playing forward or backward continuously.

The **Audio Toggle** ( ) is to enable or disable the playback of an audio file. If you have an audio clip loaded, you can use this as a mute button.

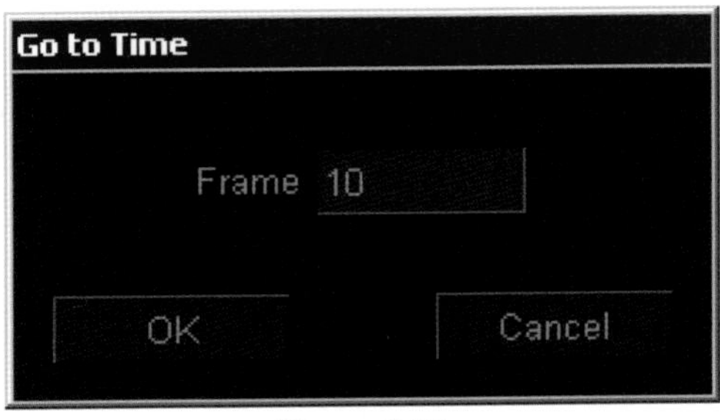

Figure 2.24

Time Indicator – On the left, reads as the current frame. Notice that this is a data entry field, meaning you can use the three different methods of data entry detailed in Chapter 1. You can also bring up the dialog seen in Figure 2.24 by hitting the '/' key on the keyboard.

There are three ways of expressing time in combustion and they can be cycled or switched on the fly. Time code, frames from zero, and frames from one are the three methods of displaying and inputting temporal values. To cycle the method, simply click the mouse in the right time indicator. In the example below, all three total exactly 15 seconds of animation at the NTSC frame rate of 30 fps.

00;00;15;00	Time code as hours, minutes/seconds/frames.
0 to 449	Total of 450 frames (frame 0 counts as the 1st frame).
1 to 450	Total of 450 frames.

Note: You can be working in a frame-based method of viewing time and enter an SMPTE time value and vice versa. For example, if you are working in frames, you can hit the '/' key to bring up the Go to Frame dialog and enter 3.00. This will take you to frame 90 in a 30 fps project. The period acts like a semicolon and identifies the value as SMPTE time code. 3.05 is frame 95 in this case (or three seconds and five frames).

Tip: To verify which of the frame-based time codes you are using, you might want to jump to the first frame (to be positive). If you know you are on the first frame and it reads zero, then you are using the second method of reading and displaying time.

View Modes

Each of the various View modes allows different ways of looking at the image data in any particular viewport. When a viewport is set to display an image, that is, when it is not showing the Schematic or the Footage Library, you can access nine different View modes. Remember that you can make any image in any viewport use any of these View modes at any time. The specifics to each View mode will be detailed after this brief exercise.

Changing the View Modes

1. Open the Workspace named *CH02_Viewports.cws*. If this is the last project you opened, you can select Revert Workspace from the File menu.

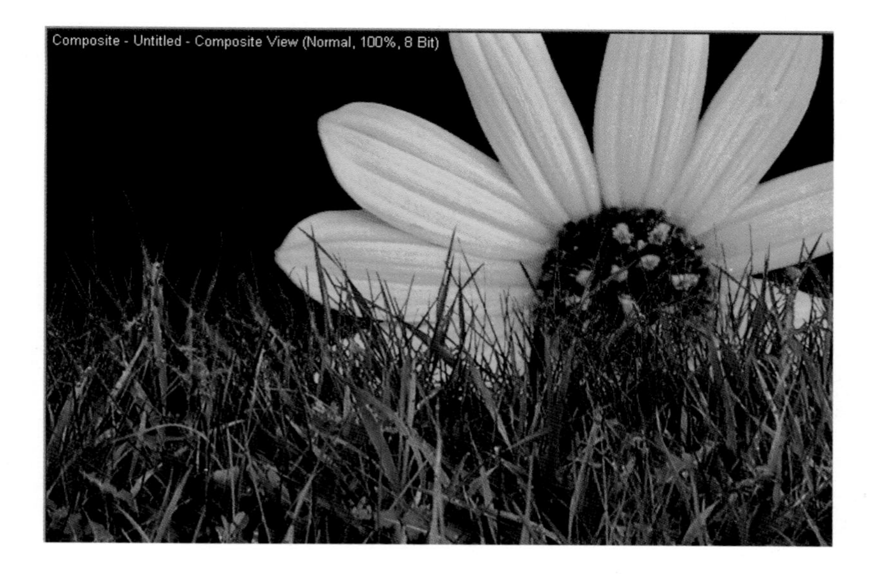

Note: This is a simple, two-layer composite. Both pieces of footage making up these layers are still images, and contain an embedded alpha channel.

2. Go to the Window menu and select the View mode flyout.

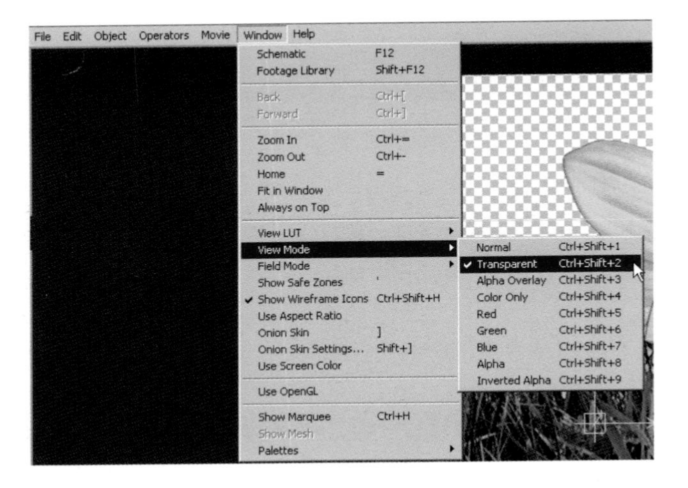

Tip: The hotkeys for all the View modes are visible here as well. While holding down the Control and Shift keys, you can tap across the numbers on the keyboard (not the numbered pad, but the row of numbers across the top of the keyboard). You can also access these View modes by right clicking on any viewport and selecting View modes from the flyout menu.

3 Select Transparent as the View mode type. You should notice that the composite window now shows the transparent areas as a checkerboard very similar to the way Photoshop displays transparency. Another thing to notice is that the label of the viewport now indicates the View mode change. At any time, this is how you can easily tell how any viewport's View mode is set.

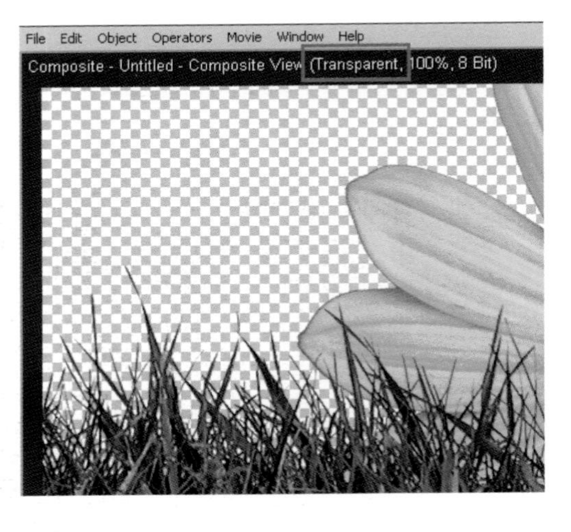

> **Note:** In the preferences, there is a category called 'Transparency'. This is where you can, optionally, change the way that this checkerboard appears. The default checkerboard should work in nearly all cases, however.

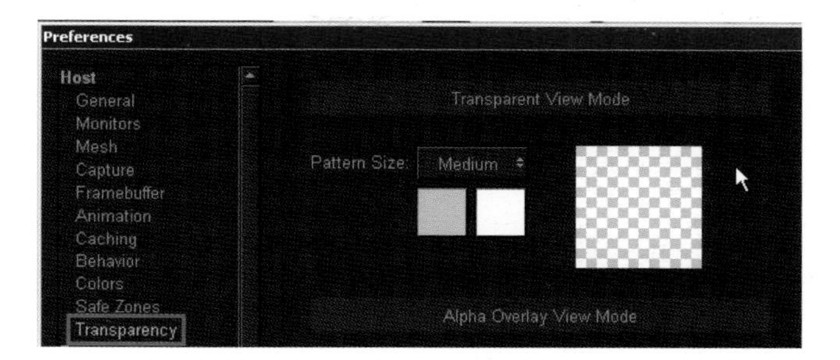

4 Switch to a four-up viewport layout if you have not already done so.

5 Using the techniques outlined above, switch the viewport layout to the following examples. When complete, your viewports should exactly match Figure 2.25.

- A Composite view, Normal
- B Composite view, Alpha
- C Composite view, Transparent
- D Layer view, Alpha (zoomed to fit entire image)

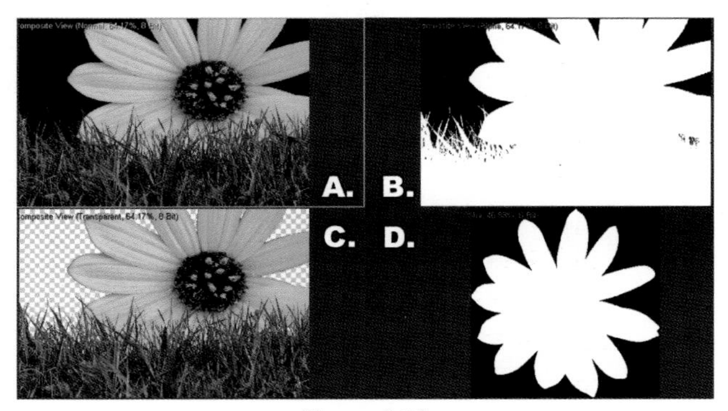

Figure 2.25

Below is a brief description of each View mode that you can enable at any time for any viewport.

Normal – Views the image as it will render. Normal mode takes into account and displays any footage settings for premultiplied alpha.

Transparent – Shows a checkerboard in areas that contain any partial or total transparency.

Alpha Overlay – Shows areas that contain transparency information in a color and opacity as defined by the user in the preferences menu.

Color Only – Shows pixel information without any alpha channel considerations. This will also view an image without addressing premultiplication issues at the footage level.

Red, Green, Blue – These three View modes all show a color channel as a grayscale version of just the specified color channel.

Alpha and Inverted Alpha – **Alpha** is also a grayscale image, but here, values represent transparency information in an image. White is opaque and black is totally transparent. Areas of pure black will completely allow underlying pixels through, while areas of white allow no underlying information to come through. Any gray value in between will result in a proportionate and partial transparency. **Inverted Alpha** is a way to look at the alpha channel reversed, but it does not actually invert or negate the effects of the alpha channel itself.

Note: These View modes are not an effect and do not change the image in any way. They are just different ways of looking at pixel information in combustion.

CHAPTER 3

PAINT AND TEXT OPERATORS

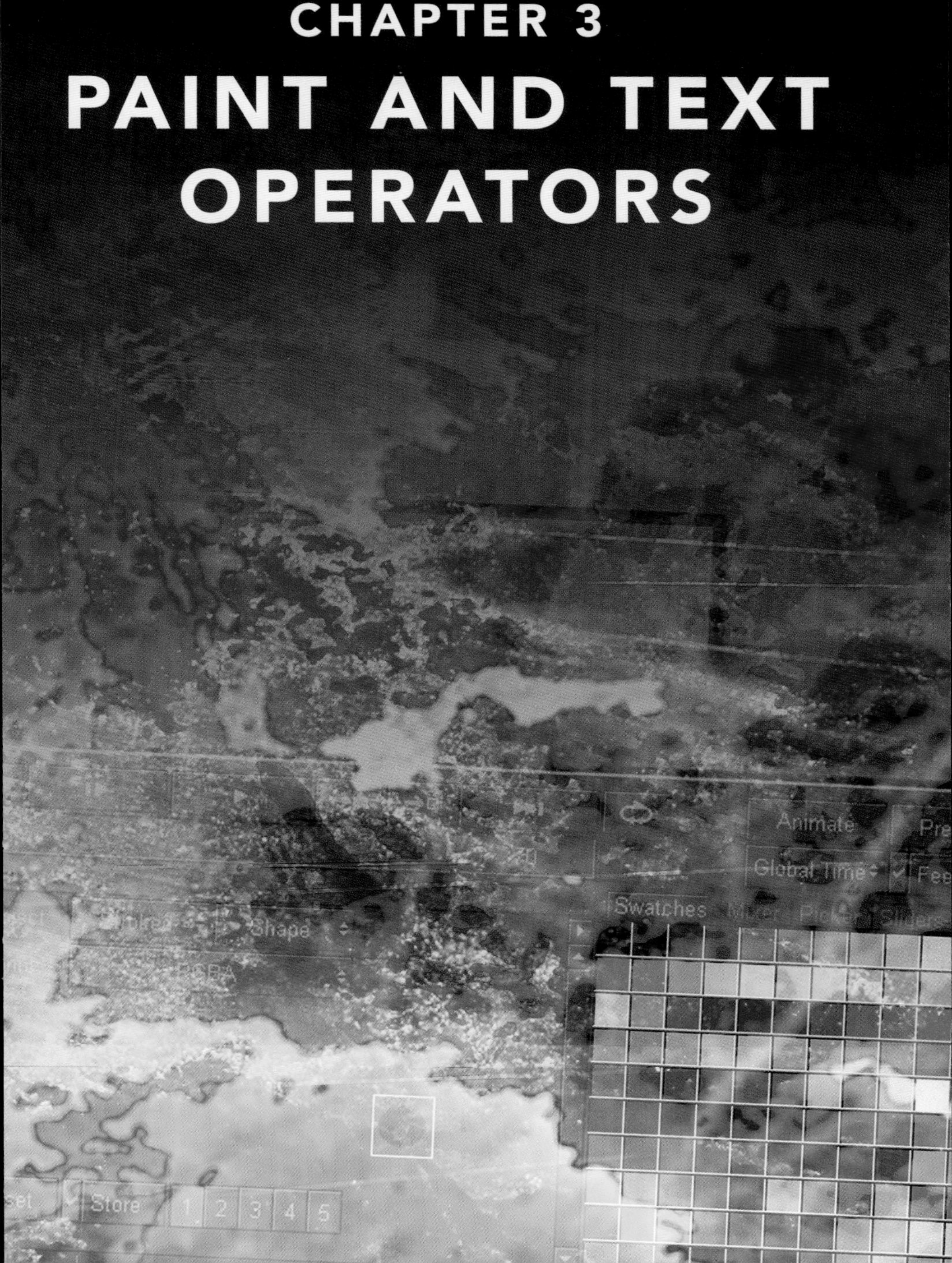

A Bit of Background . . .

Before Discreet combustion, there were two software applications made by Discreet Logic simply called Paint* and Effect*. One was a 2D paint package and the other was a 3D compositing application. It was almost ludicrous to use one without the other and, because of that unavoidable union, these two applications joined in the summer of 1999 and birthed Discreet combustion 1.0.

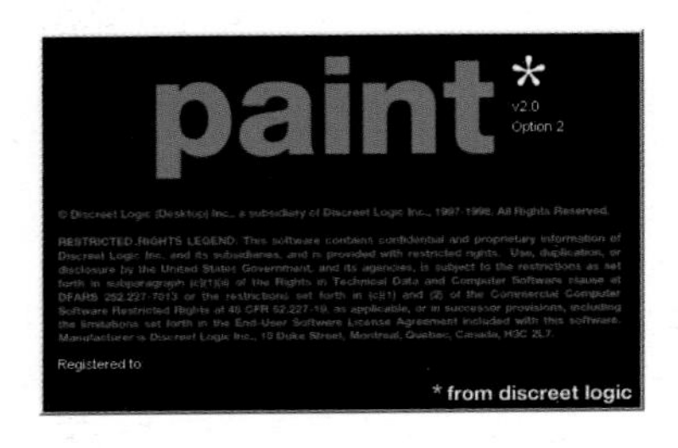

You can understand why then, arguably half the power of combustion can be found in the very humbly named 'Paint' operator. The Text operator is really just an operator that features a subset of the Paint operator toolset. Because of this depth and history, it could be conceivable to write an entire book just on the use of the Paint operator (ahh, don't tempt me). Hopefully this overview is enough of an exploration to get the juices flowing and get you painting away within combustion. Not every feature will be detailed, but the major, not-so-obvious points will be addressed so that you can explore the Paint operator more easily on your own.

There are numerous uses for the Paint operator. Examples are hand-drawn and 'tween'-driven cartoon animation, titles and character generation, wire/rig removal, actor blemish touch-ups, laser blasts, and alpha channel touch-ups when creating a chroma key shot. These are just a few uses of the Paint operator, but they collectively show how no single discipline uses paint over another. All users of combustion can find uses for the paint tools within.

For example, Real Time Roto™ is a term Discreet uses to describe a process that takes advantage of multiple viewports. You paint on a single frame in one viewport while another viewport is constantly caching and playing back your entire animation in real time as you work. This is an excellent way, for example, to see the progress of a wire removal shot as you work or even to have instant playback of cartoon animations as you draw and keyframe in another viewport. Regardless of the purpose of your painting, you can take advantage of these features.

Applying a Paint Operator

There are several ways to access the Paint operator. You can apply it as an operator on a solid, as an operator on a piece of footage or as an operator applied within a branch.

1 To examine the **first** way, select New from the File menu at the top of the UI. Use the settings seen in Figure 3.1. The name of the new paint will be especially important for clarity and comparison purposes in a moment.

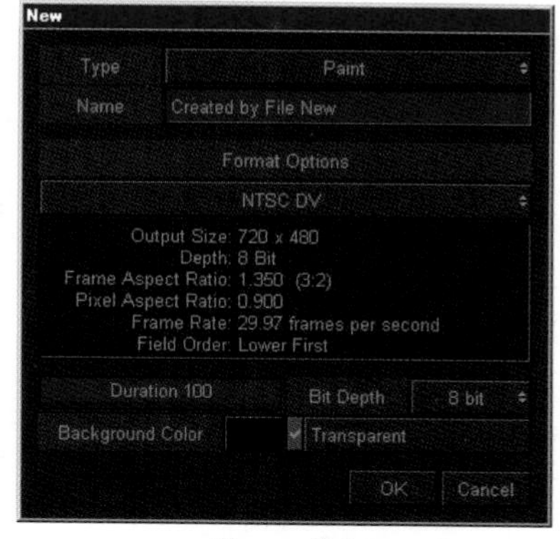

Figure 3.1

2 After clicking OK to create the Paint branch, you will be faced with a blank, black canvas that is NTSC-DV resolution. It should be mentioned here that a black color in this case does not mean the same as transparent – these are separate parameters.

3 In the Workspace panel, notice that you now have a branch containing a single Paint operator applied to one piece of footage. This footage is a solid that is created internally by combustion and does not reside on your computer's hard disk. Select this footage by clicking on its name in the Workspace panel.

4 The Footage Controls tab appears. By switching back and forth between the Source and Output categories, you will notice that all the attributes of the solid footage are the same as the settings from Figure 3.1. Of particular interest is the Source > Opacity setting of 0%, as seen in Figure 3.2.

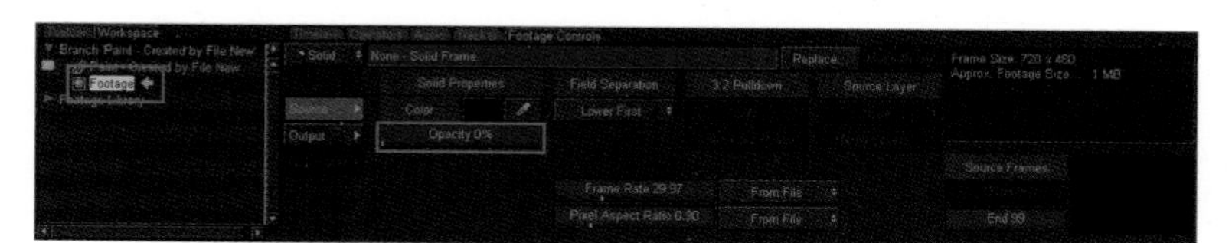

Figure 3.2

When you created the new Paint branch and enabled the 'Transparent' checkbox, this set the opacity of the footage to 0%. Creating a new Paint branch *without* this checkbox selected creates a solid piece of footage with the opacity value set to 100%. You can, however, at any time go to the solid footage controls and change this to any value between 0 and 100% (or even animate this value).

When a Paint operator is applied to a completely transparent solid, the color of the footage is irrelevant. You can think of this as if you were painting on a clear piece of acetate, much like a traditional cell animator. If the solid is not 100% transparent, the color of the solid will show as if you were painting on a canvas of that color and opacity. This only has relevance when the Paint operator is located in a composite and there are other layers behind the paint layers.

The **second** way a Paint operator can be created is to open a piece of footage directly into a paint operator. This allows you to open and immediately start painting on a still or moving image off the hard drive.

1. Leave the current project as is and select Open from the File menu at the top of the UI. You will be presented with the Thumbnail Browser.

2. Navigate to the Footage > Stills > Digital Juice directory on your hard drive and double click on the file named *vegetables.jpg*. The Open Footage dialog will appear as seen in Figure 3.3.

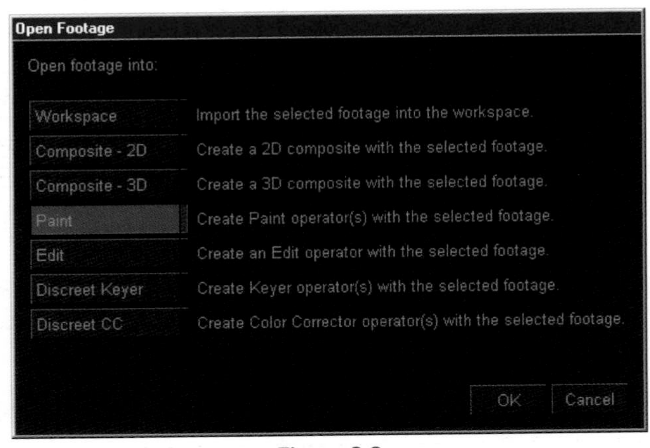

Figure 3.3

You can now open this still JPG directly into combustion with a Paint operator instantly applied. Select 'Paint' from the available choices and click OK to confirm.

You will now have two distinct branches in the Workspace panel, as seen in Figure 3.4. One is named *'Paint'* and the other is named *'Paint – Created by File New'*. The first branch created is a paint operator on a transparent solid and the second one created is a paint operator applied to an image off the hard drive. Notice the order of these branches represents their creation order, and that the new branch did not assume the name of the JPG file we opened.

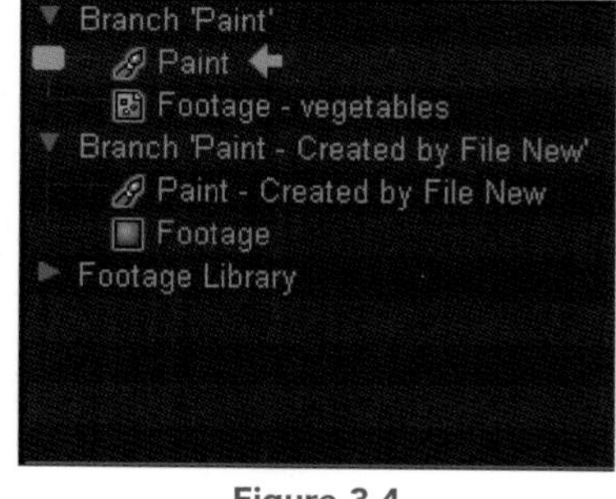

Figure 3.4

3 Select the footage named *vegetables* in the Workspace panel and you will see the Footage Controls > Source and Output settings reflect the attributes of the still image (including a larger resolution of 1600 × 1200 pixels).

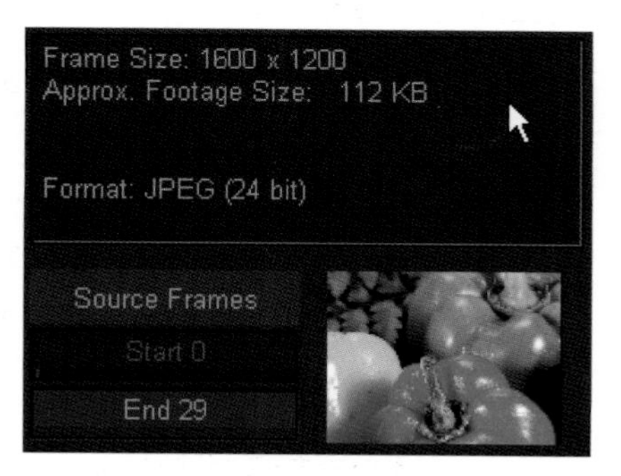

> **Note:** The duration of the still will be that of the *Preferences > Footage > General > Default Still Image Duration*. Because this is a single still image, you can edit the length to accommodate a longer or shorter duration in the *Footage Controls > Output > Source Frame > End* setting seen in here.

The **third** way to apply a Paint operator is as you would any other operator in the Process Tree. That is, you can place it before or after any other operator. To see this, we will import another project into this current Workspace.

1 Go to the File menu and choose *Import Workspace*. Select the file named *ch03_ToBeImported.cws* by double clicking on it. You will now have three completely separate branches in your Workspace: one is a composite branch and two are Paint branches.

2 Double click on the composite in the Workspace panel. This will put the output of the composite branch in the current viewport.

3 Click the triangle to the left of the layer named *Train Layer* to expand it and expose the two effect operators, as seen in Figure 3.5. The single layer in this composite is the end result of two operators applied to a piece of moving footage.

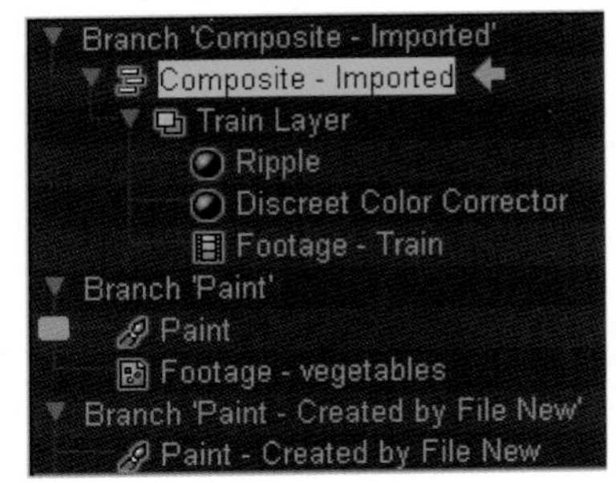

Figure 3.5

4 Single click on the Discreet Color Corrector operator in the Workspace panel to select it.

5 From the Operator menu at the top of the UI, select *Paint*. You should then notice that while the controls for the Color Corrector operator are still active at the bottom of the UI, you have now added a Paint operator in between it and the Ripple operator. The Workspace panel should look like Figure 3.6.

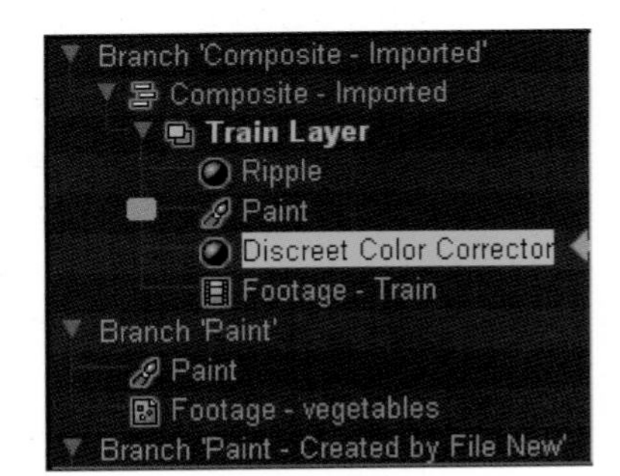

Figure 3.6

If you were to paint in this new operator, the output of the Paint operator will be fed into the Ripple operator, so the ripple will affect the elements created within Paint. To see this:

1 Double click on the Paint operator to put the output of this operator in the active viewport. You will notice that the ripple effect is not visible, because we are viewing a point in the Process Tree prior to the ripple effect. This can be seen in the Workspace panel.

2 Go to the Toolbar of the Paint operator and select the Rectangle tool ( ).

3 In the viewport, draw several overlapping rectangles about the center of the image. Make several sizes and shapes, but do not entirely cover the whole train background image.

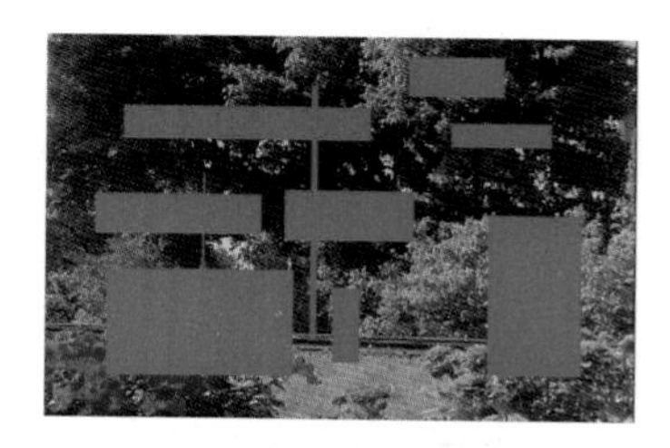

4 Go to the Workspace panel once again and double click on the composite to send the output of the entire comp to the active viewport. You will now see that the Ripple operator is affecting the rectangles you created. This is because the ripple occurs after the Paint operator in the Process Tree.

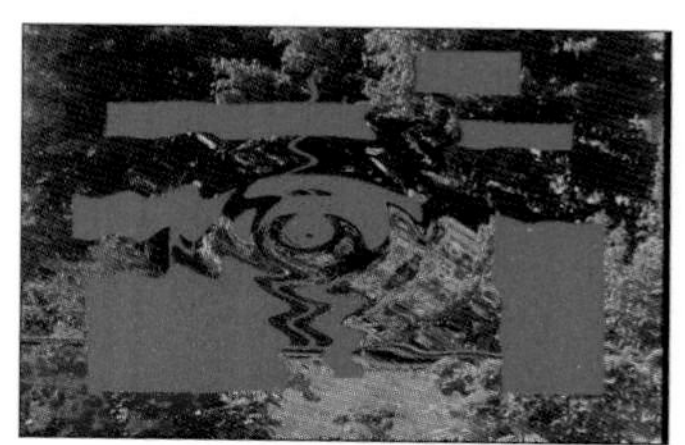

Non-Destructive Paint

Nearly every piece of literature that mentions combustion says something about non-destructive vector painting – but what does that really mean? As you may have noticed, the application keeps track of every Toolbar creation in the Paint operator as an individual object in the Workspace. These objects can be brush strokes, polygon shapes, text and the like. However, unlike many paint applications that get 'flattened' or rasterized as you work, combustion preserves every element created and lets you go back and forth at any time to do things like edit the appearance and attributes of these shapes, reorder their creation order, or even toggle them on/off individually or as groups. These elements are all contained in the Paint operator and while they are non-destructive and unique, they are not actually layers such as you might find in a composite.

This non-destructive workflow is the fundamental thing to remember about combustion's paint. This allows you to work without worry of error because you can go back at any time and modify or refine anything long after it was created. To go back and edit an existing object that is already listed in the Workspace panel, it must first be selected. Take a moment to read that last sentence again, for this is consistently the number one error made by almost every new user to combustion's Paint operator.

To illustrate this briefly:

1 Navigate the Workspace panel to the Paint branch named *Created By File New.*

2 Double click the Paint operator in this branch to send its output to the active viewport. The UI and Toolbar for this Paint operator return.

3 Switch to the Toolbar and select the Line tool ( ). Then draw several lines in the viewport. Make sure that a few of them overlap each other as seen in Figure 3.7.

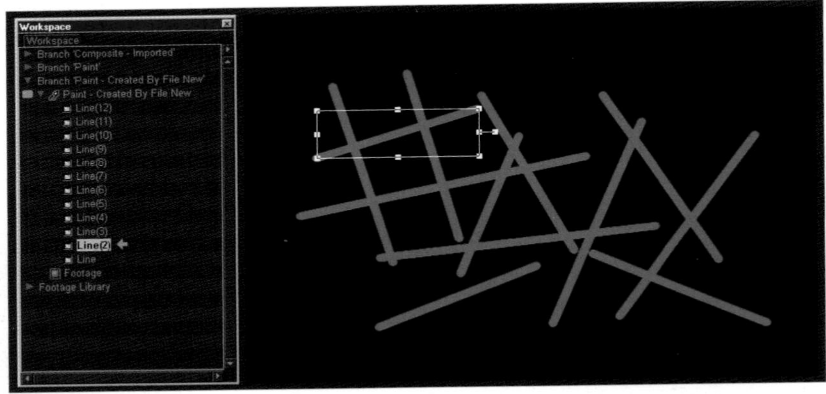

Figure 3.7

4 Go to the Toolbar and switch to the Arrow (Move/Edit) tool ( ). Then, repeatedly click directly on the different objects in the viewport. As you select different objects, notice the bounding box that surrounds the selected object as seen here.

You can also take note that even with just a few overlapping paint objects, it can sometimes be difficult to select objects using the viewports. This is not always the case and depends on the size and shape of the objects in the viewport.

5 In the Workspace panel, click on the different objects named with the prefix *Line*. This is a second way of selecting different objects created within a Paint operator. You will notice that as you pick items in the Workspace panel, the bounding box for that object in the viewport indicates that it is, in fact, selected.

Selecting objects in the viewport or the Workspace panel are both fine for many occasions, but it is here in the Workspace panel that you will be able to select items that might be out of frame, invisible, turned off, or otherwise difficult to select simply by clicking on the item in the viewport. Leave the final selection to the object named *Line(2)* before moving on.

Note: The order of these numbered objects is the order in which they were created. The 'oldest' is on the bottom of the list and the highest numbered line was the one most recently drawn.

6 In the Paint Controls > Modes panel, click on the foreground color swatch highlighted in Figure 3.8. When the Pick Color dialog appears, select a bright blue color and click OK to exit. You will notice that the selected object turns blue.

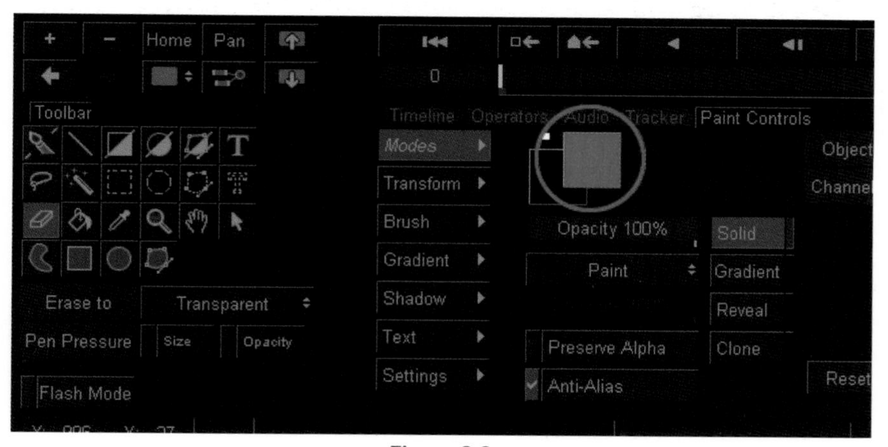

Figure 3.8

7 With this object still selected, select the thickest available round brush preset just under the right end of the Playback Controls. The selected object changes thickness. Again, we have edited an existing object by changing parameters about this object after its creation. You should get used to this ability as soon as possible, for it is the fundamental power of combustion's Paint operator.

8 If you click an empty area in the viewport or Workspace panel, you will deselect all objects. At this point, changes made such as the color and brush size (to name a very few) have no effect on existing objects.

When nothing is selected in Paint, all the operator controls are still available, but changes made to attributes like color, font, modes and so on are being pre-emptively made as presets for the *next* objects or brush strokes to be created. I cannot reiterate this point enough: existing objects typically need to be selected to make changes to them.

Tip: You can modify multiple objects at the same time by first selecting them all in the Workspace panel and then changing attributes like the color and brush size for all selected objects.

9 Reselect the object named *Line(2)*. In the Workspace panel, click and drag (up) on the name of the selected object. You will notice a horizontal bar appear, indicating where you can 'drop' this object in the stack of other objects. The order of these objects defaults to oldest on bottom, but you can use this method of reordering objects to make some appear under (or 'before') others. In the viewport, you will see that *Line(2)* moves closer to the 'top' visually.

Note: Depending on which objects overlap in your viewport, you may have to change the color and/or brush size of several objects to see the effects of this reordering.

10 Right click on the selected object and select Rename from the flyout. Name this object *ThickBlueLine*. You will immediately see the name change reflected in the Workspace panel. You can see that the naming of elements created in a Paint operator can quickly help you navigate through the potentially numerous objects. While I am not suggesting that every single paint stroke be renamed, it can be quite advantageous to identify key objects in your projects.

The Paint Toolbar

Paint Objects – The top row of icons are for creating basic shapes in the Workspace. Because they are designed for animation, these objects also have a duration that should be considered. The following chart briefly explains each tool.

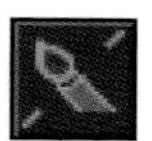

Freehand. This is for freeform drawing tasks. This tool also offers options for size, opacity, color and mode for people using a graphics tablet. These tools will not have any effect, however, if a tablet is not present. There is also an option ( ) to create shapes that are immediately created as curves that control points accessible. Control points will be detailed in a moment.

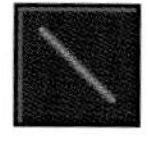

Line. This creates a straight line with a click and drag of a start and end point. The resulting objects are actually curves whose end points can be edited. You can also add additional control points by clicking directly on the line after it has been created.

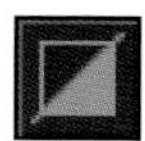

Rectangle. This is for creating simple, four-sided shapes. There are options for creating freeform shapes, constrained aspect shapes and fixed pixel-sized shapes.

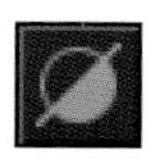

Ellipse. This is for creating ellipse shapes as a starting point. Options for this tool include creation of shapes that are oblong, constrained to a specific aspect ratio, or fixed to a specified dimension in length and height in pixels.

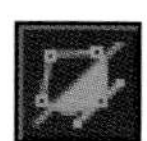

Polygon/Bezier. Shapes created with this tool can also be open or closed. You begin drawing by creating points onscreen. If you click to add a point it will be a corner edge and if you click and drag, the initial point will be a Bezier curve. To create an open shape, you draw until you want to end the creation process and then hit the TAB key to exit. To create a closed shape, you return to the first point and close the shape by clicking the last onto the first. You will not be prompted for this closure; it happens automatically.

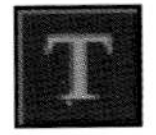

Text. The Text tool has options for creating numbers or time code. Entering the Text tool evokes a plethora of additional tools relevant to creating text. These are replicated in the Text operator. The Text tool will be detailed later in this chapter.

There is an additional function for the Freehand, Rectangle, Ellipse and Polygon/Bezier tools. These four tools have the option of initially creating their respective shapes in either *filled* or *stroked* mode. Figure 3.9 shows the results of these four tools each being used to create the same shape in both modes.

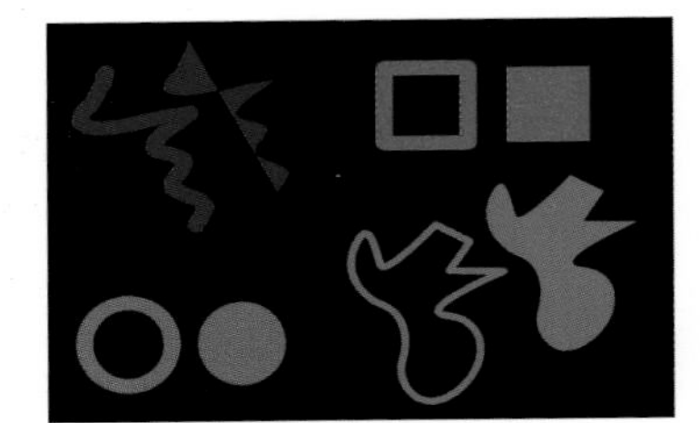

Figure 3.9

Clicking on the upper left of the icon activates it as stroked, and activating the icon by clicking the lower right will initiate the tool in filled mode. If you look closely, you can notice a thin line separating these four icons in half. To change from one mode to another, simply click the icon a second time. You can also go back, select an object, and change it from one state to the other. Briefly experiment with the top row of paint tools. Make sure you try out the different options for each tool.

Selection Objects – The second row of tools in the Paint operator are for the selection and isolation of pixels so that successive paint objects will only be applied to portions of an image. Like the first row of tools, these also create actual objects in the Workspace.

Selections within the Paint operator act very similarly to the Selection operators detailed in Chapter 6. Instead of isolating pixels for subsequent operators, Paint selections isolate pixels for subsequent objects created *within the Paint operator*.

With the exception of the Magic Wand, these tools mimic the icon and corresponding options of the tool immediately above each respective selection tool. The difference is that instead of laying down 'vector ink' like the first row of tools, the selection tools are vector shapes that act as a selection function instead of a drawing function. For example, the rectangle Selection tool has the same options and features as the Rectangle drawing tool above, but instead of creating a drawn, filled or stroked rectangle, it isolates pixels as a selection in a four-sided shape.

Lasso Selection. This allows you to draw a freehand selection onscreen. There is only one option associated with this tool. This is either to convert the drawn shape to a curve object upon completion of the shape, or to leave it as a freehand shape without control points. The same icon ( ) is used to create a control-point-enabled object. Remember that existing objects created without this option can later be converted to curves from the Object menu if the objects are selected first.

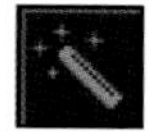

Magic Wand Selection. This tool is for isolating pixels much in the same manner as other paint application's Magic Wand tool; you pick a pixel and a predefined tolerance chooses similar, surrounding pixels that are in a range of similar RGB values. The difference is that a crosshair in the viewport identifies the pixel used for the selection. Remember, this is actually an object occurring in the Workspace. This selection may change dramatically if the pixel under the crosshair changes color as the clip plays.

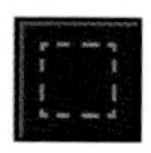

Rectangular Selection. This is for creating corner selection shapes as a starting point. These shapes are automatically objects with four (corner) control points that can be edited or added to; this allows for shapes with more than four sides/corners.

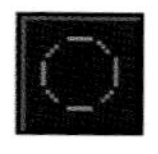

Elliptical Selection. This is for creating rounded selections as starting points. These objects have four Bezier control points to

begin with, but you can click on the line to add more. You can alternatively select and delete existing control points.

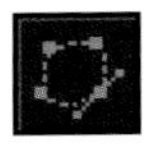

Polygon/Bezier Selection. There are no options for this tool. This is for creating a freeform shape of your choosing, but with a controlled number of points.

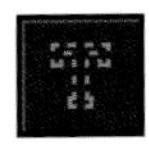

Text Selection. This tool has the same features as the top-row Text tool, but instead of creating ink it only isolates pixels in the shape of a text outline.

Miscellaneous Tools – The third row of tools in the Paint operator are various. These tools also create objects that occur in the Workspace and have duration.

Eraser. This tool is unlike many eraser tools you may have been used to from other paint applications. Like the other tools in the Paint operator, the Eraser creates a vector object that has duration, location and so on. There are tablet pressure options for size and opacity, as well as options for painting to the background color, reverting to the image beneath the Paint operator, or painting to transparent (which is similar to creating a freehand mask).

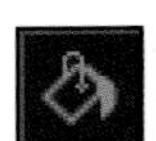

Flood Fill. This has a tolerance and crosshair similar to a Magic Wand. Unlike many other paint applications, you are identifying the pixel to fill. If this operation is done on a clip with motion, the tolerance and crosshair may affect a different range of pixels as time progresses.

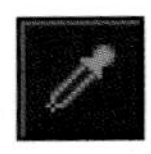

Color Picker. This is a simple Eyedropper tool similar to most paint applications. You can optionally take an 'area sample' by holding down the Control key while using this tool. All the pixels sampled will be averaged and one color value will be returned as the foreground color swatch in the Modes category.

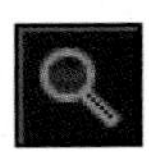

Magnify (Zoom). This is the standard Zoom tool found in combustion's Toolbar.

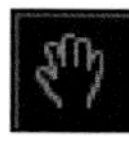

Grab (Pan). This is the standard Pan tool found in combustion's Toolbar.

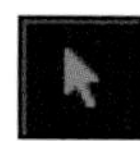

Arrow (Move/Edit). This is for picking and moving objects. It also activates the bounding box, control point and pivot point options for selected objects. Experiment directly in the viewport with the different bounding box handles and points for position, rotation, and scale.

Mask Tools – The last row of four icons in the Toolbar are for creating mask objects within a Paint operator. These use the same workflow as the masks detailed in Chapter 6. The fundamental difference is that these Paint operator objects are non-destructive and can, for example, be changed to become a shape or a selection after their creation time. This change can be accomplished in the Modes category of the Paint operator. Like the rest of the tools here, masks have duration and are objects in the Workspace.

Pivot Points

The vast majority of all paint objects have an invisible point that they use to base their transformations about. Position, rotation and scale are all performed about an object's pivot point. Open the Workspace named *ch03_PivotPoint_MakeCurve.cws*. This will be used to explain pivot points through a brief example. This is a simple paint object that has been copied and pasted several times with a rotation about an edited pivot point.

1. In the Workspace panel, select the object named *Brush Stroke(10)*.
2. In the Transform category of the Paint Controls, scrub the rotation value back and forth. You will notice that the selected object rotates about its end point. This invisible axis is actually the location of the object's pivot point.
3. Switch to the Toolbar and then click on the pivot point icon seen here. Remember, to access and edit an object's pivot points, it must first be selected.

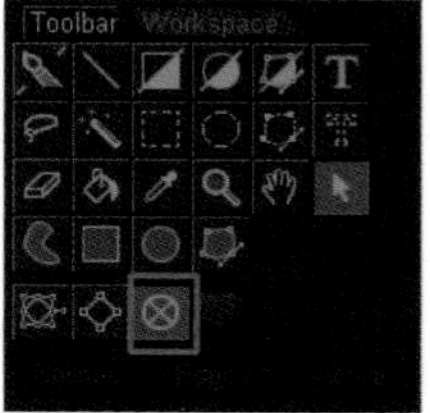

You will notice that in the viewport, instead of the Transform box surrounding the selected object, you can see a small round wire dot at the tip of the selected object. Figure 3.10 shows the pivot point visible and ready for editing.

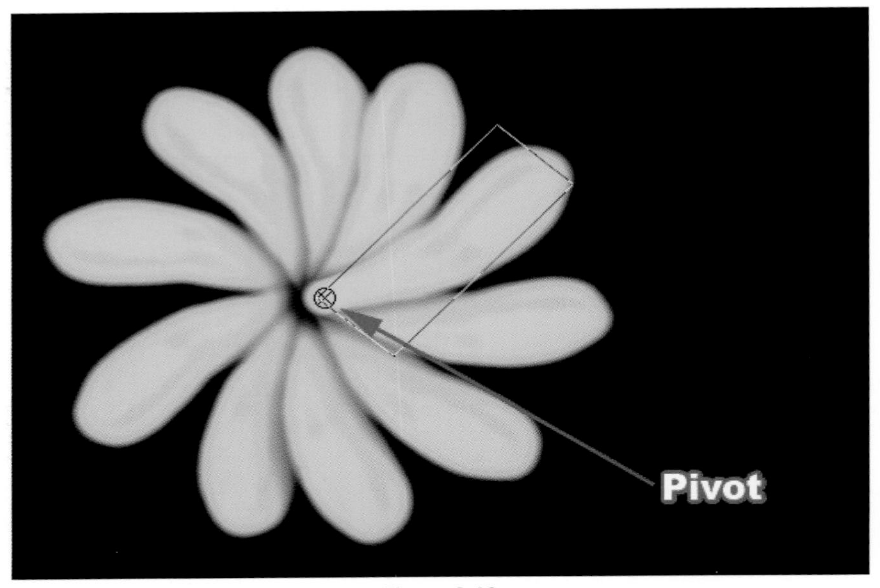

Figure 3.10

4. In the viewport, click and drag the cursor directly on the pivot point and move it to the other end of the same flower petal. Notice the shadow effect changing due to the pivot point.

5. Repeat the same scrubbing of the Transform > Rotation field and you will notice that the object now rotates about a new location.

6. Tap the TAB key to cycle to object transformation mode. The bounding box will reappear on the object.

Control Points

Many objects in combustion also have what are known as control points. You might think of these as 'sub-objects' that can, themselves, be edited, added, deleted, and even animated at will. To access the controls points of a paint object, you must first select the object and then enable the icon highlighted in Figure 3.11. In the case of some freehand paint strokes and text, you may have to do one quick step if this icon is grayed out, as it is for you currently in this example. To convert the selected object to a format that has controls points, it must be 'converted to a curve'.

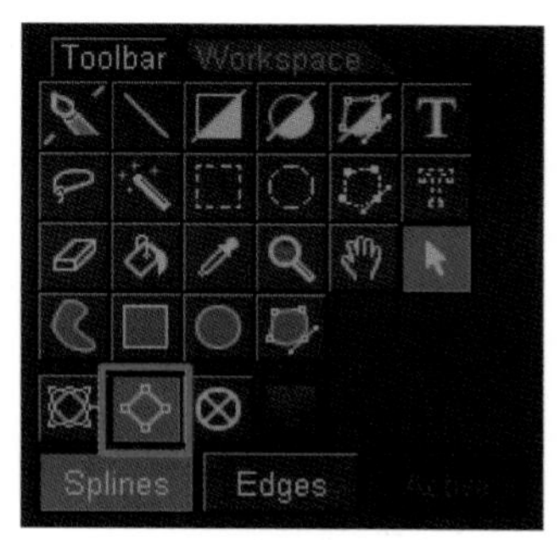

Figure 3.11

1 To see this workflow, verify you still have *Brush Stroke(10)* selected and go to the Object menu at the top of the UI. Select Make Curve from the pull-down menu.

> **Note:** Objects created using pressure input from a graphics tablet will lose pressure settings when converted to spline curves.

2 Switch back to the Toolbar, and the icon for control point access will now be enabled. Click on it. In the viewport, you will see several points appear that make up the object's stroke.

3 Click and drag on any of the controls points within the object. Experiment with editing the Bezier handles and adding control points on the line. To return to editing the transformation of the object and not its control points, simply click on the Edit object icon in the Toolbar.

Figure 3.12 shows an object that has been first made a curve, and then had its control points edited.

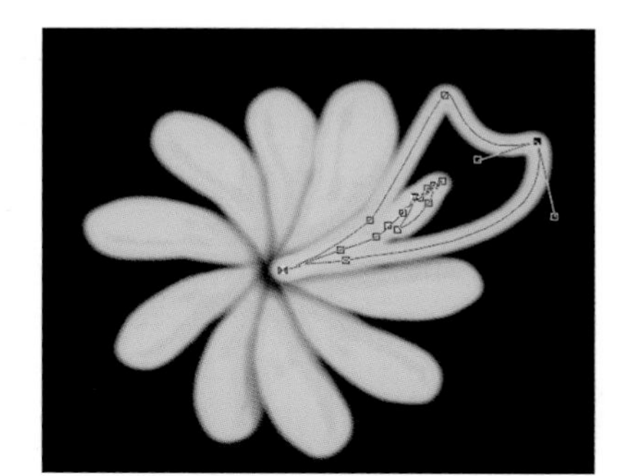

Figure 3.12

Paint Groups

Groups of vector paint objects can be created at any time by selecting multiple paint objects in the Workspace panel. These groups, in turn, can have their own transformations, keyframes, and so on.

1. Draw three tall, filled, solid-red, paint rectangles in the viewport.
2. Select (just) these three objects in the Workspace panel.
3. In the Paint Controls > Transform category, scrub the rotation slider back and forth. You will notice that each selected object rotates about its pivot point.

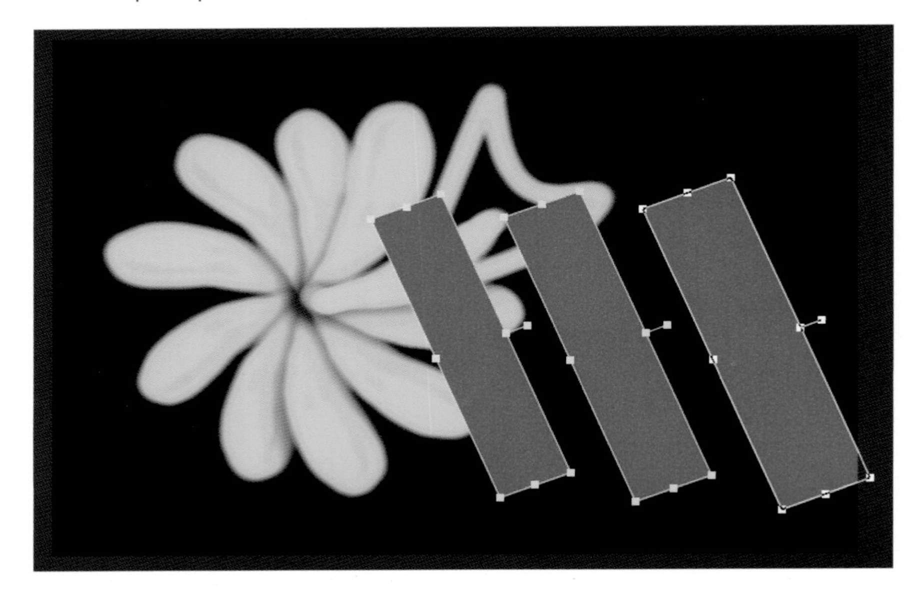

4. With the three rectangles still selected, go to the Object menu and select Group. You will notice that all three rectangles now have one bounding box around them. Rotate this group and you will see that all three boxes now rotate about the group's common pivot point.
5. In the Workspace panel, notice the selected object is named Group. You will also notice there is a small triangle to the left of the name. Click on this triangle to expand the group.
6. Select the object named Filled Rectangle(2). You can still rotate and edit the object independently of the group.

7 Lastly, select the Group in the Workspace panel and click a green color swatch. All three rectangles become green. This allows you to easily change the modes of many objects at once, while maintaining the ability to go into the group and edit the objects individually.

The Object menu at the top of the UI optionally allows you to ungroup selected groups. You currently cannot drag and drop objects into existing groups but you can ungroup, add the object to a multi-selection, and then regroup. Doing this, however, will cause you to lose any animation applied to the original group, though its contents will still have their own keyframes. You can alternatively select both the group and the object you wish to add, and group these. When you group groups, they are considered nested groups (phew . . . say that ten times fast).

Categories of the Paint Controls

The Paint operator, like many other operators, has several sub-categories of controls. Highlights and major features of each are outlined here, but you should experiment with the Paint operator's controls in tandem with one another. Go slow at first, and then combine features from several categories.

Modes

Just under the two active foreground/background color swatches and the opacity setting for paint objects is a rollout menu that defaults to 'Paint' the first time you run combustion. Each vector paint object can have a unique Transfer Mode. These modes are Paint, Additive, Negative, Subtractive and so on. **Transfer Modes** are different ways to have an element blend with other elements 'behind' it. For example, Additive adds the RGB values of selected elements to those pixels below.

> **Warning:** You should really try to get in the habit of setting this back to 'Paint' (with nothing selected) to avoid confusion the next time you return to paint. When you create shapes in certain draw modes, they can sometimes be difficult to see, depending on the image behind the object.

Say, for example, that you are painting on an image with *smear* and then continue to work elsewhere in your Workspace, you return to paint and forget that you were still drawing with smear. This is extremely easy to forget and often you might ask yourself, 'why aren't these new paint strokes I am making visible?!'. It might very well be because you forgot to return to the Paint draw mode prior to creating them. But wait! It's non-destructive! You do not have to delete them and start over, simply go to the Workspace panel, select the new brush strokes, and change their draw mode to Paint all at once.

> **Tip:** Anywhere in combustion when you see pull-down menus with arrows (such as those seen for transfer modes, fonts or viewport quality), it is possible to use the scroll wheel on a mouse to roll through the choices. Simply float your cursor over the menu and roll the mouse wheel. This allows for extremely fast previews of the effects of different transfer modes on selected items.

Regardless of the Transfer mode, you can also set another important option for a paint object. Just to the right of the Transfer mode settings are options for Solid, Gradient, Reveal and Clone.

Solid	Creates paint objects with one color. This color can be overridden by Transfer mode. For example, painting with a Negative Transfer mode will always result in inverted pixels, regardless of the color of the solid 'ink'.
Gradient	Objects that are set to gradient can be edited in the Gradient category of the Paint Controls. These controls will not be available if the object is not set to Gradient here.
Reveal	This is similar to an eraser, but you have the option of painting from another source or from a different time in the current source. This tool is often used for wire/rig removal.
Clone	This allows you to sample pixels from one place and paint in another. This is similar to the Rubber Stamp tool in Photoshop, except you can additionally clone from a still, moving image, from a different frame within the current source, or even from another source entirely.

> **Note:** The Lock button ( ) found in the Reveal and Clone tool options lets you treat the source as a still or a sequence of frames. When enabled, the input frame number is

locked and the source image will be treated as a still image, regardless of which frame you are painting. When unlocked, the source will advance a frame every time you advance a frame in the clip with the Paint operator applied. In the latter case, the frame count can be offset by the amount indicated in the Source frame field.

Selected objects can be changed from stroked to filled, as well as from a shape to mask or selection. These are tools that further make use of the non-destructive workflow in combustion.

Warning: Objects created are named according to their creation parameters. If you create a Filled Polygon and then later change it to a selection, it will still be named Filled Polygon in the Workspace panel (until you optionally rename it).

The Paint operator is just one place that you may come across the small set of **Store** buttons. Figure 3.13 shows the first two store bins in use, as can be seen by the small dot in the store bins. Other examples of operators with stores are the Color Corrector and the Discreet Keyer. Stores allow you to temporarily save certain groups of settings (in this case the Paint operator > Modes category). Store bins are not saved with the CWS file and are lost upon exiting combustion. To switch between stores, you simply click on the Store buttons.

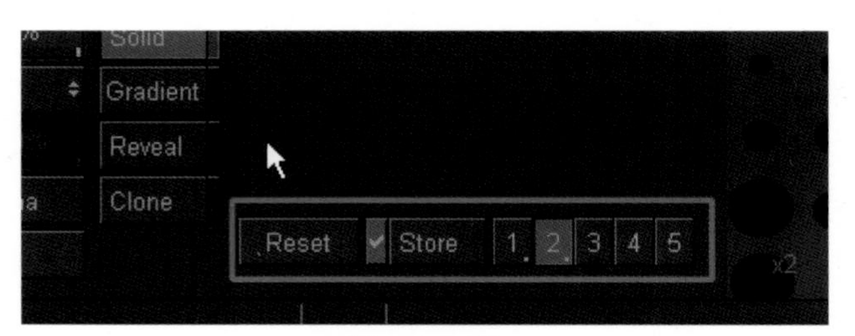

Figure 3.13

You can, for example, have a thick blue paint preset stored in 1 and a thin smear stored in 2. The hotkeys for switching through the five stores are the number keys (1–5) across the top of the keyboard. This allows you to have several paint mode types literally at your fingertips. You can easily switch back and forth from one to another very quickly, without stopping the overall workflow.

Transform Category

Transformations in Paint are measured from the upper left-hand corner of the image (0,0). You can use this dialog to precisely input data for transformations of selected objects or use the data entry fields as a slider to constrain movement on one axis. It should be mentioned that everything in Paint is limited to 2D space. You can, however, apply Paint operators to layers within 3D composites. These layers can then be translated in 3D space.

Brush Category

This is where you can control the appearance of the brushes in the Paint operator. To edit a brush for an existing object, you must first select that object. I cannot reiterate this enough. In Figure 3.14, a rectangular brush has been selected. The yellow arc is a single curved line but the repetition is due to the spacing setting in the Brush controls category.

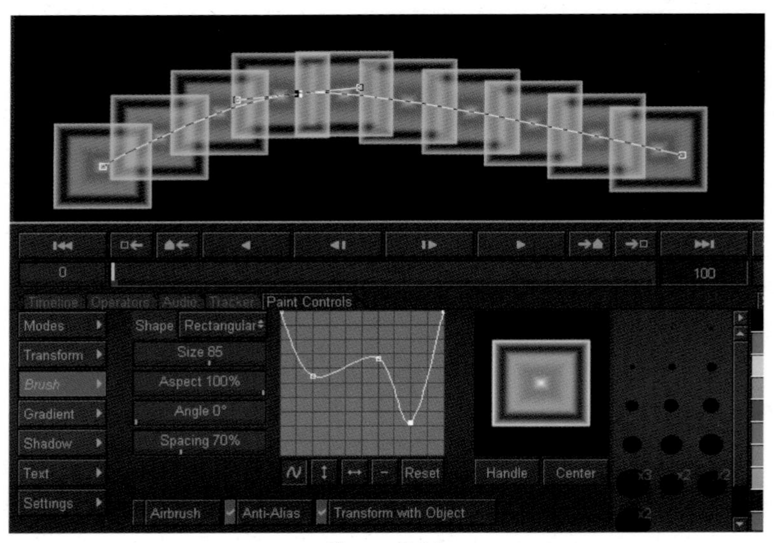

Figure 3.14

Discreet combustion 3 adds the ability to create custom brushes for use within Paint. Figure 3.15 shows a bitmap with alpha loaded into the active brush set. To access custom brush tools, you must switch the highlighted rollout.

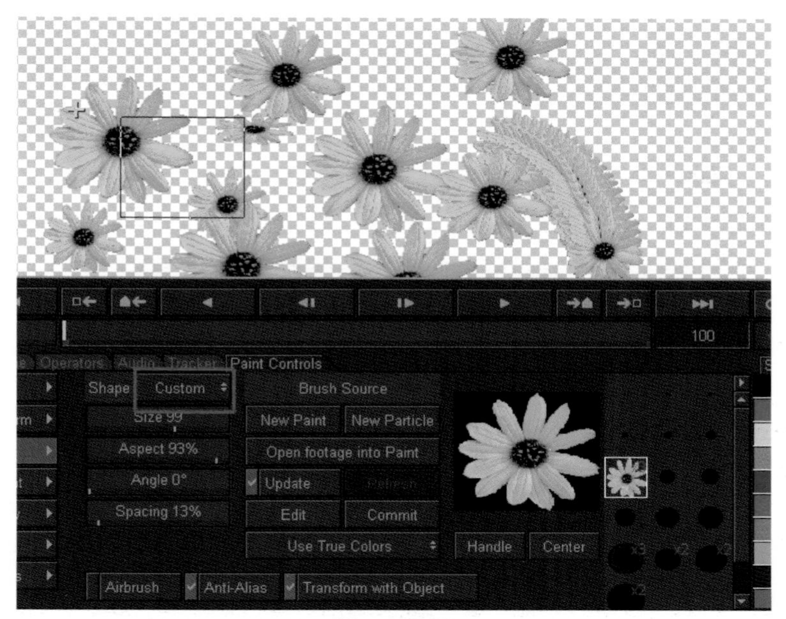

Figure 3.15

Custom brushes can be created from footage on the hard drive, a new paint branch, or a still image generated by a Particle operator. When creating a brush from a new Paint operator, the brush you are creating cannot be used within this new operator – any other brush can be used, however. This is because you are using a Paint branch to create a brush in that initial brush slot. This new brush will be saved in the brush library. It can be useful to use multiple viewports during this operation.

Gradient Category

The gradient editor will appear throughout combustion, not just in the Paint operator. To work with the gradient editor here, you must first make an object a gradient object in the Modes category. You can select an object, switch it to a gradient, and then come to the gradient editor to make modifications to the gradient ramp. In the case where an object was a solid color, switching it to gradient and then coming to this gradient editor will result in a solid gradient ramp with no change.

To add more colors to the gradient editor, click in the wide color bar to add a gradient tag. These tags can be selected and given a color using the Swatches, Mixer, Picker or Sliders to the right. There are also controls for gradient opacity. These opacity ramp color tags only use grayscale values for controlling the transparency of the above gradient. Opacity tag values are edited by right clicking on the opacity tags.

Edge Gradients options allow for paint objects to have soft edges using three different methods. To edit Spline Edge Gradients, go to the Toolbar, enable control point editing and Edges.

Figure 3.16 shows the Edit Gradient ( ) icon. When enabled, you can grab the gradient end points in the viewport or drag the gradient line through an object. Like most values in combustion, this can be animated as well as the colors of the gradient, the position of the tabs, etc.

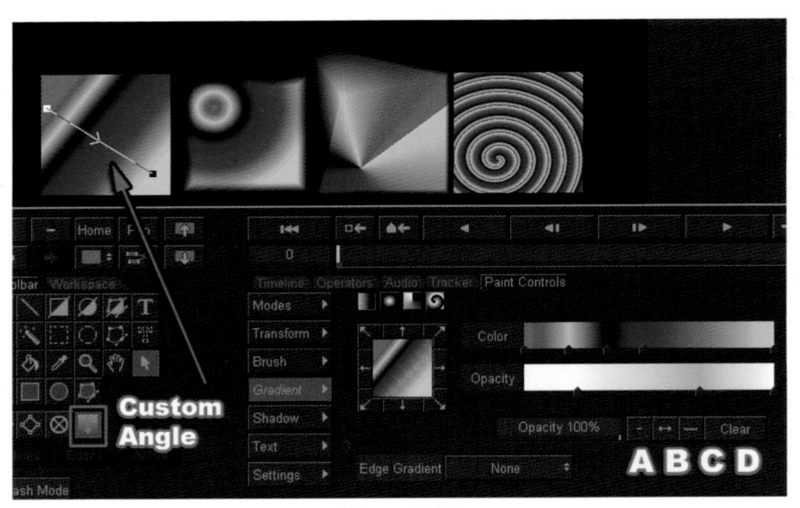

Figure 3.16

The following key identifies the gradient controls in Figure 3.16.

A	Deletes a selected gradient tab
B	Reverses the current gradient
C	Spaces all gradient tabs evenly
D	Resets the gradient editor

Shadow Category

To easily see the effects of a shadow, create several overlapping freehand brush strokes, select them all, and enable shadows from the Shadow category. In the shadow preview window, you can click and drag to place the shadow of all the objects at once so they appear to be lit the same. These shadows, it should be pointed out, are not true, raytraced shadows like the ones possible in a 3D composite. Paint operator shadows are a 2D rendered effect similar to a Stylize > Drop Shadow operator.

Text Category

This is addressed at the end of this chapter.

Settings Category

Output Selection – This allows a Paint operator to be used exactly like several of the selection operators detailed in Chapter 6. When this is disabled, selections within the Paint operator are only relevant inside the said operator. Enabling this option tells a Paint operator to output any active selections within to the Process Tree.

Flash Output – Discreet combustion 3 allows for the majority of the Paint objects to be exported as an SWF format Flash file. This feature adds the ability for combustion to generate animations geared towards the web. While combustion has previously been able to render streaming (raster) QuickTime files targeted towards the Internet, you can now additionally output vector files as well.

To export the SWF file, you stay in the Paint operator and, from the Settings category, select *Flash > Export*. This action will not only output an SWF file, but also an HTML placeholder with some statistics about the exported file (such as the file size of the SWF).

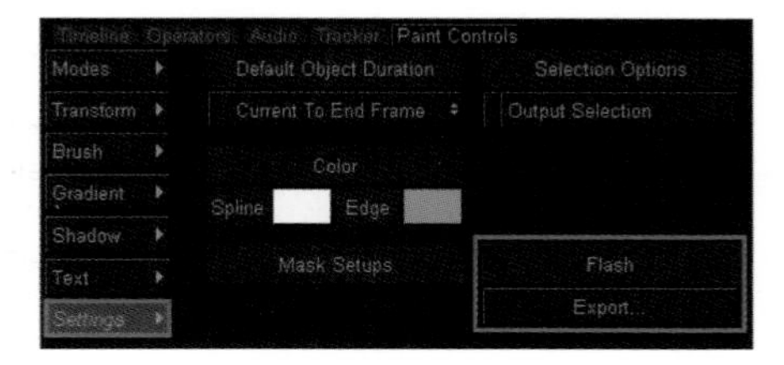

The Paint Toolbar has a button that switches the Paint operator into 'Flash Mode', as can be seen in Figure 3.17. This button disables tools within paint that are not compatible with the SWF file format. Using the Paint operator in Flash Mode assures you that the contents of the operator will appear on the web as they do within combustion's viewports.

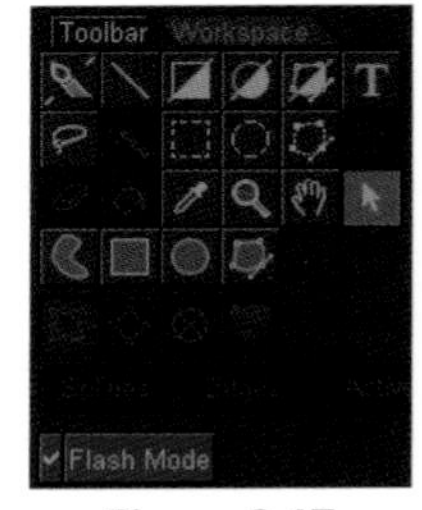

Figure 3.17

Because of the limitations of the Flash SWF format, you may want to preview an animation within combustion as it will appear when exported to the Flash file format. From the Window menu at the top of the UI, you can select Flash View to switch the active viewport to a player that is compatible with the Macromedia Flash Player. Notice in Figure 3.18 that the viewport label reflects this temporary change. After checking this, make sure to turn this feature off so your viewports will return to normal.

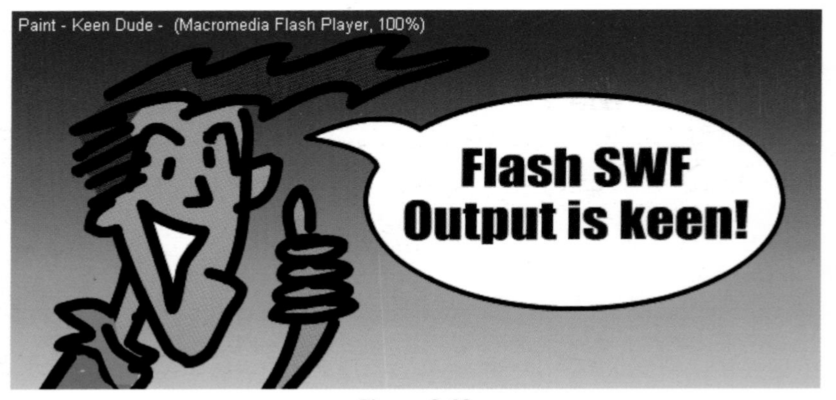

Figure 3.18

Object Duration – In addition to painting onscreen in the viewport, every object you create in a paint operator also has a specified duration value. Remember, this is a paint tool designed for the creation and manipulation of moving images. You can, for example, create a polygon selection and paint a brush stroke and have them cover many frames instead of painting individual strokes on several frames as a traditional animator might do.

The Settings category of the Paint operator is where you can set the default object duration of your paint objects. The choices are 1 Frame, All Frames, or

Current Frame to End. Remember that a paint object not only has a 'where', but also a 'when'. This is because combustion is a paint tool designed with animation in mind.

1 Frame	Object created in Paint will initially only be created on the current frame in time.
All Frames	Objects created are painted on all frames.
Current to End Frame	Objects will begin on their creation frame, and remain visible until the end of the segment.

Figure 3.19 shows the Timeline and the difference between the three types of default object durations. The Timeline will be explained in greater detail in Chapter 10, but it is briefly shown here to illustrate object duration. Notice the names of each object on the left and its corresponding Timeline representation on the right. The white, thin, vertical line represents the current frame.

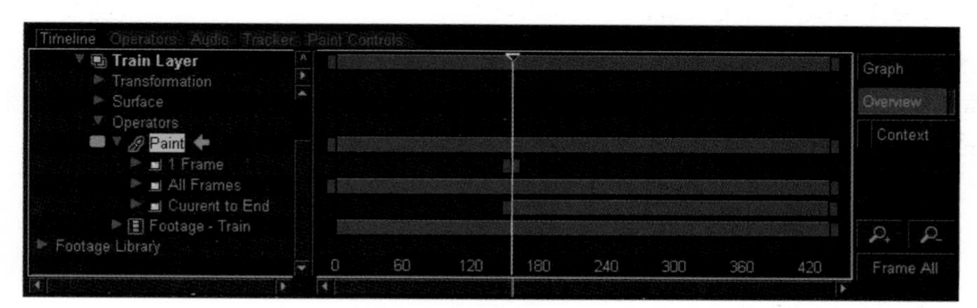

Figure 3.19

If, after creating an object with a certain duration, you decide to change its in and out points, you can use the following simple solution at any time:

1. In the Workspace panel, select the vector objects you wish to extend or reduce in duration.
2. Using the Timeline indicator, go to the frame you wish the selected objects to start and hit the comma key on the keyboard. This sets the in point of all the selected objects to the current frame.

3 Go to the frame where you want all your selected objects to end and hit the period key on the keyboard. This sets the current selected object's out point to the current frame.

Tip: To quickly extend the duration of vector objects over *all* frames, first select them all and then individually tap the following four hotkeys in this order:

Home	Comma	End	Period

Figure 3.20 shows the result of selecting all three of the previous example's Paint objects and using this simple four-hotkey combination. You can see that the bar representing each object now covers all frames.

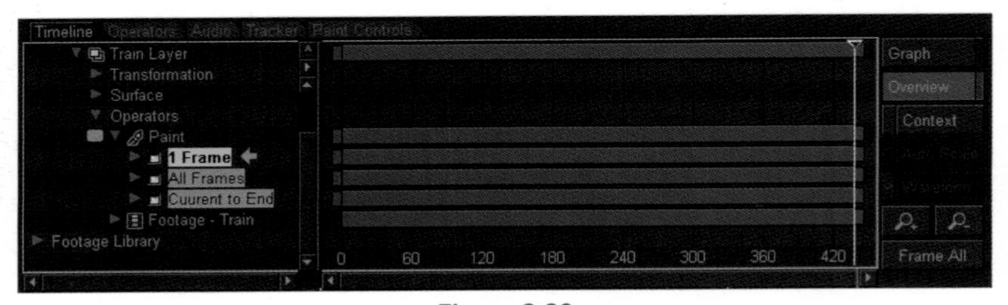

Figure 3.20

This four-key combination also works on setting the duration of a still-image piece of footage, but it does not work on multi-frame footage clips, layers or operators. Also, you do not need to have the Timeline showing for this to work, it is merely used here to illustrate the effects of this quick hotkey combination.

Vector Paint, Raster Output

We have seen that everything created in a Paint operator is a non-destructive, resolution-independent, vector-based object. Right, OK, got it. Yet another important aspect of the vector elements created in the operator is that they can be scaled up and down *inside the operator* and you will never notice the familiar 'jaggies' associated with a loss in resolution. The output of the operator, however, is raster image data. To explain this through a step-by-step example, make sure you are using Preview or Best display quality.

1 Select File > Open Workspace. If you have a Workspace open, you will be prompted to save this current project.

2 Open the Workspace named *ch03_VectorRaster.cws*. This will allow us to see the difference between resolution independence and the rasterization of a Paint operator.

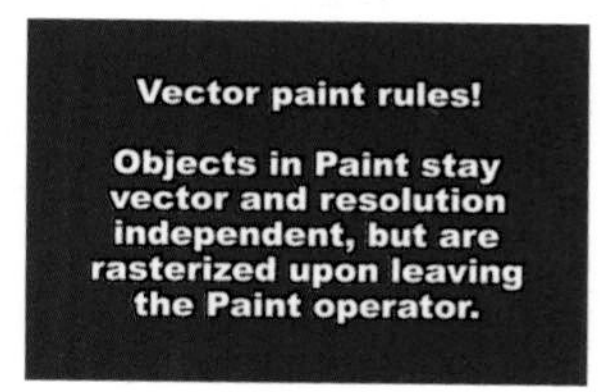

Vector paint rules!
Objects in Paint stay vector and resolution independent, but are rasterized upon leaving the Paint operator.

3 In the Workspace panel, expand the layer by clicking on the gray triangle next to its name. Then expand the Paint operator in the same way to access the text group. Select the text by clicking once on the name, as seen in Figure 3.21. When there is an arrow to the right of the name, this indicates it has been selected.

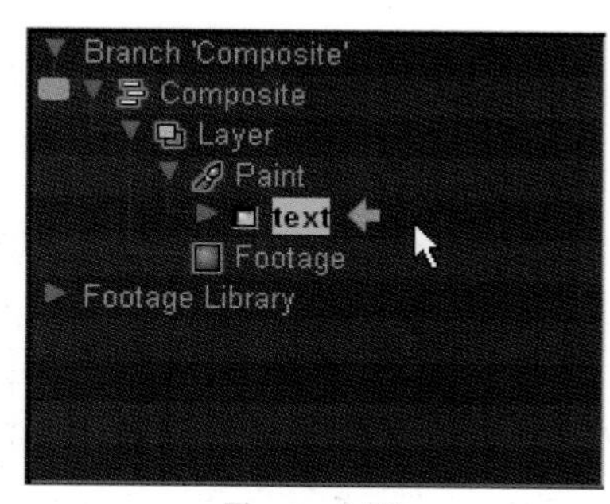

Figure 3.21

4 From the Paint Controls tab, select the Transform category.

5 Under the Scale transformation fields, enable Proportional (Proportional). Then, in either Scale field, click and drag the mouse back and forth to change the size of the text object. When the Feedback button is enabled, you will notice the text get larger and smaller. Notice that no matter how large you scale the text it stays nice and crisp. This is due to the fact that all combustion Paint objects are vector based. Figure 3.22 shows the text scaled to 400%.

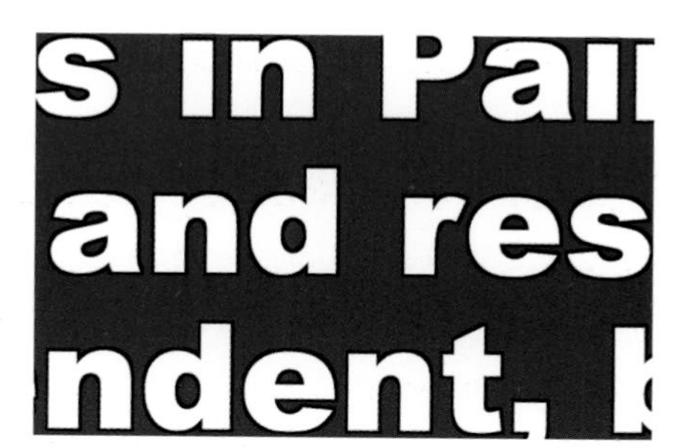

Figure 3.22

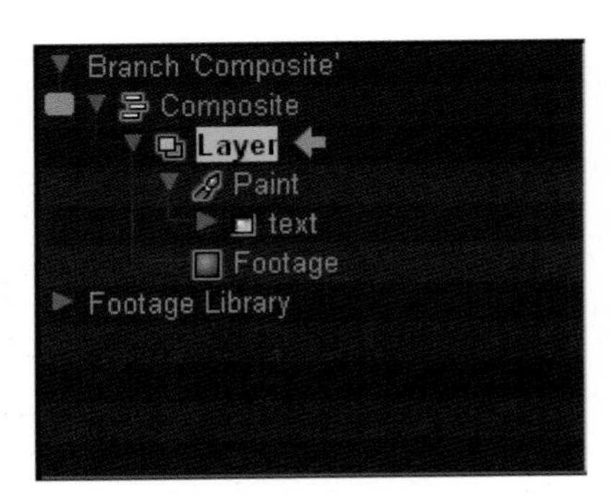

6. Click the R button next to the Scale to reset the transformation.
7. In the Workspace panel, select the layer by clicking once on its name.
8. From the Composite Controls tab, go to the Transform menu.
9. Enable proportional scaling and scrub either Scale slider back and forth to scale the entire layer. You should notice that when scaled down below 100%, the layer looks great; however, when scaled up beyond 100%, the dreaded jaggies begin to appear, as seen in Figure 3.23.

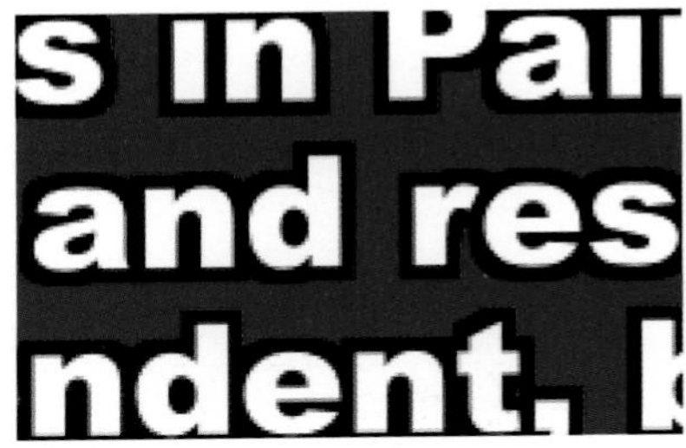

Figure 3.23

The previous exercise demonstrates that the contents of a Paint operator stay crisp and resolution independent within the operator, but pixel information exiting or 'being passed along' by a Paint operator is always rasterized and therefore prone to resolution loss just like any bitmap file on the hard drive. Because of this phenomenon, you should create any Paint branches from scratch with plenty of source resolution so that you can later scale the layer up and down without concern. You should be aware of and clear on this process before you get too involved within a Paint operator.

Working with Adobe Illustrator Files

When you open an Adobe Illustrator file with the **.AI* extension, combustion preserves the vector curves by creating a Paint operator on a solid piece of footage. Figure 3.24 shows the source Illustrator file open and as imported into combustion. Notice how the vector objects in combustion preserve the tangency of the Bezier handles for the drawn curves. These Bezier handles can be edited and even animated.

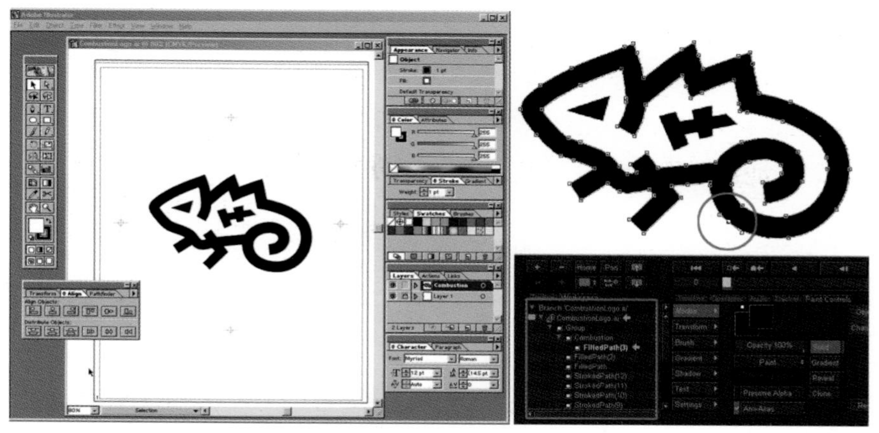

Figure 3.24

Tip: In your vector applications such as CorelDraw, Freehand or Illustrator, you can make a larger page size and combustion interprets this as a larger solid piece of footage. Then the Paint operator contains larger vector objects without the need to scale them up in combustion.

Text and Character Generation

Text in combustion can be accessed via the Paint operator or the Text operator. The Text operator is a subset of the Paint operator; that is, anything that can be created within a Text operator can also be replicated in a Paint operator, but not vice versa.

If you have a project being built that needs just a bit of simple text, then the Text operator uses slightly less overhead or system resources to cache than a Paint operator. This is, however, negligible, and after you are comfortable with the use and navigation around the Text operator, I might suggest using the Paint operator because of the additional options it presents.

For example, Figure 3.25 shows a simple project that could *not* be replicated with a Text operator alone. The blue text with black outline could be created in a Text operator, but the yellow box and red brush stroke could not, because they access paint tools that are not available in the Text operator.

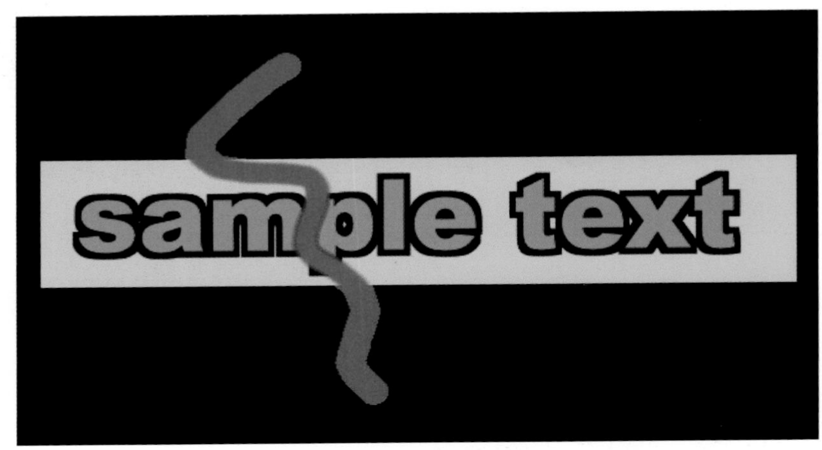

Figure 3.25

For the purposes of learning the workflow of creating and editing text within combustion, I recommend using the Text operator until you are comfortable with its use. This is to prevent any confusion as to the tools at hand. Using the Text operator instead of Paint will present only the feature set geared towards character generation and not those suited for other purposes like drawing shapes.

The most often misunderstood aspect of the Text tool is that it essentially has two modes of use. The first is when you are treating the text as a group of vector objects and the second is when you are treating it as actual text characters. When in Text editing mode (T), you will have control over changing the characters and attributes of text much as you would in a word processing application. When the Toolbar is in Text mode (T), all hotkeys are disabled so that you can enter characters in the text entry field. If you select the Pick tool ( ), the text group will still be selected, but you will be treating it as a group of vector Paint objects once again.

Figure 3.26 shows the Toolbar and controls for the Text operator. Notice the similarities to the Paint operator. You can also see here that the Text controls > Text category has four sub-categories: Basics, Attributes, Layout and Advanced.

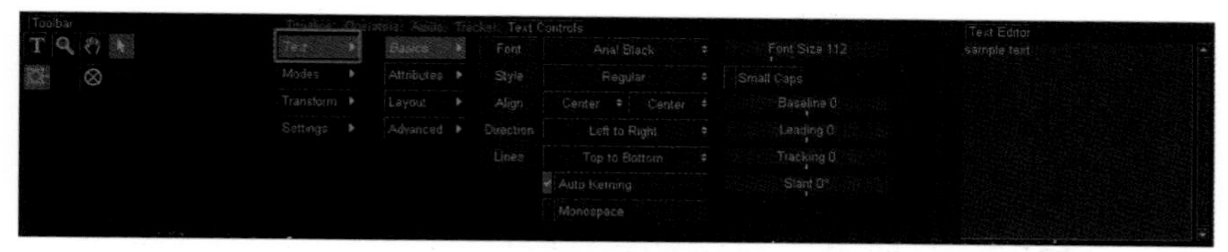

Figure 3.26

The following chart briefly summarizes the sub-categories of Text.

Basics	Font, Size, Leading, Kerning, Tracking and Alignment
Attributes	Solid/Gradient/Textured Face & Outline, plus Shadows
Layout	Static, Credit Rolls and Crawls, Write On % and Margins
Advanced	Text on path or loop, plus 4 Variation settings
Number	Only available if you use the number utility in the Toolbar
Timecode	Only available if you use the time code utility in the Toolbar

To explain the Text operator further:

1. Open the Workspace file named *ch03_TextFX.cws*. This is a Text branch consisting of one Text operator applied to a white solid. Within the operator, there are two text groups. Selecting either of these groups allows you to enter text controls.

2. Go to the last frame of the animation. You will notice that a second line of text is visible here.

3. In the Workspace list, double click on the first group, named *TextFX*. Make sure you are in the Text category of the Text Controls.

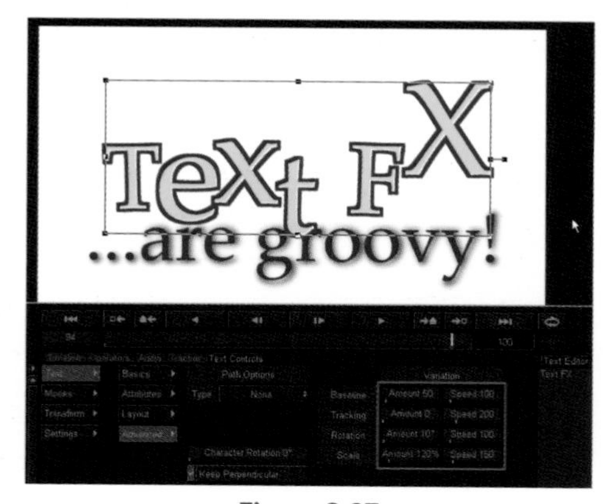

Figure 3.27

4. In the Advanced controls, highlighted in Figure 3.27, scrub the Timeline frame indicator back and forth; notice that these values

are not animated, yet the first line of text jumps all about. These Advanced > Variation controls are a great way to make complex animation without a single keyframe.

5 In the Workspace panel, double click the second line of text named *are groovy* and then go to the Text > Layout category. Here, the Write On parameter has been animated with only two keyframes, yet the many characters that make up this line of text all get typed on as if by a typewriter. Figure 3.28 shows this value.

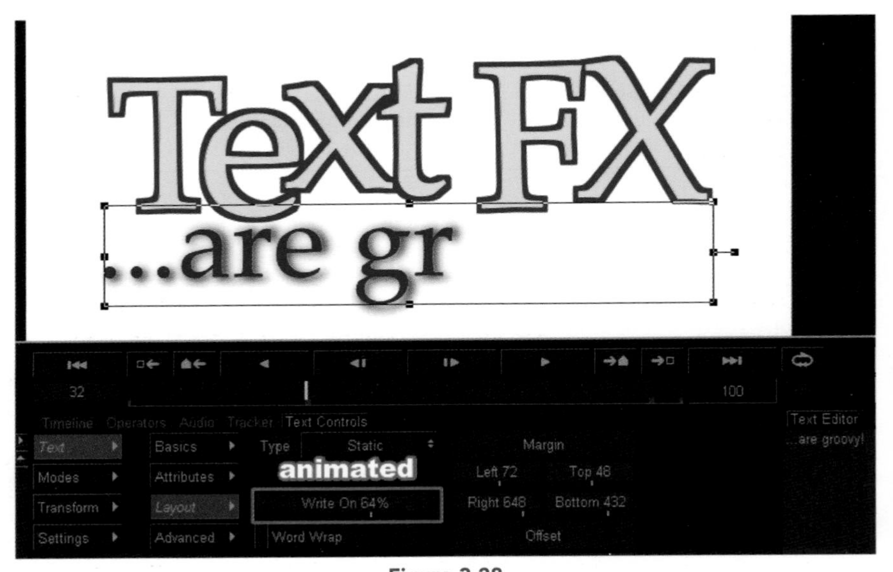

Figure 3.28

> **Note:** To see this value change, you must manually scrub the time slider in the Playback Controls. It will not dynamically update when in normal playback mode.

6 Go to the last frame and go to the Text > Advanced category.

7 Change the Path Option type from 'None' to 'Path'. This accesses the default path that all combustion text objects have embedded and available.

8 Switch to the Text mode (T) in the Toolbar to make the text's embedded path visible.

9 Now, in the viewport, edit the path. You can add/delete control points, edit tangency and edit the Path Offset value now available in the Text Controls UI.

10 Experiment with the different text tools. Try changing the second line of text in the Text Editor window. The Write On animation duration will stay the same no matter how many characters the text has.

An important thing to remember about text is that there are two modes. The text seen in Figure 3.28 is being treated as a group of vector objects because the Pick tool ( ) is active. Text mode (T) lets you edit attributes of the characters themselves.

Paint Preferences

If you access the user preferences of combustion from the File menu, you will notice there is a category just for Paint. The first two paint preference options of **Display Brush Outlines** and **Display Crosshairs** merely allow you to see a visual cue as to the location of the cursor when in the Paint operator. Figure 3.29 shows how the different options appear when in use.

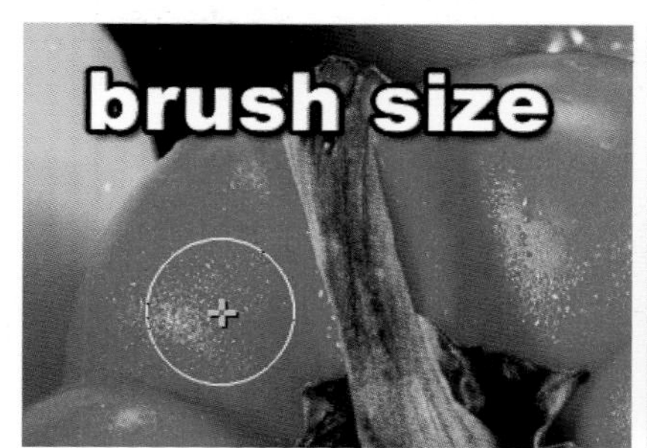

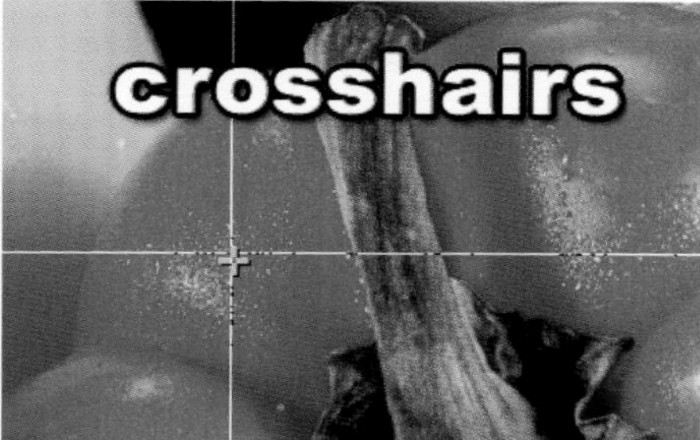

Figure 3.29

The **Render Cache Size** assigns a specified amount of your system memory to redrawing objects created on *a single frame* within any Paint operator. The general suggestion is to set this value to at least double the value of your individual, uncompressed frame size. The default 4 megabytes assigned by combustion should be more than adequate for video work. If you are working on film or HD projects, the average frame can be upwards of 15 megabytes, and therefore at least 30 megabytes (or more) would be needed just for typical painting operations.

This chapter was only a brief overview of the Paint operator. Do not be fooled by the initial 'vector-ness' of the objects created within. Transfer Modes, gradients, clone/reveal, selections and masks can work together to provide an incredibly powerful paint set that is completely removed from creating hard-edged, 'polygon' shapes. Learning to be well organized and naming the most important portions of your Workspace will help significantly, especially when dealing with all the vector objects and groups created in a Paint operator.

Closing note: The contents of the Paint and Text operators are not displayed in a Schematic viewport (which is detailed further in Chapter 5). You might have one Paint operator with 10 000 brush strokes and a second paint operator that is completely empty. They will look identical in the Schematic with the exception of the thumbnail representations of their image data. Because of this, it is in the Workspace panel where you do the majority of the reordering, selecting and renaming of the potentially numerous objects created in a Paint operator. The Schematic does not 'do' very much for working in paint, but it is extremely powerful for other things, as you will see.

CHAPTER 4

COMPOSITING IN 2D AND 3D

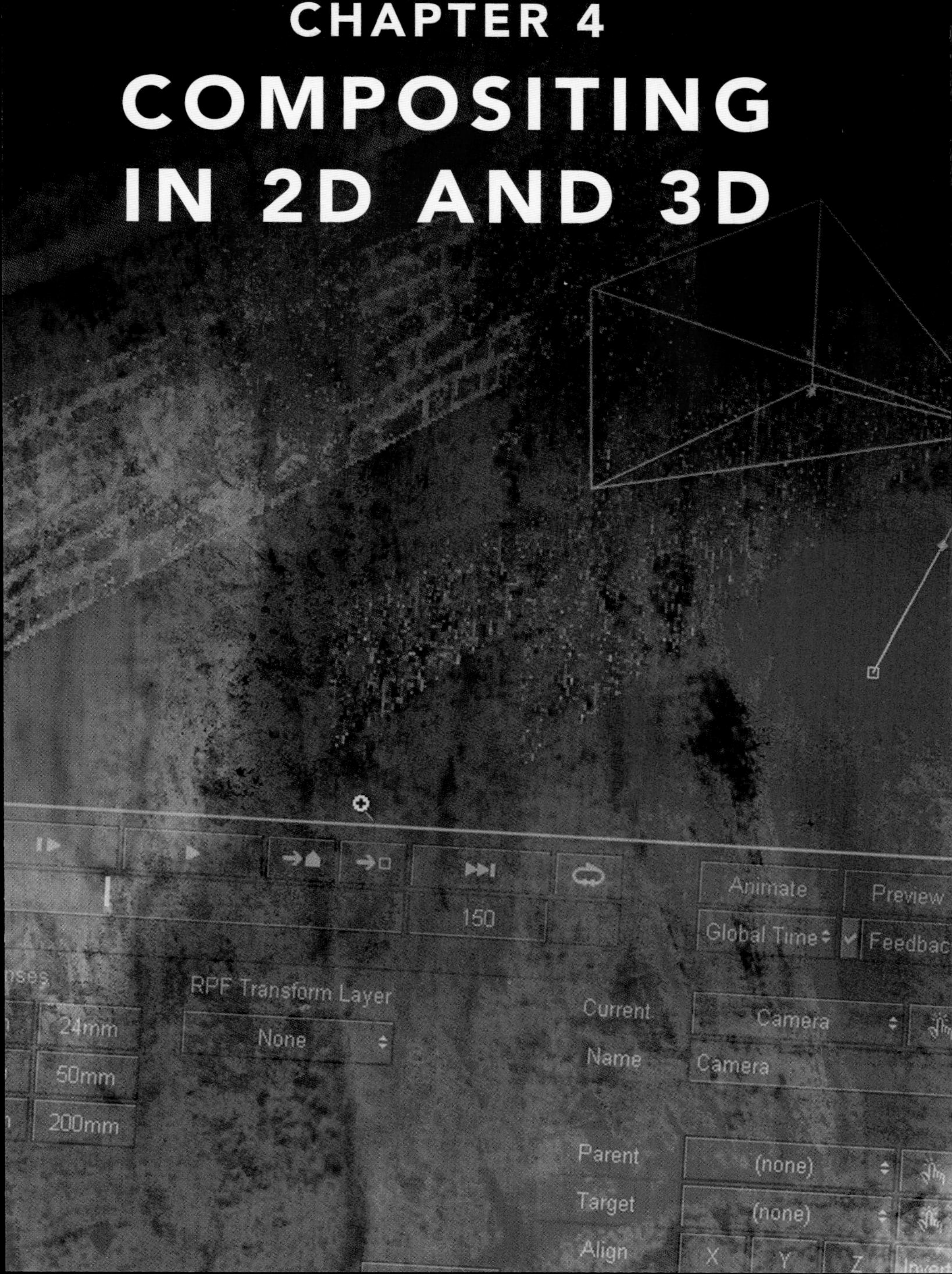

The word 'composite' is defined as a single structure or entity made up of distinct components. While you can certainly create projects in combustion that require the manipulation and editing of only one layer, the real power of the application comes from the various methods of combining several clips and operators as layers in one project. The old adage 'greater than the sum of its parts' is very much the case when you speak of building composites from several layers.

You can think of a composite in combustion as a special operator that, instead of containing footage with effects applied, is a window that 'looks' at layers within an empty void. The size of this window is the resolution of the composite, which can also have its own bit depth, duration, and so on. A composite with no layers will render blank images of a specified background color. Without at least one layer, a composite alone is like a blank slate.

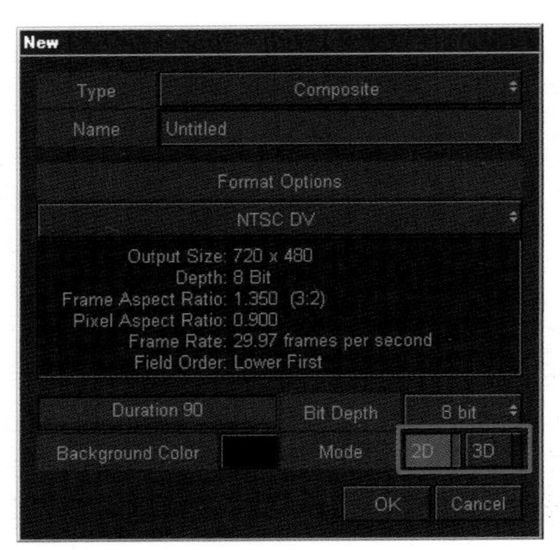

Figure 4.1

When you create a new composite from the File menu (File > New) you are faced with the option, among other parameters, to create a 2D or 3D composite (Figure 4.1). So which do you use and how do you know when to use what?

This is not a permanent decision to make or commit to. To later switch one type of composite to the other, you can access the Output category in the Composite Controls and make the switch seen in Figure 4.2.

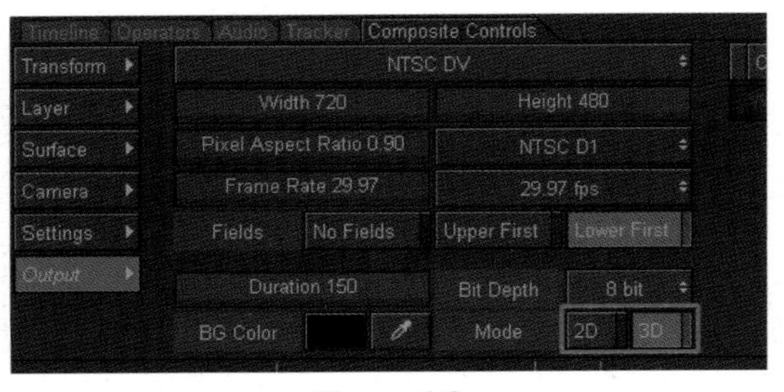

Figure 4.2

Note: A composite node can only be 2D or 3D, but you can have multiple composites of different types nested inside each other and in an unlimited number of ways.

It should also be mentioned here that instead of creating an empty (File > New) composite, you can, alternatively, select File > Open and combustion will allow you to use the Thumbnail Browser to open one or more clips *all at once* as layers in a new composite. The difference here is that the *first* piece of footage selected will determine the size, frame rate, bit depth and duration of the composite created. This can be a nice little time saver if you have a 'master' clip on which you plan to build.

One unsung hero within any composite is an entity called the **null object**. Null objects are invisible points in space that basically hold transformation information such as position, rotation, and scale. Any number of these can be created from the Object menu seen in Figure 4.3. These non-rendering helper objects can be used for a variety of things including targets for lights and cameras in a 3D composite, or as parent(s) to layers in a composite.

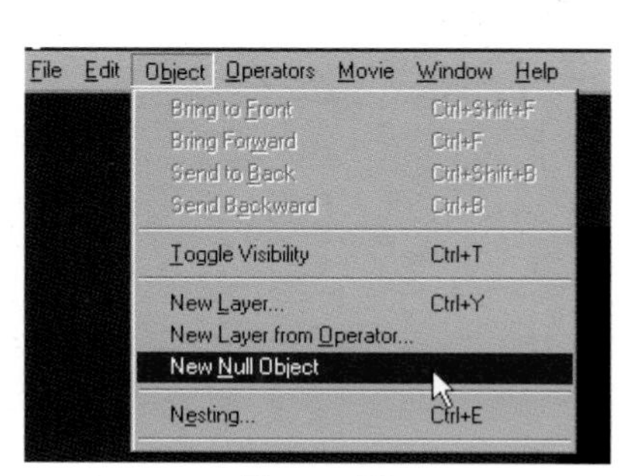

Figure 4.3

Parenting is a means to make an object control the transformations of another object. These objects can be layers, lights, camera and null objects. If an object has a parent, it will inherit the animation transformations of the parent without actually getting keyframed itself. Figure 4.4 shows the UI for creating parent relationships.

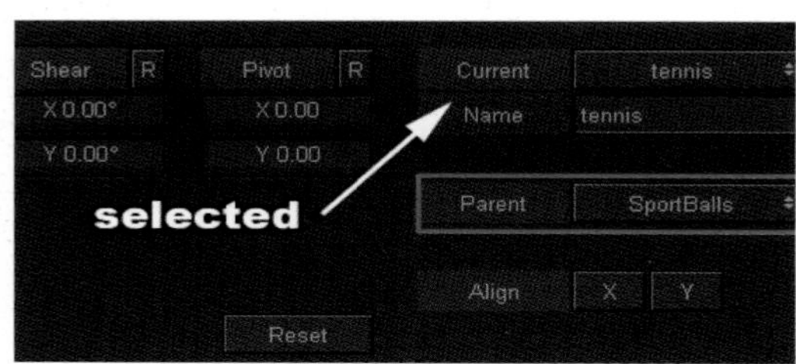

Figure 4.4

Tip: An old animation trick is to use invisible nulls as parents to objects. This lets you animate the nulls while leaving the child object's animation channels empty and, therefore, available for secondary animation such as random jitter created with expressions.

2D Composites

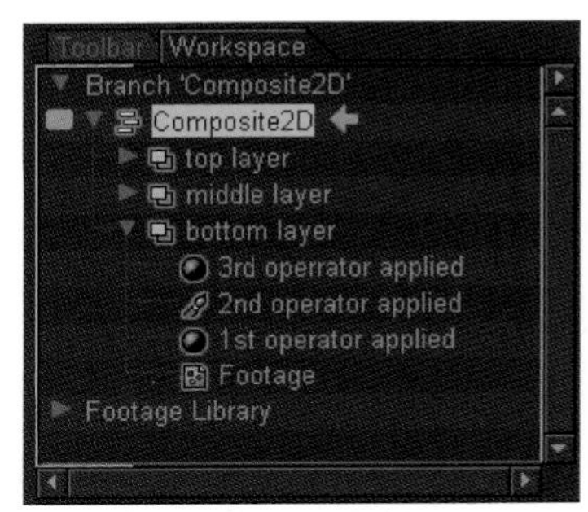

Figure 4.5

So what's the difference between 2D and 3D composites? Simply put, a 2D composite is very much like working in Photoshop; you apply effects to layers and the order in which the layers are stacked determines how they are viewed in the viewports. Like Photoshop's layers, the layers in combustion's Workspace panel are listed bottom to top; the layers at the bottom of the list can be considered at the bottom of the pile and those higher up are on top of the composite. Figure 4.5 outlines the hierarchy of a simple 2D composite.

While on the topic of Photoshop, combustion even lets you bring *.PSD files into composites and keep their layers intact. In addition, Photoshop PSD layers can take advantage of transfer modes (aka 'blending modes') that are, likewise, preserved in combustion.

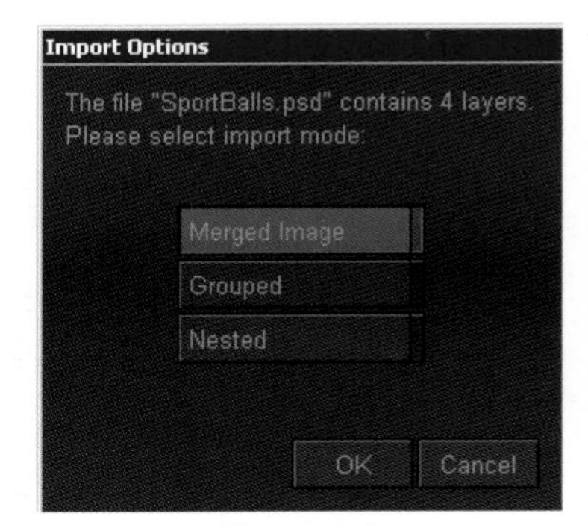

Figure 4.6

To see how combustion handles PSD layers, follow this simple exercise:

1. Open the Workspace file named *ch04_PSD_layers_BEGIN.cws*. This is a simple, one-layer composite that we will use as a starting point to add PSD layers.
2. From the File menu, select Import Footage.

3 Browse to the . . . _*footage\stills\DigitalJuice*\ directory and select the file named *SportBalls.psd*.

4 Upon clicking OK in the Thumbnail Browser, you will be presented with the dialog seen in Figure 4.6. These are the three options that will only be presented when importing images with layers such as PSD and RPF.

> **Note:** Each option is explained below and it may be worth the time to try all three individually. You may either undo each operation or merely select File > Revert Workspace to start again.

Merged Image – This is exactly like a flattened image in Photoshop with one exception. A single, new layer with the PSD document name is created in the current composite. However, if you go to the Footage Controls > Source tab, you will notice a Source Layer setting currently set to Merged Layers. Disable this and you can optionally dial in which individual PSD layer you want to use. Figure 4.7 shows the difference between the two settings.

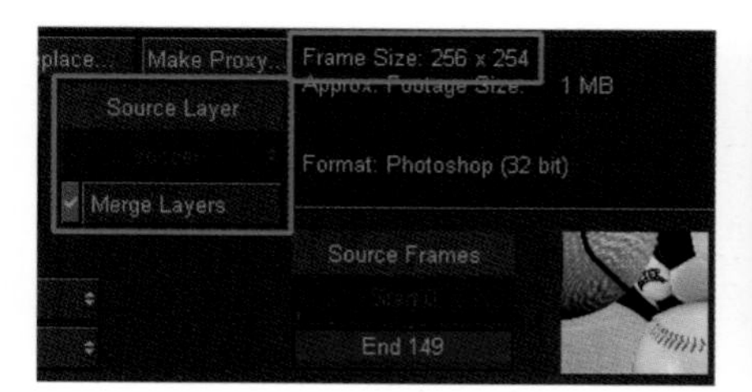

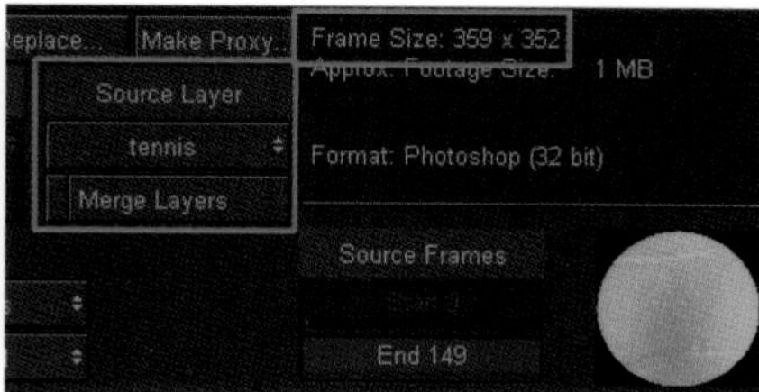

Figure 4.7

> **Note:** The difference in frame size is due to the merged image using the resolution of the Photoshop PSD file, but any 'non-merged' layers extracted from the PSD file use the resolution of the individual PSD layers. These can, in turn, be dramatically larger or smaller than the PSD file they are contained in. Notice how the tennis ball is not cut off on the right; its entire image layer is preserved and intact.

Grouped – The layers and transfer modes are preserved in their entirety and come in as footage sources for layers in the current composite. This method makes each

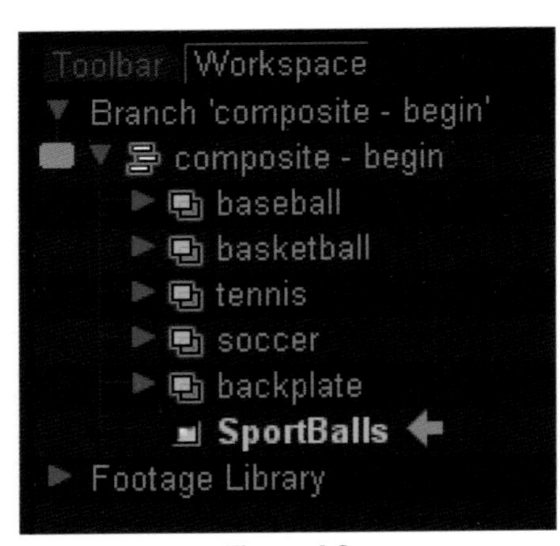

Figure 4.8

Photoshop layer in the PSD a layer in the current composite. Additionally, a null object with the name of the original PSD file is created. Figure 4.8 shows the resulting Workspace panel. All the new layers have a null object as their parent so that if you perform any transformations to the null, it will affect all these layers. This is a fast way, for example, to scale all the layers to fit into the viewport or animate all the layers as one, without nesting them.

> **Note:** Nesting layers will be explained later in this chapter.

5 Reimport *SportBalls.psd*, but this time, import the PSD files as Grouped when presented with Figure 4.6.

6 In the Workspace panel, select the null object and move, rotate and/or scale it. You will notice all the transformations are carried through the layers because each has this null object set as its respective parent.

Nested – This option for importing PSD layers creates a single layer that has the resolution of the original PSD document, but this layer is actually a nested composite containing all the individual layers. You can choose this option if you know you want to apply operators to all the PSD layers and treat them as one, yet preserve the layer information all within a single 'wrapper'.

> **Tip:** When in doubt as to which of the three import options to select for PSD files, I suggest you use Grouped. This option preserves the layers and creates a null object for easy transformations. If you later want to nest them, you can select and nest the layers.

Manipulating Layers

To create a composite with layers, you can simply open up one or more footage clips into a 2D or 3D composite. When you become more comfortable with combustion, you may begin creating empty composites and then importing footage as needed, but initially, it may be easier to just open a piece of footage directly into a composite, especially if the footage is the resolution of the target composite. Remember, opening footage into a composite branch results in a composite that starts out as the same size and frame rate as the first clip opened. If, for example, you open a still, mega-pixel image from a digital camera into a composite, the resulting composite will be set to a high resolution, and for video-resolution work you would then need to change the composite to the target video resolution. Your footage and layer would remain higher resolution than the composite 'window'. They do not get scaled to fit.

Once you have footage in a composite as layers, the three primary ways to alter and manipulate these layers are Transformations, Transfer Modes, and Effect operators. You will also make use of Layer view, which is a means to set a viewport to view any one layer in its entirety.

Transformations

Transformations are possibly the most basic way to manipulate any component within combustion. Fundamentally, they are the familiar move ( ), rotate ( ), and scale ( ), which most graphics applications use in some form or another. There are two additional transformation controls in combustion called shear ( ) and pivot ( ) that will be explained in a moment. Figure 4.9 shows the transformations available in a 2D composite.

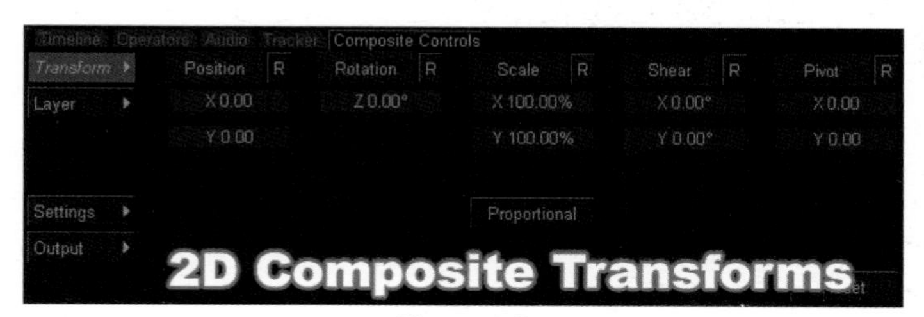

Figure 4.9

Figure 4.10 shows the transforms available in a 3D composite.

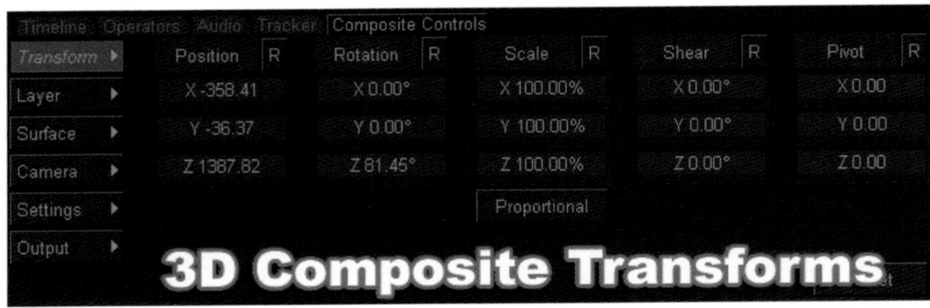

Figure 4.10

An extremely basic, yet often overlooked, concept is the simple fact that an object or element in your project usually needs to be selected prior to making a change in transformation. For example, to typically move something, you have to select it first. When using the Toolbar or the Composite Controls to perform simple transformations, items must be selected first and then transformations can be applied.

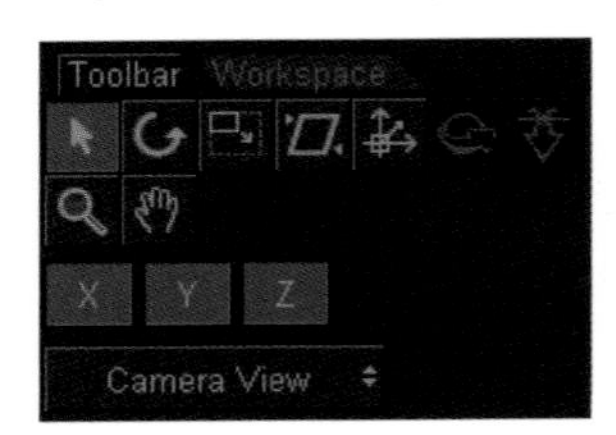

If you find yourself entering data in a transformation field but nothing is changing in the viewport, just remember that an item must be selected prior to applying a transformation.

Position – Controls the location of the selected objects or layer. Position is associated with the Toolbar arrow tool. Technically, there is no 'Move' tool in combustion.

> **Note:** Composites, unlike Paint/Text and Particle operators, use the center of the image as the origin of position (0,0). For example, in a D1 (720 × 486) video clip, the origin is at 320 × 243. Paint/Text and Particle operators use the upper left corner as the source of origin (0,0).

Rotation – Translates the object around its pivot point (defined below). In a 2D composite or another 2D environment such as the Paint, Text or Particle operator, you can only rotate on the Z axis. By definition, the other axes do not exist in 2D space. The Z axis used in 2D rotation could be thought of as an invisible line from you, the viewer, into the computer screen. Objects rotate around this line like spokes on a wheel. In a 3D composite, you are free to rotate objects and layers on all three (X, Y, Z) axes.

Scale – Changes the size of the selected object or layer. When the Proportional button in enabled (Proportional), all the scale values are linked.

Shear – Shear might best be thought of as a way to make your selected objects in an 'italics version' of themselves. That is, the layer object is skewed.

Pivot – The pivot point of a layer or object controls where that element will base the center of its transformations.

The following exercise has several purposes. First, you will perform a simple transformation using three different methods and second, you will use the three ways of entering values in a data field. Remember, this second procedure can be performed *anywhere* you see a data entry field in the UI.

1. Open the Workspace file named *CH04_SimpleTransformation.cws*. This is a simple, 2D composite with two layers. The background is a brick wall and the foreground layer is a metal grate that has a drop shadow operator added for effect.
2. In the Workspace panel, select the layer named *Grate*. You will notice a yellow outline with a small crosshair in the viewport now surrounds this layer. If you select the layer named wall, you will deselect the grate and now see the yellow outline slightly beyond the frame of the composite itself (this is because the wall footage is larger than DV resolution). Make sure you return to having the grate layer selected before moving on.
3. In the viewport, click and drag on the grate layer. You will notice it moving wherever you drag your mouse.
4. In the Composite Controls, verify that you are in the Transform category.
5. Here, you can use the data entry fields to control precise transformations. Try using these as sliders by dragging directly on them, typing in values, or by double clicking to access the calculator. You can

also try out the 'R' reset buttons to reset individual transformations. The button at the bottom that is labeled 'Reset' will reset all the transformations for the selected object or layer.

Transfer Modes

Simply put, Transfer Modes are different and numerous ways of having a layer blend with the imagery behind it. A layer does not need to have an alpha channel to take advantage of Transfer Modes, and therefore these are an excellent way to get variable transparency without alpha channel creation methods such as masks, keyers or Paint operators.

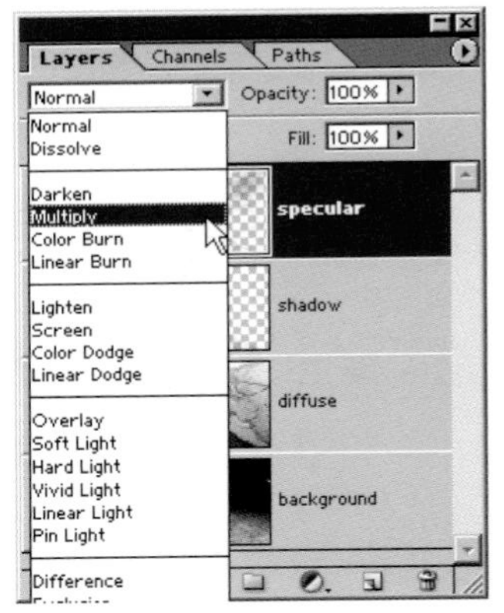

Figure 4.11

Figure 4.11 shows the Adobe Photoshop settings for Blending Modes (Photoshop calls them Blending Modes and Discreet calls them Transfer Modes).

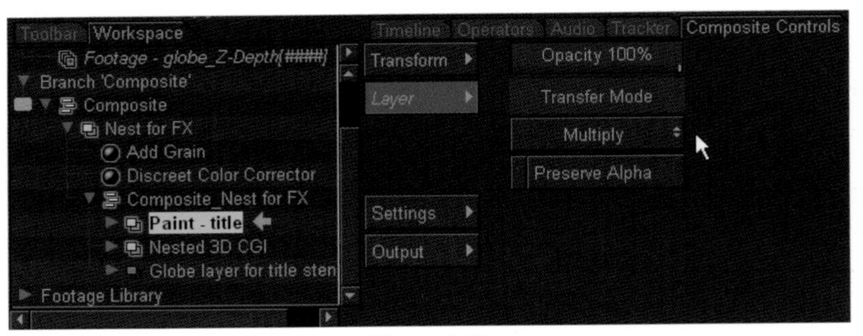

Figure 4.12

In Figure 4.12, the layer named 'Paint – title' is selected and its Transfer Mode is set to Multiply.

1 Open the file named *ch04_TransferModes.cws*. This is a two-layer composite. The top layer is a still image of color bars.

2 Select this layer and go to the Composite Controls > Layer category. This is where you can edit a layer's Transfer Mode in a 2D composite.

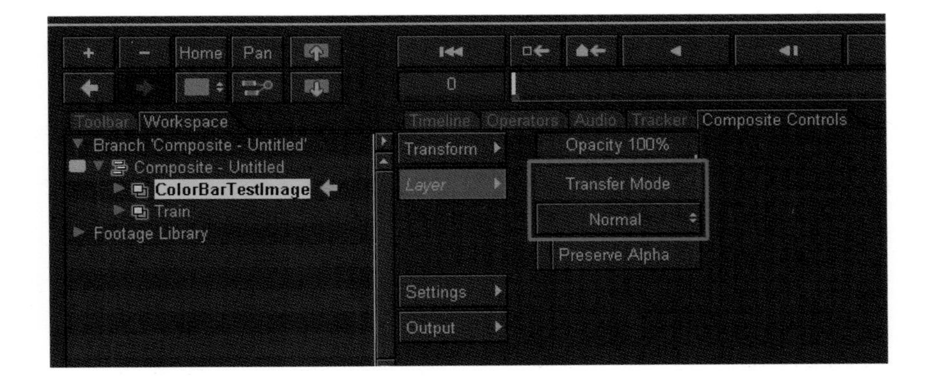

3 Change the top layer's Transfer Mode from Normal to Screen. The screen transfer mode makes light pixels show while making dark pixels transparent. If you have a scroll wheel on your mouse, you can float the cursor over the Transfer Mode setting and roll the wheel to cycle through the various choices. Notice that several transfer modes do not affect pure black or pure white.

Layer View

Recall that any viewport can be assigned to view the output of any operator in your composite. If you set a viewport to Layer view, you might initially get confused because a Layer view does not show transformations or transfer modes. The layer is shown flat and in its entirety. The advantage of a Layer view is that you might, for example, have various layers scaled and/or placed about in space where they are difficult to see. Layer view allows you to quickly look at a layer prior to any transformations or Transfer Mode settings.

To help explain what a Layer view is, let's examine a Workspace file.

1 Start with the file named *ch04_LayerView.cws*. This is a Workspace that contains the sport balls PSD layers imported as Grouped, but the layer named 'tennis' has been slightly scaled and rotated. In addition, its Transfer Mode has been changed to Multiply.

2 In Figure 4.13, the right viewport that the tennis ball is set to is Transparent View Mode, yet because the viewport is a Layer view, you do not see the scale transformation or the effects of the Multiply Transfer Mode.

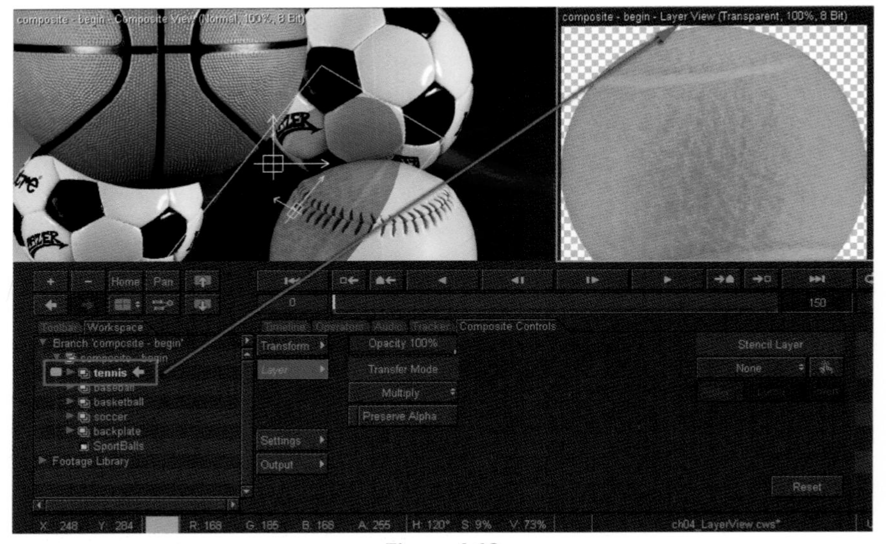

Figure 4.13

> **Note:** The setting for Transparent View Mode in the right viewport is not the reason the round edge of the ball shows through. This viewport is only set to Transparent to show where the layer is see-through.

3 Move, rotate and scale the tennis ball layer around in the left viewport. You will see it transforming about and the layers will show through below, but the Layer view on the right remains unchanged.

4 Make the right viewport the active viewport.

5 Double click on other layers in the Workspace panel. This will allow you to look at a Layer view for each layer, but leave the left viewport at the composite level.

Effect Operators

In addition to the spatial transformations and Transfer Modes, Effect operators are another powerful way to manipulate footage within combustion. No amount of time could possibly cover all the combinations of effects that the different operators can accomplish. The workflow of using Effect operators will be explained here, and key operators such as the Color Corrector and Keyer are detailed elsewhere in this book, but you should experiment with different operators on a familiar piece of footage to see how they alter your image.

The order of operators is especially critical in combustion, because the image data 'going out' of one operator is the input to the next in the series. The Schematic View is often the easiest way to visualize this, but it is in the Workspace panel that you can easily reorder operators by merely dragging one above or below the other with a single click and drag.

Effect operators are always listed in categories such as 'Keying', 'Channel', or 'Blur/Sharpen', for example. Figure 4.14 shows the Operator tab accessed. Here, you can see that the category selected is a third-party resource named Trapcode. To the right, you can see that there are three Trapcode plugins loaded and available in combustion.

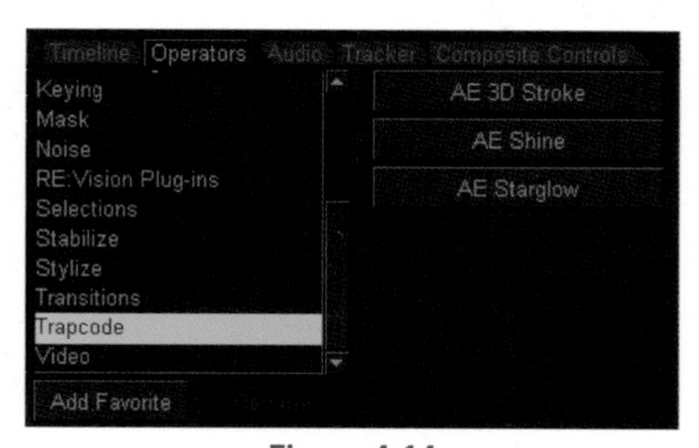

Figure 4.14

With few exceptions, third-party plugins will act and appear as part of the native combustion interface. Any third-party plugin that uses the Adobe After Effects programming guidelines typically works in combustion as an operator. Several demo plugins are included on the combustion 3 installation

CD. In addition, most plugin manufacturers offer a demo download of their products. This allows you to test the compatibility prior to purchase.

In combustion 3, you can now import and export the settings of any operator as a (*.CBS) file. Figure 4.15 shows the buttons for importing and exporting operator settings. These can even be animated values, but only identical operators can be imported into each other. For example, you cannot load a Box Blur setting into a Gaussian Blur operator because they are not the same function.

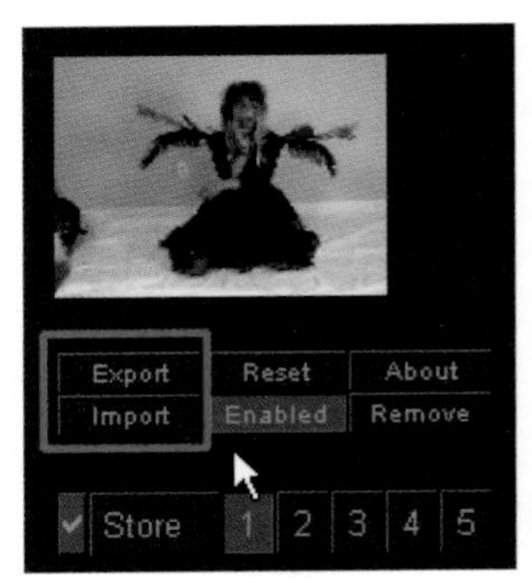

Figure 4.15

Applying Effect Operators

To apply an operator, select the object or layer to which you want to apply the effect and then pick the operator itself. This simple rule seems to be one of the most fundamental things, yet it is very easy to mistakenly apply an operator to 'nothing'. This is especially true when you use the Operators tab panel to apply Effect operators. Remember, you should first try to get used to selecting something and then applying an operator to it.

There are four primary ways to get to the same operators in combustion. Regardless of the method you use, the operators will always be listed in categories or by vendor name in the case of most third-party plugins.

To apply any Effect operator, you first select the layer or object and then you can do one of the following:

1. Access the Operator menu at the top of the UI (Figure 4.16) and select the Effect operator from the lists.
2. Right click on an element in the Workspace panel and apply the Effect operator from the Operators list.

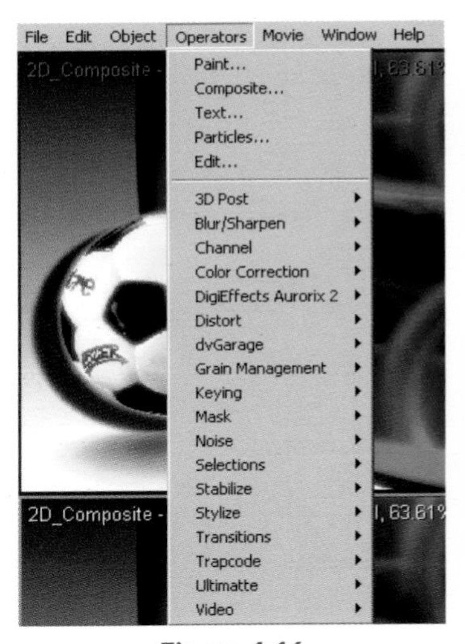

Figure 4.16

3. Right click on an element in the Schematic View and apply the Effect operator from the Operators list.

4. Access the Operators tab (F5) found next to the Timeline and Audio tabs.

Using any of these four methods will allow you to work in a manner that is efficient and best suits your particular workflow. Sometimes it literally comes down to which is the most convenient at that moment, depending on where your cursor is located onscreen.

3D Compositing

Any of the aforementioned tools in a 2D composite can be used in a 3D composite, so technically speaking you could always just work a 3D composite if you wanted to and simply not use the features unique to a 3D composite (such as Z space, lights, etc.).

You can think of 3D compositing as working in a true 3D environment similar to working in 3ds max, XSI, Maya or Lightwave, except instead of working with 3D models, you use 2D layers in a 3D world. This is actually a great way for artists to introduce themselves with 3D space without the worry of modeling and texturing.

As well as adding a few more transformation channels, making the switch to a 3D composite changes the Composite Controls > Layer category dramatically and also adds three new Composite Controls categories: Camera, Light and Surface. These add several additional features for compositing.

Layer – Figure 4.17 features the additional options to the Layer category in a 3D composite mode. The attributes of a 2D composite found in the Layer category are found in the Surface category when you are in a 3D composite mode.

Depth Order is a layer setting in a 3D composite. This is the ultimate override to (a) stacking order in the Workspace panel and (b) positioning in Z space.

For example, if you have a two-layer composite and the first layer is on top on the Workspace panel listing, then you move the layer in Z space further from the camera and, therefore, it goes behind the second layer. If you set the depth

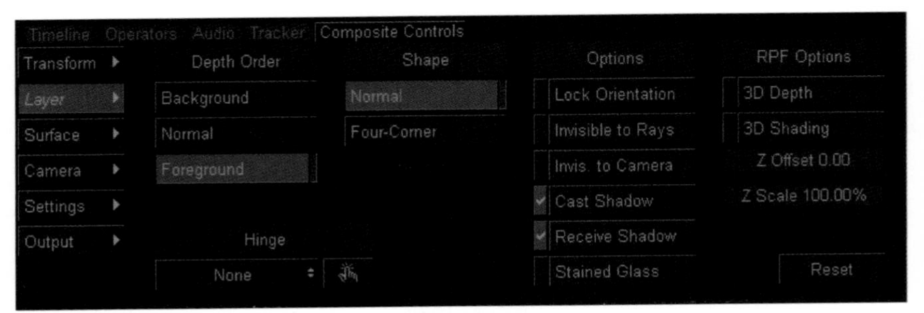

Figure 4.17

order of this layer to Foreground, the Z depth is overridden and the layer becomes visible again, even though it is physically behind the other layer. No layer in a composite will appear in front of a layer set to Foreground. This is particularly useful in the case of complex composites where you wish to override 3D space and/or stacking order and want to ensure the layer is 'on top' no matter what.

Shape – In a 3D composite, switching the Shape from Normal to Four-Corner allows for the popular Four-Corner pinning effects to be utilized. While the layer is in a Four-Corner state, you will see that each of the layer's corner points will be visible as small dots. You can select the individual corner points and distort the shape of the layer in abstract ways by dragging (or tracking) each of the corners.

> **Tip:** Selected corners of a Four-Corner layer appear as yellow dots. To select more than one corner, you hold down the Shift key while making the additional selections.

Options – These allow you to set attributes of layers as follows:

Lock Orientation	Forces a layer to ignore 3D space and always face the camera and be in front of the other layers. This is useful for burning in logos on a clip.
Invisible to Rays	This makes a layer unaffected by lights.
Invisible to Camera	This makes a layer invisible, but it will still cast shadows and reflections.
Cast Shadow	Turns off the shadow casting attribute of a layer.

Receive Shadow	Turns off the reception of other shadows on a layer.
Stained Glass	This is an option to make a layer that casts colored shadows based on the colors in the layer. This can be used to create gobo effects.

Camera – A 3D composite can only have one camera. This category allows you to choose from stock lenses, edit the field of view/focal length and can optionally get its transformation information from an RPF rendered sequence (generated in an application such as 3ds max).

Tip: To animate a camera cut effect, you must animate the camera with a jump in position from one frame to the next (possibly in conjunction with an interpolation type of Constant in the Timeline to assist this hard jump). Also, remember that cameras can be parented or targeted to any other object or null in the composite.

Light – A light must be selected for this Composite Control category to appear. There is one white point light by default and a 20% ambient white light value. You can add any number of lights from the Object menu at the top of the screen. This Light category allows you to edit selected lights, change their type, color, set targets, etc.

Distant	These lights are considered infinitely far from the objects.
Point	Casts light in all directions from a single point in 3D space.
Spot	Casts light in a defined cone and direction. This cone can have a user-defined angle and soft edge that gradates from full intensity to no illumination (outside the cone).

Note: The effects of lights will not be seen without enabling Composite Controls > Settings > Shading and/or Shadows.

Tip: The lights in combustion are additive just like in the real world. For example, if you shine a pure red, a pure green and a pure blue spot light in the same location, the resulting/overlapping area is lit white.

Surface – This is where you can set layer opacity, reflectivity (how much it will behave like a mirror when composite reflections are enabled) and the front/back visibility of a layer. Remember, in a 3D composite, layer Transfer Mode, Opacity and Stencil options get 'moved' here.

To examine some of the attributes of a 3D composite:

1. Start by opening the Workspace file named *ch04_CameraPan.cws*. This is a 3D composite made up of 2D stills in 3D space.
2. Cache the left viewport in medium or draft display quality. The only thing animated in this Workspace is the Camera, yet notice how the layers seem to move at different speeds. This is actually caused by an effect known as parallax. The camera is moving and because of the separation of the layers in the Z position, they appear to move by the camera at different rates.

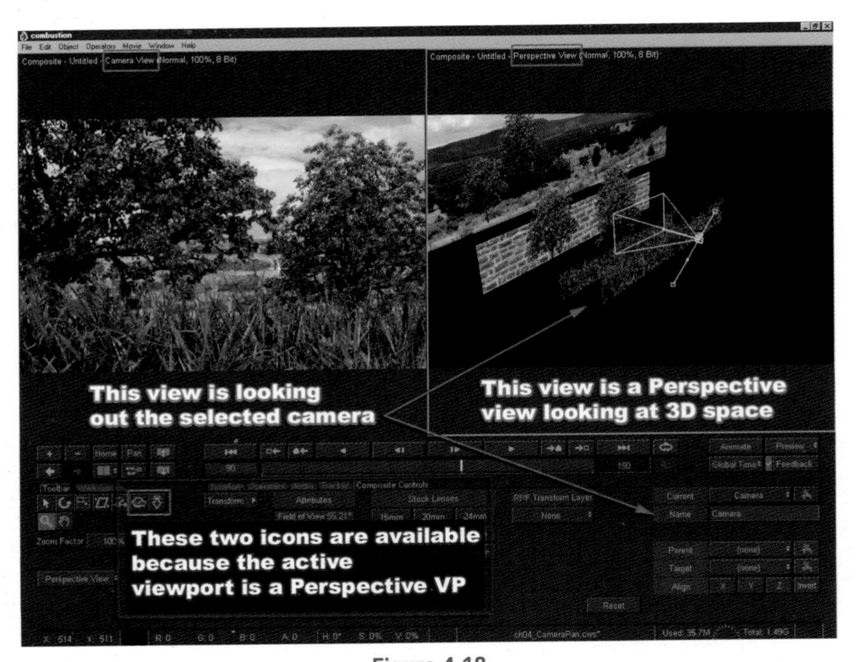

Figure 4.18

3 Stop the playback and manually scrub the time slider. Notice that now in the right viewport you can see the camera moving. To see the yellow field of view as in Figure 4.18, the camera must be selected. Elements that do not render such as wireframes do not play back in caching views and often it is advantageous to scrub the Play back Controls manually. This is especially true if you have multiple viewports open.

4 Set the current time to frame 100 by hitting the / key and entering 100 in the Go to Time dialog.

5 Pick the different layers in the left (Camera) view. Notice that they are slightly more difficult to pick in a 3D space. The more layers you have, the easier it is to pick layers by name in the Workspace panel or the dialog highlighted in Figure 4.19.

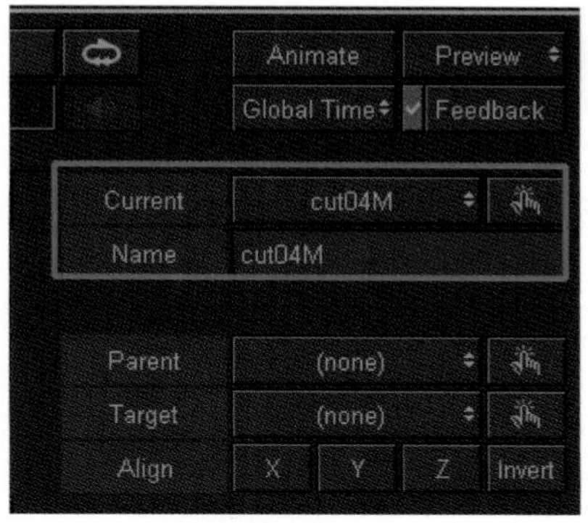

Figure 4.19

6 Select the layer named *cut04M* and rotate it using the Transform controls. Notice that if you rotate it in X or Y space, it passes through other layers in true 3D space. Also notice that Feedback is only active within the selected viewport. Only when you release the mouse do the other viewports update. This is yet another example of why you should know which viewport is the active viewport.

7 Switch to the Composite Controls > Setting category and enable the Render Effects named Shading and Shadows.

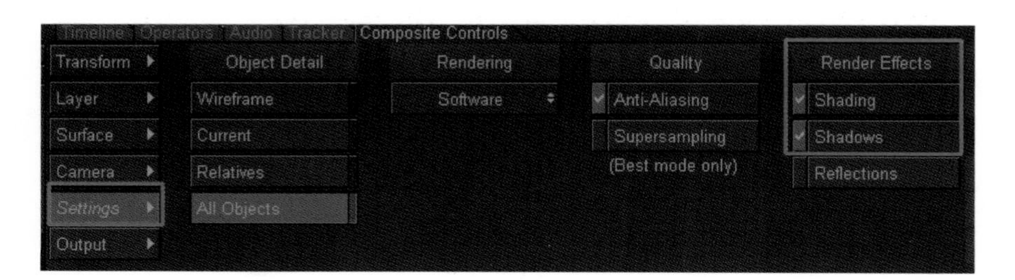

8 In the Workspace panel, select the light named 'Light'.

9 In the Composite Controls, go to the Transform category and scrub the Position X, Y and Z sliders to see the effects of moving the light in 3D space. Those are true, raytraced shadows you are manipulating, unlike the Drop Shadow operator or shadows effects in Paint and Text operators, which are a nice and simple 2D cheat for shadow effects.

10 Activate the right viewport and switch to the Toolbar.

11 Click and drag directly on the Perspective Rotate tool ( ) icon. By clicking and dragging directly on this icon, you do not even need to move into the viewport to make changes. You will orbit the viewport and 'look around' your 3D space. Clicking and dragging directly on the Perspective Zoom tool ( ) takes you into and out of a perspective viewport in a similar manner.

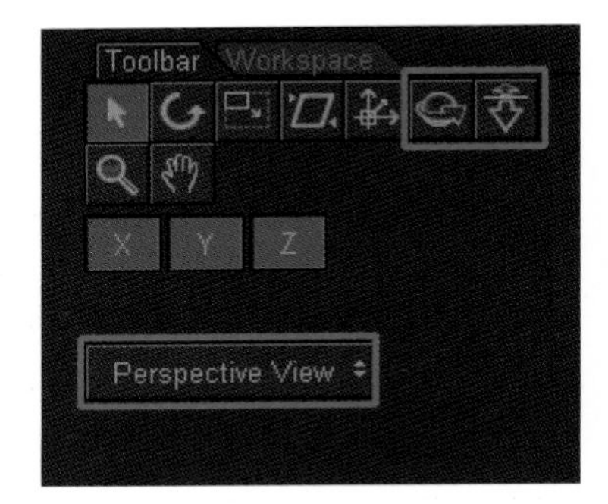

Tip: When dealing with 3D space, it can be an extremely good idea to keep track of things in multiple views, and not concentrate too hard on how just one view looks. Manipulating elements in 3D space, especially if you make transformations directly in a Perspective viewport, often confuses new users. One common solution is to do a transformation in one viewport while watching the other viewports to see the results.

Practice with multiple viewport layouts. Try setting some viewports to look at footage, others to operators, yet others to different views of your 3D composite windows (i.e. top, front, left, right and perspective).

Additional Notes about 3D Composites

3D space can get confusing at first, especially if you are used to a 2D system like Photoshop. You have been living in 3D space your entire life, however, so all of us are 3D artists at heart! Keep simple spatial rules of perspective such as parallax in mind. For example, things farther away seem smaller in scale than identical items close up.

Try using null objects and layers as targets of spotlights and cameras. This allows you to easily aim them. The lights or camera can stay in one place, but automatically rotate to aim at (the pivot point of) a moving target.

Several composites have been provided for you to examine, and I encourage you to really abuse them. Experiment in 3D space with layers, lights, shadows, reflections, cameras, layer transformations and targeting . . . and animation! The Workspace named *ch04_Nulls.cws* has been set up for your examination and experimentation.

. . . and Finally, Nested Composites

The idea is both simple in concept and complex because of the endless possibilities it opens up. Basically nested composites are a way to treat several layers as one. You can think of it like grouping layers. For example, if you have two layers that you want to apply a ripple to, you could apply two ripples, or nest them and apply one ripple operator to the nest.

> **Note:** In After Effects, nested composites are called 'pre-comps'. You may already be familiar with this workflow.

Simply put, a nested composite is a way to treat a composite as a layer inside another composite. Put yet another way, let's say you have a composite made up of layers A and B and you nest them. These nested layers are now a composite that we will call AB. You might also have a second composite in your Workspace that has two layers; the first is called C and the second is the AB nested composite you created earlier. Figure 4.20 shows this scenario and you can also open the file named *ch04_NestedABC.cws* to examine this simple setup.

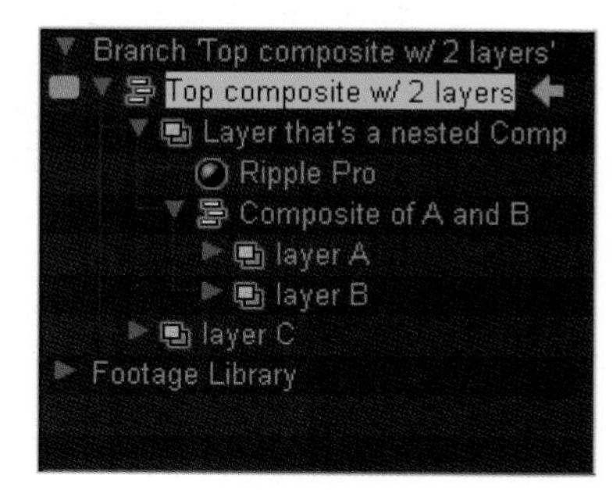

Figure 4.20

There are two composites in the Workspace, but one of them is actually a layer in the second. Because of the non-destructive way combustion works, you can go back anywhere along the way and make changes that are reflected downstream within the image data Process Tree. Notice in Figure 4.21 that the effects of the Ripple Pro operator get applied to both the A and B layers, because it is actually applied to a nested composite. Also take note of both viewport labels, which identify each as a separate composite.

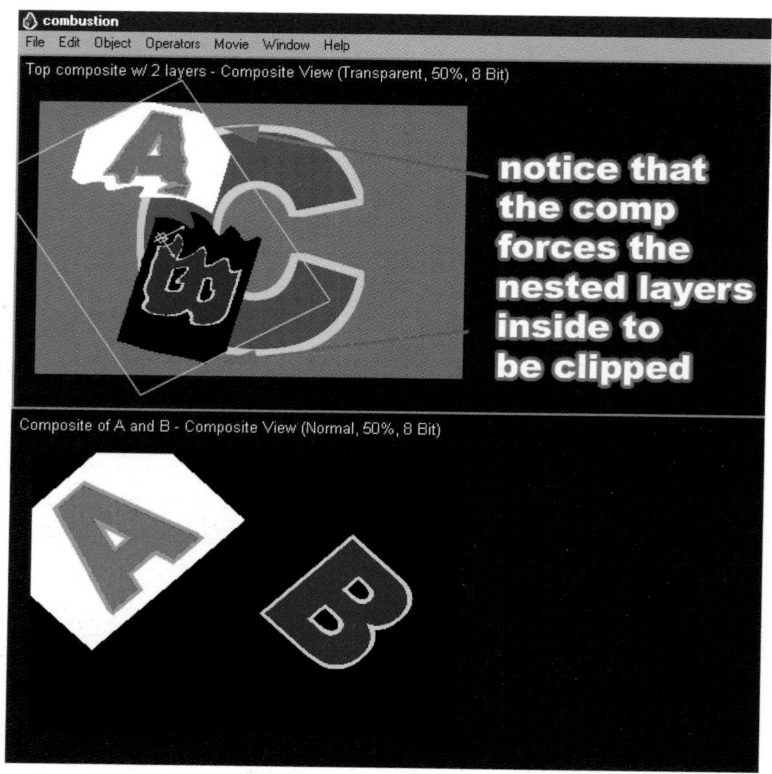

Figure 4.21

To create a nested composite, we will perform the same simple action.

1. Open the file named *ch04_Ready2Nest.cws*. This is an unnested version of the above example. There are two branches that are completely disjointed in the Workspace.

2 Expand and examine the Workspace panel. You should see that there are two branches and the familiar footage library.

Notice that *Composite AB* has two layers and *Composite C* has only one layer. The next few steps will introduce a new way to use the Workspace panel to add a layer in a composite (C). In this particular case, this new layer will be another composite, but you can use this technique to add layers from other operators in your Workspace.

> **Note:** This function can also be performed in the Schematic View with great ease and visual aid.

3 Select the composite named Composite C.

4 Right click on it and select *New Layer From Operator . . .* from the flyout menu seen here.

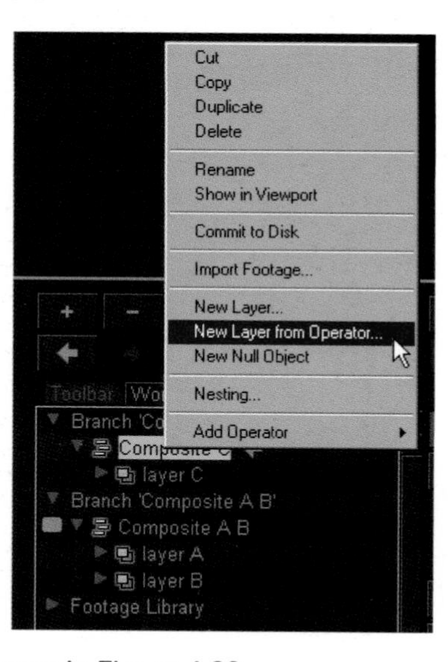

5 From the Operator Picker dialog that appears, double click on the composite operator named Composite AB. This double click makes the selection and also confirms the choice. When the dialog disappears, notice that you now only have one branch in the Workspace. This has two layers, one of which is the composite you picked. You may have to double click the top level to see the viewport seen in Figure 4.22.

You can also create a nest of layers at any time by simply selecting the layers you wish to nest and selecting Nesting from the Object menu.

You can also right click on the selected layers and choose Nesting, or simply hit Control + E to evoke the Nesting Options dialog.

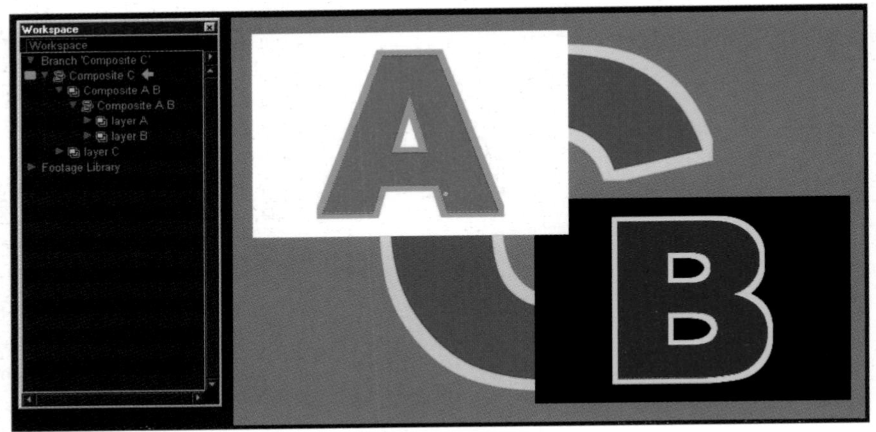

Figure 4.22

Starting with 2D composites and then migrating to the additional features of 3D composites allows you to learn features 'as they come'. This is, however, not to say that 3D composites are for more 'advanced' users; they merely add features that may prove useful for a particular task. Learning in 2D and moving to 3D may help in the initial phases of getting up to speed in combustion. Keep in mind that you can use both 2D and 3D composites throughout combustion at any time, and change them on the fly.

CHAPTER 5

THE SCHEMATIC VIEW (GO WITH THE FLOW)

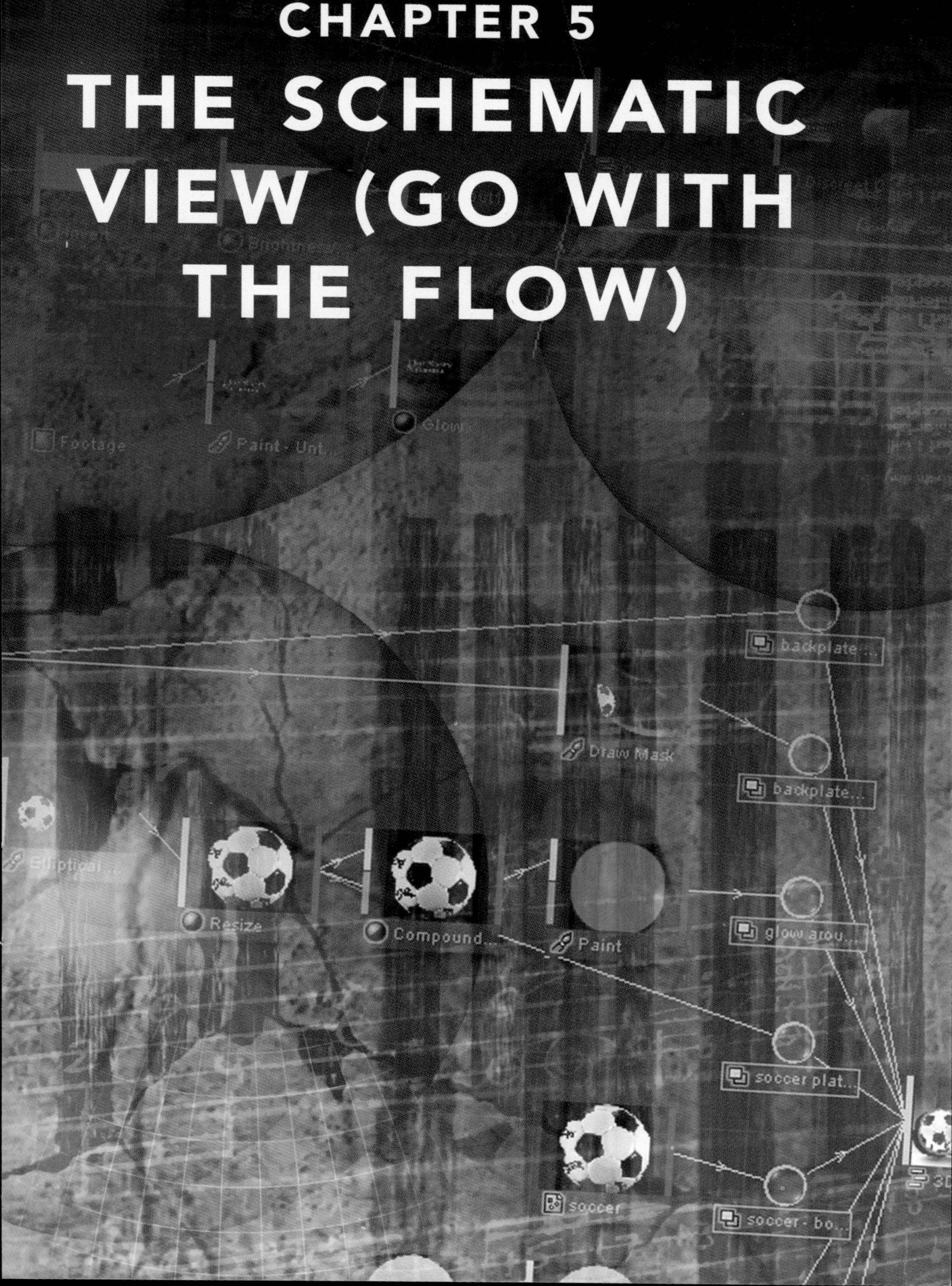

The Schematic View is similar to the Workspace panel in that it is basically a look at the entire Workspace (project) at hand. The most obvious difference is that instead of being a text-only listing and organizational layout, the Schematic is an iconic or 'node-based' system that shows the flow of image data.

The Schematic shows the sequence of events of footage and operators as nodes connected by arrows which indicate flow direction. Once again, this flow of data is known as the Process Tree. The Schematic is one place where this name begins to visually make some sense (branches, trees, etc.). It should be mentioned that this Process Tree is not 'object oriented'. For example, you do not see lights and cameras of a 3D composite in the Schematic View. This all really starts to make sense when you visualize the representation of the branches in your entire project in a Schematic View. Here, you can not only visualize your Workspace, you can also manually 'wire' nodes together to organize (rewire) the order of this pixel information.

Outlined below are various methods of working in the Schematic, as well as a few of the not-so-obvious points about it. I actually think the best way to learn the Schematic is by opening projects you are familiar with and looking at how they were put together. Likewise, when I am asked to examine any **.CWS* file, this is the first place I look because it is an immediate roadmap to the bulk of the project.

Accessing the Schematic View

1. Let's begin by opening the Workspace project *ch04_Ready2Nest.cws.*
2. This next step is a four-hotkey process. You will switch the active viewport to the Schematic, clean up the layout of the Schematic and fit the contents to the window. Carefully hit the following keyboard shortcuts individually and in this order:

F12	L	=	=

The first hotkey switches you to a Schematic View. To toggle the *active viewport* to/from a Schematic View, you can interchangeably use any of the three methods listed here:

Schematic icon ( ) in the Viewport Controls
F12 (Hotkey)
~ (Hotkey)

The remaining three hotkeys represent a hotkey combination that should be learned as soon as possible:

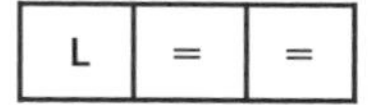

This cleans up the layout of the Schematic so that nodes are not overlapping one another, and immediately fits the entire contents of the viewport to the view. This is not just for when you start the Schematic; you can do this at any time. During the next few paragraphs, you may find it useful to experiment and then clean up the Schematic contents before moving on using this quick, three-hotkey series.

3 Try the Zoom and Pan tools in the Schematic View. All the icons and hotkeys for zooming and panning work for navigation within the Schematic as well. Always remember that a Schematic View is (also) just another viewport. It can be cached like any other viewport, but this can greatly affect the overall performance of combustion.

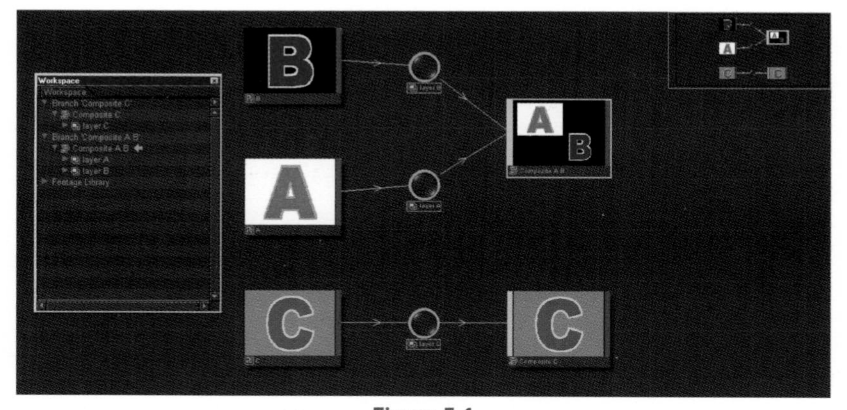

Figure 5.1

Please refer to Figure 5.1 or your current UI for the following brief descriptions of this simple Schematic.

The branch with 'C' has been moved to the bottom during this 'clean-up' procedure. This has no relevance in the Schematic, as these two branches are currently completely disjointed. The position of the layer nodes in the Schematic has no relevance to the layer order or depth in Z space.

In the upper right corner of the Schematic is the navigator. This is a small representation of the entire Workspace and is similar to the navigator found in other applications you may have used. A small rectangle representing the Schematic will be visible in the navigator; you can drag this around to control the panning of the Schematic. This can help you pilot around the Schematic if you happen to be zoomed in on one portion. Remember, the Schematic is just like any other viewport, and the icons and hotkeys for zooming and panning work just like any other view.

In this example, there are two disjointed branches in the Workspace that are both composites. One branch (C) is a composite with one layer; this layer is the end result of one piece of footage and it has no operators applied. There is another branch made up of a two-layer composite (AB). Likewise, these layers are made up of footage without any operators applied. In the composite named AB, you can see that the layers have both been scaled down and they are both slightly offset so both are visible and not overlapping.

The round nodes *without* any thumbnails are the layers themselves. The round nodes represent what get transformations and have transfer modes, among other things. To see how this functions:

4 In the Workspace panel, select the item named *Layer A* by *single* clicking on it. In the Schematic View, notice that the round node to the right of the footage A gets highlighted, indicating it is selected.

5 With *Layer A* selected, access the Composite Controls > Transform category and change the rotation value for this layer to 45 degrees. Remember, what you are rotating is the layer, since it is selected. This layer is represented by the round node, but there is no visible translation occurring to the node. That is, in the Schematic the node looks the same, yet the thumbnail of the resulting composite shows that the layer A has been rotated.

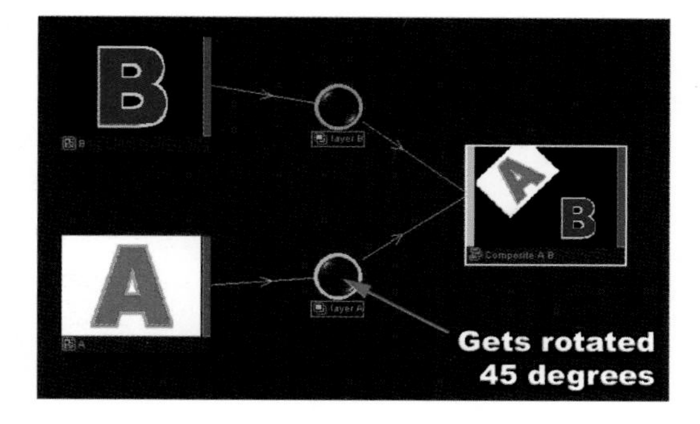

All the nodes with thumbnails represent the end result of the output of each node. The thin arrows going from one node to another indicate the flow of pixel information. Some nodes have a red stripe down one side and white stripe down the other side. The red stripe represents the output of a node and the white represents the input. Round nodes representing composite layers or edit segments will not have this coloration.

6 To change the input of a layer, carefully click and drag on the red bar to the right of the footage named B. Continue to drag the output of the *Footage B* and connect it to the round node that is named *Layer A*. You should end up with a Schematic that resembles Figure 5.2.

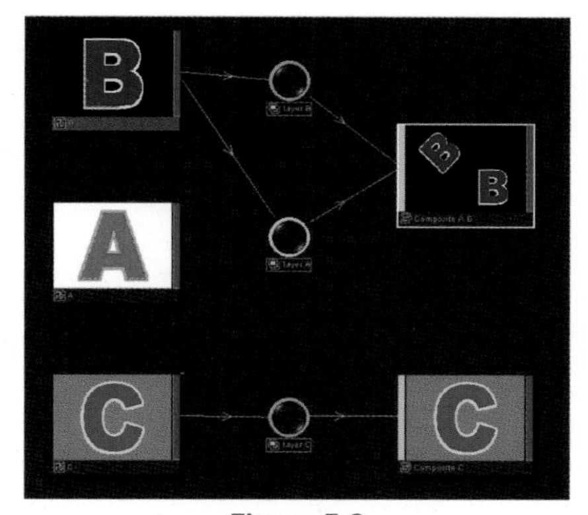

Figure 5.2

A few observations: notice that the output of A has been removed and now the footage named B is going out to two layers. One of the layers has previously been rotated 45 degrees, and whatever comes into this layer node, therefore, is seen rotated. Again, this is because what was rotated was not the footage, but the *layer*, which is represented by the round node. Layer nodes can only *ever* have one input, but this can come from the output of just about any kind of other node except another round layer node.

7 Before moving on, put this back to the starting point by either reverting the Workspace from the File menu, performing undo(s), or simply by putting the output of footage A back into the node named Layer A with a second click and drag wiring.

Using the Schematic, we will now recreate a step from the last chapter. We will create a single, new layer in composite C, which is a nested composite that contains both A and B.

8 In the Schematic, wire the output of the composite named AB to the input of the composite named composite C. Do this by taking the red output of the composite AB into the white stripe input of composite C. Figure 5.3 shows this procedure in mid-stage.

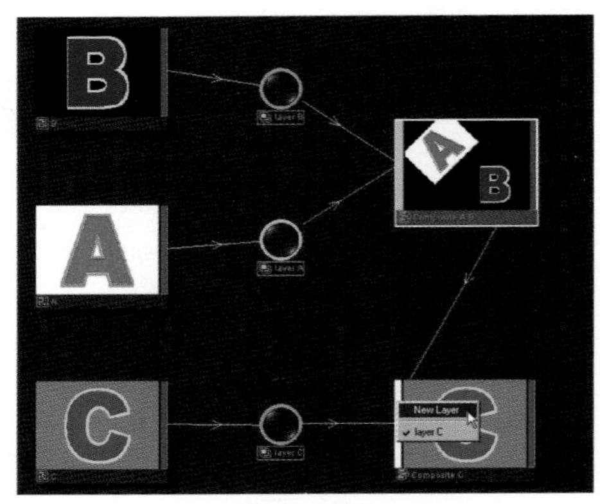

Figure 5.3

Just before you complete this task, you will be presented with a small pop-up window that indicates you need to make a new layer with this method. Depending on the layout of the current Schematic, this dialog can be difficult to see, as shown in Figure 5.3. When you complete this connection, you will have created a nested composite exactly the same way you did at the end of the previous chapter. Leave this project open at this point before moving on. A cleaned-up, resulting Schematic can be seen here:

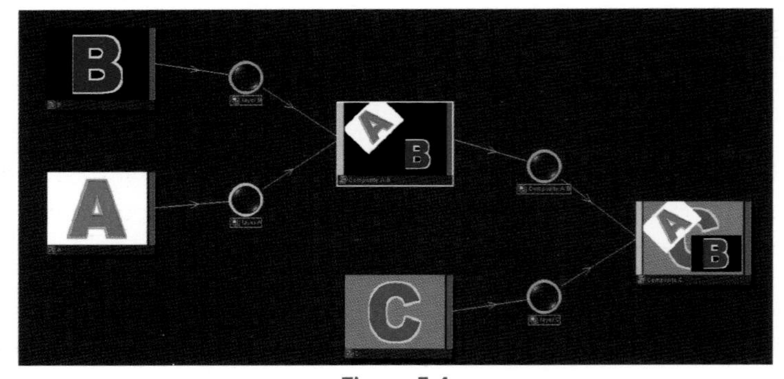

Figure 5.4

Note: Using this procedure, it is a common occurrence to end up with a layer named 'layer'. Like elsewhere in combustion, you can right click on an item and select rename elements at any time. If this occurs, it is a *really* good idea to immediately rename this layer to something more appropriate. You will rarely, if ever, want a layer simply named 'layer'. This is much too vague if you have a complex Workspace.

Tip: When you are still learning, it is also a good idea to name the round nodes something like 'layer person' or 'layer background'. This will help identify elements over in the Workspace panel. It is often ideal to enter the Schematic just to rename lots of things, because it can often be more clear what is a footage, operator, layer or composite/edit node.

Applying Operators

To apply operators, you can simply select a node in the Process Tree and then apply the new operator to it. New operators typically get applied downstream of the selected node. However, if you apply an operator to a round node, the node will end up (remain) at the end of that chain and the new operator gets applied the same as if you applied it to the last/previous operator in the chain.

1. Select the round, layer node named composite AB by clicking directly on the node in the Schematic view.

2. Right click on the node and, from the flyout, select Operators > Blur/Sharpen > Box Blur. This will apply a single operator to the nested composite.

3. In the Box Blur Controls dialog now visible at the bottom of the UI, increase the value to 30. This will blur the nested composite as seen in the thumbnail of the composite C.

4. Clean up the Schematic by tapping L==. You can see that the operator was added to the composite AB yet remains prior to the round layer node in composite C.

Switching the order of two operators can be accomplished by one click/drag in the Workspace panel, but in the Schematic you must either rewire several in and out links or you can use a cut/paste procedure on operators. However, it depends on which works best for any given moment in a project; they all have advantages.

Try using a simple Workspace such as this to apply, reorder, rewire and rename operators using the various means available in the Workspace panel and Schematic View.

Notes on Nodes

Any node or icon in the Schematic View represents a point in the flow of pixel/image information. At each of these stops, something typically happens to the image information and then gets passed along.

Again, most operator nodes have a white and red stripe down their sides. Red represents the output of data and the white stripe represents the primary input to a node.

Footage can only have output and never has an input. Footage, however, can have several outputs off the same node. This created duplicated (instances), which will be detailed shortly.

Operators such as Paint, Gaussian Blur (and the like) have both inputs and outputs. Effects operators are applied in a series, where one is applied, does its effect and then passes the outgoing pixel information to the next operator for it to do its effect. The order of operators can easily be seen here and in the Workspace panel. The outputs of an operator can also be instanced (multiple outputs). Many operators may also have what is called a **secondary input**, which is signified by a **light blue input**. A secondary input is used for special case operators when they need additional information for some effect. Figure 5.5 shows a Paint operator applied to *Layer B*. You can also see that the plant footage is coming in as a secondary input to this operator.

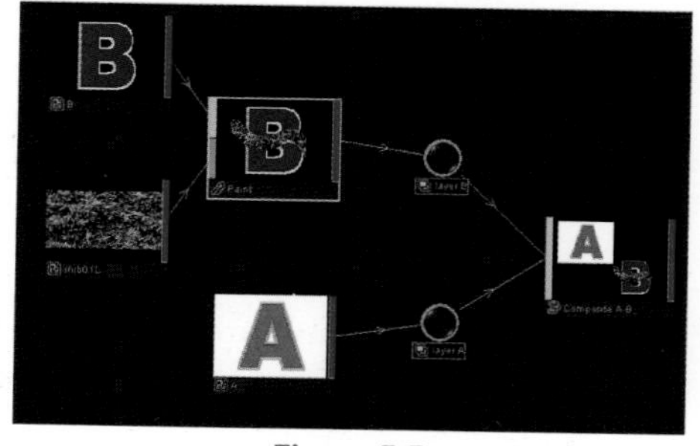

Figure 5.5

Notice that the Paint operator actually has two input bars, one white and one blue. The white input is always the primary input and the blue the secondary input. Most operators do not have a secondary input, but depending on their function, others may. The secondary inputs in the Schematic are (secondary) images being used by that operator in some fashion. In this example, it happens to be a Clone source for a paintbrush in the Paint operator. You would not be able to find this information in the Schematic View, however. A Paint operator, for example, often has several secondary inputs because of the numerous things that can be done in a single paint operator.

Layers will be represented as round nodes, not as thumbnails. This is helpful to differentiate them from other nodes in the Workspace. Layer nodes can only ever have one input. In a composite, these nodes hold information pertaining to the layer such as transformations and Transfer Mode information (i.e. Normal, Additive, Hard Light, etc.), among others.

Composites and Edit Operators can only ever have round nodes coming into them, nothing else. Layers in composites and segments in an Edit operator are both represented by a round node, but the icon next to the element's name in each case differs accordingly. These round nodes are vastly different to thumbnails of all other elements in a Schematic View, even if zoomed extremely far out. This makes them easy to identify and locate. Both Composite and Edit operators can have an output and do not always have to be the 'end of the line'. When a composite's output is the input to anything else, this is considered a nested composite.

Further Points on Schematic View

To wire and break connections, you merely drag from the output (red line) of one node to the input (white line) of another. The flow can be broken by clicking on a wire and dragging it outside of any node, thus breaking the connection with a quick flick of the wrist.

Working on the first frame of a project while in the Schematic can often be a really good habit to get into. This is primarily true if you are creating or rewiring layers because if you are not on the first frame, you will be creating layers at the new location in time. This is a powerful feature, but it often confuses new users who are not aware they are working in time on a different frame. Always be aware of what frame you are working on.

With the exception of an edit or composite, a Schematic View does not show the contents of operators, only the flow of data coming into or out of them. Therefore, operators with lots of objects are seen as a thumbnail representation of their end results. Examples of operators that can potentially have many objects within them include Paint, Text, Particles, Masks and Selections. These are the operators that might need examination using the Workspace panel.

A Schematic does not show any information about keyframes or animation. It is a Process Tree. Only the updating thumbnails can indicate any change of pixel information.

Scrubbing icons can be useful in the Schematic if you wish to see what images look like at various stages of the Process Tree. You can hold your cursor on the upper third of the thumbnail and it will change to a left/right arrow indicating a jog/shuttle wheel format.

Schematic Hotkeys

A few more hotkeys that are extremely usefully for speedy workflow in the Schematic are listed below. The majority of these tools can be accessed from the right click menu in the Schematic, if you do not want to use hotkeys.

L	Cleans up the **L**ayout of the Schematic. Overlapping nodes will be made clearly visible.
=	The same as the Home icon. This is a three-cycle hotkey for zooming viewports.
Control + A	Selects **A**ll the nodes in the Workspace.
Control + D	**D**eselects everything.
Control + click node	Adds to the current selection.
Shift + click node	Selects node and all those UP-stream.
Alt + Shift + click node	Selects node and all those DOWN-stream.
G/U	**G**roup and **U**ngroup selected nodes. This is useful to clean up an area that you may be done working on and want to hide from the rest of the Schematic. You can select several nodes and tap the G key to make them all be represented

	by one node. This does nothing for hierarchies in the Workspace; it is purely cosmetic for Schematic purposes only.
T	Toggles all the *selected* node's **T**humbnail icons on and off. While learning, it is a good idea to leave thumbnails on to help analyze things in the Schematic.
Shift + keyboard arrows keys	Cycles between the four available flow directions. By default, the Schematic reads left to right – you can, however, change this to suit your needs. Some Schematics fit differently (read: better) using different flow directions. Some 'want' to be wide and others are easier to read tall.

Duplicating (Creating Instances)

The concept of instancing is not something that is specific to the Schematic, or even to Discreet combustion. Like several other functions in combustion, it is often easier to visualize this process because of the diagrammatic nature of the Schematic View. When you duplicate something in combustion, it creates a special copy that has a connection to the original and vice versa. Changes made to one also occur to the other. This is because there is only one source used in several places. This can be a considerable time saver and also a great way to save precious cache resources. Let's look at an example of this workflow.

1 **Start by opening the workspace named *ch05_InstanceSTART.cws*. Figure 5.6 shows the starting two-layer composite as well as an inset portion of the Workspace panel.**

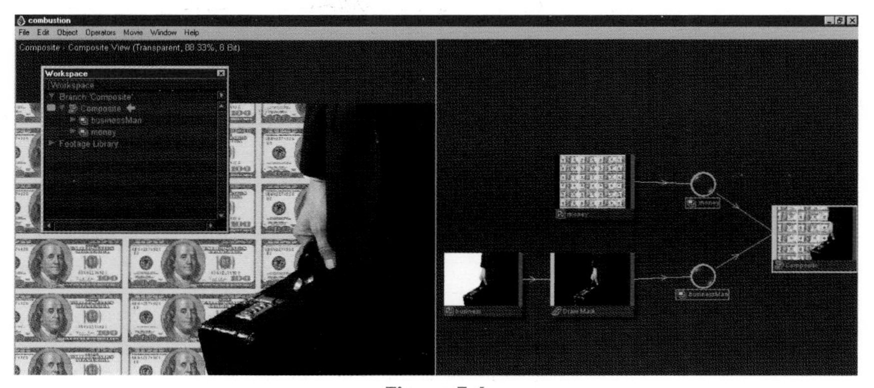

Figure 5.6

2 In the Workspace panel, select the layer named *businessMan* and copy it (Control + C). For this step, do not use the Schematic.

> **Note:** Doing this in the Workspace panel copies the entire branch below this point, which is what we want. Copying in the Schematic only copies the selected nodes.

3 Now paste it (Control + V) two times and then offset the two new layers in the X position by using the Transform category of the Composite Controls. You should end up with something like Figure 5.7.

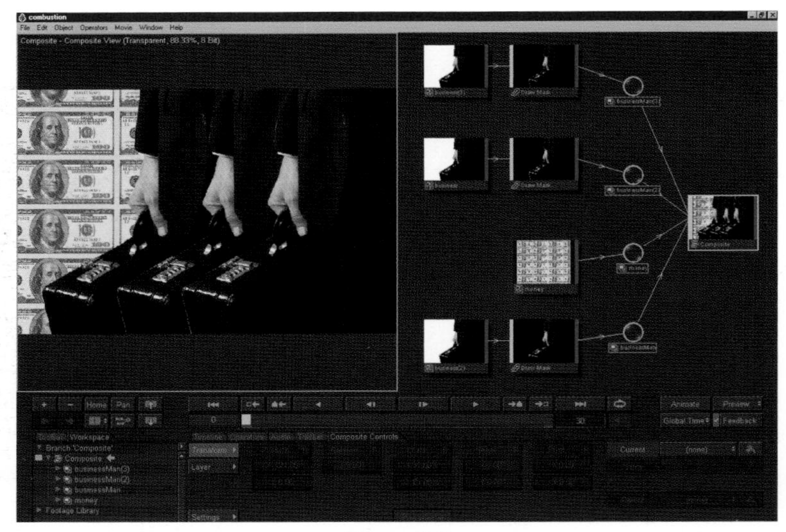

Figure 5.7

Notice that there are now four layers in the current composite and three of them are derived from copies of the same two operators. There are a total of seven operators needed to complete the composite, and caching one frame of these at Preview display quality takes about 15 megabytes.

4 Drag a line from the output of the bottom Draw mask operator's thumbnail and link it to one of the other layer nodes. This will bypass the two nodes that currently make up that layer. If you do this twice, you can end up with something similar to Figure 5.8.

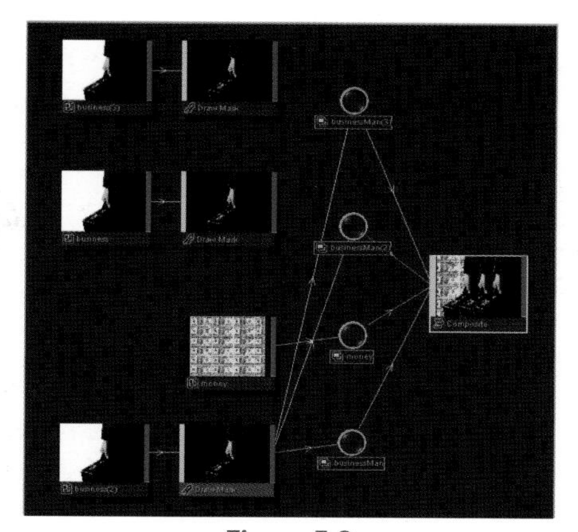

Figure 5.8

Notice in this figure that the four nodes in the upper left are no longer needed in our composite.

5 Select and delete these four unnecessary nodes by clicking on them all and tapping the delete key on the keyboard. After tapping the L key to clean up the layout, Figure 5.9 shows the resulting Schematic layout for the current Workspace. The resulting Schematic has the same visual end result as before but it only takes around 8 megabytes to cache one frame. This is because there are only three nodes and one footage operator to cache. You can see how instances can be a fantastic way to optimize the use of system resources, especially precious RAM.

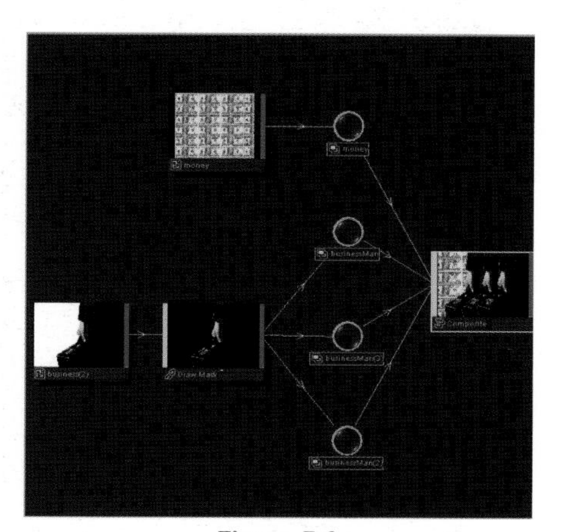

Figure 5.9

Note: If, in step 2, you used 'duplicate' (Control + Alt + D) instead of copy/paste, you would have initially created instances and have a resulting Workspace like the one seen here.

6 If you apply operators to the layers at this point, the new operators will be applied after the instance point but be placed before the layer node. This allows you to have instances at one point and then break off individual branch elements to perform unique operations from that point on.

Figure 5.10 show an example where three separate color correction operators have been applied to the layers. As you can see, their unique settings result in each layer being colored differently, yet as the Schematic shows, changes made to the raw footage or the Mask operator will affect all of the branches downstream from the point it was instanced.

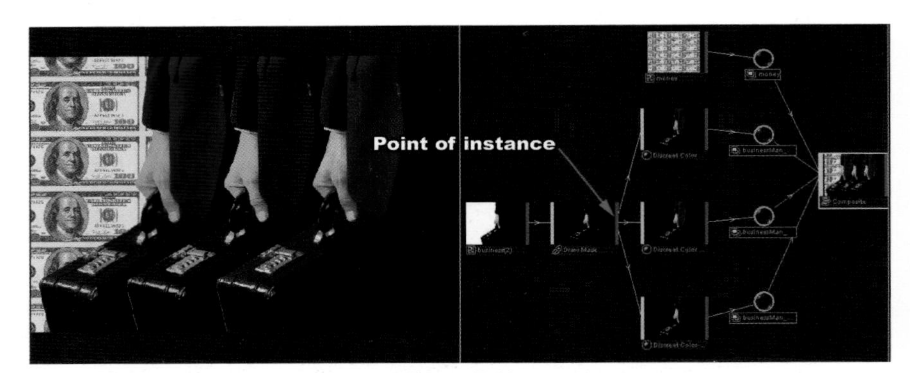

Figure 5.10

Remember, items in the Workspace panel and Timeline that are labeled in italics are instanced in combustion. The Schematic is often the best place to find out where these instances occur. Anywhere a node has multiple outputs, it has been instanced somewhere in the Workspace. You could, for example, have one branch being used in many different composites.

7 Go back and edit the Mask operator applied at the beginning to the single source footage clip. You will notice that the changes are reflected downstream to all three of the colored layers. This shows how an instanced operator can save you valuable time while building a project.

Schematic Preferences

In the user preferences for combustion, there is a category specifically for the Schematic. Here, you can set several options for Schematic grid size, layout, emphasis and overview position/size. Experiment with different preferences but I suggest the defaults at first.

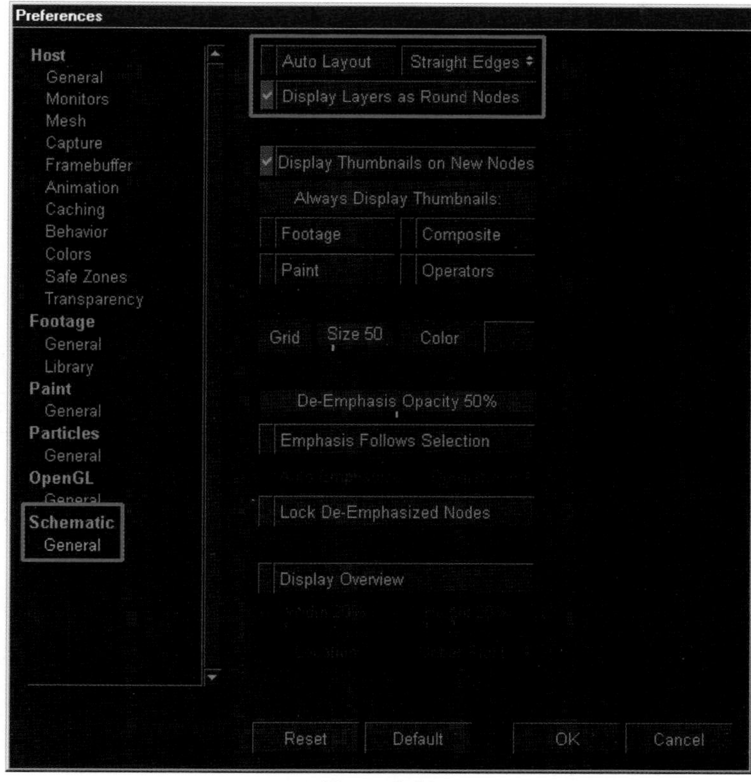

Figure 5.11

In the Schematic preferences seen in Figure 5.11, I *highly* recommend leaving the option for Auto Layout *off* (the default). Auto Layout redraws the Schematic with every single operation and this can get confusing when trying to organize your nodes. Likewise, the option for Display Layers as Round Nodes should be left *on*. Round nodes easily identify a layer because their appearance is different to the other operators. Again, these are just suggestions for a starting point. The rest of the preferences here are primarily cosmetic.

Try opening different CWS project files and initially examining them in the Schematic. Here you can quickly find out how many layers there are in the entire project, how many composites there are, if there are instances, etc. I have heard people say, 'I never use the Schematic' or 'I only work in the Schematic'. In my opinion, either of these decisions is a bad move. The Schematic and the Workspace panel both have their strong points and advantages over one another. The Schematic allows you to easily visualize the overall flow of pixel information starting at the source footage, while the Workspace panel allows you access to every single brush stroke, particle emitter and text object within different operators, for example.

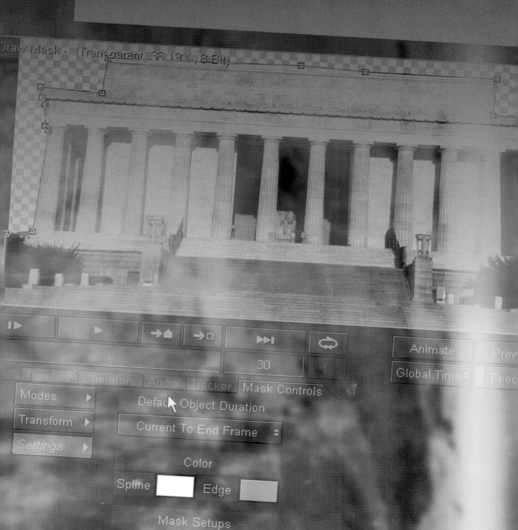

CHAPTER 6
SELECTIONS AND MASKS

Selection and masking operators are used for quite different purposes, but the toolsets used in each are derivatives of Selection and Mask tools previously discussed within the Paint operator. Selections are used when you want other operators and effects only to occur on part of an image. Masks are used when you only want part of an image to be visible, while other portions are made partially or completely transparent to allow the images or pixels below/behind to be visible.

Shared Terminology

Because selection and masking tools share so many of the same terms and common tool workflows, the common verbiage is listed here only once. For example, feathers, edge gradients, and Boolean functions apply to selections and Mask operators alike.

Feather – A feather is a gradual change in the amount of opacity of a mask or selection. As in other graphics applications, this means a gradual change from full effect to no effect whatsoever. The amount of feathering is typically measured in pixel values starting at 1. Within combustion, feathering a mask or selection often helps blend the area that is being modified with the rest of your image. In both selection and mask objects, a feather alone is a uniform amount around the entire perimeter of the object's boundary.

Edge Gradients – These are derived from the Discreet Systems products and are a very powerful tool in the combustion arsenal. There are four types of Edge Gradients detailed here:

None	This disables Edge Gradients. You can still use the feather setting for the object, however.
Offset	Provides an offset amount (in pixels) that can be +/− the border of the selected object in question. For example, you can have an inner offset of 5 pixels that will create a feather of 5 pixels inside the vector shape. You could, in turn, change this to 5 pixels outside the drawn shape. There is also an Opacity setting that controls the visibility of the feather.
In/Out	This allows you to independently control the inner and outer offset amounts as detailed above. This setting, however, does not have opacity for the Edge Gradient, as does the Offset type.
Splines	This is the real powerhouse. With spline-based Edge Gradients, you get the ability to have a non-uniform, variable feather around a vector-based selection

or mask object. To see the splines and edges, you must be in control point editing mode.

Booleans – In many computer graphics applications, Booleans can be thought of as a way to resolve intersecting shapes. In 3D modeling and animation software, for example, you can Boolean an overlapping sphere and a cube to get a resulting 3D object that may be one added to the other, one carved out of the other, and so on. In many other applications the result of a Boolean is one shape. In combustion, however, these shapes are not permanently joined; instead, Boolean functions of each vector shape dictate how they interact with one another for a resulting, single function. The shapes are left independent of each other for a non-destructive workflow. Discreet combustion uses four Boolean functions within several operators, especially Draw Selection and Draw Mask.

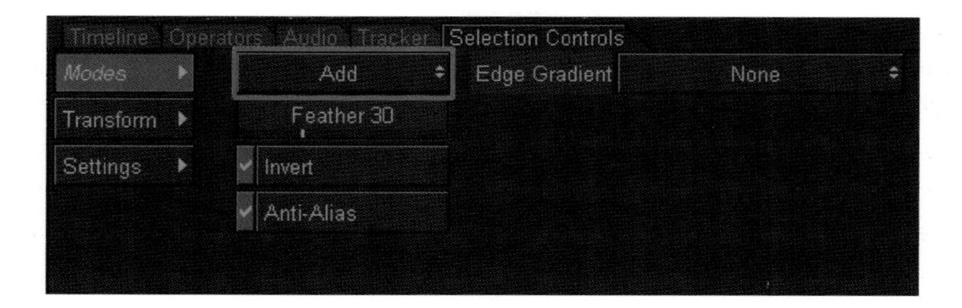

There are four types of Boolean operations vector objects can be set to use. These are listed and detailed below.

Replace	This overrides any object drawn prior to the current object. For example, if you have a number of objects drawn using the Replace mode, then only the last object drawn will remain active, because each subsequent object replaces the preceding object.
Add	This takes into account selections or masks below and adds to the area. For example, if a vector object set to Replace is followed by an object drawn using the Add mode, the result is the union of the two objects.
Subtract	A vector object that has a subtraction setting will 'carve out' from preceding selections or mask objects.
Intersect	This option is used when you only want to leave behind the area where two vector objects overlap.

The first object you create in an operator should typically be set to Replace or Add. Subsequent objects and their Boolean values will result in an infinite number of combinations, because of the infinite shapes and overlapping potential.

In Figure 6.1, the red square can be thought of as the first object drawn and the blue circle is the second; thus, the 'start' point. Each of the four resulting examples indicates the result if you were to change the circle to the Boolean setting described below each sample.

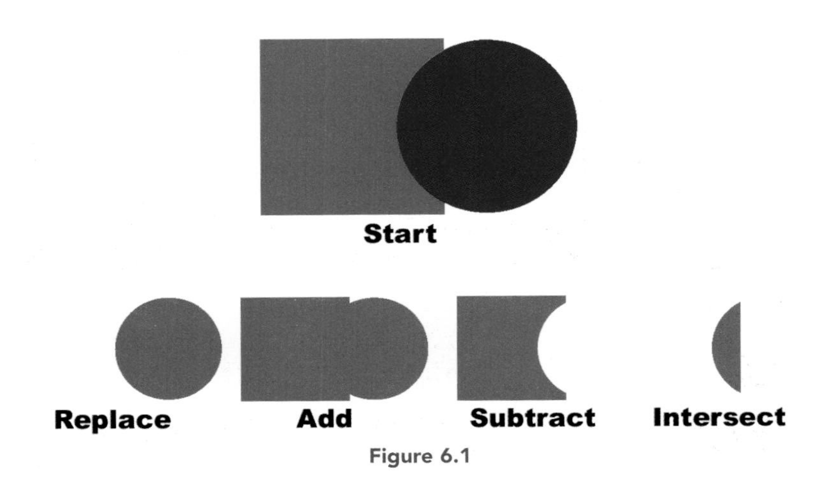

Figure 6.1

Selections and masks will be detailed after a brief, introductory lesson. Keep in mind that the majority of the tools and settings used in this lesson apply to both selections and masks.

1. Open the file named *ch06_FeatherExamples.cws*. This is a composite with one layer. This layer is made up of a still image with two operators applied to it. The first is a Draw Selection operator that contains three vector objects, the second is a Color Corrector operator set to tint incoming pixels purple.

Figure 6.2 shows three vector selection objects in one Draw Selection operator. These three selection objects are all the same shape, but one is hard edged, one is feathered and one uses a spline-based (variable) Edge Gradient. The output of this operator is passed along to another operator which tints selected pixels purple. The left viewport is set to view the output of the Color Corrector node and the right viewport is set to view the Draw Selection operator that occurs prior to the Color Corrector operator.

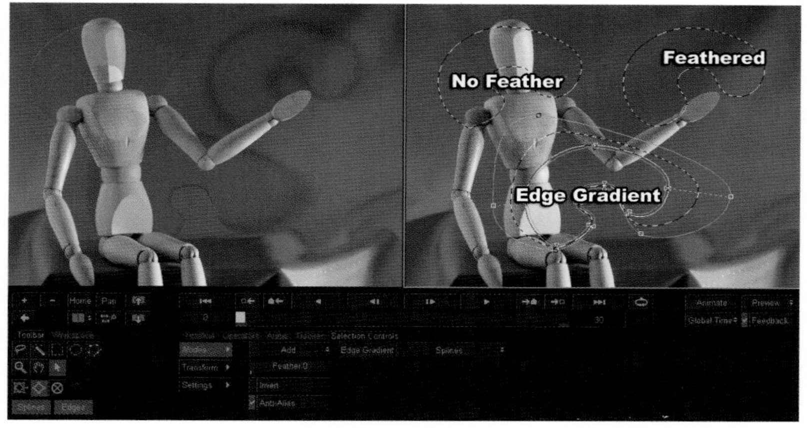

Figure 6.2

2 Make the right viewport the active view by clicking on it.

3 Expand the *WoodDoll* layer and then expand the Draw Selection operator all the way. Then double click on the name of the vector object named 'feather'. It will become selected in the right viewport.

4 Go to the Modes category of the Selection Controls now available at the bottom of the UI.

5 Change the feather amount from 30 to 5. Notice that in the left viewport, you see the effects of the feather, but in the right viewport where you are working, you cannot actually see the result of the feathering. This is because, by itself, selections don't alter an image; they only pass pixel information along to the following operators applied in the series. These selections indicate which areas should and should not be affected by operators further down the Process Tree. Scrub the feather amount input field as a slider and notice the 'marching ant' marquee change shape in the right viewport. When you are finished, put this feather value back to 30.

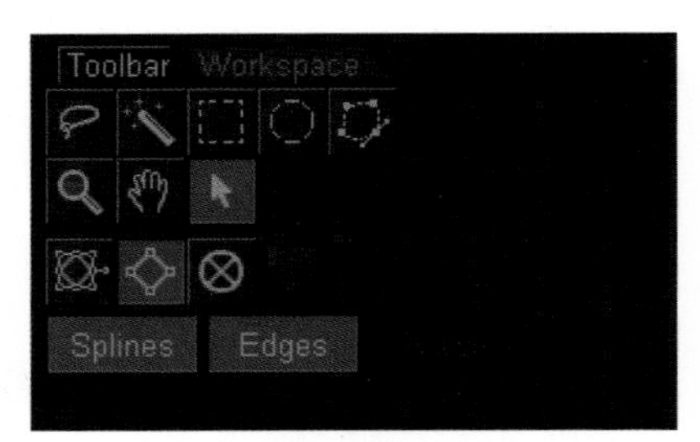

Figure 6.3

6 With the right viewport still active, double click on the vector selection named Edge Gradient.

7 Go to the Toolbar and click on the control point editing ( ) button. Then, enable the Splines and Edges options as seen in Figure 6.3.

In the active viewport, you should see the green and white splines representing the Edge Gradients set for this object. If you go to the Modes category of the Selection Controls, you will notice that there is no feather amount set (amount = 0) but, instead, the Edge Gradient type has been set to Splines for this object. This gives you a powerful, variable edge gradient that can change across the perimeter of this selection object.

8 You can edit the control points directly in the right viewport. Notice that the white spline is the master shape and the green splines represent an inner/outer variable feathering effect. The table below outlines the various ways combustion edits control points and tangency handles.

Move control points	Click and drag on the control point.
Add control points	More over an empty portion of the white line until the cursor becomes a plus sign. Click where you wish to add a new control point.
Remove control points	Select the control point and tap the delete key.
Extend the tangent handles for a point	Hold Control key down while dragging on a control point.
Retract tangent handles	Hold Control key down and click once on a control point.
Break tangent handles	Hold Control key down while dragging tangent handle.

Important: The procedures in this chart work for all spline curves in combustion, not just mask and selection objects. For example, you can break the tangency in an animation Timeline curve using the last technique listed above. Another point to mention is that all of these functions listed here are animatable!

To examine 2D vector object Booleans in a Selection operator:

1. Select File > Revert Workspace to start again, or simply reload the workspace named *ch06_FeatherExample.cws.*
2. In the Workspace panel, select the vector object named 'none'. This is the first selection object applied. It has no feathering, as can be noticed in the upper left-hand corner of the left viewport.
3. In the right viewport, move the object over to the right and down slightly until it overlaps the other two vector selection objects. You should end up with something that resembles Figure 6.4.

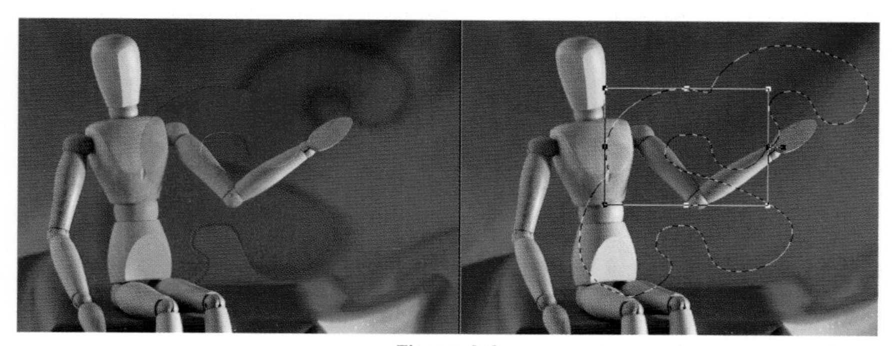

Figure 6.4

Notice that one marquee seems to encompass all three objects and the image on the left has one ameba-shaped area of purple. While this certainly is the case, each vector selection object still has its own marquee working with the other two. This purple area is made up of several different selections and feather types working in tandem due to Boolean operations. Remember, this process also works for masking operations in almost the exact same manner. You do not need to do all the work with one vector selection or mask object.

4. Select the vector object named 'feather'. This is the second vector object applied within this operator.
5. In the Selection Controls > Modes category for this object, toggle the Invert button repeatedly. Notice while you do this that the inversion of

this selection object means that the pixels outside the area drawn are selected instead of the pixels inside the marquee boundary.

Tip: Quite often when drawing a mask or selection, you will invariably create the object inverted when you did not want to and vice versa. Just select the object and then switch this parameter. There is no need to recreate the shape from scratch. You are in non-destructive land now!

6 Before moving on, return the Invert state to disabled.

7 With the object still selected, switch the mode from Add to Subtract. The selected object is used as a 'cutter' and the resulting selection has been carved out of the other selections. Notice that the feather of the cutting (subtractive) object is still utilized.

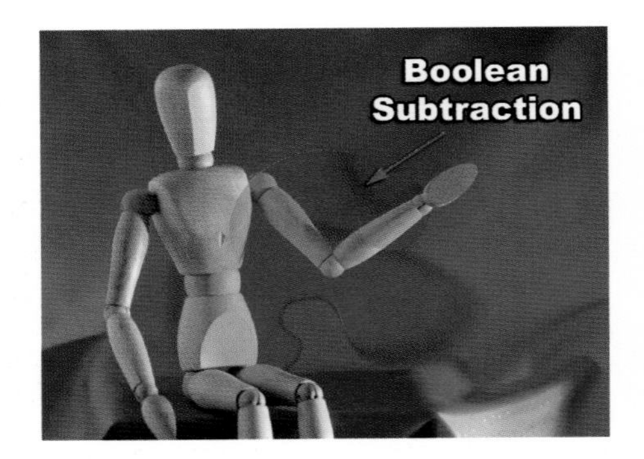

Selections

If you only want to have an effect take place on part of the image, you typically use a Selection operator first to isolate the portion of the image you want to affect. For example, to turn an actor's eyes a different color, you select them with a Selection operator and then apply a color corrector. Only the selected region of pixels will be affected.

Selection Operators

Channel Selection – If you want to make a selection based on a particular color channel in an image, you can use the Channel Selection operator to derive the selection information from red, green, blue or the alpha channel. For example, suppose you are forced to chroma key a subject against a rough-textured key wall. You can select and then slightly blur the green or blue channel (only). This will then help with the keying process, which occurs later down the flow of operators by eliminating the extra detail in the rough surface of the key wall.

Compound Channel Selection – This is exactly like the Channel Selection operator, except that the secondary input of the operator can come from another node elsewhere in the Workspace.

Draw Selection, Elliptical/Rectangular Selection – These three operators provide the basic toolset for manual creation of a selection. The Draw Selection operator adds an empty operator but does not initially create any vector objects within the operator. You are provided with five different tools to create a selection object in the viewport. The second two operators are identical to the Draw Selection operator in every way, except they initially add one default selection object of the named type at their creation time. In this case, the default vector object can then be edited to become the shape needed. In all three cases, you can add and manipulate multiple selection objects in the same operator. These can overlap using the aforementioned Boolean functions.

Feather Selection – Most selection objects and/or operators you create have a built-in feather control. The Feather Selection operator can add a feathering amount to an existing selection, perhaps if the selection was the result of several vector objects, for example. Another case when this might be useful is if you use the output of a Discreet Keyer as a selection and you want to add feathering.

GBuffer Material/Objects Selection – These two operators only work on files with extra metadata information such as RLA/RPF files from Discreet 3ds max. Frames rendered must have Material and/or Object ID values set in the 3D application prior to bringing them into combustion for these operators to be able to get the extra data needed to perform the selection.

Invert Selection – All the pixels in the current existing selection get flipped once this operator has been applied. The exact opposite selection is the result of applying this operator. This includes an inversion of any feather information.

Remove Selection – This operator has no controls, yet performs an extremely important task within combustion. You use the Remove Selection operator when you want to end the selection chain or branch in order to be able to affect your entire image once again. Adding this operator is a good idea when you want to finish off the inclusion or exclusion of prior Selection operators.

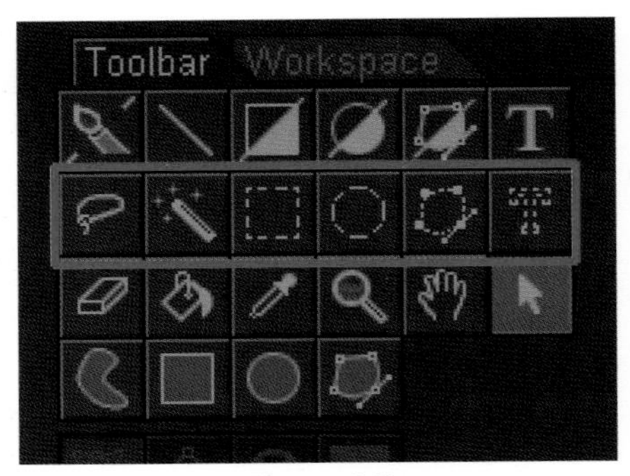

Figure 6.5

Paint – The Paint operator can be used to create selections by using the second row of tools seen in Figure 6.5.

To finish the procedure of using the Paint operator as a selection, you need to drop down to the Settings category of the Paint operator and enable the option for Output Selection (Figure 6.6). This is useful if, for example, you want to output a Magic Wand or text-shaped selection out of the Paint operator.

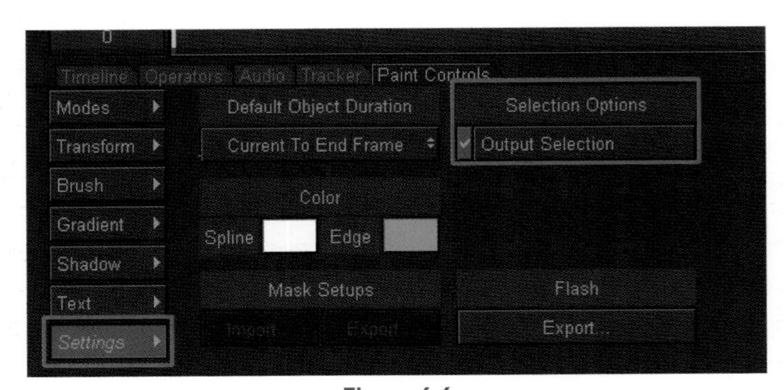

Figure 6.6

Mask Operators and Alpha Channels

When you want to see only part of an image, it may be a good time to ask yourself if masks and masking techniques are the right solution(s) for the task at hand. There is an entire category of effects operators simply called 'Mask' to handle the majority of these cases. There are additional means to add alpha channels to an image that will be outlined in a moment.

Unlike footage obtained via a real-world camera, computer-generated animation frames can optionally contain an alpha channel rendered directly into the image for compositing purposes. Footage obtained from real-world cameras has no alpha channel. If an image has no alpha channel but you need one, masks are one common way to create it. Masks remove or leave parts of an image and show other layers below the area 'masked out'. These alpha channels are typically an embedded image file that is represented by grayscale values, but in combustion you can create and view an alpha channel as part of the Process Tree.

Animated, frame-by-frame masking or selections is often referred to as rotoscoping. Ideally, a subject would be isolated on a blue screen, but often this is not the case. To remove the subject from the background in these cases you can isolate the subject with a mask.

Draw Mask Operator

This operator is applied and within it you create and manipulate vector shape objects. Instead of 'laying down ink', these vector shapes obscure or leave behind pixels depending on whether they are inside or outside of the shape. Pixels left behind will be visible and those obscured are made invisible. In these areas, images behind the current layer show through. The **Elliptical Mask** and the **Rectangular Mask** operators add a single, default vector mask within the operator at the time of creation. These simply save you one step if you know you need an oval- or rectangular-shaped mask as a starting point. These shapes can, however, be changed to any shape using the same vector drawing tools that you have seen elsewhere throughout combustion.

To quickly create and see the effects of a mask:

1. Open the project named *ch06_ForMasking.cws*. This is a two-layer composite of two still images. You will remove the sky from the memorial using a Draw Mask operator. This will allow the sky in the second layer to become visible around the building in the resulting composite. Take a moment to notice that the foreground layer has been scaled down to

30%. The source footage for this layer is 1600 × 1200 resolution.

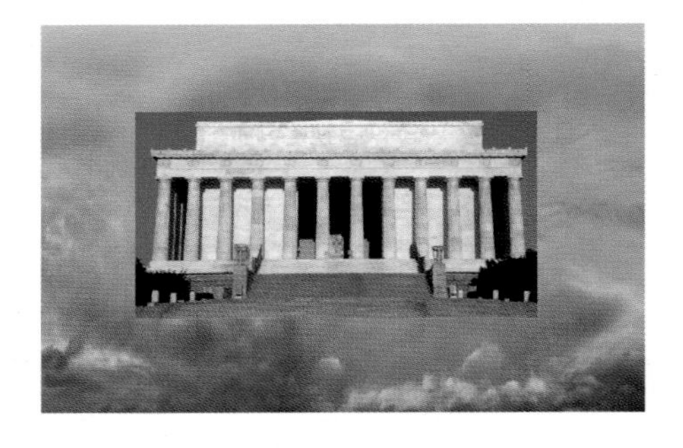

2 Apply a Draw Mask operator to the layer named Memorial and then double click this new operator. This will fill the viewport with a Layer view of the memorial.

3 Zoom out until you can easily see the edges of the image.

4 Switch to the Toolbar and select the Polygon/Bezier Mask tool ( ).

5 Start drawing an extremely rough, basic shape around the edge of the memorial. To close/complete the mask object, click the first point again for closure. Notice in Figure 6.7 that there are several mask points *outside* the visible frame.

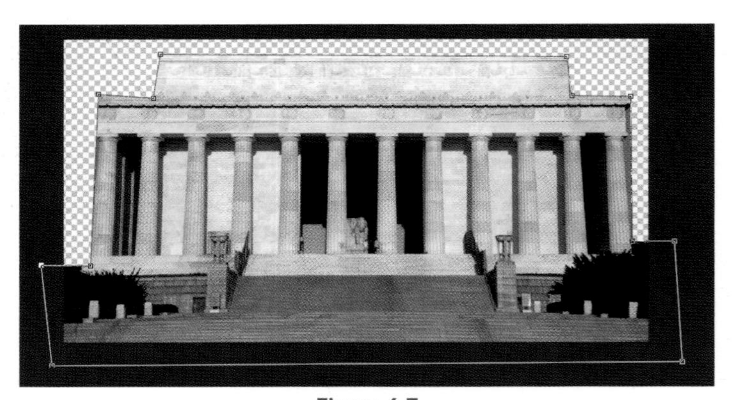

Figure 6.7

Tip: Keep in mind the non-destructive nature of these vector masks. You can initially rough in the shape and then go back and refine it later. Often, new users initially and painstakingly draw the exact shape of the mask, forgetting that they can adjust the shape of the mask later. Just draw a starting mask to see the effect and refine it once you know it is what you need.

Note: If upon closing/completing the mask, the memorial disappears and the sky is left behind instead, you need to select the mask object in the Workspace panel and invert the mask in the Modes category of the Mask Controls. You might also verify the mask's mode is set to either Add or Replace. Either will work fine in this case.

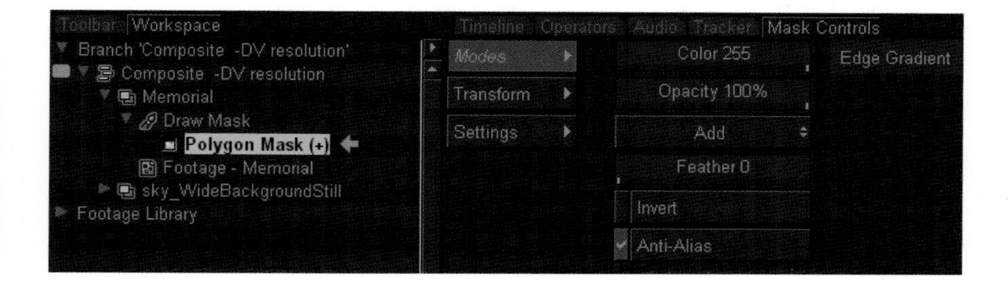

6 Double click the Composite node in the Workspace panel. This will send the output of this composite to the current viewport. You may need to zoom back to 100% to work full screen once again.

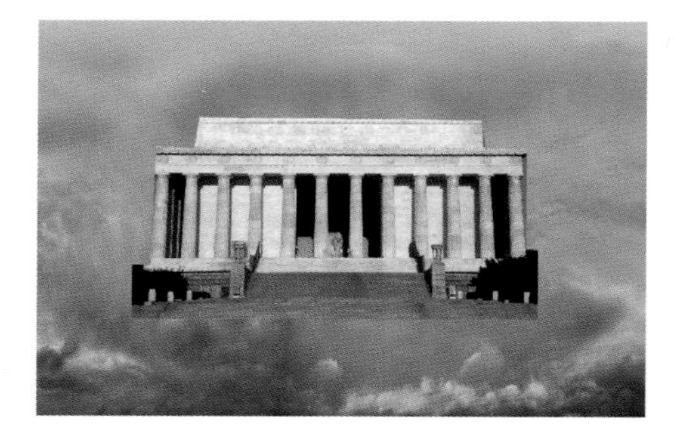

7 Scale the Memorial layer and notice that the mask scales with it. Scale and position the layer until you end up with a simple composition that suits you.

8 For a slight challenge, set a dual viewport layout. In the left, have the composite in full view. In the right, put the output of the Draw Mask operator by double clicking on it, etc. These two views can be at two different zoom levels if, for example, you wanted to see the entire result in one viewport, but work at 100% zoom scale in the other. While you work on refining the mask in the right viewport, you will see the changes appear in real time in the left viewport. Figure 6.8 shows this workflow. You can see that points have been added and edited.

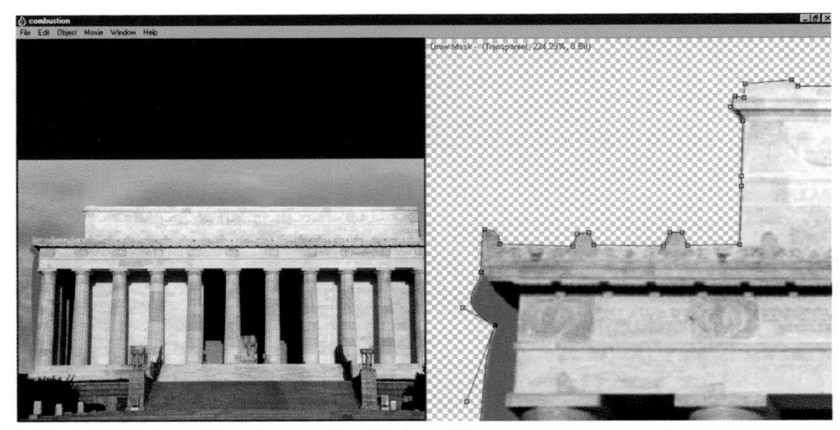

Figure 6.8

> **Note:** Keep in mind that all of these points can be animated to accommodate movement in the footage.

G-Masks – The Edge Gradient feature seen in selections works identically in masking operators. You may, however, hear of the term 'G-Masks' when dealing with the Discreet product line. G-Masks are the nomenclature for masking with a spline-based variable feathered edge. G-Mask is an abbreviation for garbage mask, an industry term for masks that are used to remove unwanted elements, or 'garbage' in a shot.

Paint Operator

This operator keeps popping up all over the place! The fourth row of tools in the Paint operator's Toolbar is identical to the Draw Mask operator's Toolbar and can be used freely at any time within a Paint operator. Figure 6.9 shows these similar tools in the Paint Toolbar.

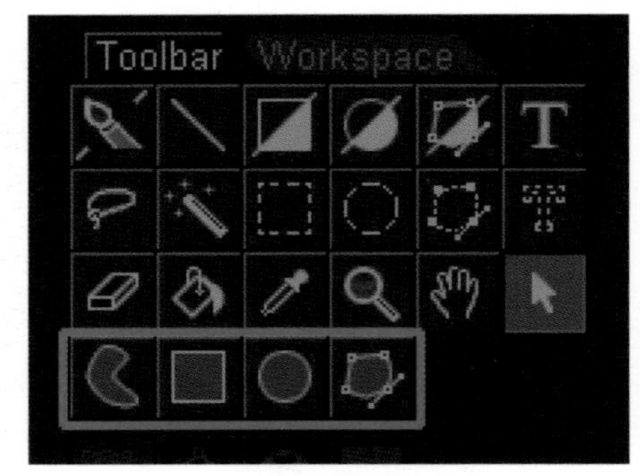

Figure 6.9

In addition, painting only on the alpha channel has the same effect as painting with a mask. In this case, remember that pure black is transparent and white is opaque. For paint objects to draw only on an alpha channel, access the Modes category of the Paint operator. Then, with the objects selected, you change the channels to draw on to 'Alpha'.

Using any of the methods outlined in this chapter allows you to isolate parts of an image. Selections isolate some pixels while ignoring others. Masks completely block or leave behind pixels. Feathering and Edge Gradients are ways to add a falloff to an effect and nearly all of this is animatable.

Set Matte Operator

This operator is not in the Mask category of operators, but it has several resulting characteristics common to a mask. The Set Matte operator can be found in the Channels category of operators, and allows you to pick any node in the current Workspace as the source for another branch's alpha channel. This is one way to quickly generate an alpha channel when there may not be one present.

1. Open the file named *ch06_SetMatte.cws.*
2. If you look in the Workspace panel list you will notice that the composite only has two layers, named DollHeads and Autumn, yet the flower image is loaded in the Workspace and being used as a secondary input to the Set Matte operator.

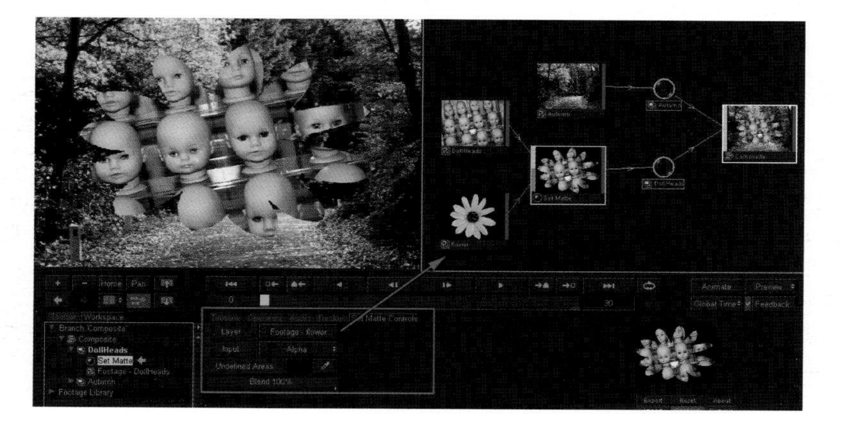

3 Move, rotate and/or scale the layer named *DollHeads*. You will see that the alpha channel of the flower also scales with this layer. This *DollHeads* layer has the Set Matte operator applied, and this operator has identified the flower footage's alpha channel as the input source. The alpha channel that results can be considered embedded in the layer. They cannot be moved independently of one another.

4 For a challenge, try applying a Paint operator to the flower footage in the Schematic. Then paint on the alpha channel in this Paint operator. The output of the Paint operator will automatically be rewired to become the secondary input of the Set Matte operator, and the effects will be seen downstream on the *DollHeads* layer.

Stencil Layer

This is a special case and is actually not an operator. Any layer can have what is known as a Stencil Layer. This can be set in the Layer category of a 2D composite or in the Surface category of a 3D composite. This function is similar to a Set Matte operator in that you are pulling pixel information from one place to create an alpha channel in another place, but the difference is twofold.

First, the Stencil Layer must reside in the same composite as the layer using this feature. The Stencil Layer does not need to be visible and in fact can be turned off if you like. The second difference is that any transformations to the Stencil Layer source are seen in the alpha channel of the layer using this information as a stencil.

1 Open the file named *ch06_StencilLayer.cws.*

2 Go to frame 30 using the frame indicator bar in the Playback controls. Notice that the text is hidden behind the globe and in front of the background image.

While this might seem simple to do with three layers (background, text and globe), the text is actually a layer in a composite with only one other layer, a nest of the globe and background. In this example, the nest was created so that the globe and background could both get a single color corrector and a glow applied, but the text would not be affected. The alpha channel of the original globe sequence provides a stencil for the text. The entire resulting composite is then Color Corrected and Grain is added to all elements (including the text).

3 In the Workspace panel, navigate to the layer named '*text with Stencil*' and select it. Then go to the Composite Controls > Layer category as seen in Figure 6.10.

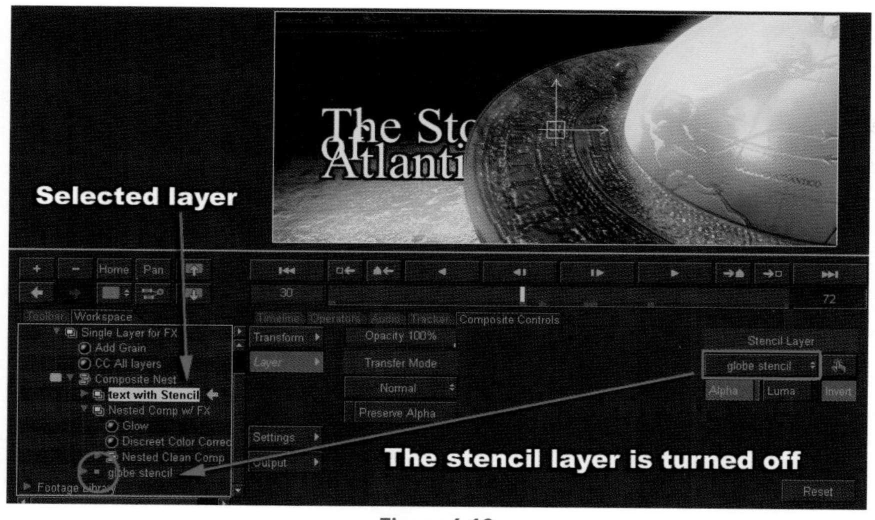

Figure 6.10

4 Toggle the Stencil Layer setting for Invert on and off. You will notice that the pixels in the viewport that make up the text are inverted in visibility. Return this value to Invert when finished with this examination.

5 Select the layer named *globe stencil* and then go to the Transform category of the Composite Controls.

6 Move the layer. Even though it is turned off, its position is irrelevant as you can see when you move the globe stencil.

7 To see this layer, double click on the *globe stencil* layer name. This will make the current viewport a Layer view. Try switching the different view modes to Alpha and Transparent. This will allow you to see where the alpha channel exists for that image sequence.

Preserve Alpha

Like the Stencil Layer detailed above, this is not an operator, but another means to affect the alpha channel of an image. Therefore, it is listed in this chapter. Just under the setting for a layer's Transfer Mode is a checkbox for Preserve Alpha. This means that objects or layers below this point will be considered cumulatively, and their resulting alpha channel will be used as a mask for the objects with the Preserve Alpha option set.

1 Open the file named *ch06_PreserveAlpha.cws*.

2 Select the layer named 'flower'.

3 Go to the Composite Controls > Layer category and enable Preserve Alpha.

You will notice that even though the flower layer has an embedded alpha channel, enabling this option causes it to take into account the layers below as well when calculating transparency.

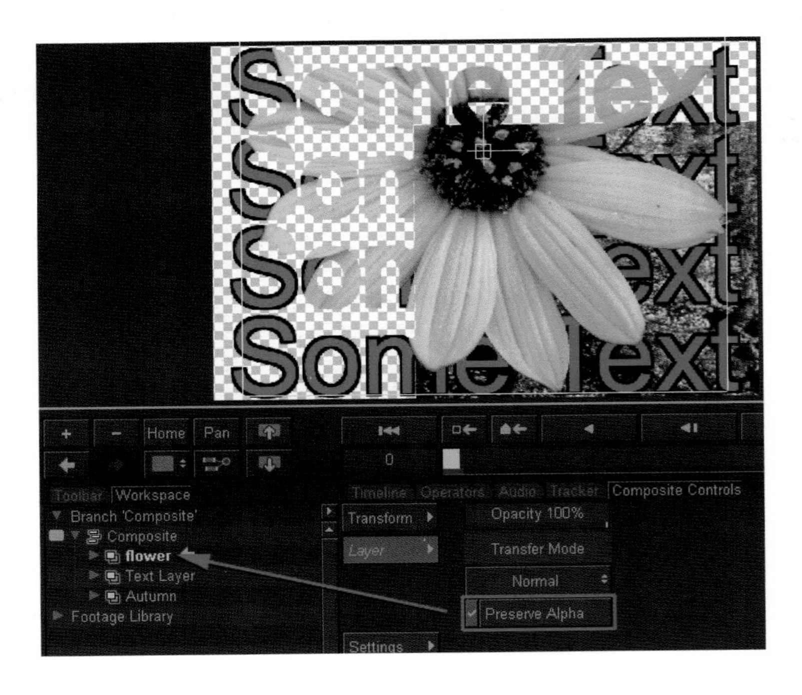

4 Move the flower layer around in the viewport to examine it further. If you move any of the other layers beneath the flower, the flower layer will only be visible where there are pixels below.

Note: Within a Paint operator, individual objects can use a Preserve Alpha option that is identical in function to this layer-level option.

Preferences

As you saw in the previous example, a marquee of dotted lines, often referred to as 'marching ants', indicates the area of a selection object. The location of this line of marching ants can be adjusted in the User Preferences > Host > General category, where there is a setting for Marquee Threshold (Figure 6.11). The default value of 128 means that if there is a feathered selection, the marching ants line will be right in the middle of the boundary between full selection and no selection. If you change the Marquee Threshold to 1, for example, the very outer limits of a feathered edge will be where the marching ants occur on a selection. You can adjust this to suit.

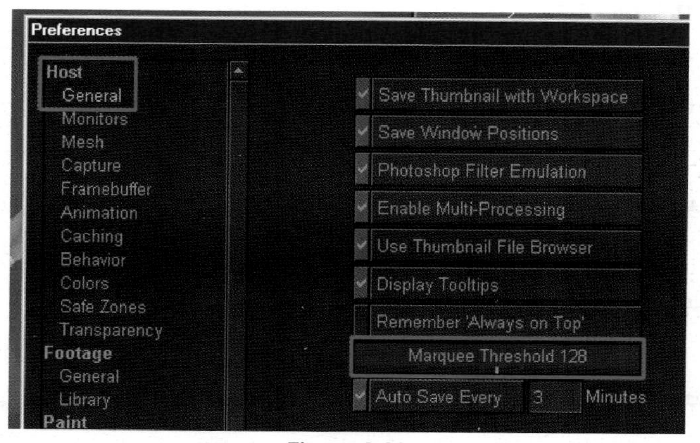

Figure 6.11

Tip: You can temporarily disable the marching ant marquee from the Window menu by turning off 'Show Marquee' (or tapping Control + H). I *strongly* recommend, however, turning this back on immediately after you have seen what you need to do. This is because a hidden marquee is one of the most sure-fire ways to ruin your day. You may end up troubleshooting a project looking for objects that are turned on, yet have completely invisible marquees.

CHAPTER 7
WORKING WITH COLOR

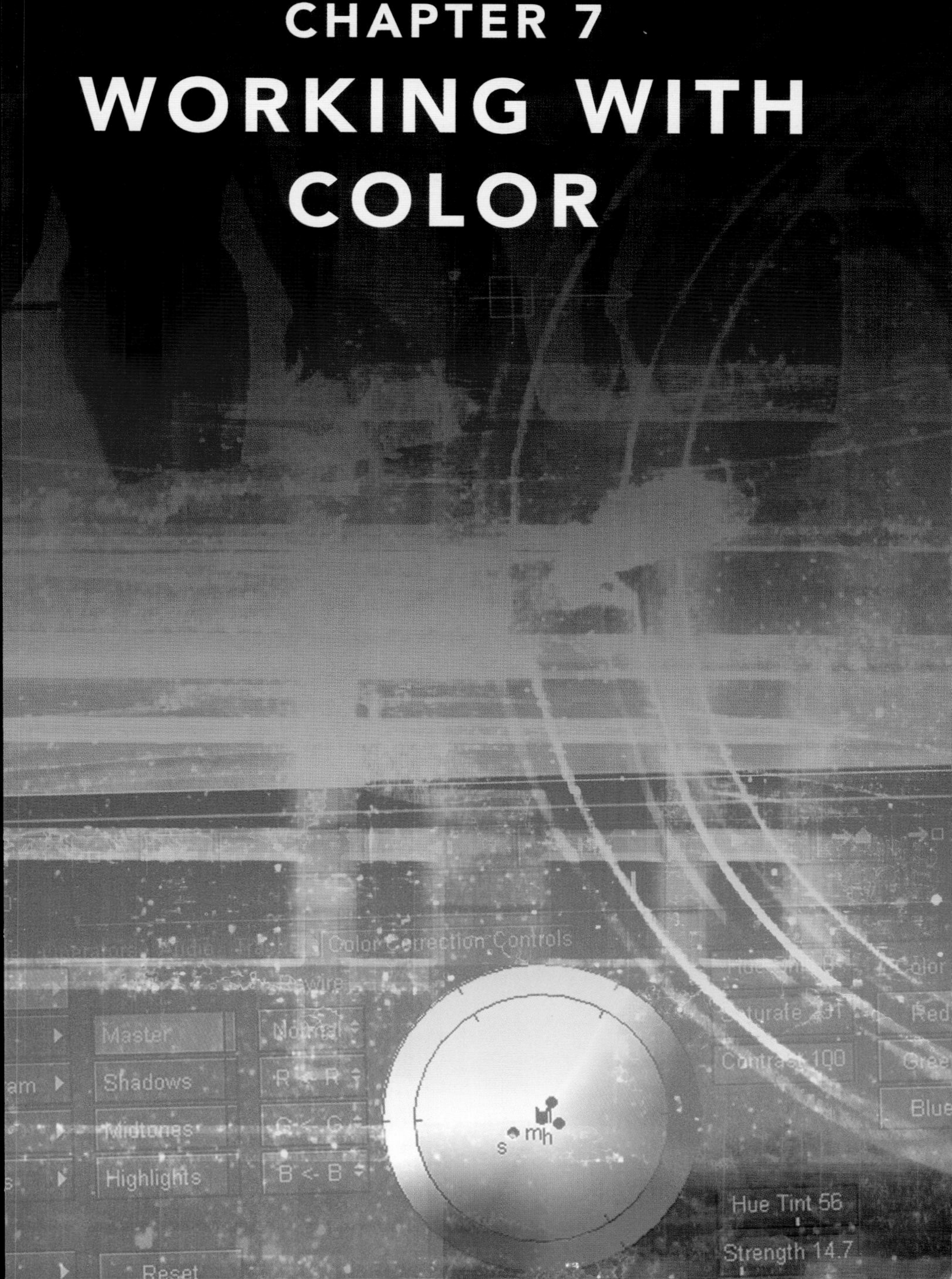

Discreet combustion has the ability to work with color information in many different ways, as can be seen in Figure 7.1. It may seem easy to pick a pixel that represents the color that you are after, but understanding the basics of the different color spaces, color channels and bit depths will help you create and alter images with more control.

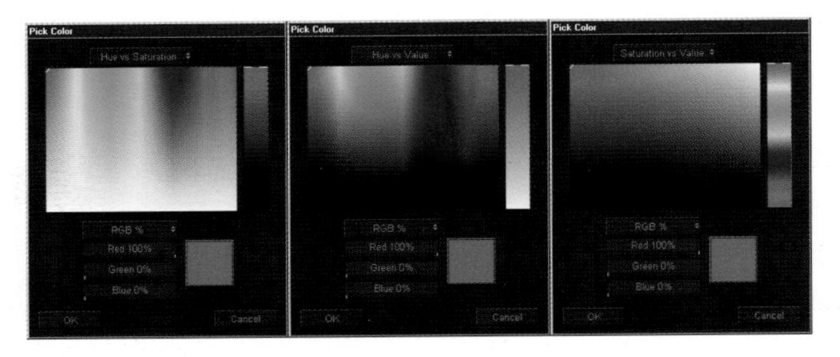

Figure 7.1

Color Spaces

Figure 7.2 shows four different ranges that all represent the same thing: a transition from dark to light. The first example represents the familiar 8-bit color range 0 to 255 that you may be used to when dealing with paint applications such as Photoshop. Many video software and hardware systems use the second and third means of describing color values. Regardless of the method, the absence of any color information is black and complete values represent pure white.

0	128	255
0.0	0.5	1.0
0%	50%	100%
shadows	midtones	highlights

Figure 7.2

Discreet combustion can use any of the above methods to describe color depending on what tools you access. For example, the sliders in the Paint operator use the first and third samples in Figure 7.2, as well as a third named HSV.

RGB – Red/Green/Blue. This is probably the most familiar color model in which other graphics applications you may have used operate. RGB is actually three separate color components that add up to one color. Mixing low values results in darker colors and higher numbers are proportionately lighter. For example, (0,0,0) represents zero amounts of red, green and blue, respectively. Pure white is represented as (255,255,255) in an 8-bit color space. Pure green would be represented as (0,255,0). Mixing 256 RGB values results in the familiar 16.7 million colors in an 8-bit color model (QuickTime's 'millions of colors').

HSV – Hue/Saturation/Value. This color space is often represented graphically as a color wheel or spectrum of color.

Hue is measured in degrees and can be considered a true 360-degree color wheel, as seen in Figure 7.3. Notice that it begins and ends with pure red. The hue represents color.

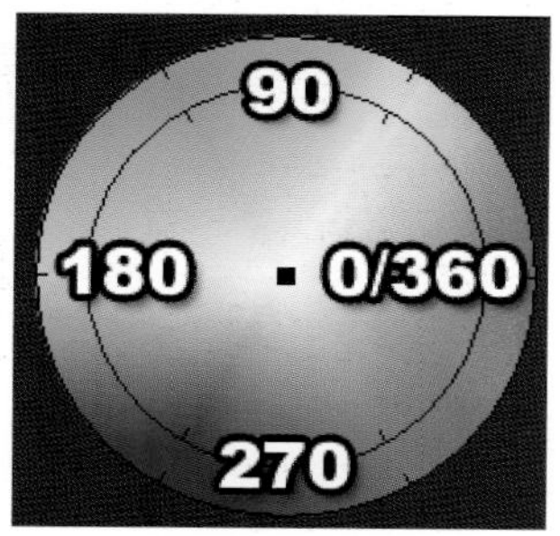

Figure 7.3

Saturation is typically a percentage. The more saturated a hue is, the more it resembles that pure color. The less saturated it is, the closer that color approaches white. In Figure 7.3, colors closer to the center of the wheel are considered less saturated.

Value is also typically a percentage. This can be thought of as a grayscale multiplier of the hue and saturation. Value represents the brightness of a color. A value of 0% means pure black, regardless of the hue and saturation quantities.

CMYK – Cyan/Magenta/Yellow/Black. This is a color space designed with the process of prepress printing in mind. While these colors can naturally be used, they are typically expressed in terms of RGB. For example:

Cyan is the combination of green and blue.
Magenta is the combination of red and blue.
Yellow is the combination of red and green.

Black is the absence of any RGB. In combustion, the amount of black is measured in luminance. Therefore, CMYK is referred to as CMYL in combustion.

Discreet combustion does not typically express color in CMYK except in the rare occasion of the Discreet Keyer. There you have the option to use RGBCMYL as a color space for keying.

Color Channels and Bit Depth

Within combustion, pixel information is treated as RGBA, which stands for red, green, blue and alpha respectively. The combination of the first three represents the color of the pixel and the alpha channel represents how transparent that pixel is.

Tip: Remember, you can look at these individual color channels at any time by enabling the View modes from the Window pull-down menu. This workflow is detailed in Chapter 2.

Depending on how many values are available to each of the RGBA channels determines the bit depth of an image. As you may have read, combustion can work at mixed bit depths within the application. This means that you can use footage with different bit depths all within the same Workspace. It is important to understand the terminology of color when working within combustion, especially if you are coming from a background that 'only' uses 8-bit color depth.

Most of the applications and file formats that are commonly used in computer graphics use the 'millions of colors' that QuickTime vaguely distinguishes, or the 16.7 million colors that more accurately describe the number of colors available. In most paint applications, there is color represented in R, G, B and optionally an alpha channel.

Quite often, people will identify an image that only has a grand total of 256 colors as '8 bit'. An example of this is a grayscale image or a color GIF file. In the world of the Internet, an '8-bit' image refers to the total number of colors available.

In the realm of video, film and animation, '8-bit color' typically refers to 8 bits of color information *per channel*: red, green and blue. This is the bit depth that most digital video equipment uses to capture and manipulate color. When you go to the cinema, chances are that the image you are looking at was shot on films and then converted to 10-bit color, which has a higher range of values than video equipment. The chart below outlines the different bit depths that you can utilize in Discreet combustion.

Bit depth	Color range per channel of RGBA	Total available colors
8 bit	0–255	16,777,216
10 bit	0–1023	1,073,741,824
12 bit	0–4095	68,719,476,736
16 bit	0–65535	281,474,976,710,656
Float*	0.0 to 1.0*	*

*Float bit depth uses a floating-point value between zero and one, and is often represented by a decimal number. The range is technically infinite, and is one of the only color models to use decimal values.

Tip: When you are working in combustion, you should make sure that your operating system desktop is using a full range of 8 bits of color per pixel. This is often referred to as True Color. High Color is only 4 bits of color per pixel, and does not represent color well when you are dealing with applications such as combustion.

The following is a simple exercise demonstrating the different ranges:

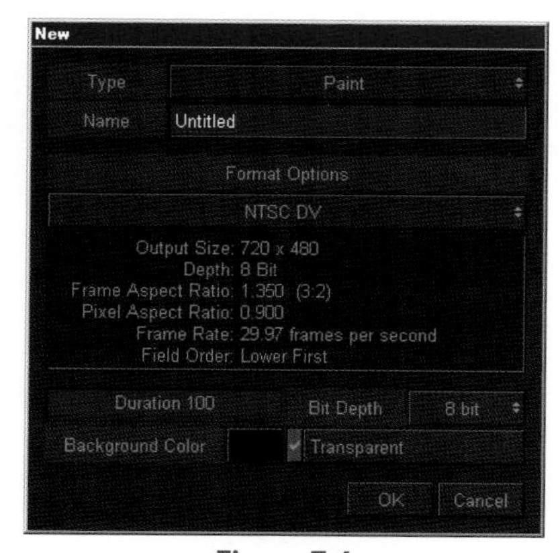

Figure 7.4

1. Create a new Paint branch from the File > New with the settings seen in Figure 7.4.
2. Go to the Paint Controls by double clicking on the Paint operator in the Workspace panel.
3. In the Modes category, click once on the foreground color swatch.
4. In the Pick Color dialog that appears, notice how the sliders have a range from 0 to 255. This is because 8 bits of color are made available to the RGB channels, since we initially created an 8-bit Paint branch by setting the bit depth in the new dialog window.

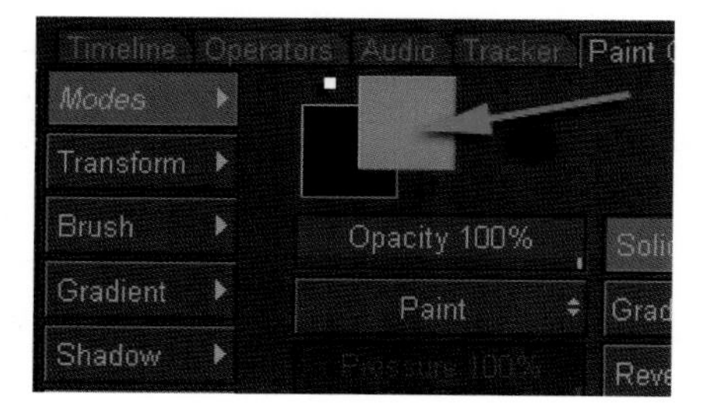

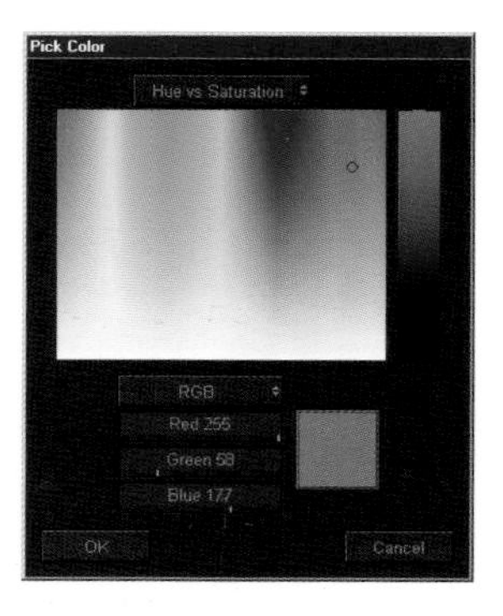

5 Click the cancel button to leave the color the same as you found it when you evoked this dialog.

6 In the Workspace panel, select the solid beneath the Paint operator.

7 Switch to the Footage Controls > Output category and change the bit depth from 8 to 16.

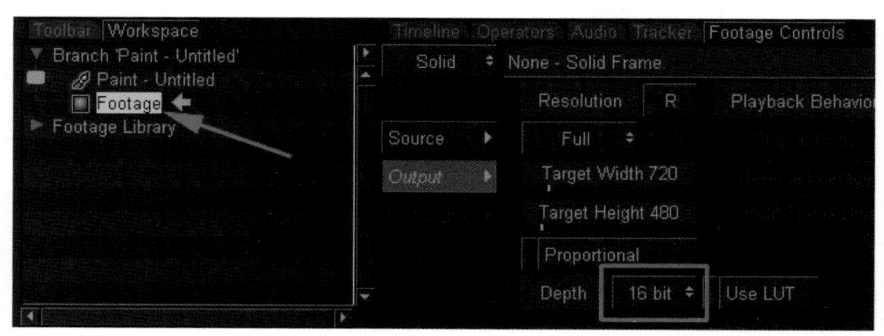

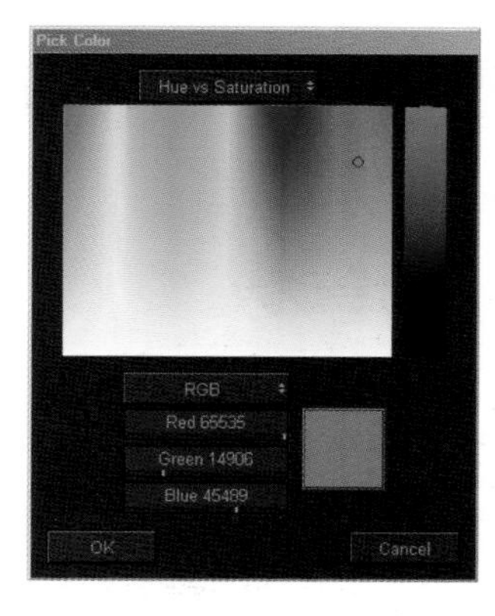

8 Once again, select the Paint operator in the Workspace panel.

9 Bring up the Pick Color dialog again by clicking on the foreground color. You will notice that now the color sliders go from 0 to 65535. This is because 16 bits of color are available to the RGB channels; thus allowing an exponentially larger range of color to be available to an image of this bit depth.

Color Correction

Arguably the best thing about the general process of color correction is the truth in the old saying, 'If it looks right, it's right'. While this may certainly be the case, it requires a bit of understanding about how most color correctors work before we can talk about the specific buttons in combustion's Color Corrector operator(s).

Any color correction system of merit will be able to deal with color using three sets of three values. These all interact and can affect each other at any time to achieve the look you desire.

Red/Green/Blue (RGB) – These are the color channels for red, green and blue, as outlined above.

Shadows/Midtones/Highlights (SMH) – These could be thought of as the dark, middle and bright colors in your image. For example, any pixel that is (0,0,0) is pure black and therefore a Shadow, whether or not it resides in an element of the image that is in shade.

Gamma/Gain/Offset – There is obviously a lot of math going on under the hood here, but when dealing with the three primary ways of manipulating color, I will refer to the simple diagram in Figure 7.5. As you can see in this example, the values across the bottom of these three charts represent shadows, through midtones on up to highlights from left to right.

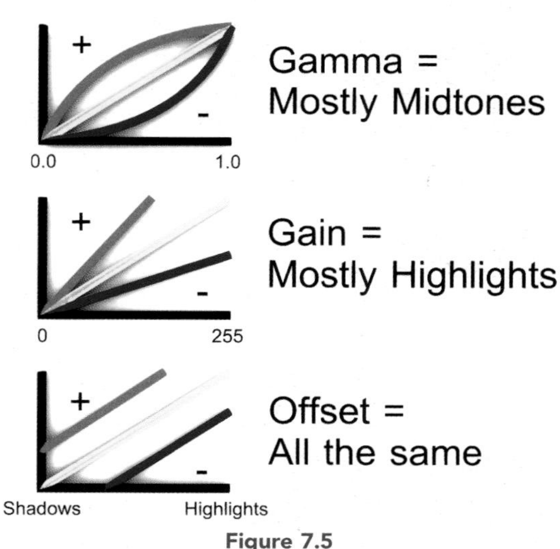

Figure 7.5

These simple charts represent color 'response curves'. Each of the three charts shows color ranges of equal value, but they are represented in (0.0–1.0), (0–255) and (Shadows to Highlights) scales to remind you that all of these are interchangeable. The white lines represent unaffected color prior to color correction. The red lines represent a positive adjustment of a particular type and the blue lines are a negative change.

For example, the red and blue Gamma curves in the Shadows and Highlights have changed little from the original white value, but the midtones are greatly affected.

Gain value changes have little effect in the Shadow range, but the brighter a color is, the more it is altered from the original value.

Since the red and blue lines representing change for Offset are parallel to the original color, this means that Offset affects color the same across shadows, midtones and highlights values.

Note: As you can see, none of the three affects shadows more than the others. This is an important aspect of Color Correction.

Tip: Often in video and film, it is desirable to keep blacks as dark as possible so the footage does not look washed out. Avoiding changes in Offset and only using Gamma and/or Gain will allow you to preserve your darks much easier. In the case that your shadows are already washed out and far from black, you will have to use tools to 'bring them down' to this level, should you so desire.

The Discreet Color Corrector

The Academy Award winning Discreet Color Corrector (often hereafter referred to simply as 'CC') is an extremely powerful yet surprisingly simple system for manipulating an image's data. With little effort, you can master dramatic looks and change the mood of an image very quickly.

If you look in the Operator tab at the Color Correction category, you will see several choices listed, as seen in Figure 7.6.

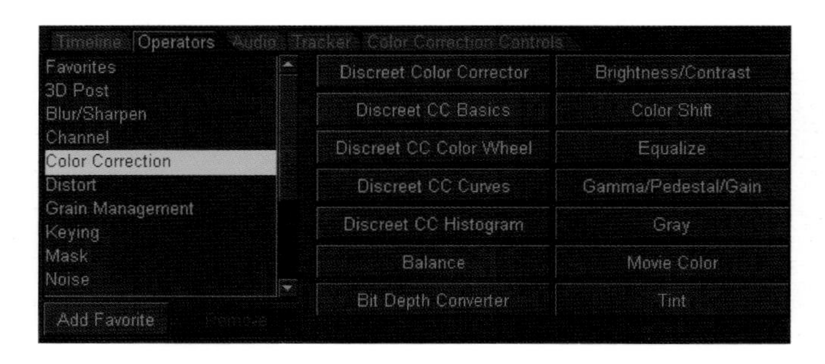

Figure 7.6

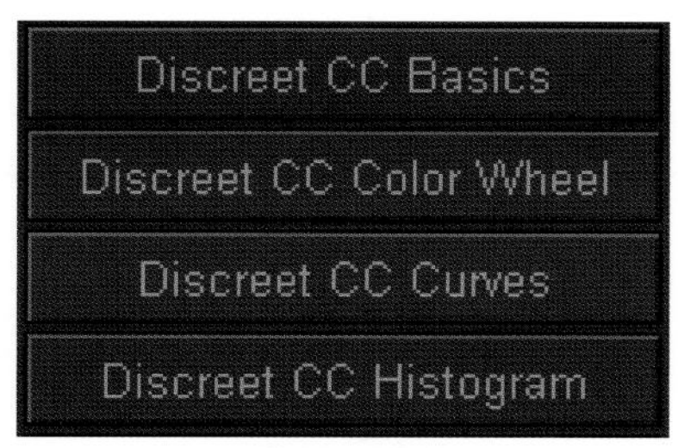

Figure 7.7

The first choice, the Discreet Color Corrector, is the operator in its full form. The next four available below it are subsets of the first – meaning that the Discreet CC contains all of the controls of the Basics, Color Wheel, Curves and Histogram in one operator. Those listed in Figure 7.7 are all available as individual operators, should you know that you only require one aspect of the Discreet Color Corrector. Another reason to break them apart is if you wish to have utmost control of the processing order of the color correction process.

For an explanation of the CC operator, open the Workspace named *ch07_ColorCorrect.cws*. This is a colorful sequence that contains primary and secondary colors, as well as a good range of shadows, midtones, and highlights. For the best interaction, go to frame 200 as seen in Figure 7.8.

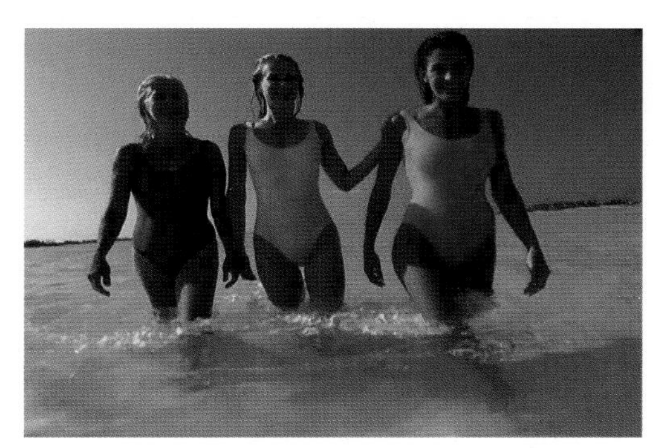

Figure 7.8

Master/Shadows/Midtones/Highlights – These four buttons are visible at all times in the CC operator, as seen in Figure 7.9. These buttons are not just for the Color category seen here; they will be visible for the Color, Basics and Histogram categories of the CC operator.

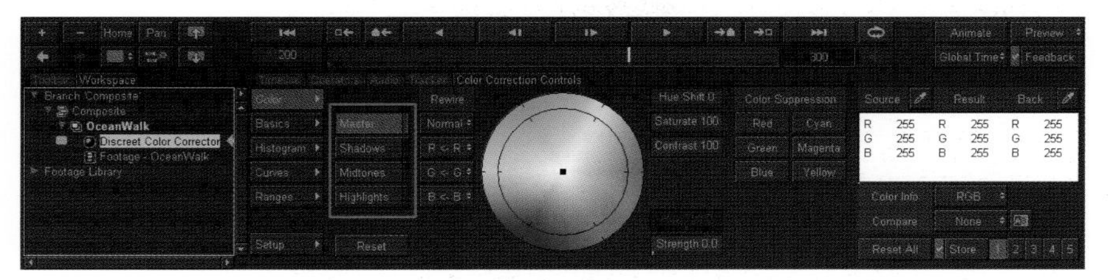

Figure 7.9

When Master is selected, you are dealing with a global color correction process across the entire range of the image. When Shadows is selected, you are isolating the darker colors to work on. When Midtones is selected, this allows you to, for example, 'Gamma up' and affect just the middle range of colors. Selecting the Highlights will isolate just the brighter portions of the image for manipulation.

Color – This category allows you to push color in your image selectively. In Figure 7.10, notice how there are four letters in the color wheel. These represent (M)aster, (s)hadows, (m)idtones and (h)ighlights respectively.

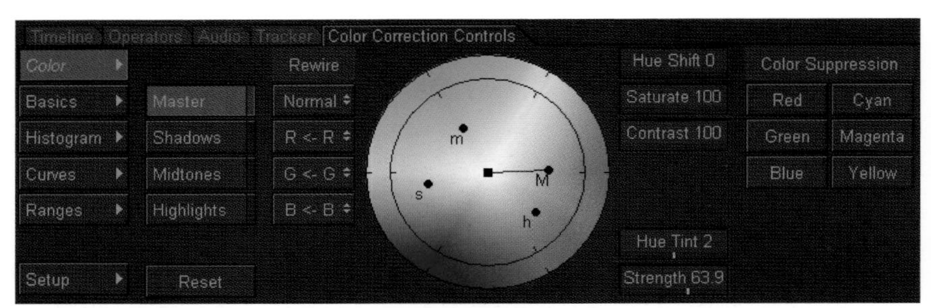

Figure 7.10

For a simple exercise using the color wheel, follow these brief steps:

1. Select the Shadows by clicking on the Shadows button.
2. In the color wheel, click and drag the mouse from the very center to the pure blue. Notice the small 's'. You will see the dark areas of the image become blue.
3. Select the Highlights by clicking on the Highlights button.
4. Drag from the center of the color wheel to the yellows. Only the brightest area in your image will become tinted yellow. Notice the small 'h' in the color wheel.
5. Experiment with isolating different values of color and pushing color in various directions. Also try using the color suppression buttons to the

right of the color wheel in different combinations. You will see that with very little effort, you can accomplish a great deal just by using the color wheel alone.

6 At any time, you can hit the Reset button (Reset) for each category, or the Reset All button (Reset All) for the entire operator.

Basics – It sure isn't the most interesting part of the UI, but this is where a lot of the magic happens. Here are all the controls for affecting the Gamma, Gain and Offset of all the RGB channels individually or all at once. The Basics category also gives you control over image saturation, contrast, temperature, and overall value.

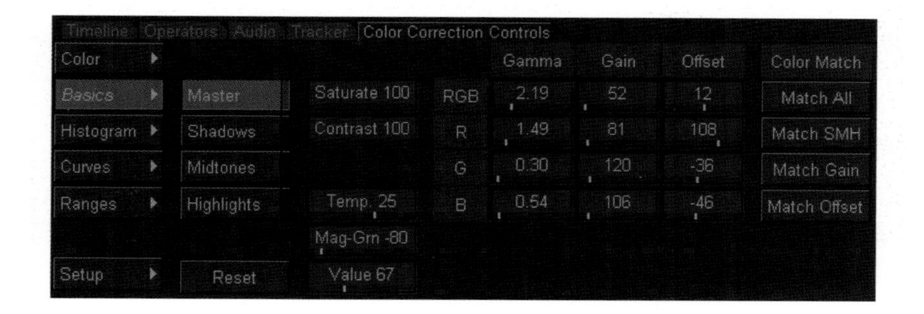

Note: The functions for Temperature, Magenta-Green and Value are directly tied to the Gain settings, all found within the Basics category.

For a quick challenge, isolate the highlights and then bring the Offset down in just the red channel. Now you are color correcting with finesse. Continue to play with color for a moment by isolating and manipulating SMH, RGB and Gamma/Gain/Offset.

Tip: Use the input value fields as sliders with the viewport preview enabled. This will allow you to scrub the sliders back and forth while observing the subtle variations and extreme control you have over color aspect.

Histogram – The histogram of an image is like a map showing the amount of any particular color. In the example in Figure 7.11, the image has a nice spread of color with three major peaks in the shadow to midtones, and a falloff to little highlights (read left to right).

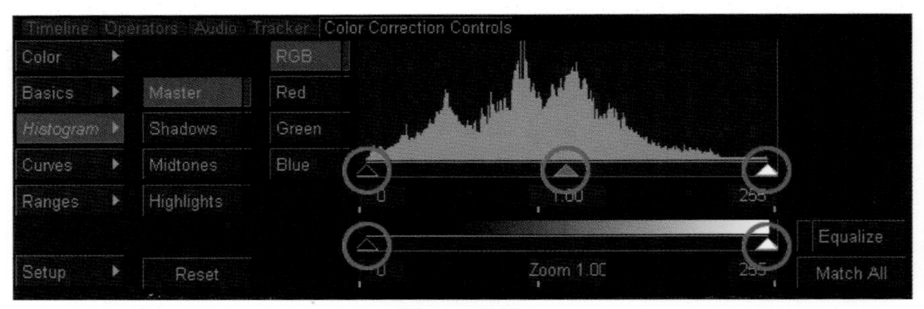

Figure 7.11

The small arrows indicated in Figure 7.11 are input sliders for shifting the bias of an image's color. For example, you can move the middle, gray arrow in the top set to affect the bias of the midtones of your image towards shadow or highlights while you leave the shadows and the highlights alone. The result is an overall darker or lighter image.

The bottom sliders are for output. If your project, for example, calls for no blacks below RGB value 7, then you can remap the darkest color to 7 by dragging the black arrow slightly to the right. This 'clips' color.

To the left of the histogram are buttons for working in all RGB channels at the same time, or isolating the histogram for viewing and manipulation in red, green or blue individually.

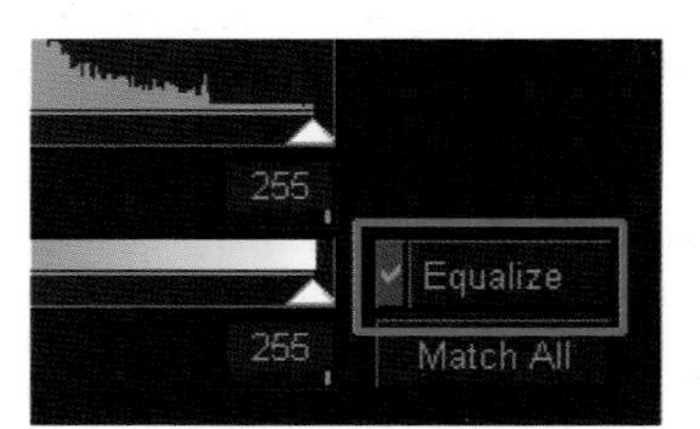

Figure 7.12

The Equalize button seen in Figure 7.12 will smooth out the histogram values evenly when enabled.

Curves – The Curves category allows you to remap color values in a visual manner. These curves can be used to replicate the diagram seen in Figure 7.13.

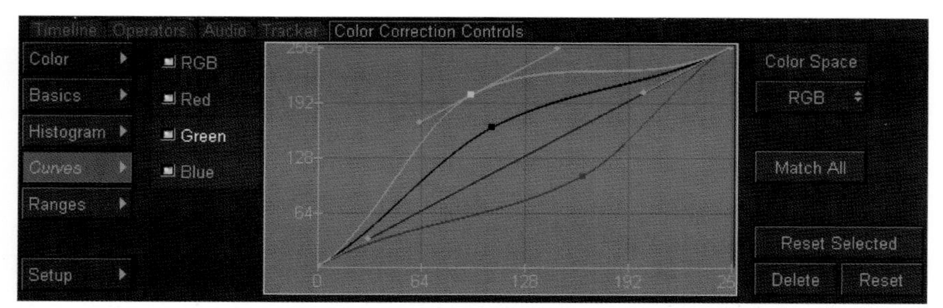

Figure 7.13

The Curves category can also be applied individually as the operator named Discreet CC Curves. It should be mentioned, however, that as an individual operator, it does not have the Ranges category (below) embedded, as do the other three CC operators that are broken out as individual operators.

Ranges – This is where you define what in your image is a Shadow, Midtone, or Highlight area. This can therefore be used in conjunction with the rest of the CC controls to dramatically change the effects of the other controls. Since midtones fall between shadow and highlights proportionately, only controls for the two extremes are made available. This does not affect the image itself; it only defines the area that will be affected when you use the Shadows, Midtones and Highlights options.

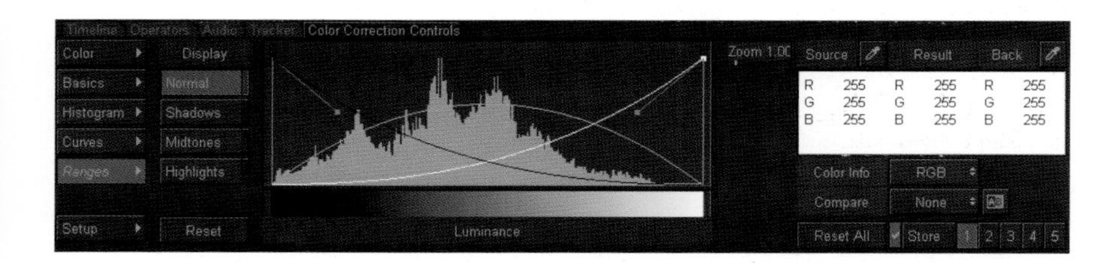

Setup – This last category is not so much for manipulating color as it is for saving your CC settings. Here, you can import and export files to other combustion stations, as well as the Discreet systems such as Smoke, Flame and Inferno.

Color Matching

Open the project named *ch07_ColorMatch.cws*. This is a simple, two-layer composite of a girl that has been masked to allow the bridge clip to be seen beneath.

Quite often, you have two images that you wish to combine as one. This is frequently the case when you are chroma keying an image and, even though you did an excellent job of eliminating the greenscreen, the subject still does not look like she was shot at the same time as the backplate. Using color matching you can adjust the colors of one image to closely match those of another, target image.

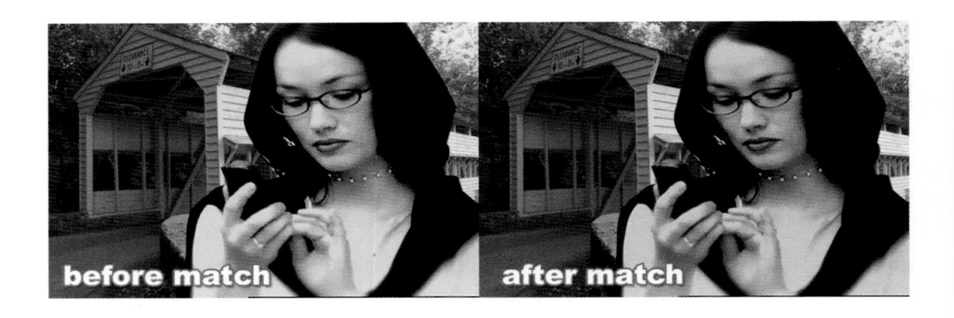

Source		Result		Back	
R	255	R	255	R	255
G	255	G	255	G	255
B	255	B	255	B	255

Color Info RGB

Figure 7.14

Regardless of the category of tools you are currently looking at within the Color Corrector operator, to the far right you will always have access to the color matching tools seen in Figure 7.14.

The vernacular of the color match tool is that the Source is the image that the CC operator is applied to and the Back is the image that you are trying to push the color towards, or match. This area provides color pickers (eyedroppers) to use to identify different pixels in your images.

To perform a color match:

1. Open the Workspace named *ch07_ColorMatch.cws* and expand the *PhoneDial* layer to reveal the Discreet Color Corrector. Select this operator.

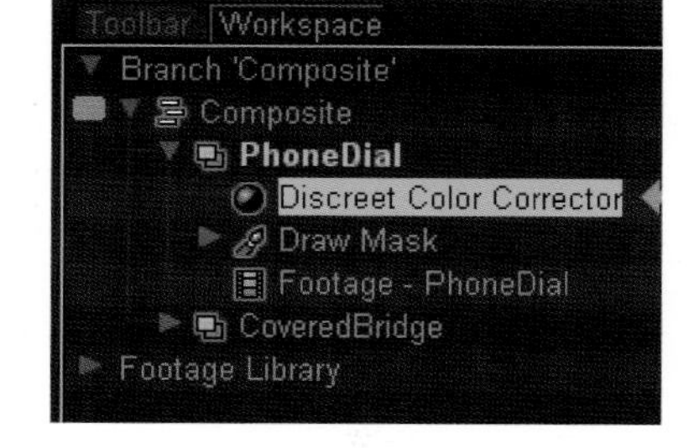

2 In the CC controls, select the Shadows by clicking on the Shadows button.

3 Select the 'Source' color picker and sample the darkest value in the image that the CC operator is applied to. This might be a pixel from the woman's hair, her phone, or her glasses, which all seem to be near black. To do this you simply highlight the eyedropper icon and then pick a pixel in the image.

4 Switch to the 'Back' color picker and sample the darkest area of your target image. This might be the dark area under the bridge canopy, for example.

5 Select Midtones and repeat the previous two steps.

6 Select Highlights and repeat.

7 Now try any of the Match buttons in the Basics (Figure 7.15), Histogram and Curves categories of the CC operator. The result should be the color shifting on the Source image to more closely resemble the colors in the target image.

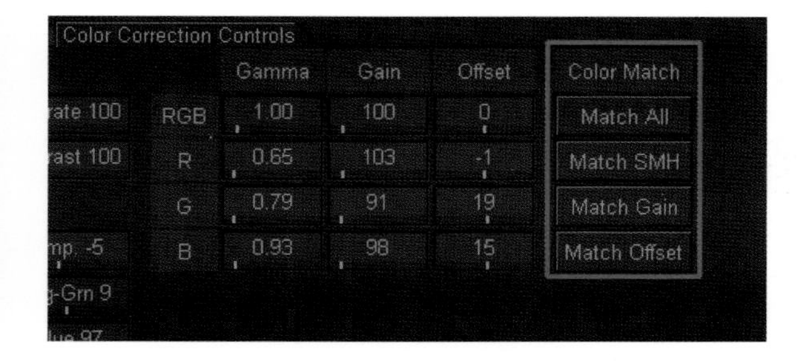

Figure 7.15

A Few Tips for Successful Color Matching

When sampling the shadows and highlights, a single pixel is often the preferred way to go; however, when you sample the midtones, using an area sample will often provide better results. Remember, an area sample can be achieved by dragging a box around the area in question while holding down the Control key.

You do not have to sample all three shad/mid/hi to achieve a successful color match. If it looks right, then it is right.

When sampling shadows and highlights, you do not need to pick the absolute darkest or lightest pixel in an image to achieve good results. You should, however, take a moment to zoom in to the image to pick what closely represents the darkest or lightest pixel in the image. By zooming in and click-dragging your cursor in these areas, numerical values representing colors will be visible and changing in the color swatches of the color Match utility. You do not need to find *the* darkest pixel, just get as close as possible without spending too much time looking.

When going to sample color from the Back/target image, it is often helpful to quickly turn off the layer that the CC operator is applied to, pick the color, and immediately turn the layer back on. This will allow you to pick from the entire, unobstructed back image. Remember, you can easily turn off elements in the Workspace panel by clicking on the icon left of the item's name.

The Store and Compare Features

Because of the subtlety of the effects you can achieve with the Discreet CC, you may often want to get the feel for what a before and after comparison may look like.

Stores – The Stores features highlighted in Figure 7.16 are similar to those found in many other operators such as Paint and the Keyer. These allow you to make subtle (and dramatic) changes in the CC while keeping values you may want to return to for comparison.

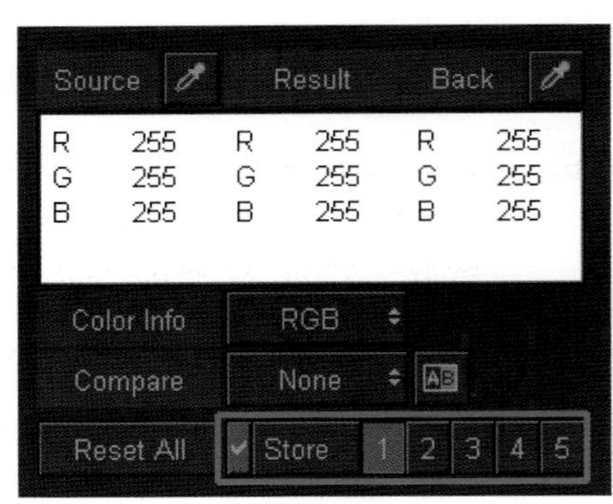

Figure 7.16

Compare – The Compare feature can be utilized to see the 'before and after' effects of the Color Corrector operator.

1. Open the Workspace named *ch07_Compare.cws.*
2. In the Workspace panel, double click on the composite node to send the output of the current branch to the current viewport.
3. Single click on the CC operator to select it and make its controls visible.
4. Click on the Compare rollout in Figure 7.17 and select the last entry named *Operator* . . . This will bring up the operator picker seen in Figure 7.18. The dialog presented will allow you to select an operator to compare to.

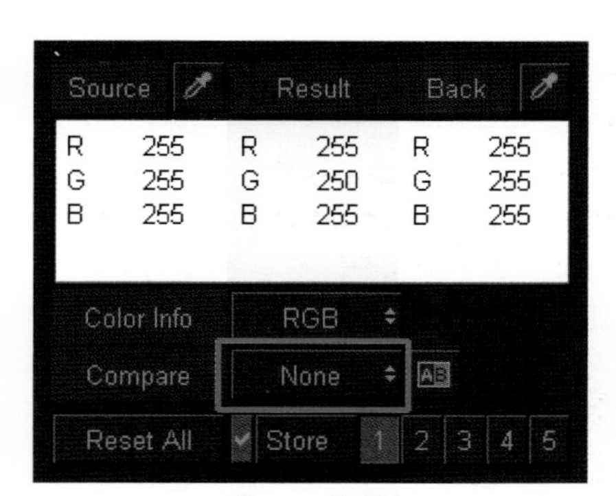

Figure 7.17

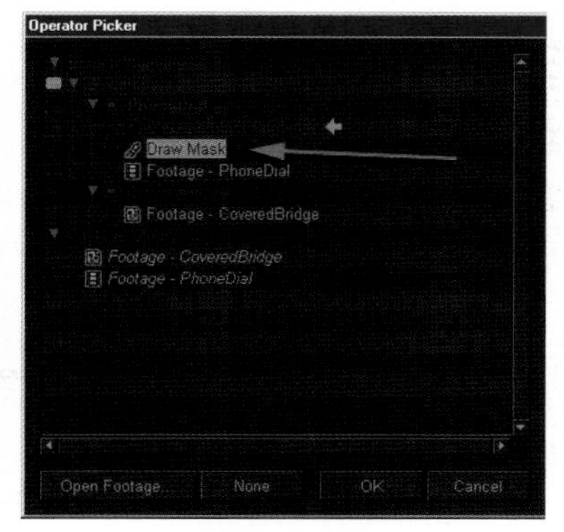

Figure 7.18

5. Double click on the Draw Mask operator to select it for the comparison. This is the operator just prior to the CC operator; therefore, you will be comparing the CC results with the element just prior to any color changes.
6. Enable the A/B Compare toggle seen in Figure 7.19.
7. Go to the Toolbar and notice the Compare option is now available in Figure 7.20. The images in this figure have been overly changed to illustrate the split vertical feature.

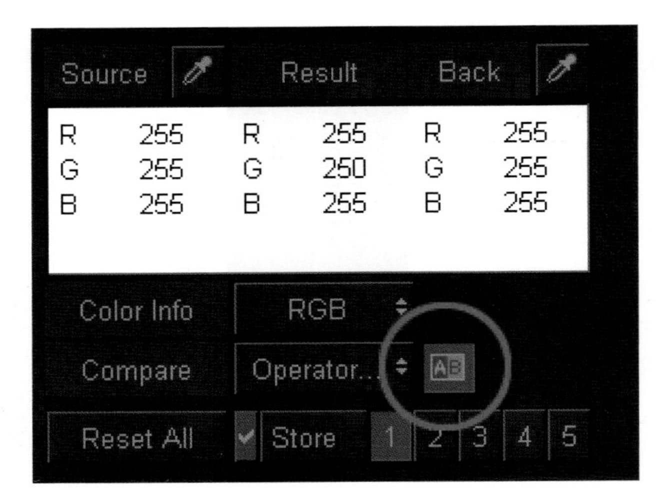

Figure 7.19

8 In the viewport, drag the mouse back and forth on the image. You should notice a before and after effect occurring on just the layer with the CC operator applied. To stop the comparison, simply change the compare option to 'none'.

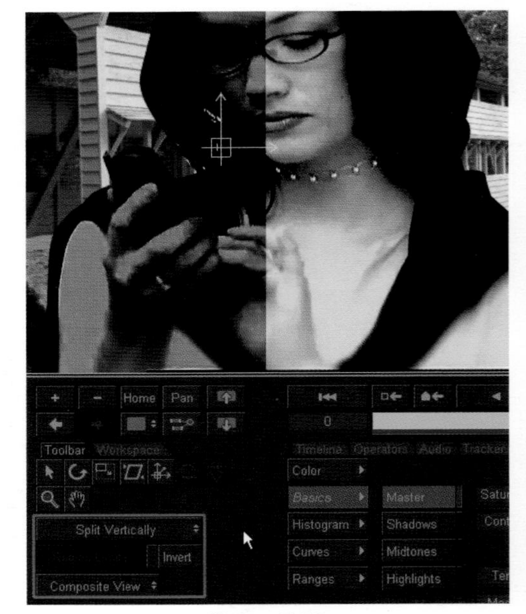

Figure 7.20

9 As a closing exercise, try storing different Color Corrector settings and use the CC's Compare feature to analyze the differences at the same time. This allows for both broad- and fine-tuning of color and easy analysis of different CC settings.

Note: The Compare feature in the CC operator(s) is not specific to the category of color correction, but because you use the Compare feature often in the process of color correction, this functionality has been included right into the Color Correction operators. It should be mentioned that a Compare feature can also be accessed at any time, by using the Render to RAM utility detailed in Chapter 14.

Closing CC Tip: If you make any adjustment and wish to tone down the effects of the operator without changing the values, you can apply a *Channel > Blend* operator and crossfade to the node just prior to the color correction. This can be done with any operator, for that matter.

For additional information on color correction and color space, I highly recommend Brinkmann's *The Art and Science of Digital Compositing*.

CHAPTER 8

KEYING AND THE DISCREET KEYER

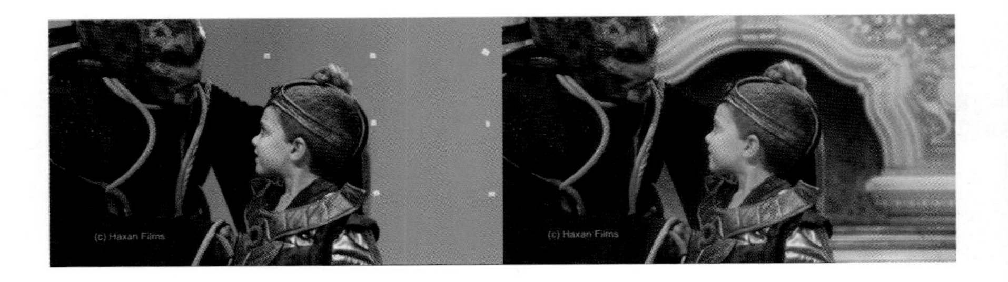

There usually exists a lot of excitement when work involves chroma keying. The results you can achieve using this process are so diverse and the benefits of its use are essential when you cannot actually capture a shot in reality. Making the blue or green go away is merely the beginning of creating convincing composites, and understanding a few basics about keying can help you when using combustion. There are, however, other means of keying in addition to using a blue or green screen.

Keying is a generic term that typically means procedurally creating an alpha channel where there typically is not one present. Most computer graphics programs of merit can generate or render images with an alpha channel embedded right in the file. In doing so, you are assured a seamless composite because even in areas of partial transparency, the footage has been prepared for compositing applications via this embedded alpha channel.

> **Note:** In the case of most computer graphics applications, the terms 'matte' and 'alpha channel' mean the same thing.

Under ideal circumstances, you will only use a keying process on uncompressed media that was filmed in reality and never on computer-generated imagery (CGI). Alpha channels embedded in the frames rendered by animation software will always result in a better composite than a keyer-generated alpha channel on the same clip. Keying of any kind is *not* the preferred way of creating mattes in CGI animations for compositing purposes. The included PNG image series named *Globe####.png* is a good example of CGI footage with an embedded alpha channel.

Footage of real-world subjects that is obtained through a camera of some kind cannot contain an alpha channel. 'Life' has no alpha channel; therefore, you must create one if you want to put image A over image B. To create an alpha channel, you can either do it manually using Paint or Masking operators, you can use another image as the alpha channel source (with the Set Matte operator or Stencil Layer feature) or you can use a keying process to identify areas of the image you want to keep and those you want to eliminate. This last option is often referred to as 'pulling a key'. With careful planning, lighting and shooting of your subject, you can capture footage that is geared towards the process of keying in one form or another.

In many cases, no single keyer does it all. You might need to use multiple keyers, paint touch-up and garbage mattes to obtain the results you want. Quite often, new users have high expectations and when one click is not the solution, frustration ensues. Even if you shoot with the same camera, same film or tape stock, lights, actors and same chroma key wall – every shot will still key differently and present different challenges. It is virtually impossible to say, 'I always use these settings with keyer X'.

Keyer Types in Discreet combustion

Discreet combustion implements all of its keyers as Effect operators. There is an entire category named simply 'Keying' that provides all built-in keyers. Many third party plugin keyers will be found in other categories according to manufacturer. Regardless of which you use, the operator manipulates the alpha channel (aka 'matte') onto the image to which it is applied. On alpha channels, black is transparent and white is opaque. Therefore, dark areas on the alpha channel allow the background to come through.

Linear Keyer – This operator is a down and dirty keyer that should not be overlooked. This is a simple chroma keyer that uses a color range to determine what will be transparent and what will be left opaque. The linear keyer can often be used with great success on solid subjects that do not contain transparency. Objects such as glass, hair or lace fabric may not work well with the Liner Keyer. If you are keying an inanimate object such as a scale model, often the Linear Keyer can work great.

Difference (Keyer) – This operator uses two separate pieces of footage to generate a matte. Simply put, you have a clean background plate and another matching image with the subject in frame, the pixels that differ between the two shots are kept and the pixels that are the same are eliminated. For example, if you video an empty wall and then have a separate shot of a person walking by the wall, you could extract a matte around the person because the pixels in the background that do not change from one image to the other are easily identified. To make practical use of a Difference Keyer, however, you must use a good tripod to ensure an *extremely* stable shot (no pan/zoom/tilt).

Luma Keying – This process forces darker areas of an image to become transparent. For example, if you photograph a person on a black curtain or night sky, you can often eliminate the black while keeping the subject intact. For example, pure (0,0,0) black is the first color to be dropped out and as colors get brighter, they are more visible. Luma keying is done within the Discreet Keyer operator by setting the Keyer Mode to 'Luma'. Remember that 'lightness' = luminance or keying out pixels based on how light or dark they are.

Chroma Keying – This is the one that most people refer to when they say 'you know, like the weatherman on TV over the weather maps'. The vast majority of chroma keying is performed on a blue or green backdrop, but any color can be used. Blue and green have been adopted primarily because the colors in the human skin tones are opposites of these on the color wheel. Yellow, orange and reds found in human flesh tones have dictated that the cooler colors are easier to remove while leaving skin tone. If you are capturing footage of an inanimate object that is blue or green, you can get great results with a 'red screen' shot. When performing this type of keying, it is known as chroma keying because you are isolating the area to be removed based upon pixel *color* values. Remember that color = chrominance or chroma. Think of it as 'color keying'.

More than Just Making the Blue or Green Vanish . . .

Eliminating the blue or green screen from your shot is hardly the entire process of creating a convincing composite. Often your footage will have elements in

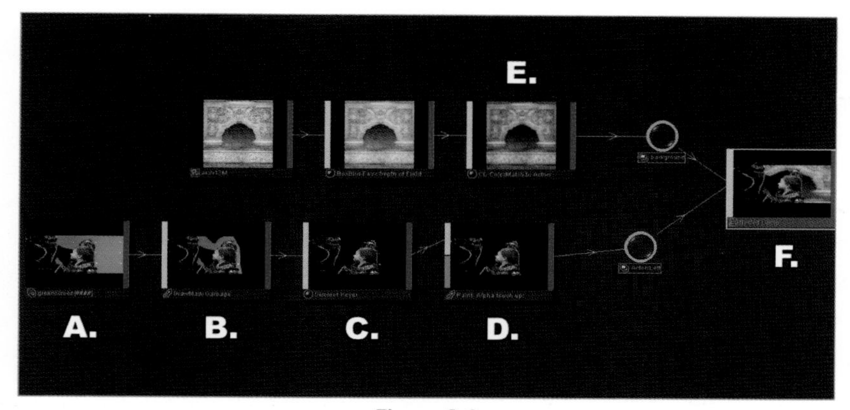

Figure 8.1

frame that no keyer could eliminate. Examples include microphone stands, tracking markers, or even the edge of the chroma key screen itself. The workflow seen in Figure 8.1 can be considered one common workflow in the processes of working with chroma key subjects. This is the bigger picture, if you will; it is more than just making the blue or green disappear.

- **A** Raw footage
- **B** Garbage mask
- **C** Pulling a key
- **D** Paint touch-ups
- **E** Color match one plate to the other
- **F** Nesting both layers for further, shared effects operators

Step C is technically the only one that actually involves a keying operator. For a more detailed look at this step see the One Keying Workflow section on page 183. First, each step will be briefly explained.

The following details may be clearer when viewing the project named *ch08_KeyingDONE.cws*. It may be advantageous to reverse-engineer this finished project while reading the steps below, and then follow later with a step by step of the actual chroma key (step C). All of these actions have been performed on the layer named *ActorsLeft* that lies in the Nested Composite. One way to examine each operator is to double click on it in the Workspace panel. This will send its output to the active viewport. Then turn the operator on and off to see what it actually does. I also encourage the use of multiple viewports and View modes during your analysis of this project.

> **Note:** The source footage of the chroma key actors is highly compressed to reduce download times. Using compressed footage for chroma key subjects is not recommended and should only be performed when uncompressed footage is not an option.

A. Raw Footage – This is the source clip of the subject on a chroma key screen.

B. Garbage Mask – Often, footage contains extraneous pixels caused by objects such as microphone stands or tracking markers on the key wall. Using a Mask operator prior to keying can quickly eliminate these pixels. This step can typically be done very quickly, because you are only eliminating elements that should not be in the shot. If this mask needs to be animated, you should use just a few controls points and keyframe it as quickly as possible. Remember, this is just a garbage mask and should be generated with minimal effort in a few minutes.

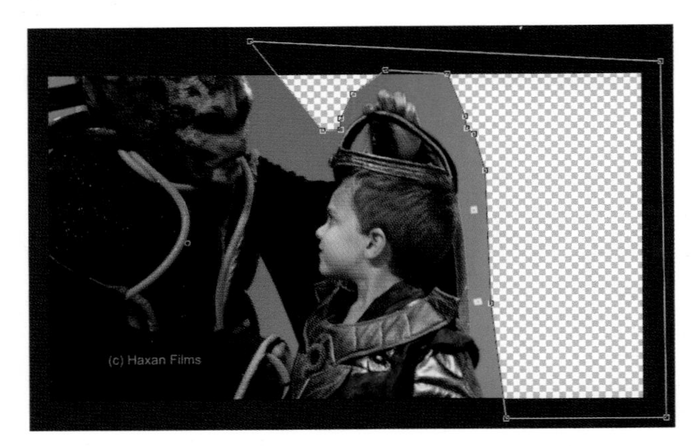

Figure 8.2

Figure 8.2 shows an example of a quick garbage mask. The green screen left over after the garbage mask will be handled by the keyer. The white tracking dots that are still visible are left because they intersect with the moving actor at some point during the clip. These will be eliminated in step D.

> **Tip:** A garbage mask should rarely, if ever, be feathered. This feathering will actually make the keying process more difficult because of the gradient edges.

C. Pulling the Key – Next is the actual keying process to automatically remove the rest of the chroma key wall. One workflow will be outlined later in this chapter, but it is mentioned here briefly to demonstrate (again) that making the blue or green transparent is often not the entire solution, but just one step in a larger process. Figure 8.3 shows that white tracking dots on the wall near the child are not eliminated by the keyer.

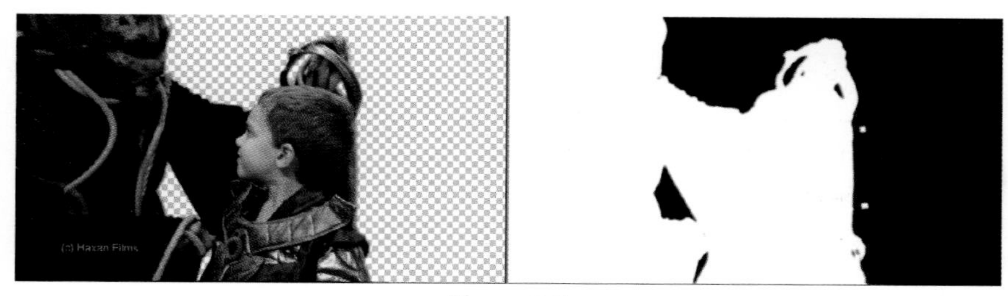

Figure 8.3

D. Touch-up Matte – No keying solution in the world is bulletproof. You may work for several minutes or several hours on 'pulling a key' and still have areas of the subject and/or background that are just not cooperating. For example, you might be able to eliminate the chroma key wall, but in doing so, you also eliminate some of your subject by creating unwanted 'holes' in them. Using a Paint operator, you can easily put back or add holes in the alpha channel as a 'post-keying' process. This is the reality of chroma keying and a perfect example of how essential it is to have a non-destructive, vector paint application right in your compositing environment. This is the manual clean-up that often cannot be avoided no matter how much care went into obtaining the source footage. Figure 8.4 shows three selected objects that were created using the Paint operator and animated to compensate for movement by the actors.

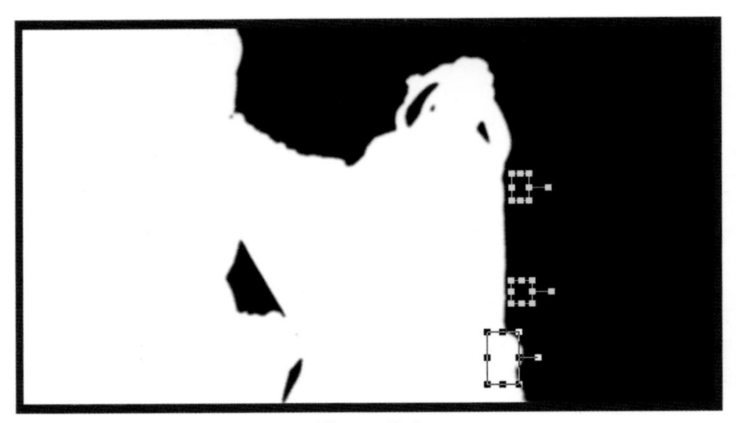

Figure 8.4

Note: All three of these objects are painting on the alpha channel. Two of these are black 'holes' in the alpha to eliminate the tracker dots and one is pure white to 'put back' the actor's robe. You can toggle these on and off to see which is which.

E. Color Match – After the subject has been chroma keyed and the alpha channel is as clean as possible, the subject may still not look like it is 'in' the composite. For example, if you have an actor lit in a studio but they are supposed to appear as if they are in a dark, night shot. No matter how perfect the key is, the two layers do not look like they were shot under the same conditions. Using the Discreet Color Corrector operator to match either the background to the subject or the subject to the background can often be the most important step in creating convincing/seamless composites. Figure 8.5 shows the original background on the right has been pushed to an orange hue to match the actors on the left.

F. Nest and Effect – Many compositors also want to add effects to both the subject and the backplate to help 'tie' them together visually. By creating a nested composite out of your subject and backplate layers, you can apply operators to the nest so both layers get affected equally. Film grain, additional color correction and specular blooming are common examples of popular looks in many recent commercials and feature films. Figure 8.6 shows one example.

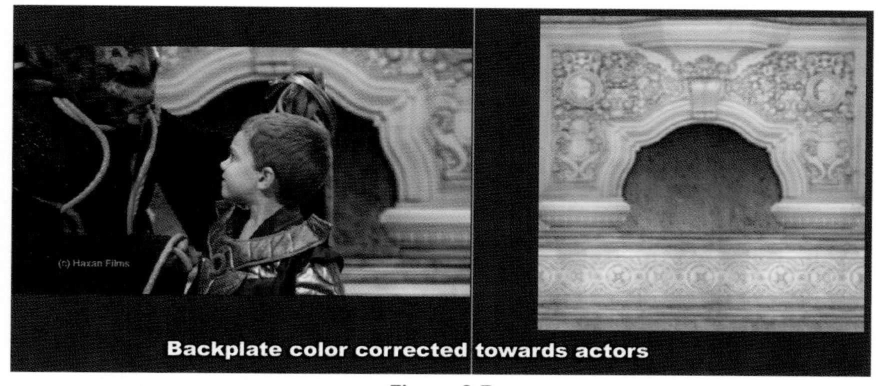

Figure 8.5

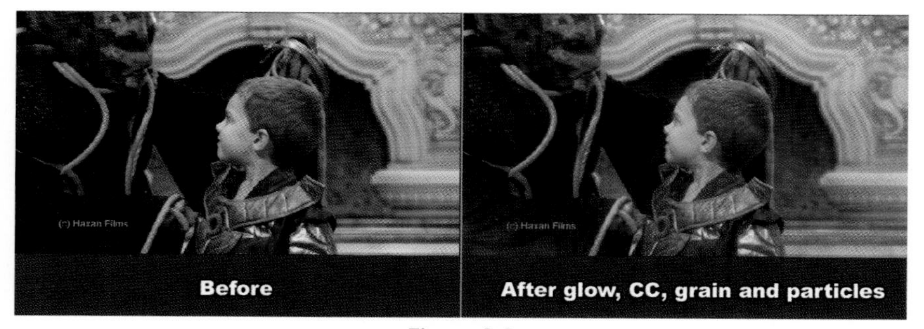

Figure 8.6

The Discreet Keyer Operator

The Discreet Keyer operator is a robust tool that provides many categories of tools in combustion for doing chroma, luma and channel keying. As with the Discreet Color Corrector, the Discreet Keyer provides a myriad of controls that should be understood prior to attacking key shots. Each of the following is a brief description of the categories found within the Discreet Keyer operator.

Key – This category is where you isolate a color or a range of colors in a specific color model such as RGB, YUV and HLS. The Key Color eyedropper is provided to sample the image and begin the keying process. With it, you isolate a single color and add transparency to the alpha channel where pixels of this color reside in the image. The color fields to the right provide a visual representation of the colors and ranges you set in this category of the operator. In these color fields, the ramp between the yellow and cyan vertical bars represents a softness falloff. If there are two cyan bars in any of these three fields, then the space between represents a range of tolerance. These cyan and yellow bars allow you to adjust softness and tolerance globally or locally to each channel by dragging directly on them in the color fields.

The Tolerance controls found here are one way of increasing or decreasing the range of color to be keyed out. This should only be done after you have chosen an initial color with the Key Color eyedropper. To extend the range, select the Add Tolerance picker and sample the pixel(s) you wish to add. To restrict the tolerance and remove a color from the keying process, use the Remove Tolerance eyedropper and the pixels will 'come back'. It is recommended to use Tolerance sparingly.

The Softness controls here are for defining areas in the matte that are transparent. Subjects that are glass, lace and thin cloth are a few examples of items with partial transparency. You can add or remove softness as needed.

The Plot eyedropper seen in Figure 8.7 can also be found in several other Discreet Keyer operator categories. This provides a means to pick a color in the viewport and have its value returned to you for examination. Here, the value is returned in real time as a color swatch and also as a thin red line in the color bars.

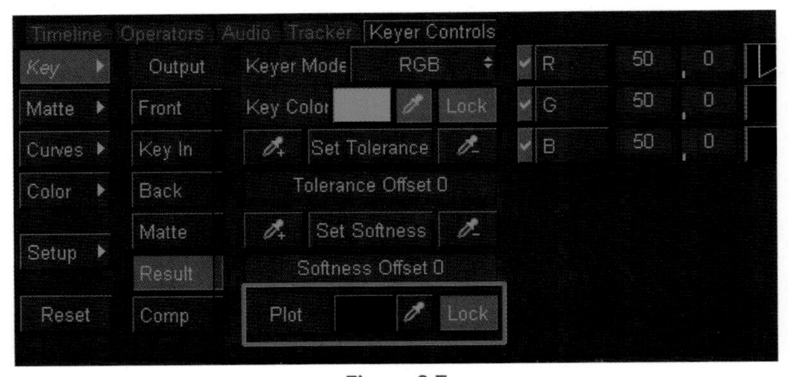

Figure 8.7

Matte – This is where you can manipulate the range of gray values in the matte that is created by the Discreet keyer. You also have controls to 'choke' the matte using shrink, erode and blur functions at the matte edges.

The steps of defining and editing the Key Color, Softness and Tolerance are the primary ways to generate the matte within the keyer. It is here in the Matte controls that you refine the alpha channel created by the keyer. The histogram in this section represents the alpha channel of the resulting matte generated by the Keyer operator. Sliders below the histogram allow you to remap the overall brightness of the matte.

The three buttons for Shrink, Erode, and Blur allow you to optionally manipulate the edges of the alpha channel by a defined width (measured in pixels).

Shrink	Adds or removes pixels from the edge of the matte.
Erode	Adds transparency to the edge of the matte.
Blur	Applies a blur to the matte. This option has independent settings for width and height of the blur applied.
Lift	Offsets all the matte pixels equally. This value can be negative to darken the matte 'down' to pure black, if needed.
Gain	This applies a multiplier to the pixel values of the alpha channel. This primarily affects the brighter pixels of the matte.
Zoom	Changes the scale of the histogram to the right. This is purely cosmetic and has no effect on the matte.
Invert	Enabling this button is the same as flipping the alpha channel of the image. Areas that are transparent become opaque and vice versa.

Curves – This is where you can alter how the front matte and the back matte meet. The default is an equal blending of the two, but if you want to bias towards one or the other, you can use the Curves controls to blend the front and background images together. To add a matte curve, simple click on either the Front or Back setting and then click on the highlighted curve. This new point can be edited using standard Bezier editing.

The Plot picker here will result in a red line within the Curves editor window. This helps you determine a pixel's matte values. Quite often, you can get by with little or no editing within the Curves section.

Color – This category is where you can correct color 'spill' that remains on your subject after the initial key has been performed. Often, in the case of thin elements such as hair, color spill will be left around the edges of a subject, even after the initial keying process has eliminated much of the chroma key wall. Editing here allows you to disguise pixels instead of eliminating them from the image.

The seven labels on the left represent seven different color curves available in the color spectrum. To isolate any one of them, you click on the name to the left and edit the corresponding curve. The two primary options to concern yourself with here are Hue Shift and Supp(ression).

Hue Shift pushes a color towards the user-defined Hue Shift Target color. This is the color that will be put in the place of color spill and is often set to a color similar to the background of the image and/or the inner edge of the key subject. In the case of our sample image, you may use a yellow-orange as the target color, for example.

'Supp' is for suppressing color from a specific hue by reducing the saturation of the Color Suppression Target. This target color, in turn, identifies a color to suppress. This can often best be found by using the Plot tool to identify color spill pixels in the image.

The Plot eyedropper here allows you to click and drag across the image and the pixel color selected will be identified in the Color Histogram by a red vertical line. This can be useful to help select Hue Shift and Color Suppression Target colors. Quite often, the naked eye will see the edge spill as one color when, in fact, it is another color when examined by the eyedropper.

Setup – This is an area that controls how the keyer will function. You could almost consider this preference local to each Keyer operator. This is also the area where you can import and export setups for the Keyer operator. These **.KEY* files can be loaded by many Discreet products such as Flame, Smoke and Inferno. A few different finished **.KEY* files are provided for your examination.

There is also a useful option here for 'Output Matte As' (the choices are Key or Selection). In many cases, you may find it useful to use the keyer as a Selection operator of sorts. To output the alpha channel as a selection, simply change the setting from Key to Selection. More information about selections is described in Chapter 6.

Output – There is also a vertical column of Output options for Front, Key In, Back, Matte, Result and Comp. These Output choices dictate what information is sent out of the operator in the Process Tree. For the most part, you will want the output to end up as 'Result', but often during the process you may want to briefly check another, such as the matte generated by the operator.

Additional Keying Operators

There are three additional operators that can be considered subsets of the Discreet Keyer operator, yet useful in their own right. As you have seen, the Discreet Keyer has several categories of functions. There may be times, however, when you need some of this functionality but do not need the entire toolset of the Discreet Keyer. An example of this is where you use a Linear Keyer operator but just need to choke the matte slightly to finish the effect.

Alpha Levels – This is an operator that adds some of the functionality of the 'Matte' portion of the Discreet Color Keyer. With it, you can push the whites and blacks of the matte.

Color Suppression – This operator uses the spill suppression technology of the Discreet Keyer. This can optionally be used as a color correction tool, completely removed from the matte extraction process of keying.

Matte Controls – This operator allows you to choke the matte of any image, including images that never even utilized a keyer. For example, to blur the edge of a 3D rendered CGI alpha channel, you could use the Matte Controls operator.

One Keying Workflow

Outlined here is one method of pulling a key with the Discreet Keyer. You may learn and use a different workflow with great results – this is just one take on the matter. Again, different methods and different keyers may be required from shot to shot. The end result of a convincing blend of foreground and background is what ultimately matters, not how you get there.

1. Open the file named *ch08_KeyingStart.cws*. This project has the garbage masking and touch-up steps outlined above already completed

for your examination. The following lesson is just to isolate the second step (of keying out the color) in the bigger picture.

Take notice that there are two layers: one of actors shot against a green screen and a still image background to put them over. This lesson will walk you through keying the layer named *ActorsLeft*.

2 You can examine the effects of each operator either by turning them on and off, or by double clicking on each operator to send its output to the active viewport. Figure 8.8 shows how the project loads: with two operators and one layer turned off. Again, these are provided for your analysis of the big picture, but this particular lesson is simply the procedure of making the green go away using the Discreet Keyer operator.

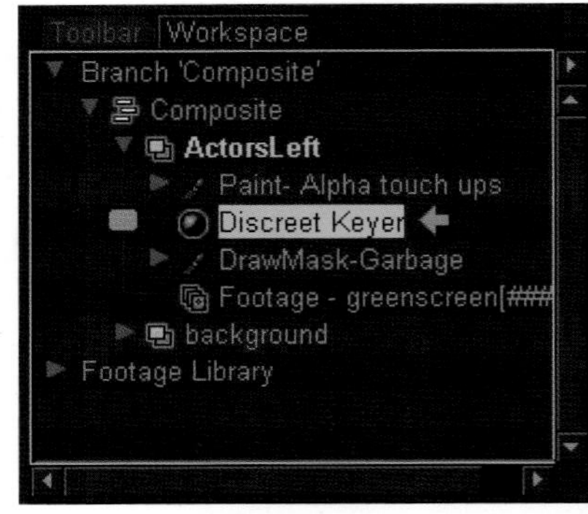

Figure 8.8

Before moving on, return the on/off states of elements to the starting point (or revert the Workspace from the File menu). Also, make sure you are looking at the composite in the active viewport by double clicking on it in the Workspace panel.

3 Switch to a two-wide viewport configuration. In the left viewport, put the output of the entire composite by double clicking on the Composite in the Workspace panel.

4 In the right viewport, send the output of the Keyer operator of the *ActorsLeft* layer by double clicking on the Keyer operator in the Workspace panel. At this point, the viewports should look the same, the right viewport is set to be active, and the Keyer controls are visible at the bottom of the UI.

5 In the Key category, activate the eyedropper tool and click in the RIGHT viewport on a point of green screen behind the child. Now pause to take notice of a few things: the left viewport now shows the keyer starting to work, because the background layer is becoming visible. The right viewport drops out some green, but there is still plenty left over. No worries at this point.

> **Tip:** If the 'big picture' dictates that you are going to use a garbage mask, then you might not want to sample color from the area getting masked out because it will already be handled by the Mask operator. At that point, you should only concern yourself with the chroma key pixels that are left over after the mask has done its thing. Also, remember that you can turn the garbage mask operator on and off while taking this color sample if you need to.

6 With the Key Color eyedropper still selected, click a point of the green screen between the two actors' faces in the right viewport. Notice that picking this color results in a completely different 'starting point' for the rest of the keying process. The first major step in keying is finding the most useful key color. In the case of actors with loose hair, this is often the most difficult area to key and, therefore, a good place to start your keying process (near the areas with fine detail to preserve).

The Key Color eyedropper is only picking one color to start keying, but it also adds a value of 50 on each side of this color value for Softness. You can also opt to hold down the Control key and drag a rectangular region around a larger portion of the green screen. This is an 'area sample' and does not create a range of color; it still only generates one key color – however, this color is the *average* of all the pixels sampled. Figure 8.9 shows an area sample being performed on the right side of the frame. For this lesson, you may want to area sample above the actors' heads. Make sure you do not sample pixels of a white tracking marker on the chroma key wall.

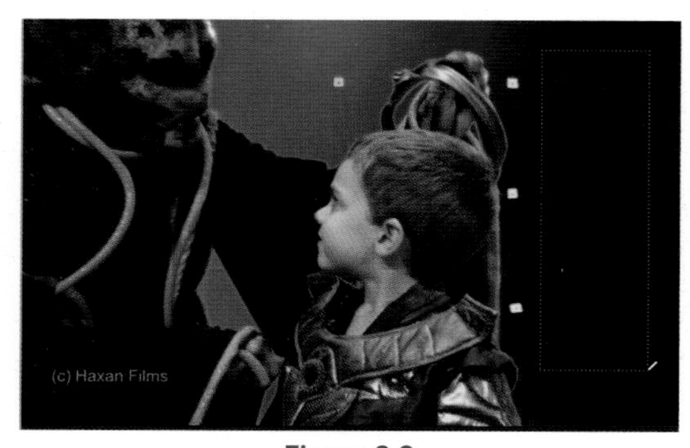

Figure 8.9

7 Switch this right viewport to *View Mode* > *Alpha* by tapping Control + Shift + 8 (at the same time). This will result in looking at the alpha channel generated by the Keyer operator in the right viewport, while still looking at the resulting composite in the left viewport.

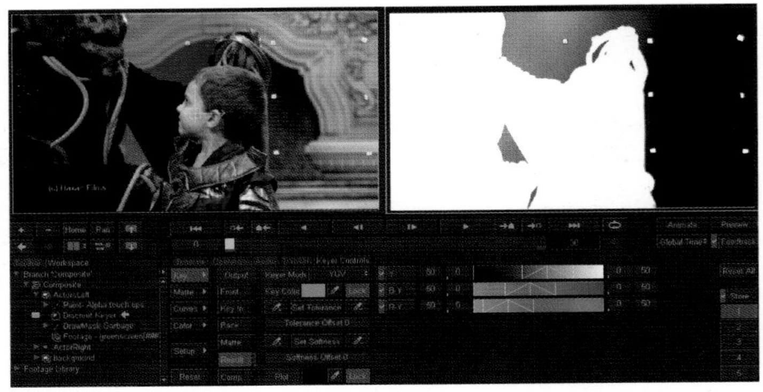

Figure 8.10

This workflow, seen in Figure 8.10, is a fantastic way to chroma key because while the final result is what ultimately matters, the matte being created is what you are actually working on. This side-by-side viewport layout allows you to see both at the same time. This can be useful because sometimes you cannot see if your key has 'holes' in it. This is typically due to the color of your background. Alpha View Mode allows you to see these faults in the matte clearly.

8 Just above the key color swatch is a Keyer Mode rollout. Toggle between the first three choices of RGB, YUV and HLS. These are different color spaces in which the Discreet Keyer can operate. When the key color is locked (Figure 8.11), the color selected in steps 5 and 6 remain constant, but it is put in a different color space to determine how the resulting matte is generated.

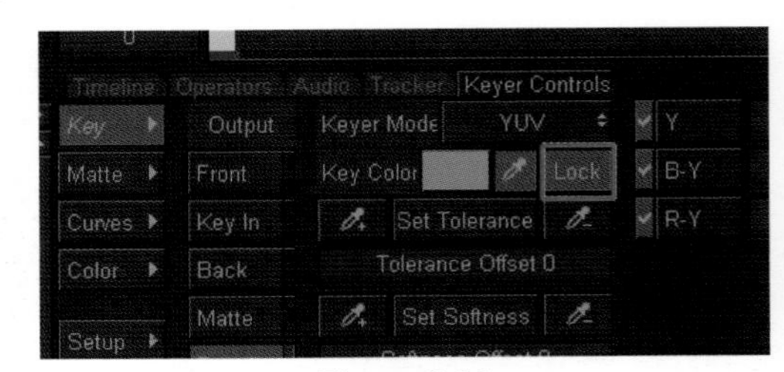

Figure 8.11

Figure 8.12 shows one key color result in RGB, YUV and HLS from left to right, respectively. The printed reproductions here probably do not represent the subtle differences well, but they are often dramatic on the computer screen. What you are trying to determine is the one that seems to do the best job as a starting point. Making this selection gets easier with practice, but what you are looking for is the setting that eliminates the most chroma key color while still leaving the fine detail in areas such as hair.

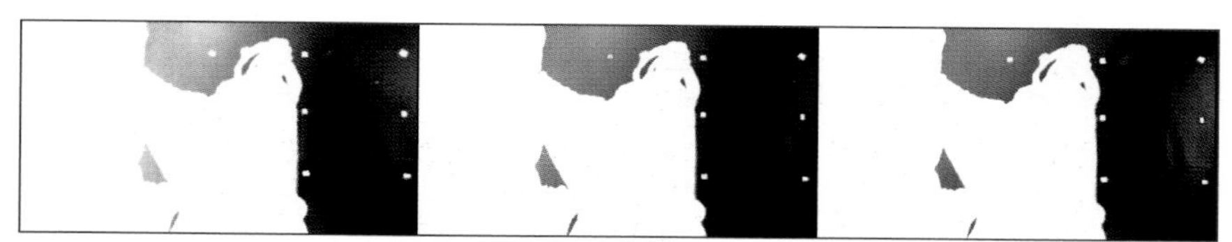

Figure 8.12

Note: If one of the Keyer Modes creates a nice, soft edge around hair but creates 'holes' in the subjects, this can actually be an acceptable starting point because you can easily remove these holes with either the keyer tools detailed in a moment, or simply by using the Paint operator to paint on the alpha channel.

9 For this example, we will use the YUV keyer. After deciding on a Keyer Mode, you may find it useful to add a bit of Tolerance to the key color. Select the Add Tolerance icon and *tap the cursor once* in the right viewport where the remaining chroma key pixels are most dense. In this example, it is somewhere between the actors' heads or under the alien's arm. You do not need to eliminate *all* the green, but the dense areas of green screen should be largely gone at this point.

Tip: Try to avoid clicking and dragging the Add Tolerance eyedropper around in the chroma key color. This will add every single pixel you drag on to the range of colors being keyed out. Many new users are tempted by Tolerance because it seems to 'do a lot of the work' at the outset. You should use Tolerance sparingly.

> **Note:** The initial key color you picked and the pixel(s) selected with the Add Tolerance eyedropper will undoubtedly be different to the ones used for this example. Once again, this shows how every single keying shot must be treated independently of one another.

10 Switch to the Matte category and slide the black and white value sliders back and forth with Feedback enabled. Figure 8.13 shows these sliders being adjusted.

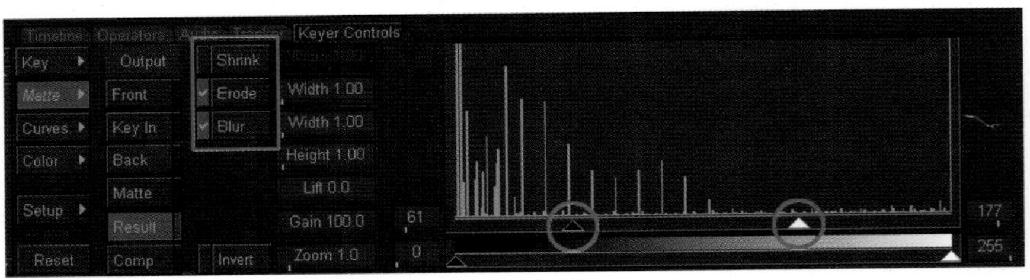

Figure 8.13

This process is often called 'choking the matte'. You are essentially limiting the range of gray values available to the alpha channel; therefore, you do not want to pull the black slider too far right or the white slider too far left. This is another feature of the keyer that has no 'right and wrong' – you just get better at determining what works best with practice. Choking the matte reduces the total amount of gray values made available to the alpha channel resulting from the keying process. If you limit this range too much, you will reduce the ability for objects to have partial transparency and edges will become hard like a cutout.

The Shrink, Erode and Blur options also highlighted in Figure 8.13 might be considered 'last resort' tools and not 'jump right to them' tools. These three buttons also tempt many new users because they seem to reduce color spill around the edges. However, if you have loose hair or other extremely thin or transparent elements in your subject, then these three options in the Matte category may actually work against you. In this particular clip, there is actually little stray hair detail. Try repeatedly toggling these on and off while watching both viewports to see if they help or hinder your final result. It may be a good idea to momentarily hold off and then come back to these three buttons after the next step.

11 Go to the Color category to suppress color spill. Use the Plot eyedropper to select a pixel on the actor that represents remaining color spill.

> **Note:** You will need to identify this pixel in the left viewport. Use a bit of caution, for if the eyedropper tool is selected prior to this clicking on the left viewport, you may disable the tool when you activate this viewport. If this occurs, simply reselect the eyedropper tool. Also remember that you can zoom in to sample the spill pixel color.

The spike in the color spectrum represents the color that has been keyed out. You typically want to suppress a color to either side of this, because the 'spike colors' have already been removed from the image. This means that your lowest point on the suppression curves would not be in the spike, but instead to the yellow-greens or light blues on either side of this spike (in the case of the example seen here).

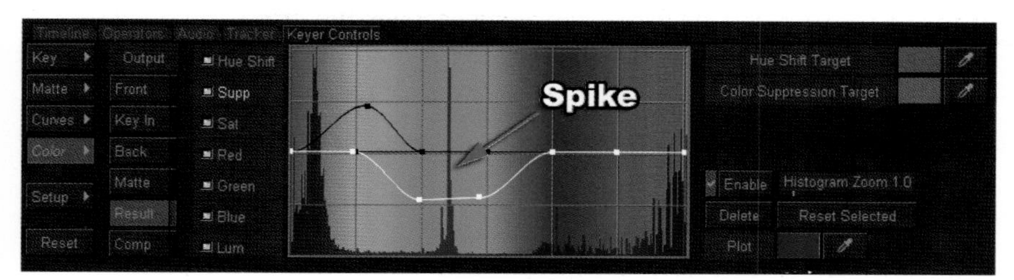

Figure 8.14

Figure 8.14 shows the color Suppression curve isolated with two suppression points dragged down to the gray, horizontal bar. This means that color range is suppressed as much as possible without adding in a new color. Dragging suppression points below this 25% height gray bar results in the complementary color being added (instead of just suppressing one color you are adding a second). This example also shows that the Hue Shift curve has isolated some yellow-green in the spectrum, and it has been pushed (up) towards a tan-brown target.

At this point, you should experiment with fine-tuning the key using a mixture of color suppression and Hue Shift. Remember that the Hue Shift allows you to change the color of the spill to another color picked from the image.

A few different *.*KEY* files have been provided with the materials for this book. If you like, you can go to the Setup category of the Discreet Keyer operator and import these settings. Then, you can look to see how one keyer solution for this particular shot was executed. It should be reiterated that these steps are only one brief guide to the Keyer operator workflow in combustion. There are numerous controls working in tandem in the Keyer operator. While the Discreet Keyer may not be a one-button solution, it has proven time and time again that it can handle extremely fine keys with just a bit of practice.

I encourage you to try several approaches to the Discreet Keyer. This operator, by the way, is one of the best places to take advantage of the Stores feature in combustion. If you get to a point that is looking good and you do not want to 'mess things up', simply store those settings and move on. Quite often, I do one complete key, store it, reset the keyer and do another. Then I can click on the different stored keyer results to see which I like the best.

On-Set Tips for Chroma Key Shoots

Quite often, as a compositing artist, you will be handed a videotape of images and that's what you have to work with. However, if you can get involved with the actual on-location shoot, there are several steps that might help you obtain footage more suitable for keying.

If possible, light the chroma key wall and the subject separately. Using soft, warm backlighting (or rim lighting) on your subject often helps separate the very edge from the background color when keying.

Without going into the physics of it all, video equipment responds better to chroma key green and film emulsion responds better to blue. Often you don't have a choice because the studio or location has a specific color already in place. It is fine to use blue for video and green for film, but if you are given a choice, it does not hurt to choose your color according to your acquisition source.

If you are shooting on video of any kind, using a 3CCD or 'three-chip' camera will produce a superior image than if you only use a single-chip camera. This is because there is a separate CCD for red, green, and blue color information.

Avoid using auto focus, auto aperture, or auto white balance on a chroma key shoot. These will almost always make keying more difficult because the camera is changing your image dramatically on the fly. Even if you cannot tell so in your viewfinder or preview video monitors, the range of colors is dynamic and presents problems when pulling a key digitally. Manual 'everything' is always the preferred way to go.

If possible, use a shallow depth of field if you can. This will cause the chroma key wall to be slightly out of focus and will aid in eliminating it with a keyer because minute shadow or fabric detail will be reduced.

When shooting your subject, shoot the subject in focus and do not try in-camera tricks like blurring the image for effect. It is much easier and vastly more flexible to add blur as a post-process in combustion. Acquire the source footage of the subject as crisply as possible so that the edges where the subject meets the chroma key wall are clean and in focus.

Make the subject as large in frame as possible. Many people make the mistake of framing their subject as they want it in the final composition. The only thing that actually matters is the lighting and the camera angle, not the placement of the subject in the frame. You can always scale down and move the layer after you have pulled a successful key. This might not be the case with a camera that is moving, but for locked down shots, get the subject as big in frame as possible.

Additional Resources for Chroma Keying

For chroma keying DV and other compressed footage, there is an excellent third party plugin available at www.DVgarage.com. *DV Matte Pro*, by Ben Syverson, is an inexpensive chroma key plugin that you can use in combustion that is very forgiving when generating a matte from a compressed source clip.

www.Ultimatte.com is a company that is synonymous with chroma keying and has been creating hardware and software for decades. The *AdvantEdge* plugin is a chroma keyer that has years of development behind it, but at a price.

Currently the plugin for Mac and PC is more than the cost of combustion itself. However, if you are heavily involved with chroma keying, this is well worth the investment in the long run. Just like any product, remember that no single chroma keyer does it all and, in some circumstances, you might use several different keys to get the job done. Ultimatte is a great solution in many cases.

www.StudioDepot.com is an excellent reseller of portable chroma key screens of all sizes, including a portable/cloth model that is 5 × 7 feet and is also collapsible. Studio Depot also carries different assortments of chroma key paint, fabric, tape, etc. Find the Special Effects section in their website for tons of great goodies.

For a more permanent chroma key wall, check out www.procyc.com. This solution is a bit more costly than fabric or merely painting a wall. However, these cyclorama components are beautiful, believe me. Custom quotes via email only.

CHAPTER 9

THE TRACKER

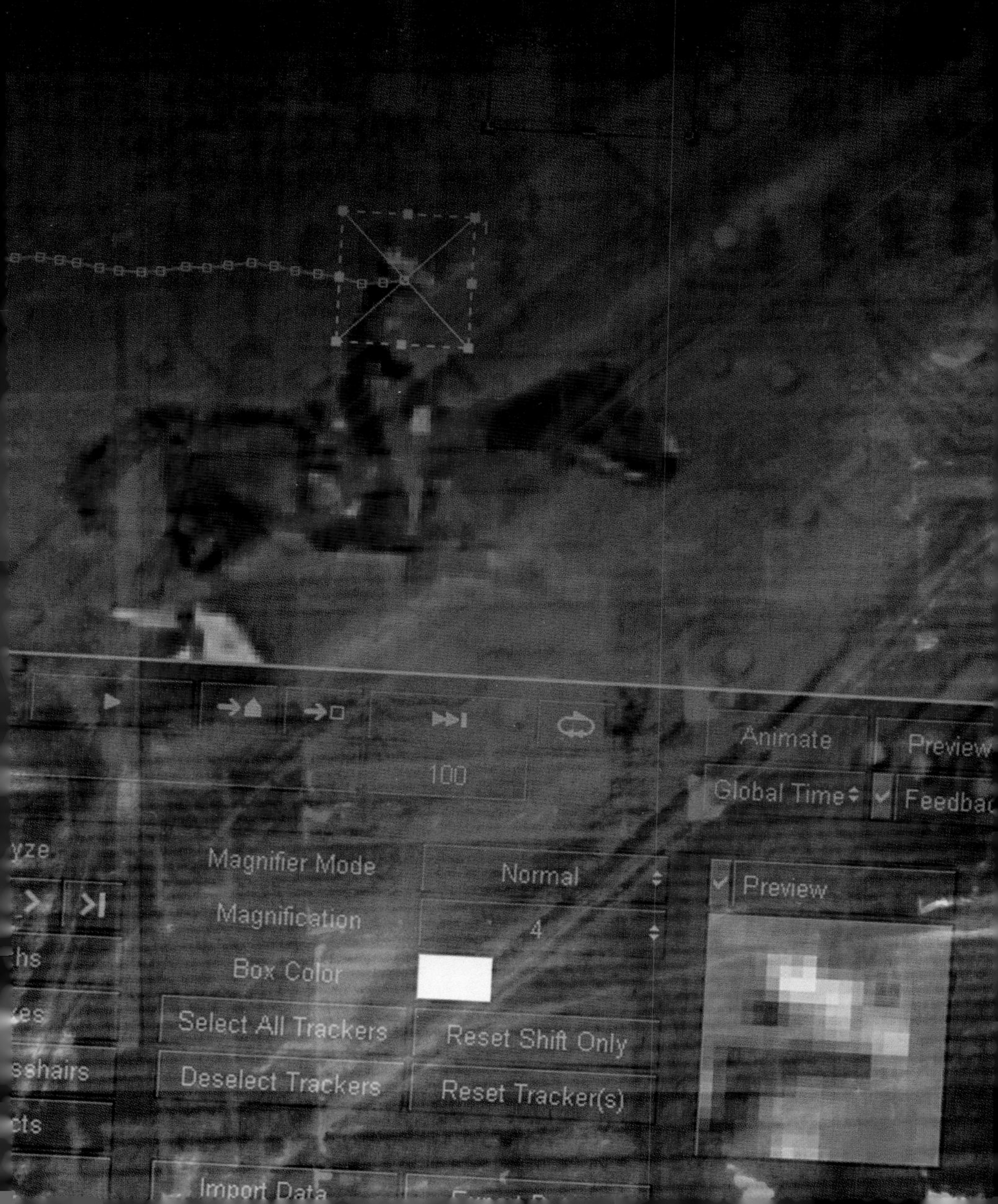

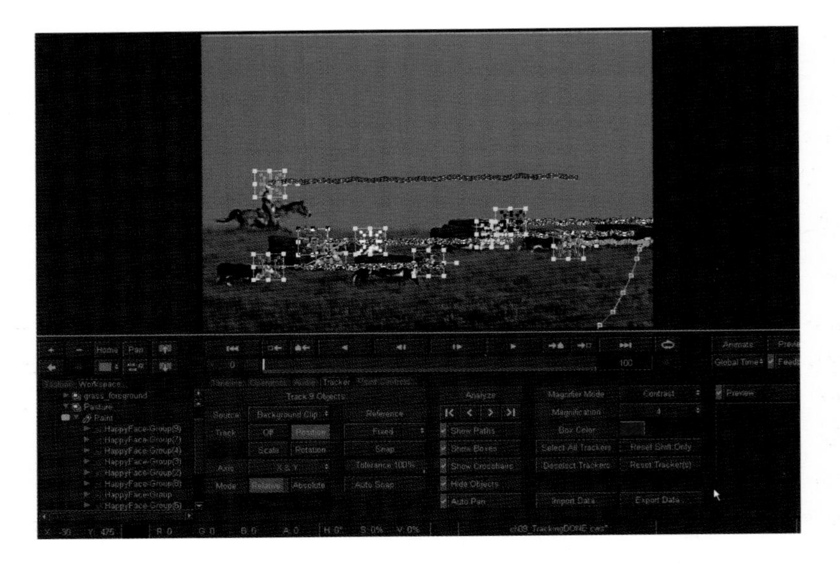

The Enigma Unveiled

While the Tracker is, most definitely, an extremely powerful tool within combustion, it should be said that it really does nothing magical and is not bulletproof (no tracking software is for that matter). The success of the Tracker is largely due to input from you, the user.

Fundamentally speaking, the Tracker is really just a keyframe-generating assistant. That's it. The Tracker does nothing that you could not do by hand; it just aids in creating keyframes, but hopefully speeds up your workflow in the process. It does this by analyzing the image and calculating the pixel shifts based on areas of defined interest.

> **Note:** Discreet combustion 3 uses a 2D tracker that follows changes in pixel data in the images. It does not track 3D camera data.

To immediately reiterate a critical point, the Tracker only generates keyframe data. After it has done this, you move on and the tracking data gets applied to an element in your Workspace as keyframes of position and/or rotation and/or scale information. *At that point, the data no longer resides in the Tracker.*

Two Questions to Consider

When you are dealing with a tracking solution of any kind, there are two fundamental questions that you should ask yourself to help you with the tracking workflow:

1. In my image, what is the best reference to provide each tracker?
2. What am I going to apply the resulting data to?

You can consider this pair of inquiries the axioms of tracking, if you will. These two questions, or more importantly, the answers to these questions, will help you determine the workflow of the Tracker within Discreet combustion at any given time.

The first question is typically the more difficult to answer. Here, you have to look at clips in your viewport(s) to determine what can be isolated and used to extract keyframe information.

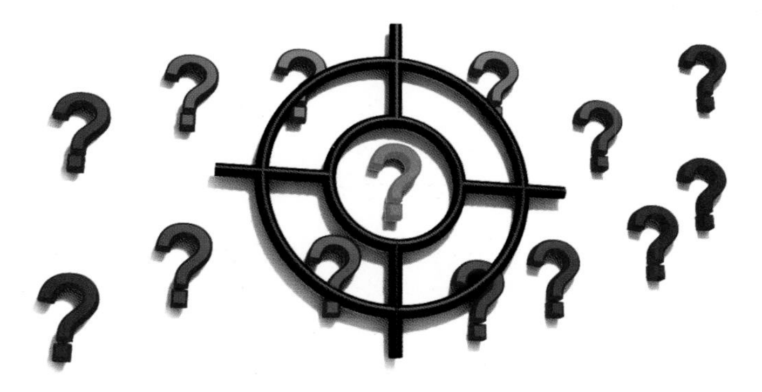

The second question is usually a bit easier to answer. The fact that you even thought of using the Tracker probably indicates that you want to use it to apply keyframes to an element within your project.

For example, if you say to yourself 'this clip is shaky and I want to stabilize it', then the Stabilization operator is where you are going to apply the data.

> **Note:** You can track multiple objects in your shot at the same time. Depending on the use for the Tracker, you can have numerous trackers being utilized at any given time.

Applications for the Tracker

You can utilize the Tracker for any number of things within combustion. Its applications are really up to you and your specific project requirements and footage. Below is a brief summary of some common workflow solutions that take advantage of the Tracker.

You can track the motion of part of an image to pin another element to it. For example, if you have a clip of a person walking through frame, you could take an image of a hat and track it on top of their head. This would make the hat move in sync with the layer of the clip with the person walking. Another common use for the Tracker in combustion is to keyframe an emitter in a Particle operator. This would allow you to have a single source of particles follow an element within footage – for example, smoke coming out of a panning chimney.

You can track the control points of a vector object within combustion as seen in Figure 9.1. Remember that vector objects can occur within a Paint operator as well as in others such as the Draw Selection or Draw Mask operators. For example, using the Paint draw mode of blur or smear, you could paint a small dot on an actor's blemish to remove it.

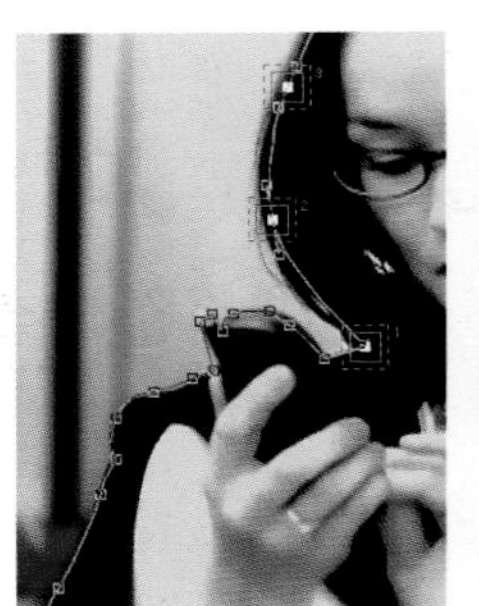
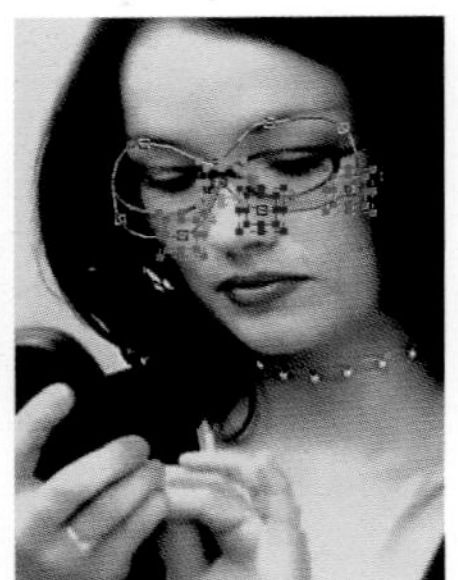

Figure 9.1

For garbage masks commonly used in chroma key shots, you can often track the control points of the mask shape to the object that the mask is meant to obscure. This is often used with great success to track several mask control points at once, so that the mask can distort and drastically changes shape over time, if necessary.

For simple wire-removal shots, you might paint a straight line using a clone source and then track the end points (not the object, but the control points at each end) of the line to an item in the footage containing the rope or wire rig.

You can use the Tracker in combination with the Stabilizing operators to make handheld or vibrating source footage smooth. There is one- and two-point stabilizing within combustion, and both are operators that rely on a symbiotic relationship with the Tracker.

You can track a 'pick point' for an operator tool. Examples include the center of Dolly Blur or Lens Flare operators and the center of the Magic Wand tool within the Paint operator. This would allow the effect of the operator to travel along with an element in your clip.

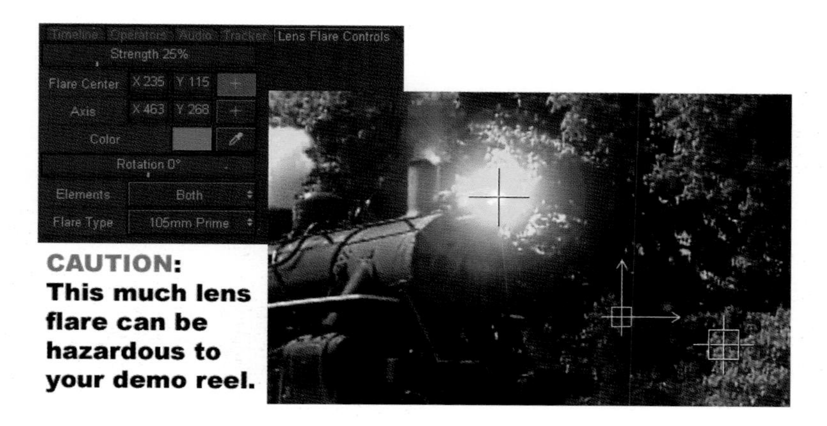

In a 3D composite, you can use the Tracker to attach the four corners of a layer to elements seen in another layer. This technique is called 'four-corner pinning' and can be accomplished by first making the layer shape a four-corner layer, as seen in Figure 9.2.

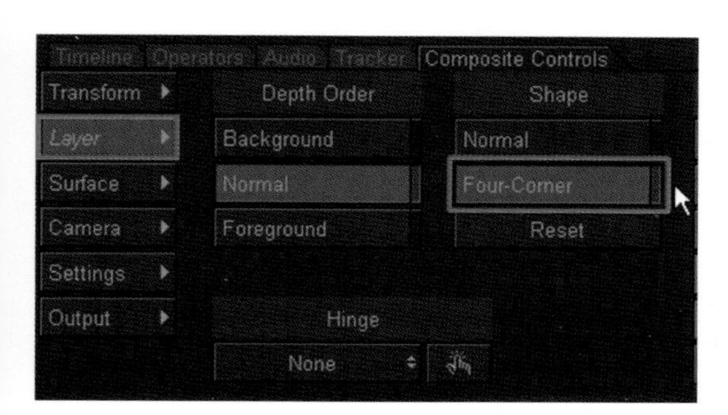

Figure 9.2

Then, while holding down the Shift key on the keyboard, each corner can be selected and then tracked to elements in another layer. This is typically used in cases such as replacing a sign on a moving vehicle or putting an image onto a blank television screen.

Let's Make Tracks, Already!

To make some sense out of all of this tracking business, let's first skip the details of the Tracker and go through the motions of performing two simple tracking operations. The first will be tracking a group of vector paint objects onto an element in the footage onto which the paint operator is applied. The second will be to simply track one layer in a composite to another.

1. Open the Workspace named *ch09_Tracking.cws.* This is a composite containing two layers; the top layer is temporarily turned off for the moment.

2. In the Workspace panel, expand the layer named Pasture and the Paint operator applied to this layer until you see the group of vector paint objects named *HappyFace-Group.*

3. Double click on the name of this group to assign the output of the Paint operator to the viewport. This double click will also select this group at the same time. Your Workspace panel should now resemble Figure 9.3.

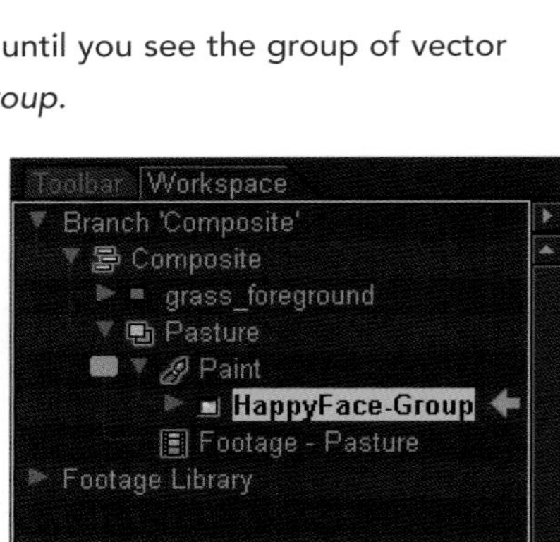

Figure 9.3

4. Access the Tracker tab under the Playback Controls or by hitting the F7 key. At the top of the

Tracker controls, it should say *Track 1 Object*, as seen in Figure 9.4. This one object is the group making up the happy face.

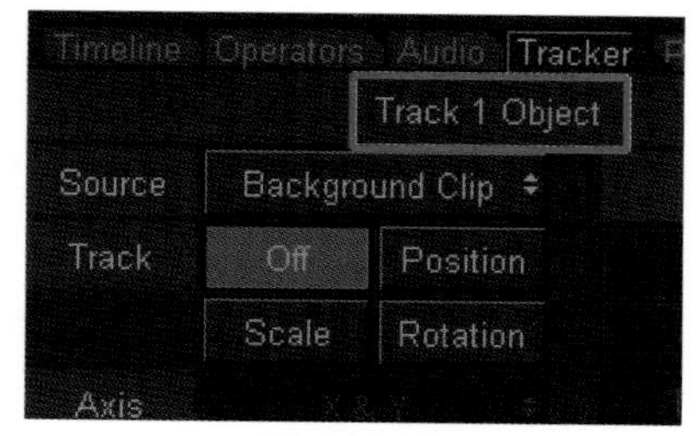

Figure 9.4

5 Click on the Position button (Position) to turn on the Tracker and also specify the type of tracking data you wish to generate. The happy face will disappear. It has been temporarily turned off by the Tracker to allow you to place the tracker object without obstructing your view of the reference image.

6 Carefully float your cursor to the center of the Tracker boxes (now visible in the viewport) until your cursor changes to a light-blue crosshair pointing in four directions.

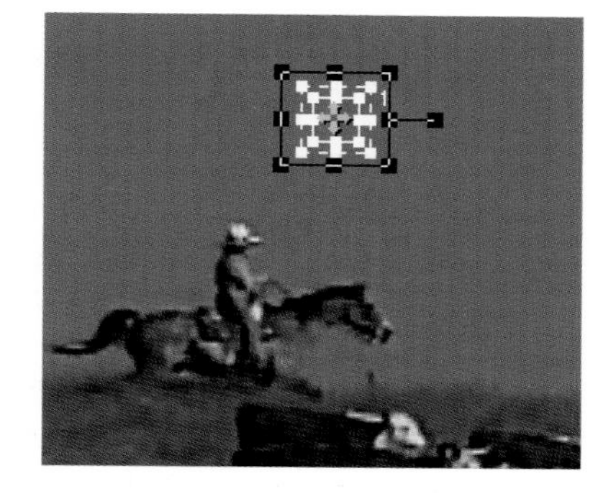

7 Click and drag both the Tracker boxes down to the cowboy's head. The Tracker will temporarily switch to a magnified mode to allow precision placement of the Tracker. When you are finished, the Tracker Preview window should look very similar to Figure 9.5.

8 Leave all the Tracker settings to the defaults and click the Analyze forward button (>). You will notice the Tracker begin working. The Preview window at the bottom right-hand side of the Tracker palette will update, showing the matching reference found by the Tracker as it goes, and there will be a green dotted line representing the keyframe results of the track in progress.

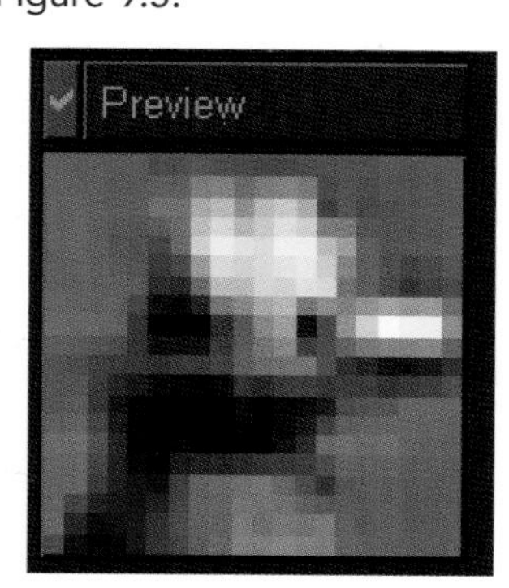

Figure 9.5

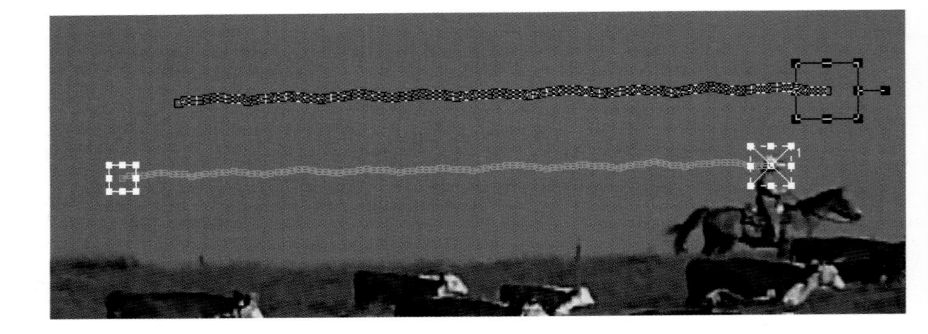

9 When the Tracker is complete, click the off button highlighted in Figure 9.6. This will turn off the Tracker and apply the data to the happy face.

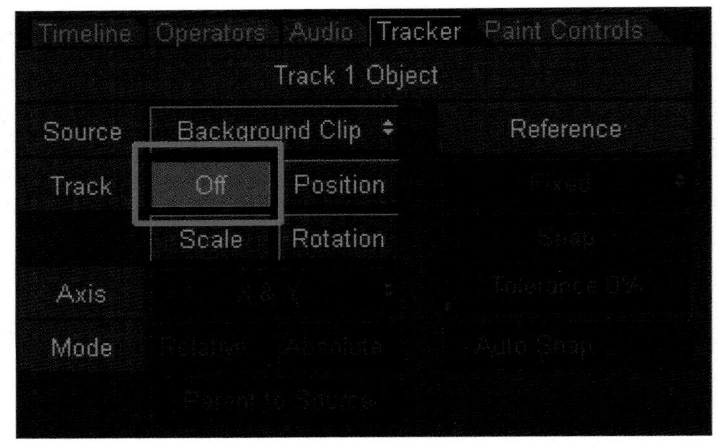

Figure 9.6

10 Play back the clip. You will notice that the happy face now travels along and bobs up and down in the exact same manner as the cowboy's head, but with an offset in position.

11 While the animate button is off, you can now select the happy face and position it anywhere. Using the arrow keys on the keyboard, position the happy face over the cowboy's head. The animation keyframes that have been applied by the tracker will remain applied to the group of paint objects, but you will offset the location of the entire animation.

> **Suggestion:** Now try turning on the top layer named *grass_foreground* and tracking its position to the cowboy layer. The only real difference in the workflow is that you will have to change the Source to the layer named *Pasture*. At this point, you may want to ensure you are looking at the output of the composite by double clicking on it in the Workspace panel.

Trackers

Before you use the Tracker, the object(s) that you wish to apply the keyframe information to must be selected. If you switch to the Tracker Palette (F7) and nothing is selected, the Tracker will not be available for use, as seen in Figure 9.7.

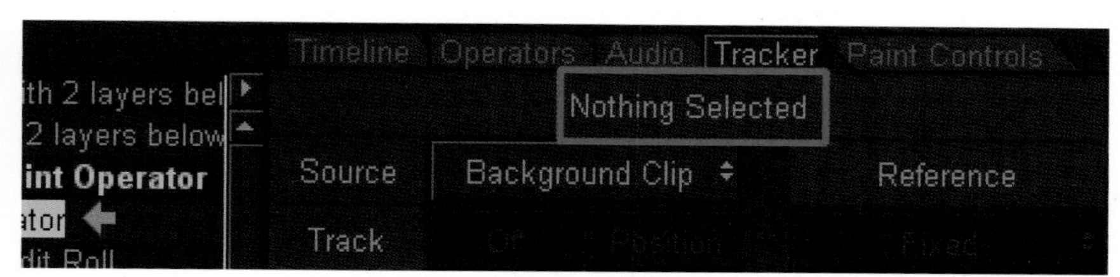

Figure 9.7

The Trackers themselves consist of a few items that all work in tandem with one another. In Figure 9.8, a color-coded version of the Tracker boxes has been recreated for clarity. The Tracker boxes in combustion will all be the same color, typically white.

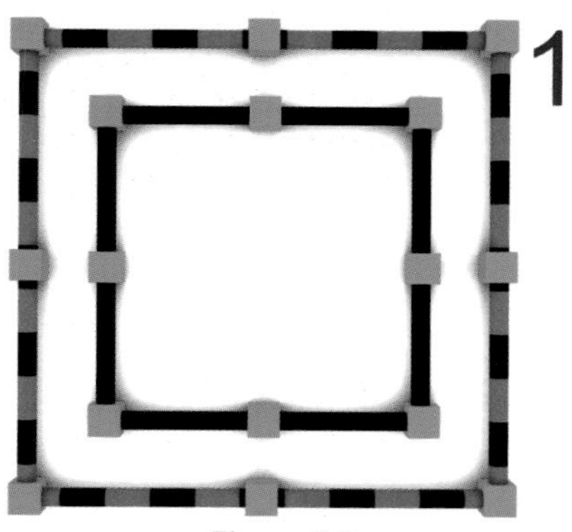

Figure 9.8

Reference Box – The solid black inner box represents the image data you are providing the Tracker as a reference to look for from frame to frame. The contents will be visible in the Tracker Controls preview window. You can move the Reference box by clicking and dragging within the shape. Your cursor will change to a four-way arrow indicating you are ready to make the move.

Tracker Box – The dotted, outer box represents the area (from frame to frame in your source image) where the inner Tracker box will look for the reference. If the element being tracked does not have a lot of extreme movement from frame to frame, this box can be small. Conversely, if the item to be tracked jumps around from frame to frame, then this box will need to be expanded to allow the Tracker to look for the item within a larger range of pixels. The larger this box is, the slower the Tracking process. The Tracker box should be made big enough to accommodate the largest movement from between any two frames.

Scaling Handles – The green dots on both boxes represent scaling handles for each box. You can resize the Reference and Tracker boxes by pulling on these handles. Your cursor will change to a two-way arrow indicating a resize.

Number – Individual trackers are often numbered for clarity. This becomes especially helpful when you use two or more trackers at the same time.

Picking an Element to Track

In Figure 9.9, the top row of red boxes indicates elements that the Tracker would follow well and the bottom row of blue boxes displays elements that the Tracker would probably have real problems with. Now why is this?

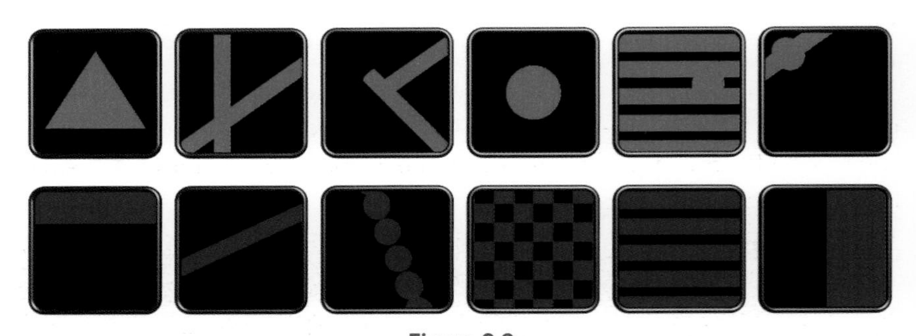

Figure 9.9

Notice in each of the red examples, there is something distinct within the Tracking box that the Tracker could 'lock onto'.

In all of the blue examples, there is nothing distinguishable in any of the samples. What you need to provide the Tracker with is a unique reference in X and Y.

One might think that the fourth, checkerboard pattern would be OK because of all the distinct edges, but the repetition will cause the Tracker to find the solution in a number of places and not just one. In this case, the Tracker will jump all over, as is potentially the case if you try to track a clean, brick wall. The reference can be found in more than one place in those cases.

The rest of the blue/bad Tracker items will cause the Tracker to slip along the pattern, because elements within these boxes will, undoubtedly, continue outside of the reference box. This will cause the Tracker to slip up and down or diagonally along these items. You may think it is doing a fine job when it is not because, in these cases, the Tracker will actually find what you asked it to look for. Imagine that the second blue pattern was a limb on a tree. This limb undoubtedly extends past this reference point in both directions and therefore will cause problems for the Tracker without greater detail.

When looking for an element in your footage to track, it is a good idea to first cache your footage before tracking. This will allow you to quickly scrub through the frames and concentrate more easily on the procedure of locating a good reference for tracking. Ideally, the reference item will be visible in all frames.

The Tracker Interface in Depth

Source

The Tracker can be accessed at any time by accessing the Tracker tab under the Playback Controls, from the Window > Palettes menu at the top of the combustion UI, or by tapping the F7 key. The interface for the Tracker is seen in Figure 9.10 as it is first encountered.

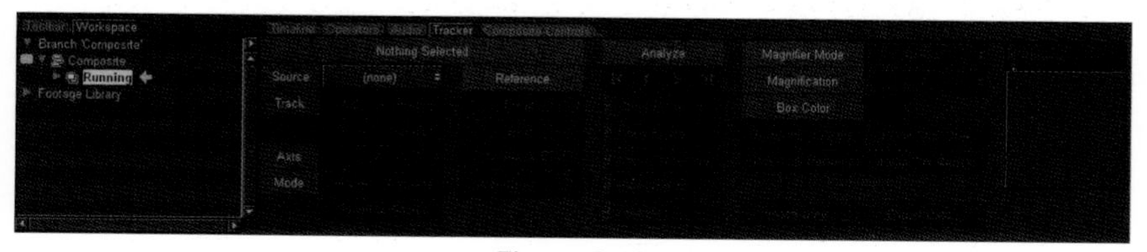

Figure 9.10

Notice that, in this example, all the controls for the Tracker are disabled with the exception of the Source (none) rollout. This is because the Tracker is turned off when you initially access it.

Composite – When dealing with a composite, the source should be set to the layer that contains the element(s) to which you intend to track your layer or object. This may or may not be the same layer as the one that contains the element onto which you intend to apply the data, as is the case if tracking one layer to another, for example.

Paint Operator – In the case of tracking elements within a paint operator, the options for (Tracker) source will not show layers, but will, instead, allow you to either track the **Background Clip** or the **Clip and Objects** within the Paint operator. Background Clip ignores other paint objects and Clip and Objects will consider them when tracking.

Track (Options)

Position – This option enables a single tracker to follow the position of the reference data.

Rotation – When you enable rotation, two numbered trackers are created, as seen in Figure 9.11. If one tracker's position goes up or down, then this indicates that the source is rotating. Remember, an individual tracker can only track position. Two trackers are needed to calculate rotation and/or scale.

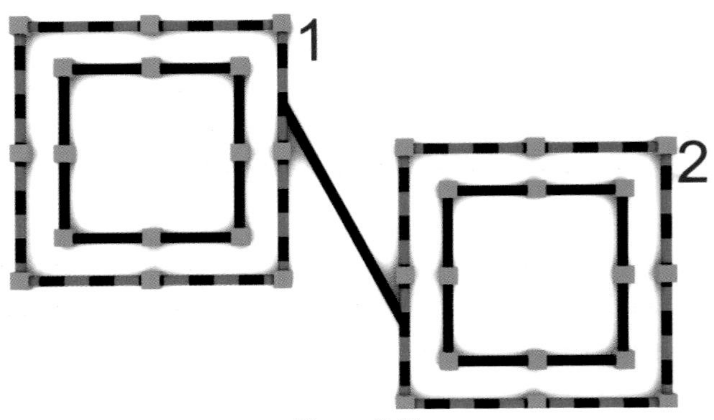

Figure 9.11

Scale – When you enable scale, two numbered trackers will be used as when you track rotation; however, instead of measuring the up/down changes between the trackers, the distance between the two trackers is used to calculate scale changes. If the pair of trackers grow apart over time, there is a scale increase applied. If the distance decreases over time, there must be a decrease in scale.

Off – As simple as it indicates, the Tracker's off button is undoubtedly the most often forgotten step in the tracking process. After you have performed a track that you are happy with, the data does not automatically get applied to the layer or object(s) that you are tracking until you turn the Tracker off. It should also be mentioned that after you turn the Tracker off, the data is then transferred from the Tracker to the object or layer in question. The entire process has been applied and there is no undo. While you can certainly retrack something by repeating the whole process over, you might want to either be completely certain of your work before turning the Tracker off or take advantage of the Export Data feature while the Tracker is still enabled. All the keyframes generated by the Tracker can now be found on your object or layer's X and Y channels and can be modified from that point on.

Axis

X & Y – This option means that the horizontal and vertical position of the item that you are tracking will be analyzed and that keyframes will be generated for both channels.

X Only – This option means that you will only be tracking the horizontal motion of a tracking target. This is useful if, for example, you had footage of a ball bouncing across frame and only wanted the lateral motion tracked, but not the bounce.

Y Only – This option tracks only the vertical motion of the tracking target. In the case of a bouncing ball, only the bounce would be tracked, but not the lateral movement across the frame.

Mode

Relative – If your reference is in a different location in the image than the object or layer you are tracking, then this is a Relative track. In the example of the cowboy, you performed a Relative track at first and the result was that the happy face was offset from the element you tracked.

Absolute – If the reference in the source and the item you are applying the tracking data to are in the same location in the image, then you want to perform an Absolute track. For example, if you want to do a four-corner pin for a label replacement, the corners you are tracking are in the same location as the destination layer's four corners.

Parent to Source – This option will be available when you are tracking within composite but not when you are tracking a Paint operator. Enabling this checkbox means that after you finalize your track and turn the Tracker off, the layer that you applied the tracking data to will have the source layer as its parent. This is useful if you think that the parent layer may, for example, go through transformations such as position, rotation, or scale, and you want the object that was tracked to this layer to inherit the same transformations.

Reference

Fixed – Selecting this option tells the Tracker that the reference identified for that particular tracker does not change in appearance over the course of the clip. A common misconception is that Fixed means the items being tracked are locked down and immobile, such as a fire hydrant is to the ground.

Roaming – Any image-based tracking system looks for a reference pattern that is identified by you, the user. Ideally, these items do not change in appearance or shape over time within the clip. If the pixels representing the items that you are tracking change in appearance over the duration of the clip, then this is considered a Roaming reference. This means the reference will be updated based upon the Snap and Tolerance settings.

Snap – If the reference being tracked changes shape drastically at some point in your clip, you can stop the Tracker – click the Snap button to update the contents of the reference. From that point on, the new reference will be what the Tracker will look for in your image.

Tolerance – This feature adjusts the leniency of the Tracker so that if it cannot find an appropriate match for the tracking reference base on the Tolerance value, a keyframe will not be created on that frame. The default tolerance of 100% will generate a keyframe on every single frame no matter how poor the match to the reference is. Lowering the tolerance makes the Tracker more rigid in its search for the target. A Tolerance of 0% will only create a keyframe if an exact match is found (which is extremely rare). If a reference is briefly obscured, for example, then you can adjust the Tolerance to accommodate this brief obstruction.

Auto Snap – You can enable Auto Snap to let the Tracker do its best with the Tolerance settings. If it does not like the results it gets on any given frame, it will snap the tracker reference to the last acceptable match found.

Analyze

The four icons in Figure 9.12 are for stepping through the actual process of tracking. The outer buttons are for single frame forward (>I) and backwards analyzing (I<). The inner are for letting the Tracker analyze forward (>) or backward (<) automatically.

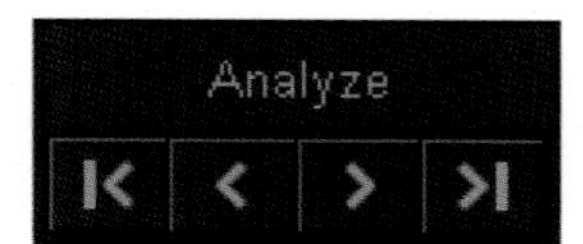

Figure 9.12

> **Note:** When using the inner buttons for automatic tracking, you can click the same button again to stop the process part way through. This can be useful if you see a tracker lose its goal and begin to jump about on screen.

For the options in Figure 9.13, the defaults are typically fine and actually helpful, especially when learning combustion.

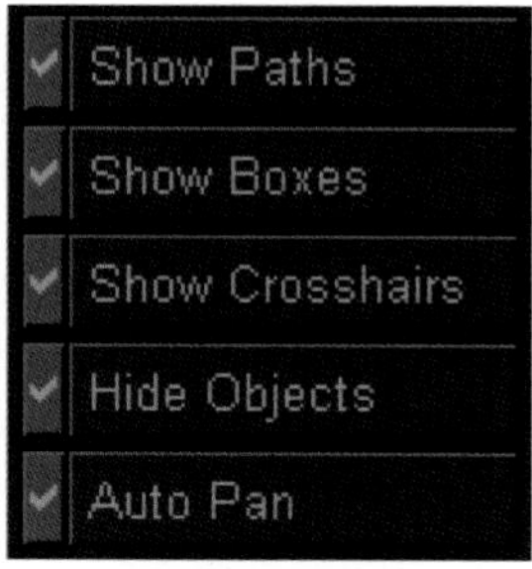

Figure 9.13

Show Paths/Boxes/Crosshairs – These options are to toggle the visibility of the keyframe data from frame to frame, the Tracker Boxes, and the crosshairs of the reference to be tracked.

Hide Objects – This option forces the Tracker to temporarily hide (turn off) the elements that you will be applying the data to. In the previous exercise, the happy face was disabled during the track and then turned back on when the Tracker was disabled.

Auto Pan – This feature will pan the viewport automatically if you happen to be zoomed in when performing a track.

Magnifier Mode

When you move a tracker in the viewport, these options change how the tracker reference data is displayed while being dragged.

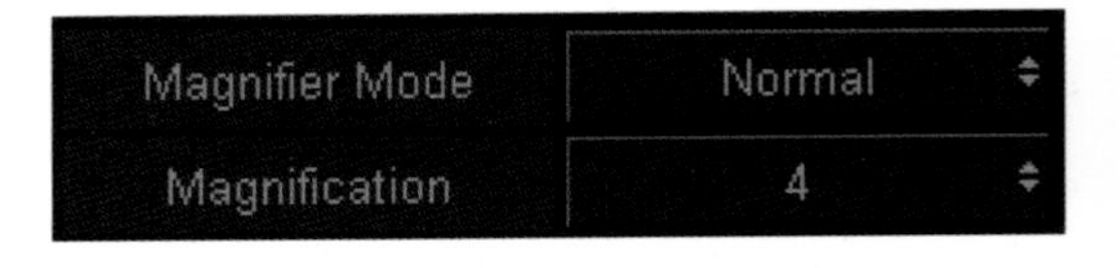

None – The contents of the reference box will be the same as in the viewport.

Normal – This option uses the magnification setting (below) to determine how the reference box will be displayed.

Contrast – This option changes the contents to a high-contrast, black and white version of the reference box while it is being placed in the viewport.

Edge – This is similar to Contrast in that the contents are displayed in black and white, but the image is an edges-only version of the reference.

The Rest of the Options

Magnification – This is a multiplier of the reference size.

Box Color – This is a color swatch (Box Color) that allows you to change the color of the box of any selected trackers. You can use this if your trackers are difficult to see against the background footage.

Select All Trackers/Deselect Trackers – This is a quick way to select all (Select All Trackers) or none (Deselect Trackers) of the trackers onscreen. While you may sometimes want to analyze trackers one at a time, you can also perform multiple tracks to all trackers by clicking the *Select All Trackers* button before you do the analysis.

Reset Shift Only (Reset Shift Only) – Only tracking data gets reset, but not the shape and location of the Tracker boxes. Often, if you perform a track and the tracker mistakenly flies all over the place, you may just want to reset the (bad) data without changing the shape of the Tracker boxes. If you have manipulated the shape of a tracker to accommodate a large or small reference, this will keep these boxes sized per your edits.

Reset Tracker(s) (Reset Tracker(s)) – This will reset the position, shape and any keyframe information for a tracker. When things go really wrong, this is a way to start over for the selected trackers without having to turn off the Tracker itself.

Import/Export Data (Import Data... Export Data...) – Since the tracking data is lost when the Tracker is turned off, this can be a way to avoid the loss, should you think you may want to edit the information within the Tracker at another time. In addition, the Tracker utility in combustion is yet another toolset that was derived from the Discreet systems products such as Flame, Smoke and Inferno. This is also a way to get data to/from these other Discreet products.

Preview – This window will show frame by frame the match for the reference by the current tracker. When you have more than one tracker selected, it will show the contents of the last tracker that you select.

Image Stabilizing

There is a category of operators named Stabilize that contains two operators. One is for one-point stabilizing and the other is for two-point stabilizing. These operators are used in conjunction with the Tracker to make footage that has some form of vibration or shake appear as if it was shot mounted on a tripod. The Tracker essentially follows a reference in the frame, the data generated by the Tracker is inverted, and then this negated information is applied to the image so that the new keyframes cancel out the unwanted movement.

To see the workflow of stabilizing a clip with one- and two-point stabilizing operators, we will apply each operator to the same clip to see the differences between the two.

Stabilize 1 Point

This operator is typically used when there is just lateral and vertical motion in a clip, or positional changes in X and Y. This operator uses one pick point and one tracker to invert the motion within a sequence.

Stabilize 2 Points

This operator can also be used to remove positional X/Y data, but it can also optionally eliminate rotation and/or scaling information. Rotation in frame would be caused by an in-camera tilt and scaling is typically caused by either an in-camera zoom or when the camera physically moves closer or further away from the subject. If you want to remove rotation/scale information from a sequence, two pick points and two trackers must be used.

To perform a quick, one-point stabilization:

1 Open the Workspace file named *ch09_Stabilize.cws.*

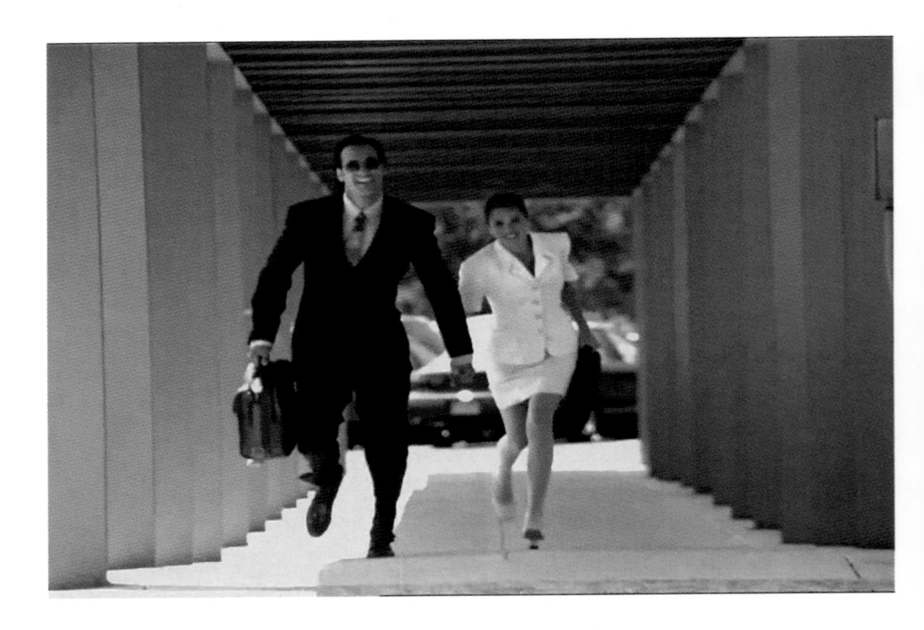

2 Cache the clip with the looping playback option selected. As the clip plays back, notice how there is camera movement and that this movement is in both lateral and vertical directions in the frame. When you are finished, stop playback and return to the first frame.

3 Select the layer named Running in the Workspace panel.

4 Apply a *Stabilize > Stabilize 1 Point* operator to the layer and then, with the newly applied operator selected, switch to the Stabilize 1 Point Controls tab seen in Figure 9.14.

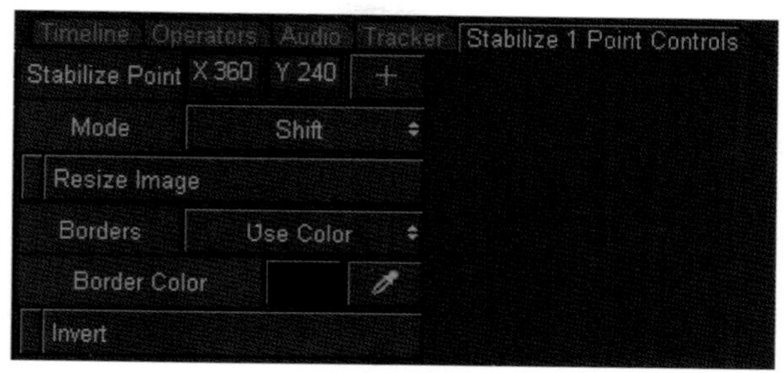

Figure 9.14

5 Pick the crosshairs icon for the Stabilize Point ( ). You will notice there is now a crosshair located in the viewport in the center of frame at (360,240).

6 In the viewport, click the cursor on the edge of the column indicated in Figure 9.15. To position the crosshair, simply click on the image. There

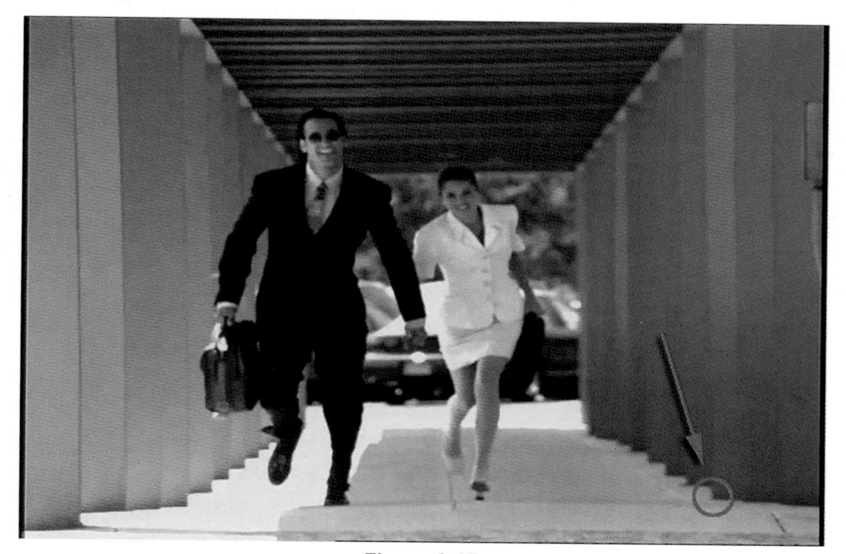

Figure 9.15

are, certainly, many good tracking options in this clip, but this is a nice predominant edge and it also stays in frame and unobstructed for the entire duration of the clip. You are looking for a reference that remains fixed throughout the clip.

7 Click on the Tracker tab to access the Tracker Controls and then click the Position button (Position) to turn on the Tracker.

8 Use the default values and click the analyze forward button (>). This will start the tracking process and the track should complete without difficulty. When satisfied with the tracking results, turn the Tracker off.

Note: The image stabilization does not occur until you turn the Tracker off.

9 Replay the clip and you will notice that while the layer named Running does not move, the pixel information in the frame is now shifting about to compensate for the motion in the clip. In Figure 9.16, the border has been changed to red for illustrative purposes, but your border is black and changes shape as the piece plays back.

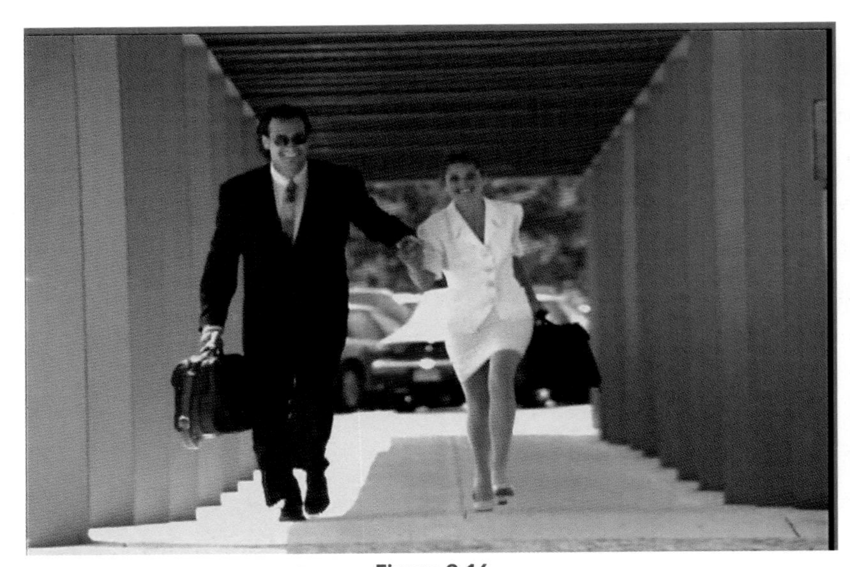

Figure 9.16

10 Exit the Tracker by clicking on the Stabilize 1 Point Controls tab. Then switch the operator controls Mode from Shift to Fit. You will notice that the border goes away and the image is scaled to accommodate the image shift caused by the stabilization.

> **Tip:** For a really strange effect, redo this process but in step 6, pick the woman's face instead. The end result is that the stabilized clip still seemingly has camera motion, but the woman's head is kept perfectly still in frame. This is one way they achieve the effect in those car commercials where the world dramatically changes around a perfectly static (yet rolling) automobile.

Stabilizing Options

Now that you have seen the basics of the stabilization process, the following descriptions of each feature will hopefully be clearer.

Stabilize Points – In one-point stabilizing, this is a reference point to calculate how much movement is in your image. You typically pick a reference that you will later use in conjunction with the Tracker. In two-point stabilizing, point 1 is the reference for X and Y movement and point 2 is used in determining the rotation or scale changes.

Mode – This option determines how the pixel information will be displayed after the stabilization data has been calculated.

Shift – Pixels are not interpolated in any way and a border of color is left where stabilization compensation is needed.

Fit – This option scales the image to fit the size of the layer. Technically speaking, this causes up-scaling and interpolation of pixel data, which means a loss in resolution. In small amounts, the viewer would never know it, but in shots containing gross amounts of movement, this option will introduce the jaggies associated with up-sampling raster images.

Wrap – This option is only available in one-point image stabilization. This ensures that no pixel information is lost. As the image compensates for movement in frame, any pixels 'lost' on the left side of the frame are wrapped around and now visible on the right side, etc. This is often used in conjunction with the invert options, so that you can return pixels to their original location, should you so choose.

Resize Image – Enabling this option means that the layer will become larger or smaller according to the results of the stabilization. When disabled, the layer will remain the same size and the pixel information within the image will do all the compensation.

Borders – This controls how the edges of the frame will be treated after the stabilization has been calculated and applied.

Use Color – This option allows you to change the color of a border that may show up when the Mode is set to Shift. This feature was used to change the border to red in Figure 9.16.

Transparent – This means that the edges of the clip will become a transparent alpha and pixel information below will be allowed to show through in these areas.

Invert – This option is only available in one-point stabilizing. This allows you to negate the effects of the stabilization process. An example of when this can be particularly useful is when you track camera shake not to remove it but to actually introduce it to other elements in your Workspace. You could, for example, go through the process of removing camera shake, then cut the entire stabilize operator off the source of the camera shake and paste it onto one or more other layers. Then, if you invert the data, the elements will all appear to have the camera shake as well.

Position/Rotation/Scale – (See below.) These will only be available as options in two-point stabilization because they involve the comparison of two references. Scaling and Rotation cannot be calculated with just one reference.

Position – This option acts just like a one-point stabilizer and only uses the first pick point (point 1) for calculations.

Rotation – Point 1 is used as the axis of rotation and point 2 is used to actually calculate the amount of rotation. Ideally, you will pick points that should be immobile in the shot. In addition, the further away from each other the points are, the more accurate the results will typically be.

Scale – The distance between the two pick points is used to determine if the image data is scaling up or down. When you attempt to remove the effect of an in-camera zoom, you should pick two points that are the same distance from the camera so that the changes in distance of the two trackers reflects a common, relative change.

Closing Tips

Two things to remember when using the Tracker are: (A) the items that you are going to apply the tracking data to must be selected before going into the Tracker; (B) you have to turn the Tracker off to apply the data to those items. When you do, the tracking process is done and actual tracking data is lost (unless you exported it before turning the Tracker off). The data is then transferred to the items, as can be seen in the Timeline and in the viewports.

Try the default Tracker box sizes first and only resize them if you need to. New users almost always edit the inner and outer Tracker boxes way too big (for reasons I cannot explain). When initially placing and sizing your Tracker boxes, remember that you can zoom in well beyond 100% to get right in on them. Quite often, the default Tracker boxes are very small and when you go to move one, you resize it by accident, or vice versa. Do not worry too much about this, as it is an undoable function.

Take advantage of the ability to change the color of Tracker boxes if your footage makes them difficult to see or if you have several trackers all overlapping and crossing each other.

Lowering the tolerance, using Auto Snap and Roaming track mode are all fine options to use, but they are prone to introducing error. Use these as needed but not as a first-pass solution.

Tracking backwards can sometimes work better than tracking forwards. This can be accomplished by using the backward facing analysis buttons within the Tracker UI. Ask yourself if the item you wish to track is more clearly defined at the beginning or end of the sequence. Quite often, the results from tracking an element backwards can be more successful than the exact same element tracked forwards. This might be especially true when using a roaming reference.

This is just an option, however, and not always the case. Every shot and every track presents its own challenges.

When you are tracking an element with low contrast, you can apply a Brightness/Contrast operator prior to doing the track. By forcing a higher contrast in the clip, the Tracker may provide you with better results. Then, when satisfied with the tracking, you can disable or delete the operator.

You can often do partial tracks and then manually keyframe the rest. Do not be disappointed if you have to do a partial track. Letting the Tracker do some of the tedium and doing the rest by hand is often a reality. For example, if you had a 500-frame sequence and, no matter how careful you were, you could only perform a successful track on the first 400 frames, you could manually keyframe the rest of the animation.

When Stabilization operators have been applied, you can easily see the before and after by letting the cached clip play back and toggling the Stabilize operator on and off in the Workspace panel. Another method is to switch to two viewports and have one show the output of the Stabilize operator and the second showing the output of the node just prior to the Stabilize operator. Both of these options will, however, require both to be cached. You can also use the Render to RAM feature outlined in Chapter 7. This utility can utilize the Compare option that allows you real-time playback of a before and after in the same viewport.

CHAPTER 10

ANIMATION AND THE TIMELINE

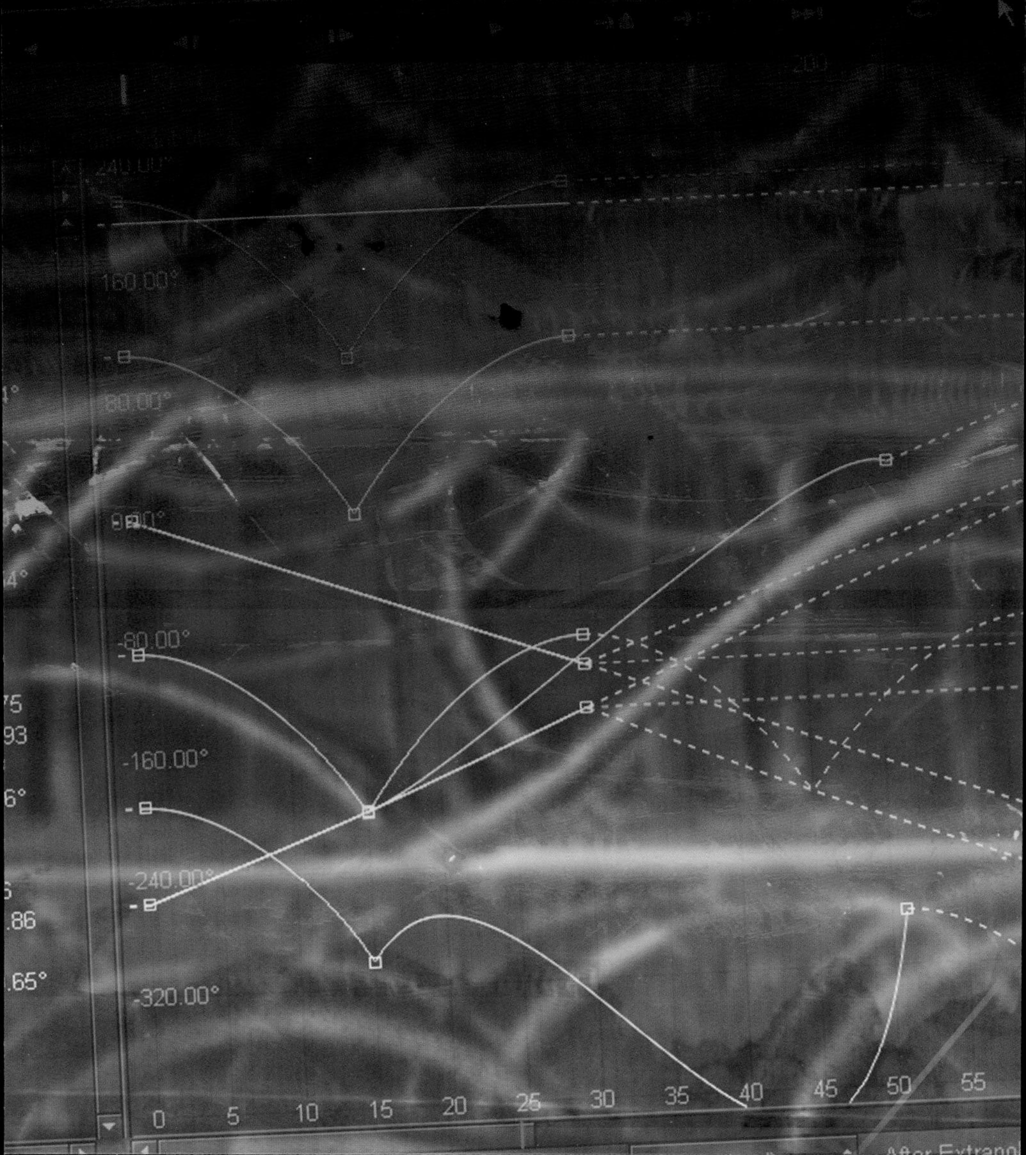

When and How Much?

At its heart, combustion is an application which has the vast majority of its toolset designed for animation. Using several different methods, most parameters allow you to change and keyframe their values over time. One way I like to define computer animation of any kind is by thinking in two terms: when and how much.

The 'when' is typically measured in frames or time code and the 'how much' can be just about any value in the application. Changes in *when and how much* equate to animation. For example, if something is invisible at the start and over three seconds becomes totally visible – the 'when' changes from the first frame to three seconds in, and the 'how much' changes from 0% visibility to 100%. Measuring the time (when) is easy, but there are so many potential values for the different 'how much' settings. How much red? How much feather? How much Z rotation? . . . and so on. These values in combustion are all considered 'channels' that can be animated.

While examining previous Workspaces to discuss other features, we have already seen some examples of animation within combustion; however, we have not discussed the different ways of creating these animations in depth. In this chapter, I will continue to use this simple *when and how much* vernacular to describe certain aspects of creating and editing animations within combustion.

When = frame number or time code
How much = a value of an animation 'channel'

Methods of Animating in combustion

Flipbook – This can be considered the simplest, brute-force form of animation, whereby you manually make changes on every single frame and then play them back in rapid succession. Computer graphics obviously allow for easier ways of animating, but quite often, one still has to resort to frame-by-frame work to accomplish certain tasks. **Onion Skinning** is a utility in combustion that aids in the flipbook/cartoon method of animating. Onion skinning can be used at any time for any reason, but it is often extremely valuable when doing frame-by-frame animation similar to traditional animators using clear acetate.

You can access the dialog seen in Figure 10.1 by selecting Onion Skin Settings from the Window menu at the top of the combustion UI. What onion skinning does is show you proceeding and successive frames as transparencies over/under the contents of the current frame. These transparencies will not render, but are merely there to help you work without flipping the Playback Controls back and forth. To actually use the onion skin options, you must enable Onion Skinning from the Window menu (or by hitting the ']' hotkey).

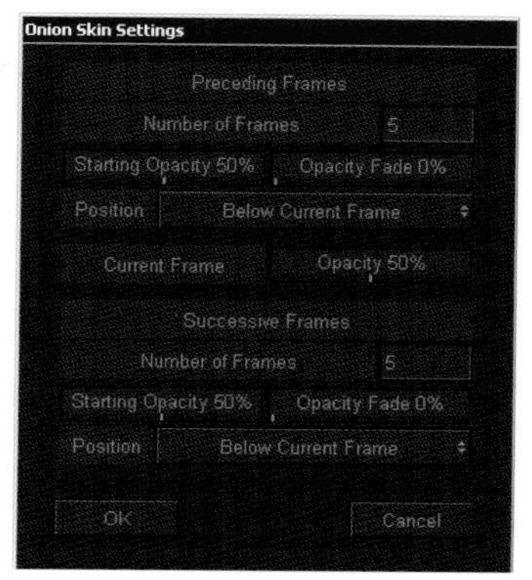

Figure 10.1

Keyframing – Keyframing is, perhaps, the easiest way to create and control animation. Keyframes work by setting a start and end value (when) for something (how much) and then letting the computer calculate values in between. This is also known as interpolation, which is the generation of data based on two different versions of something. You provide a start and end point and the computer interpolates the values in between.

Keyframing in combustion can be done in several ways but the easiest is by using the Animate button (Figure 10.2). When the Animate button is on, it turns red and changes in values (how much) are being recorded and keyframed on the current frame (when). The Animate button will always be visible and can be used at any time. For example, you can simply enable the Animate button, go to a new frame, and move an object or layer across the viewport. You can then play back the animation and see the translation across the frame.

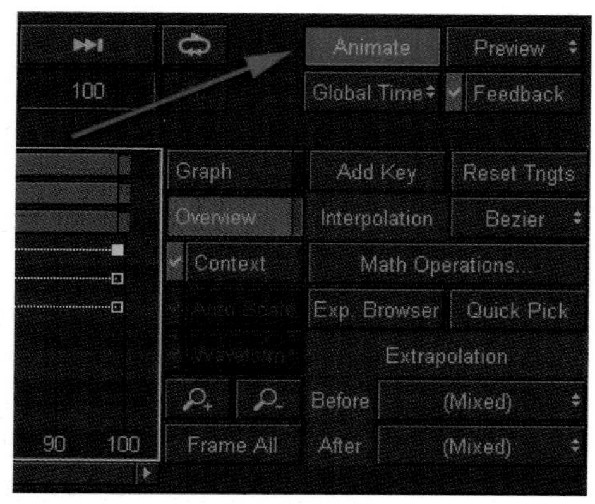

Figure 10.2

Note: The Timeline, which will be detailed in a moment, does not need to be visible to use the Animate button.

As simple as this method is, it is extremely common for new users to forget to turn this Animate button off when finished with it. I almost wish there was a warning buzzer when the Animate button was enabled, for if this button is red and you are creating and editing anything in combustion, then you are recording these changes (how much) on any given frame (when). This is another point that comes up again and again to most new users. You must always be aware if this Animate button is enabled, and turn it off the second you are done animating values. Another *really* good work habit is knowing what frame you are working on at *all* times, especially when this Animate button is enabled. This can easily be accomplished by looking at the number or time code to the left of the Playback Controls.

You can also build keyframe animation by creating keys directly in the Timeline. Figure 10.3 highlights the Add Key button, which is always available when viewing the Timeline. You can also simply click directly on the Timeline to add a keyframe.

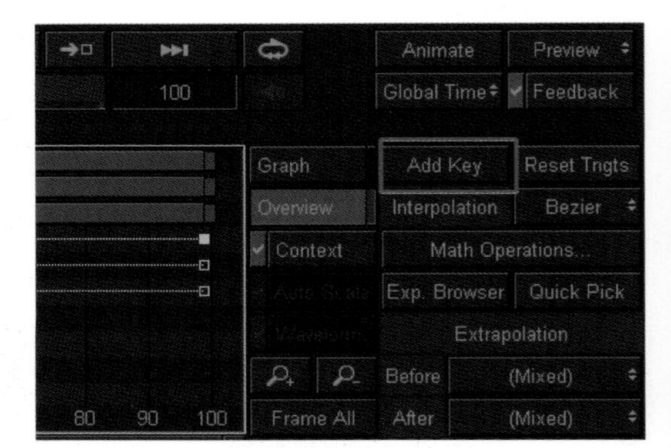

Figure 10.3

When you are starting out using combustion, I recommend using the first 'Animate button' method and only using the Timeline to edit existing animations, not to create new animations from scratch in the Timeline. This will allow you to become comfortable with the Timeline and not confuse yourself with learning keyframing, animation and the Timeline interface all at once.

Tracker – The Tracker generates keyframe data that can then be manually edited in the Timeline. The Tracker is discussed in greater detail in Chapter 9.

Expressions – Expressions are a means to use the JavaScript programming language to procedurally animate different channels in many, many different ways. Expressions in combustion are discussed in greater detail in Chapter 12.

Creating Simple Keyframe Animations

We will start by creating an extremely simple animation to keep things clear. Keep in mind that all animation is merely changes in 'when' and 'how much' of any parameter in combustion. As simple as this is, this technique can be applied to nearly every value in combustion.

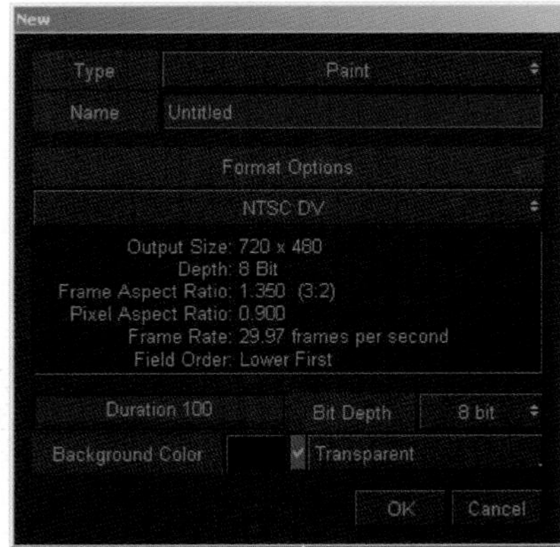

1. Create a new, 100-frame paint branch using the DV preset.
2. Make a simple shape on the first frame using the Freehand Paint tool ( ).
3. Select this object by using the Arrow tool ( ). Your viewport should resemble Figure 10.4.

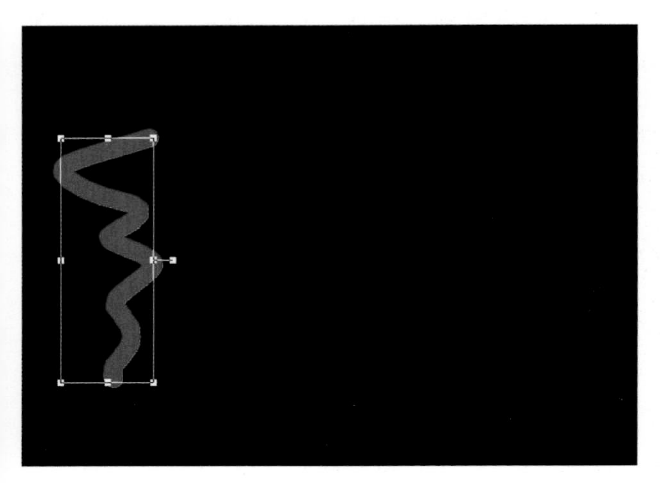

Figure 10.4

You will now animate the object across screen with three keyframes.

4 Enable the Animate button to the right of the Playback Controls. It will be red when turned on.

5 Go to the last frame and drag the paint object across screen from left to right by clicking on it with the Arrow tool. You will notice a green path in the viewport. This is an indication of the motion of the object.

6 Go to frame 50 and pull the object down in the viewport. Notice that you just created keyframes out of order, which can often have its advantages.

7 Turn off the Animate button and leave this simple project open.

> **Tip:** This method is a very good way to animate in that you start and end the object when/where you want it, and then let the computer interpolate the in-between values. You, as the animator, decide when/where refinement is needed. This is in contrast to a method in which you set a key, advance a certain number of frames, set another, and continue doing this to the end. This second method often generates too many keyframes, which can result in jerky animation.

With the object still selected, you should be able to see the resulting animation path in the viewport similar to Figure 10.5. This path can be edited directly in

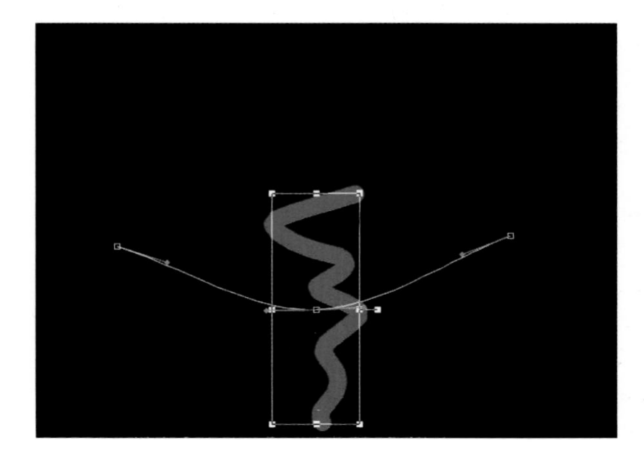

Figure 10.5

the viewport (with the Animate button on or off) or by editing the animation curves in the Timeline. If the Animate button is turned off, editing the keyframes and their tangent handles will change that particular point, but transformations to the selected object will offset the entire animation curve.

Now that you have created some keyframe animation, let's go into the Timeline and explore different ways of editing and manipulating keyframes.

The Timeline

The Timeline can be accessed at any time by hitting the F4 key. This is an interface for viewing, editing and creating keyframes of animation, and is also where you will create and edit expressions. Down the left side of the Timeline, you view and select different animation channels in a vertical order identical to the Workspace panel. Across the bottom of the Timeline is a measurement of time. This measurement corresponds to the setting in the Playback Controls (frames from 0, from 1 or time code).

> **Tip:** To temporarily expand the Timeline, you can hit Shift + F11 and the entire combustion UI will redraw for a moment. Then, you will have a much larger space to work, should you so desire. You can toggle this back to normal size by hitting Shift + F11 a second time.

The Timeline can be viewed in two distinct ways: Overview and Graph modes. These two modes can be toggled just to the right of the Timeline. They both have their advantages and it is certainly worth understanding the differences.

Overview – This is the big picture of 'when' keyframes. Overview allows you to see when keyframes occur and on what channels, but does not display the 'how much' of a value. For example, in Figure 10.6, there are four keyframes on both the X and Y position channels. You can see that there are keyframes on the first and last frames, and also around frames 30 and 72. Because you are in Overview mode, you cannot see what the values are for each of these keys – only that there are keyframes on those channels at those locations in time. The numerical values next to an animation channel only reflect the value of that channel on the current frame. When you move keyframes left or right, you are changing when they occur, but not the value of the keyframe. My recommendation is to always enter the Timeline initially in Overview mode so you can easily find the channels and/or keyframes you wish to edit. Then switch to Graph mode for fine-tuning of the keyframe curves.

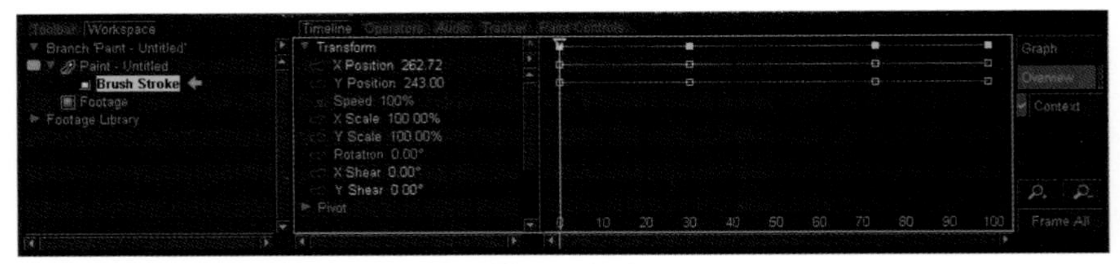

Figure 10.6

Graph – This is the nitty-gritty. Here, you can see function curves that represent the changes in both when and how much. Time (when) is always represented across the bottom and 'how much' values of any kind are viewed on the left, vertical scale. This scale can change depending on the animation value selected. For example, transparency can only range from 0% to 100%; other values can be infinite in positive and negative. Some values in combustion must be whole numbers while other values can be fractional or decimal values. There are even times when the vertical scale will be words, as in the case of Transfer modes (Normal, Multiply, Hard Light, etc.). This scale will change to reflect the measurements of the animation channel(s) selected, but time will always be measured across the bottom.

Note: The Particle operator is the sole exception to this. In a Particle operator, time is still measured across the bottom of the Timeline, but instead of time code or frames, time is represented as a percentage of the particle life.

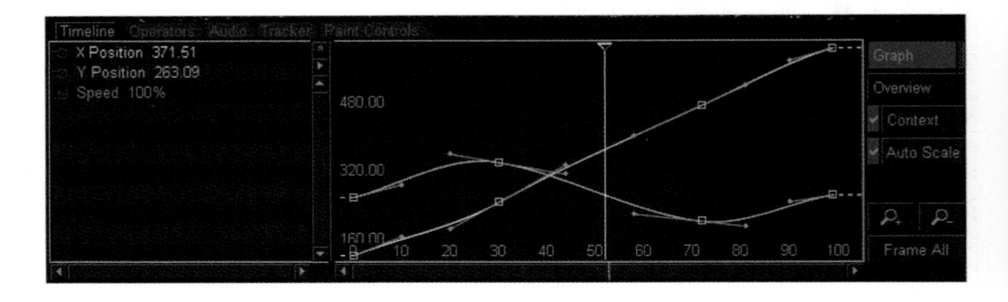

When in Graph mode, the cursor defaults to changing the value of a keyframe as indicated by an up/down cursor. Dragging keyframes up and down in the Graph mode changes the 'how much' of a value. To change the time of a keyframe in Graph mode, hold down the Alt key and the cursor will change to a left/right cursor. This changes the 'when' of a keyframe.

Auto Scale – This option is only available in Graph mode. When enabled, the Timeline scales to fit the selected channel's curves in the window. If you want to manually override this, you must first disable Auto Scale, and then you can use the following shortcuts:

Control + drag up/down	Vertical scale of Timeline
Control + drag left/right	Horizontal scale of Timeline
Alt + drag	Pans Timeline

Animation Channels and Filtering

By default, the Timeline has much more detail listed down the left side than is listed in the Workspace panel. The Workspace panel has a small flyout option tab that can be seen in Figure 10.7. For most purposes, this should be left to the default setting of *Show Operators . . . and Objects*. This will allow you to select layers, operators, and objects without looking at animation channels for every single object. In the Workspace panel, this is a time saver.

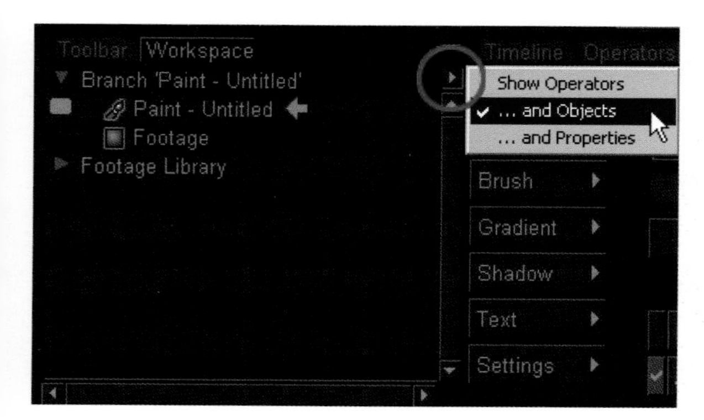

Figure 10.7

In the Timeline, however, you want to have access to all the individual channels of everything in your Workspace. This is because the Timeline is one place where you will potentially keyframe and edit any parameter. Figure 10.8 shows the Timeline options filters. For the Timeline, I highly recommend leaving the default setting of *Show Operators . . . and Properties* selected.

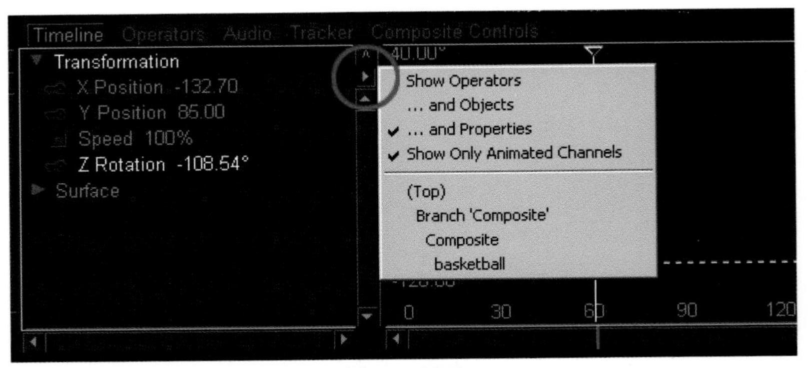

Figure 10.8

> **Note:** I would like to reiterate that the defaults described above for the Timeline and Workspace panel should be how they typically work in combustion. These controls provide 'what you need, where you need it' for almost all occasions, and changing them from the defaults often leads to confusion in new users. If you make a change to experiment and see the difference, I strongly encourage you to return these settings to the default values.

The **Show Only Animated Channels** is a nice option to turn on and off as needed when working in combustion. This filters out all the channels in the entire Workspace that have not been animated. If you know you are only editing existing animation instead of creating new animation, then this option weeds out the empty channels and presents only those with keyframes. This is another powerful feature that sometimes confuses new users. If this is enabled and you are not aware of it, then you many end up hunting in the Timeline for something that is not currently available for editing; it is filtered out and hidden. Lastly, it should be mentioned that expressions do not show up when this option is enabled.

Context – Figure 10.9 highlights the Context option for the Timeline. When enabled, this option causes the Timeline to automatically show you channels of information pertinent to the current selected item in the Workspace. 'Contextual Timelines' will only show you values for objects you have selected. When Context is disabled, you have to navigate the Timeline manually and this can take some practice. It is a great idea to leave the Context Timeline option on when learning combustion. Once again, this enforces the adage, 'When in doubt, double click its name in the Workspace panel'.

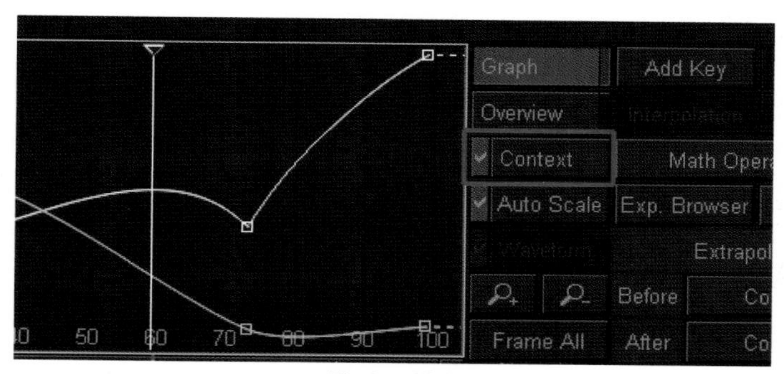

Figure 10.9

Back in Figure 10.6, the object named Paint Stroke is selected in the Workspace panel and because Context is enabled in the Timeline, only the animation channels pertaining to this object are visible. In addition, you can see that there are only keyframes in the X and Y position channels.

Frame All – This button forces the Timeline to quick-zoom to the width of the range of keyframes for the selected channels. Often when you are zoomed in, clicking on this button is the fastest way to zoom back out to full width.

You select animation channels by clicking on their names in the Timeline (Control + click to select multiples). It should be made immediately clear, however, that selecting an animation channel not only isolates and displays this channel in the Timeline, but also selects all the keys in this channel. Keyframes that are not selected are white and keyframes that are selected are yellow. If you select a channel by clicking in its name in the Timeline, you will notice that all the keys on that channel turn yellow. Quite often, users select a channel by clicking on its name and they are unaware that all the keys are selected. Then, when they go to move one keyframe, they offset every single keyframe on this channel, not just the one they intended to move. This can be a powerful feature, but often confuses new users. To rectify/prevent this from occurring, you can select an animation channel and then click in a blank area of the Timeline to deselect the keyframes. Then you can edit them individually.

The key icon next to the left of an animation channel's name indicates that the keyframing functionality is active for that channel. If you toggle this icon off for any channel, the animation for that value is temporarily turned off (and the value is held at the amount of the current frame). The keyframes, however, are still present, but they are inactive, not deleted. If you move the object at that point, the entire channel will be offset. It can often be useful to toggle an animation channel on and off while the clip plays back. This allows you to see the effects of that channel's animation in the overall, larger picture.

Ease Curves

Keyframes are usually defined in detail in animation manuals and tutorials, but there seems to be little emphasis describing ease curves. While keyframes, by definition, are essential 'poses' of animation, it is the ease curves *between* these keyframes where a lot of the finesse separates good and bad animation technique.

To explain the use of ease curves, I like to use a variant example of the old story of the tortoise and the hare. In my version of the tale, I will ruin the ending and tell you the race ends in a tie. That is, they begin the contest at the exact same time and they tie in the end; however, the race in between is where some interesting things occur.

1. Open the Workspace named *ch10_TieRace.cws*. This is a simple Paint branch with several animated groups.
2. Cache the clip and let it play back while looping.

To briefly explain what you are looking at, four paint groups have been animated from left to right and they all cover the same distance in the same amount of time. While this might be the case, it is obvious that the rabbit accelerates at the beginning and the turtle gets off to a slow start. The word 'linear' is the only one that remains at a constant velocity, yet all three groups start and end at the same time. What is interesting about these three groups is there are only two keyframes for each: one on the first frame and one on the last. It is the shape of the animation curves in between these keyframes that creates the variation of the three animations. Because of this, the animation for all three groups will look the same in the Timeline Overview mode, as seen here.

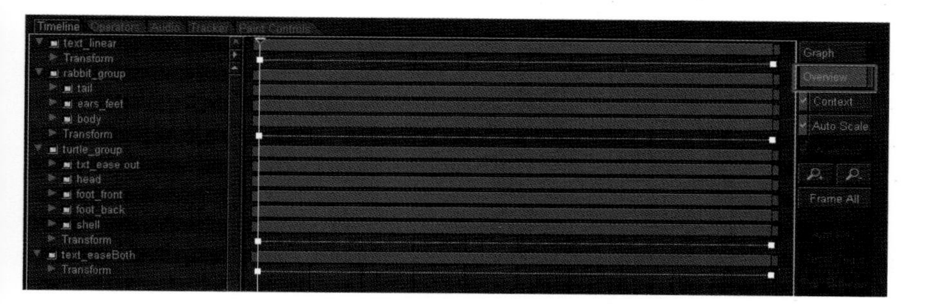

Figure 10.10 represents the Graph curve for the word 'linear' using a linear interpolation type (go figure). This shows that the transition from one value to another is performed at a constant rate.

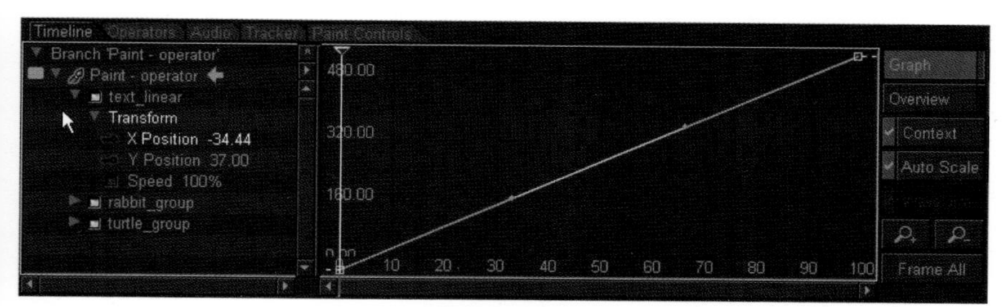

Figure 10.10

Figure 10.11 represents the Graph curve for the rabbit; it shows a curve that accelerates in the beginning and then slows to a stop at the very end. The tangent handles have been edited to customize the shape of the animation curve for the X position channel.

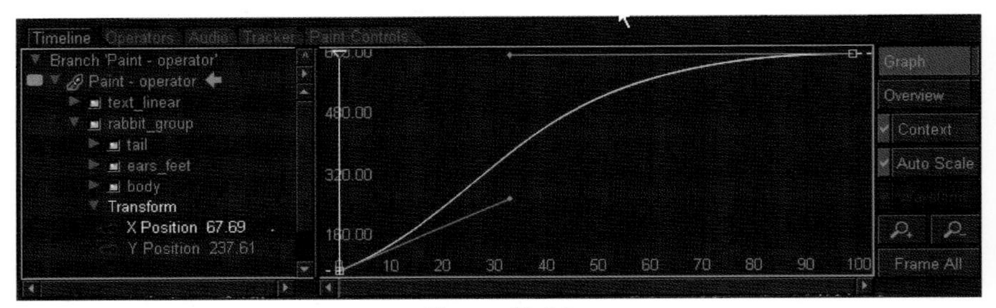

Figure 10.11

Figure 10.12 represents the Graph curve for the turtle; it shows a curve that has an extremely slow acceleration that increases in speed until the very end.

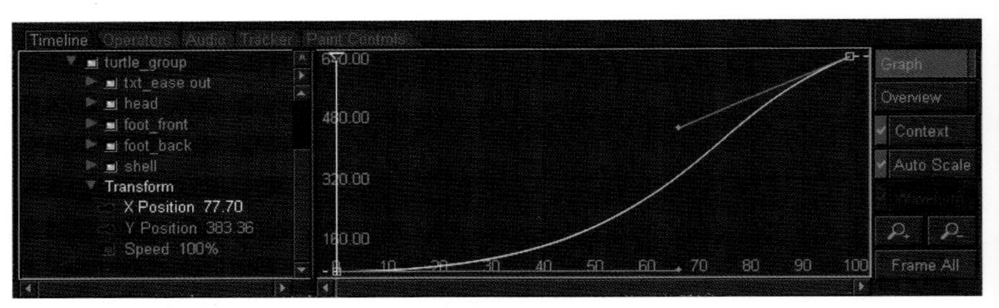

Figure 10.12

Figure 10.13 represents the Graph curve for the 'ease both' text. This curve accelerates slowly to full speed and then slows down to a nice, easy stop.

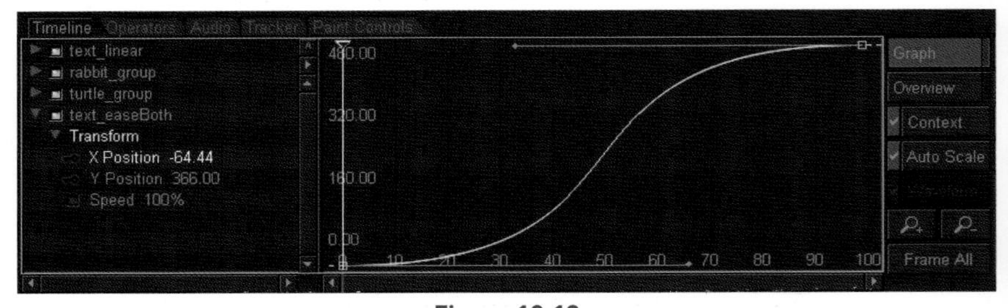

Figure 10.13

As a rule of thumb, when you go into the Timeline, always start in Overview mode to navigate and more easily locate your keyframes. Then, when you have found the specific keyframes you wish to edit, switch to the Graph mode to see the animation curves. Without looking at the Graph mode of the Timeline, you may never know if you have a 'tortoise or a hare' type animation curve and will only be able to see when keyframes are in time – not how they interpolate in between.

Extrapolation

No matter how many keyframes you may have on a given channel, the time between the first and last keyframes can be thought of as one cycle of animation in that channel. Extrapolation is a means to continue this cycle before the first or after the last keyframe you created. Depending on the animation cycle, different extrapolation methods will result in similar or dramatically different animations. What extrapolation does is create 'virtual keyframes' that really do not exist in the Timeline. The resulting animation curves can be seen as dotted lines in the Graph curve editor.

To see the different types of extrapolations, open the Workspace file named *ch10_Extrapolation.cws*. Cache this clip and loop the playback while you examine the file. Keep the Timeline in Graph mode with Context enabled and then single click on each layer in the Workspace panel to see its animation curves in the viewport. If you want to see the corresponding animation curves in the Timeline, you have to open the layer, then the transformation and finally click on the X and/or Y position channels.

Constant – A value will remain the same at the beginning or end of the cycle, regardless of the ease curves coming into or out of the cycle.

Linear – This type continues the tangency in a straight line for a constant rate of change.

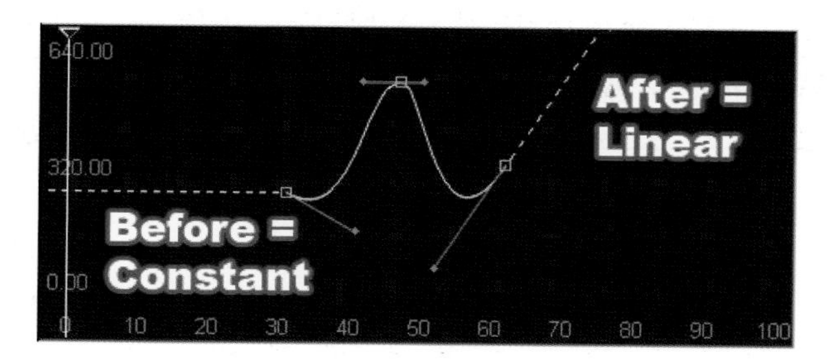

Loop – The animation cycle will play forward and then appear to jump back to the beginning and repeat playing forward indefinitely.

Ping Pong – The cycle will play forward, then backward and continue this repetition indefinitely.

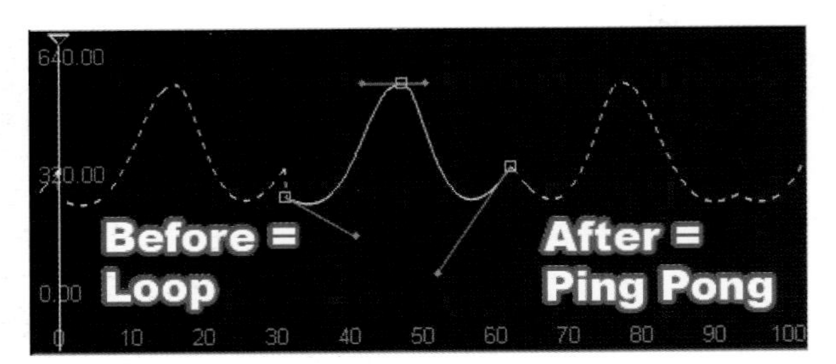

Relative Repeat – This might be thought of best as 'keep on going'. This extrapolation type takes into account the shape of the animation curve, including the ease curves, and continues prior to or after the animation cycle in a manner that continues the curve shape in either direction.

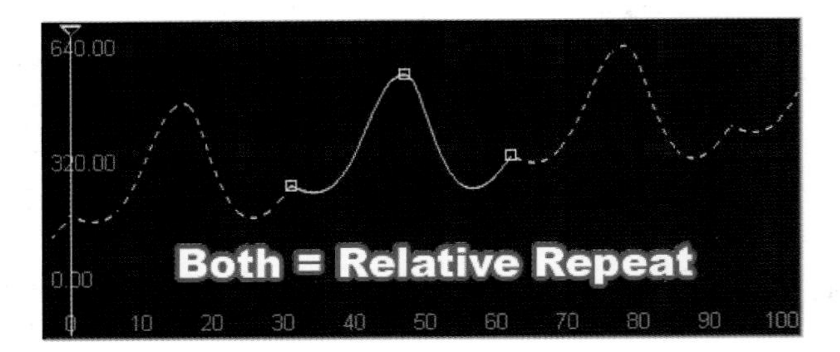

Mixed – This extrapolation definition means more than one type of the choices above is used in the animation channels you have selected.

> **Note:** Virtual keyframes generated by before/after extrapolation cannot be viewed in Overview mode. You must switch the Timeline to Graph mode to see these curves.

> **Tip:** Quite often you may not know which type will best suit your needs. Since the dialogs for before/after extrapolation types are flyouts, you can have an animation playing back while you roll the mouse wheel over these menus to cycle through the different choices.

Math Operations

The Timeline button that says *Math Operations . . .* evokes the menu seen in Figure 10.14. These options can perform transformations either to an entire animation channel or to a selected range of keyframes.

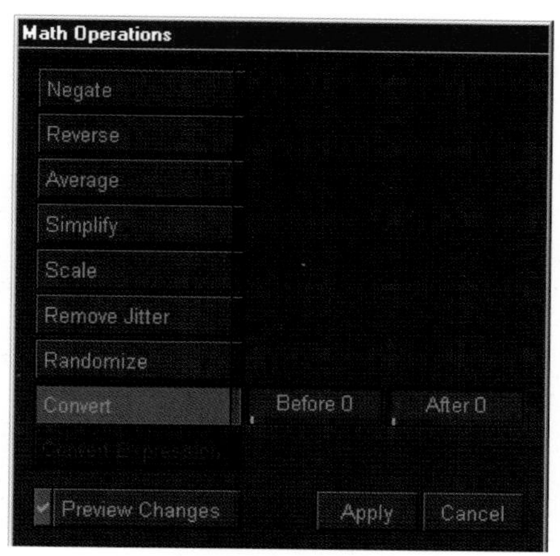

Figure 10.14

Negate	Makes positive values negative and vice versa.
Reverse	Flips the keyframes backwards so the animation is inverted in time.
Average	Averages the 'weight' of keyframes over a user-defined divisor value.
Simplify	Performs a keyframe reduction while trying to preserve the shape of the keyframe animation curve.
Scale	Independently scales the horizontal and vertical axes of the Timeline (or the *when and how much* values).
Remove Jitter	Smoothes keyframe values.
Randomize	Adds or subtracts a random amount, as specified by the user, to selected keyframe values.
Convert	This makes a user-defined number of cycles of virtual keyframes (created with extrapolation) become real, editable keyframes.
Convert Expression	Turns virtual animation curves resulting from JavaScript expressions into real keyframes that can then be edited normally. The expression is lost after this conversion.

Markers

Markers are available to aid you in many ways while keyframing and editing in the Timeline. You can add markers to operators and layers using the techniques outlined here. In Chapter 11, you will also see that you can apply Edit operator markers as well. Markers are helpful to annotate and point out key locations in time where you might want something to occur in an animation. In the case of the ch10_Exprapolation.cws project, there is an operator marker at the composite level on frame 30. This marker identifies the end of the keyframe cycle(s).

> **Note:** You need to be in the Overview mode of the Timeline to view markers.

To Add an Operator Marker (to the Composite)

1. Switch to the Timeline (F4) and enable Context.
2. In the Workspace panel, double click the Composite operator onto which you wish to add markers.
3. Click the small up arrow in Figure 10.15 once. This will take you up one level in the Timeline so you can see the Composite operator duration.

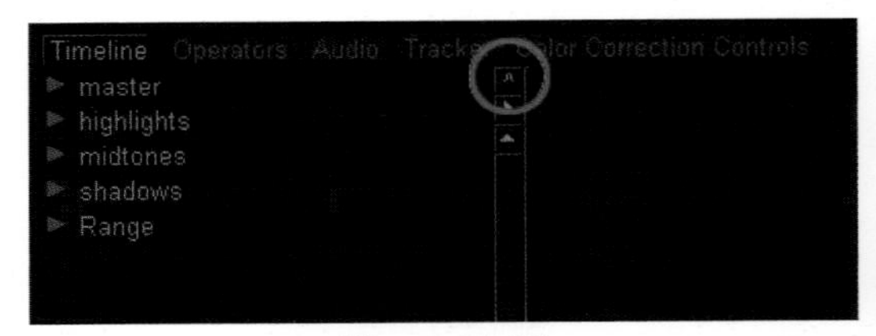

Figure 10.15

4. Go to the frame where you want to add a marker and tap the M key. You can alternately go to *Edit > Add Operator Marker*. This will add markers to the Composite operator.

To Add a Layer Marker

1. In the Timeline, select the layer onto which you wish to add a marker.
2. Control + M adds layer markers to selected layers on the current frame. You can alternatively select Edit > Add Layer Marker. You can also add layer markers by holding the Alt key down and clicking in the layer bar in the Timeline.

> **Tip:** When a clip is cached, you can tap Control + M to add layer markers during playback.

Editing Markers

You can move the location of a marker simply by dragging on it.

To edit a marker, right click on it and select Edit from the flyout seen in Figure 10.16. Note the other options presented here.

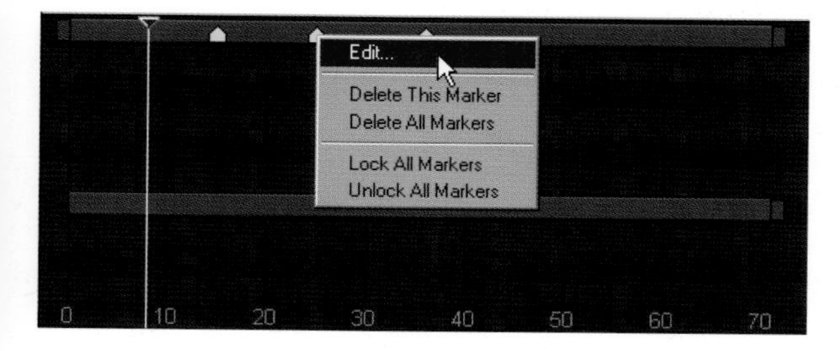

Figure 10.16

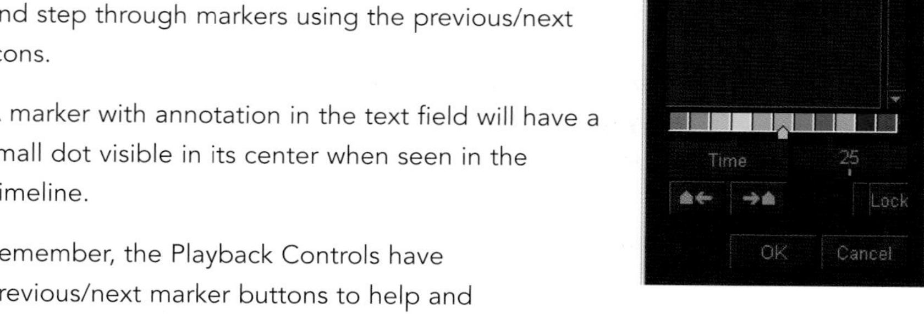

You will then be presented with the dialog seen here. This small interface allows you to change the color of markers, annotate markers, lock markers, and step through markers using the previous/next icons.

A marker with annotation in the text field will have a small dot visible in its center when seen in the Timeline.

Remember, the Playback Controls have previous/next marker buttons to help and encourage the use of markers throughout combustion projects.

Discreet combustion is a tool designed for the creation and manipulation of moving images. Since the possibilities of animation within combustion are literally endless, you are encouraged first to step through the basics of animation, and then begin to combine various methods outlined in this chapter and elsewhere in this book. Remember, creating animated, changing values of nearly anything in combustion is as easy as enabling the Animate button and making the change on the frame you wish the change to happen.

CHAPTER 11
A/V EDITING

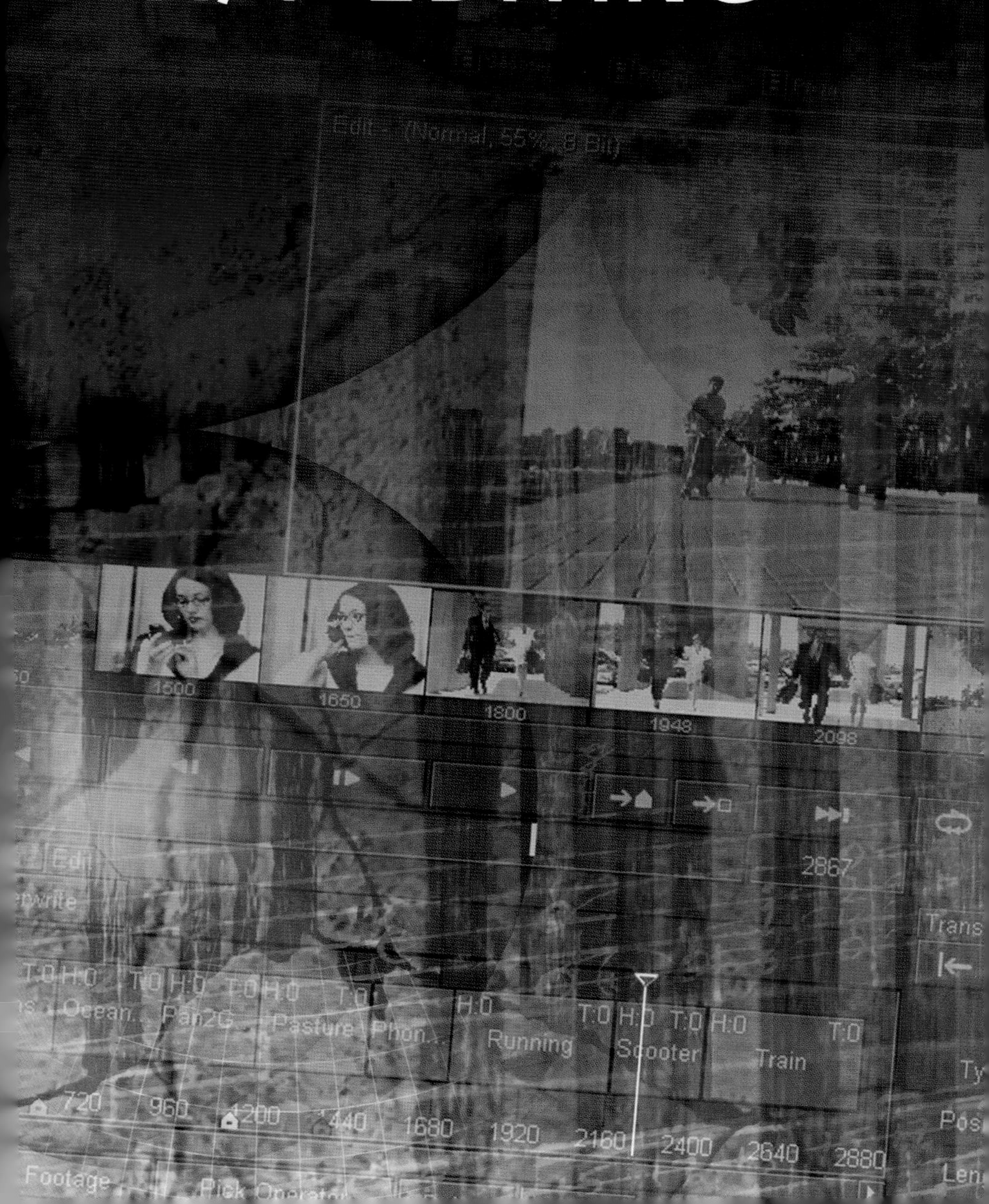

Combustion has the ability to work with audio and video in a manner much like a non-linear editing application; however, it should be understood that the tools in combustion are designed for different purposes than the likes of long-form editors such as Avid, Premiere or Pro-Tools. First and foremost, combustion is an effects tool for motion graphics and the like. If you want to cut a feature film or remix the next number one hit album, you should not look to do it in combustion. You could, but you probably don't want to. You can do a lot with a hammer, but you would not use one to drive in a woodscrew. It is really about picking the right tool for the right job.

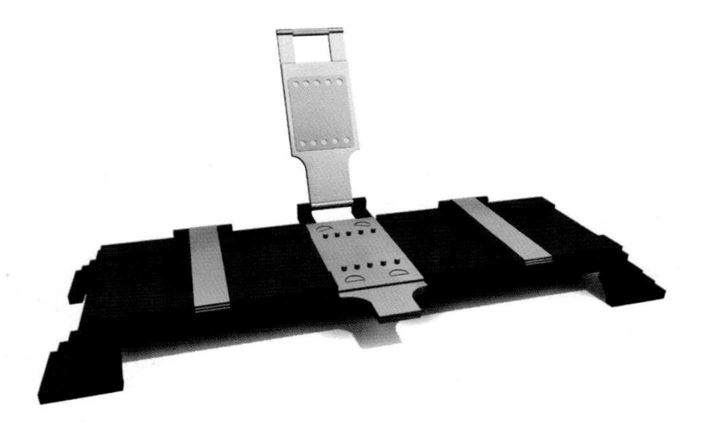

Audio

Discreet combustion has the ability to load what is often referred to as a 'scratch track' audio clip. This is done by going to the Audio tab just below the Transport Controls. When you enter the Audio Controls, the only option available is to browse to a directory containing an audio file. In addition to the common WAV, AIFF and MP3 formats for audio, you can load just the audio portion of an AVI, MOV or MPEG file.

Note: When you work elsewhere in combustion with MOV or AVI files as footage, any audio contained in those files will not be loaded unless you use the feature outlined here or the 'Set As Audio Source' option in the Thumbnail Browser. Files obtained using the Quick Capture utility can optionally have audio loaded automatically, but they will still be separate files on the hard drive.

1 Click the Browse button and select any audio file you have handy. If you need to, you can use the file named *renderdone.WAV* found in the . . . *combustion**Data*\ directory.

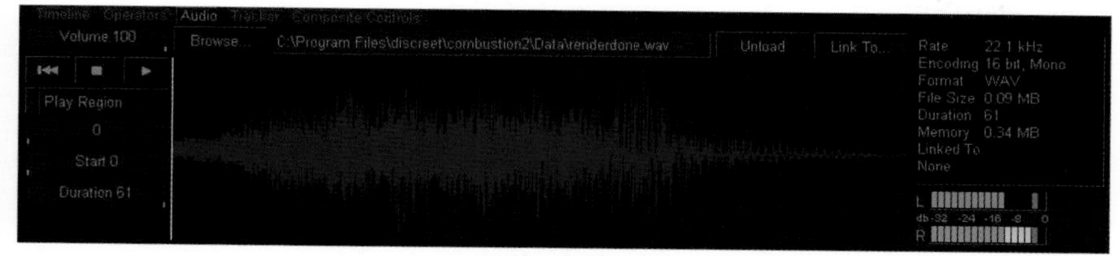

Figure 11.1

You should now see the waveform of the audio clip you selected. In the case of the *renderdone.wav* file seen in Figure 11.1, notice that the amplitude of the sound gradually increases then fades out. To the far right, you can also see basic information about the properties of this file and audio level meters.

Rewind/Stop/Play – These ( ) are for basic playback to test the audio segment. The Rewind button here takes you back to the time set by the Start fields below. If you enable the Play Region option ( ), only the range set by Start and Duration will play back.

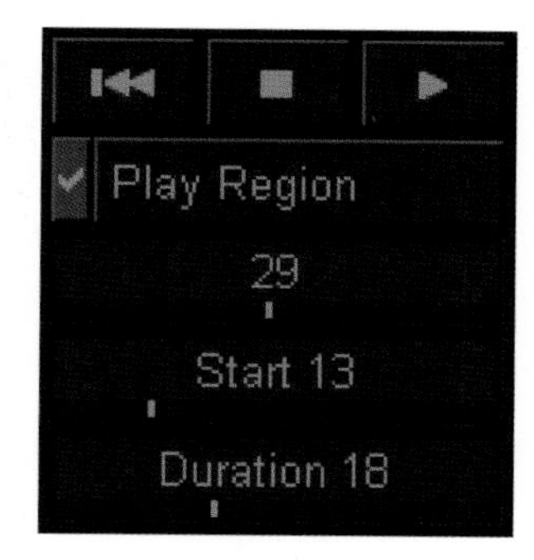

The **Start** and **Duration** values let you trim the audio in and out points of the audio clip. Use these as sliders to change the range of the audio clip. You should notice the highlighted area change accordingly as seen in Figure 11.2. The highlighted area will be the only portion available to the rest of combustion. Notice how the fade in and out has been trimmed. You can also drag the bars directly in the UI to create a section for the audio section.

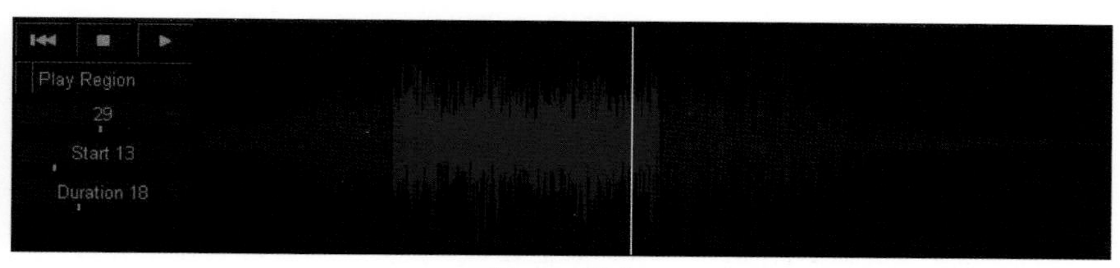

Figure 11.2

2 Switch to the Timeline tab and notice that the waveform is visible and that only the trimmed portion of the clip is being used in the Workspace. You can enable and disable the visual representation of the waveform in the timeline by disabling the Waveform checkbox seen in Figure 11.3.

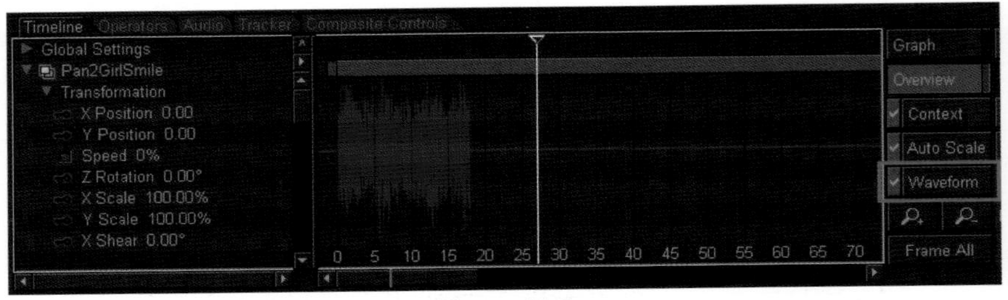

Figure 11.3

3 Return to the Audio tab (tap F6).

The **Link To . . .** button seen to the right of the file name will bring up the Operator Picker dialog seen in Figure 11.4. This allows you to tie the audio clip to an operator or piece of footage in your Workspace. Then, if you make changes in the Timeline to the element picked (such as slipping the in and out points of the footage), the audio file will come along for the ride, as it were, staying in sync.

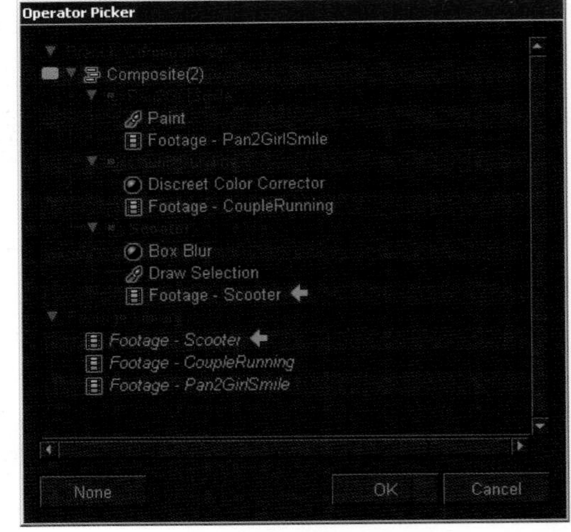

Figure 11.4

If your Workspace has an audio file loaded, you can optionally include the audio in the render as well.

The Filmstrip

You can certainly use the Filmstrip at any time when working in combustion, but it seems to be particularly useful when doing hand-drawn flipbook animation and especially when using the Edit operator.

To quickly introduce the Filmstrip:

1. Open the Workspace named *ch11_Editing.cws*. This is a simple project that contains all the sample MOV files from Digital Juice.

2. Go to the Window menu and select Windows > Palettes > Show Filmstrip. The screen will briefly redraw and then you should see a small series of numbered thumbnails appear as in Figure 11.5.

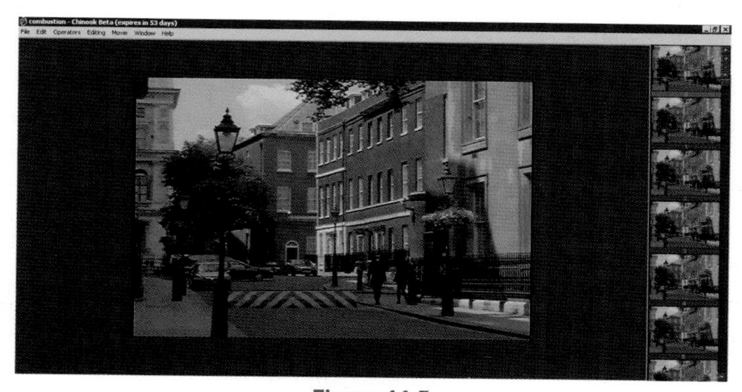

Figure 11.5

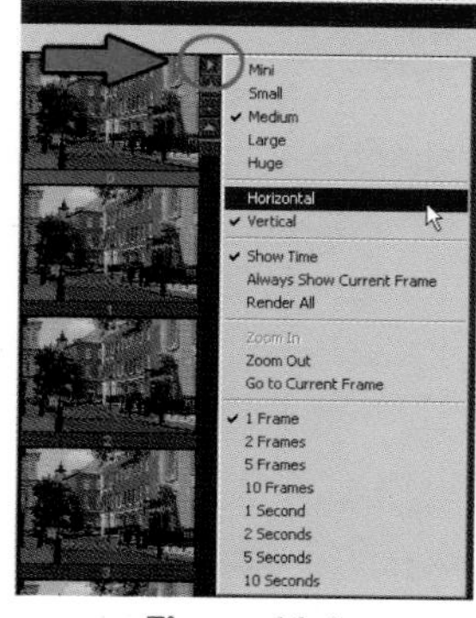

Figure 11.6

3. In the very upper corner of the Filmstrip, you can see a small arrow pointing right (Figure 11.6). This opens a menu with several options including thumbnail size, layout of the Filmstrip, and the time scale that the Filmstrip uses.

4. From this list, switch from Vertical to Horizontal. The screen will redraw and you will now see the Filmstrip across the bottom

of the viewports. The controls for the Filmstrip are now just above the Viewport Controls, as seen in Figure 11.7.

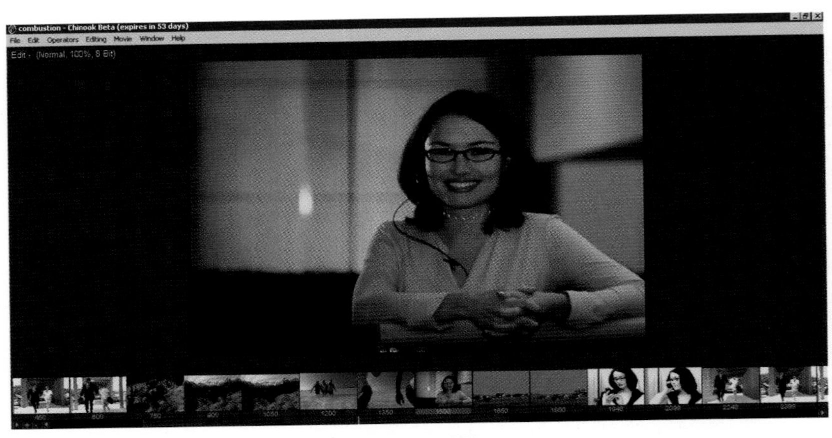

Figure 11.7

5 Reaccess the Filmstrip controls and try out the different settings for thumbnail size. They range from 'mini' to 'huge' (you have to love those naming conventions). Just as using the Filmstrip is, in itself, an option, so too is the size of the thumbnails used within the Filmstrip.

> **Tip:** The Filmstrip uses system memory to cache, just like anything else in combustion. Because of this, the smaller thumbnails require less memory. 'Mini' thumbnails, therefore, will use the least memory and cache faster than the rest of the available sizes.

6 Try scrolling though the Filmstrip by using the red frame slider just under the thumbnails. You can also drag the entire range of the Filmstrip by dragging the wider, gray bar. Lastly, you can jump to a frame by merely clicking on a thumbnail that represents the location where you want to go in time.

The Filmstrip options seen in Figure 11.6 are briefly outlined below. Remember, you can show and hide the Filmstrip at any time from the windows menu at the top of the combustion UI.

Show Time – This will toggle the visibility of the frame count or time code that is under each thumbnail.

Always Show Current Frame – This option will force the Filmstrip to scroll along in time to continue displaying the current viewport.

Render All – This will force combustion to cache all the thumbnails in the filmstrip. Then, you can quickly scrub back and forth in the Filmstrip's time slider just like a traditional NLE system.

Zoom In/Out – This changes the time settings in the Filmstrip by setting a number of frames to be skipped. You can also use the small + and – icons that are visible on the Filmstrip itself.

Go to Current Frame – The current frame will be visible in the Filmstrip. This can be used as an alternative to Always Show Current Frame.

Time Settings – This is where you can set the Filmstrip to skip a predetermined number of frames so that more of the entire project will be visible in the Filmstrip. The first four choices are in frames and the rest are in seconds; the last four use the frame rate of the current project.

Using the Filmstrip for lengthy projects such as those involving editing operations can help you navigate longer sequences. However, technically speaking, the Filmstrip slightly slows combustion down. Use it as needed, but be aware that it is slightly pulling from your total available resources. If you are not actively using it, disable the Filmstrip by accessing the *Windows > Palette > Hide Filmstrip* option.

The Edit Operator

Before moving on, revert the Workspace from the File menu or (re)open the project named *ch11_Editing.cws*. In the Workspace panel, select the Edit operator and the Edit Controls will appear at the bottom of the UI.

Like the Composite operator, the Edit operator can be thought of as a window of a defined duration, frame rate, and resolution that lets you look at elements within your Workspace. An Edit operator is also similar to a Composite operator in that it brings several clips together as one. The fundamental difference between a

Composite and Edit operator is that instead of layering your images on top of each other or using 3D space, you assemble segments head to tail so one plays, then another, then another, and so on. Like composites, the Edit operator has a single, defined resolution regardless of the resolution of the clips being edited. The Edit operator interface is extremely straightforward and only has one primary interface – the Edit Timeline.

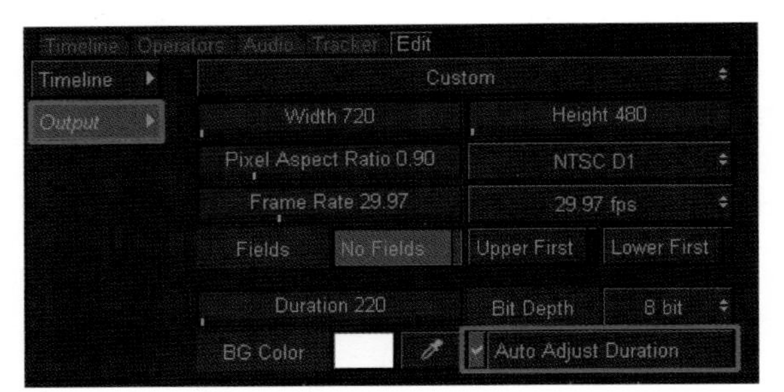

Figure 11.8

Output – This second category of the Edit operator is largely the same as a Composite operator, with one exception. Figure 11.8 shows the Auto Adjust Duration option of an Edit operator. When enabled, this will use the duration of the Edit operator's contents to determine the entire duration of the operator.

Timeline – The Edit operator Timeline is where the majority of all the editing operations occur. Figure 11.9 shows the entire interface. This is not the same Timeline detailed in Chapter 10. The Edit operator Timeline is where you will perform non-linear editing functions, not keyframe animation. If you bring together several segments into an Edit operator as seen here, you can tell where one begins and another ends by the separation of the clips by name and also by the (default) cut edit from one to the next.

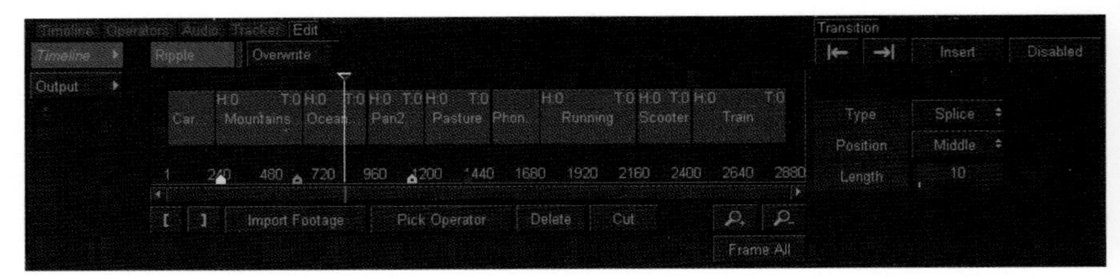

Figure 11.9

Below are descriptions of the primary buttons found in the Edit operator:

Ripple	When enabled, the Timeline will change the overall duration longer or shorter (as needed) to accommodate the edits you perform. Start and end times of clips are edited when you change the duration of any other clips.
Overwrite	When enabled, the overall duration of the operator remains the same, regardless of any edits you perform. This option causes frames to be replaced to adhere to this duration.
[ ]	Mark in and out points on the Edit Timeline. These are for one- and two-point editing, which is detailed later in this chapter.
Import Footage	This brings up the Thumbnail Browser to bring in footage off the computer directly into the Edit operator. The footage will be inserted at the current time using current (ripple/overwrite) settings.
Pick Operator	This retrieves a node from within the current Workspace as a segment source for the Edit operator.
Delete	This is used to remove transitions and clips from the Edit operator. A transition or clip must be selected (highlighted in yellow) first.
Cut	This creates a cut transition at the current time indicator.
	These are typical tools for zooming the contents of the Timeline.
Frame All	The Frame All button zooms in or out to accommodate the entire Timeline.

Trimming Heads, Middles and Tails

The beginning and end of a clip within the Edit operator are called the head and tail, respectively. In the case of merely playing clips end to end, you often do not need to worry about these, but when you want to trim a clip shorter than its potential full duration, you can either shorten the head or tail, or cut out a portion of the clip from the middle.

1. Open the Workspace file named *ch11_EditingABC.cws*. This is a simple, three-segment clip of stills each having a 150-frame duration.

2. To edit the head or tail of a clip, merely place the cursor over the edit splice and the cursor will change to indicate which 'side' of the cut you will edit. Figure 11.10 shows both the new cursor editing the tail of clip A and also that 20 frames have been trimmed off the tail of this clip.

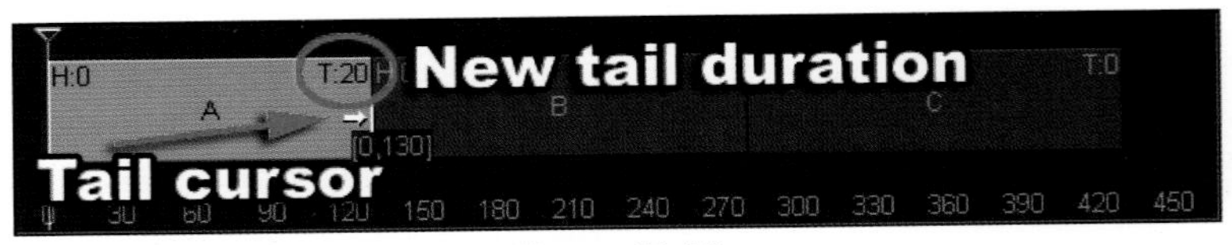

Figure 11.10

3 This example shows a Ripple trim of clip A. You can tell this is a Ripple edit because as the tail of a clip is adjusted, the following clips move to compensate for the loss of duration in clip A. Undo the previous action and switch to the Overwrite mode of the Edit operator.

4 Trim the tail of clip A again and notice that a gap is left this time, as seen here. This is due to the nature of Overwrite mode.

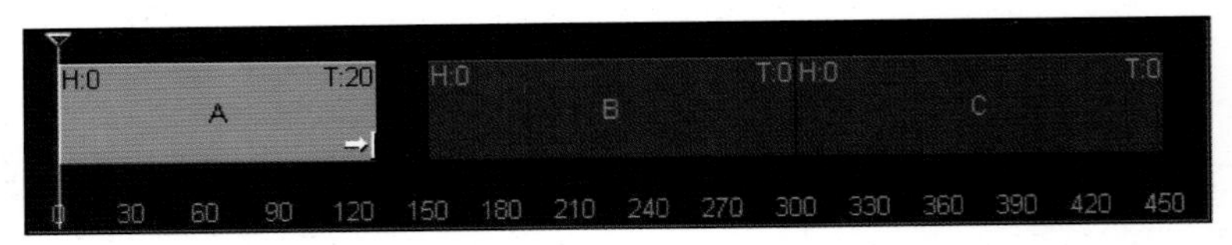

Experiment with Ripple and Overwrite modes while trimming the heads and tails of clips. Notice the effects upon the duration of the clips and the duration of the Timeline as you work.

5 To take a section out of the middle of a clip, you position the Timeline indicator over a point in a clip and click the Cut button below the Timeline. This will make two clips out of one. Each of the resulting clips will play back end to end without any indication of the cut, but there are head and tail frames now available on either side of this cut edit you created.

> **Note:** This last step may be more obvious on moving video clips and not the ABC still samples currently loaded.

Simple Editing

1 To see how a few more functions of the Edit operator work, let's begin anew by choosing Revert Workspace from the File menu (or reopening the Workspace named *ch11_EditingABC.cws*). Figure 11.11 shows the

Edit operator Timeline and segment 'B' has been selected, as is indicated by the yellow coloration.

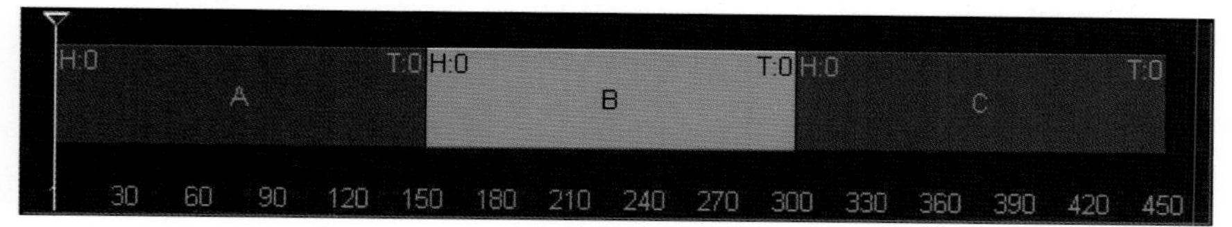

Figure 11.11

2 Verify you are in Ripple mode.

3 Click and drag segment B up and to the left. During this operation, your Timeline window should resemble Figure 11.12. Notice in this example how the head and tail frame numbers are displayed as you drag the segment.

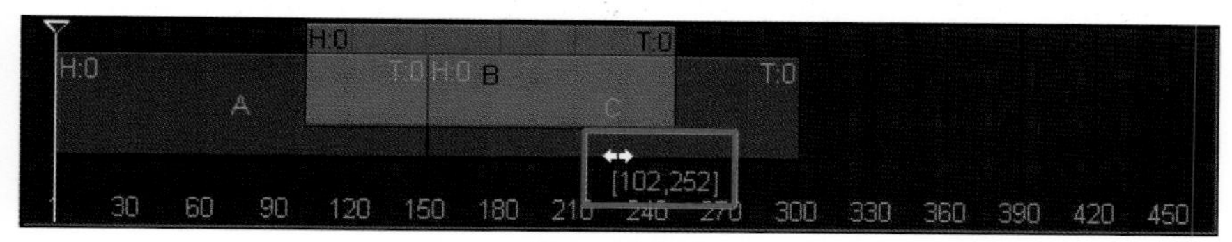

Figure 11.12

4 Release the mouse when the segment is partially over segment A. The resulting Timeline will look like Figure 11.13.

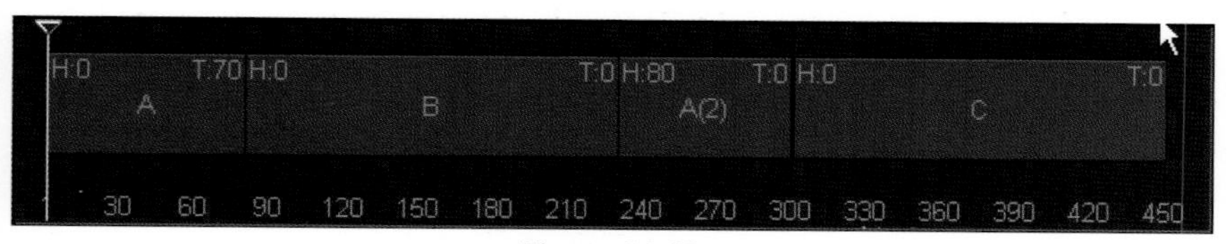

Figure 11.13

Because of the Ripple edit function, segment A was split in two and segment B was inserted in between this split. The overall duration remains the same. Also notice that the tail of segment A and the head of segment A(2) have been changed from zero to a number representing the new duration of each. You can scrub time or cache the clip to see the cuts-only edits switch ABAC.

5 Undo the last operation and switch the Edit operator Timeline from Ripple to Overwrite mode.

6 Repeat the segment B movement up and to the left over segment A. This time, when you release the mouse, you should notice there is a gap left where the end of segment A was and where segment B used to be. Figure 11.14 shows these results of this Overwrite edit.

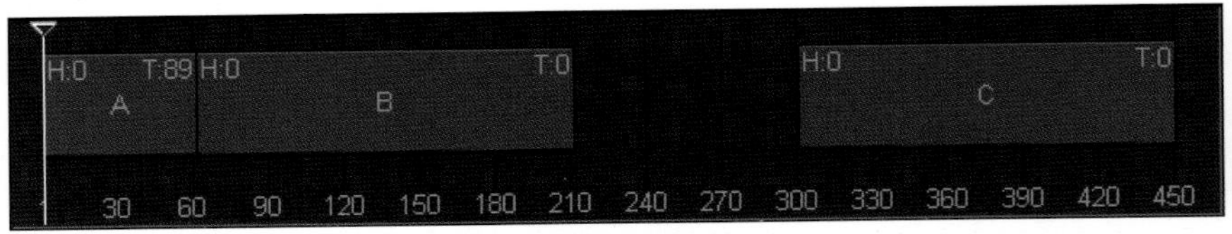

Figure 11.14

7 Switch back to Ripple mode and then, while holding down the Shift key, drag segment B in front of segment A. You should notice that dragging segments with the Shift key held forces them to snap to heads and tails of other segments, even when in Ripple mode.

Transitions

The Edit operator has the ability to add simple wipes and dissolve transitions between two segments in the Timeline. By default, cuts-only (aka splice) transitions are enabled. You can add dissolves or wipes manually, but for these types of transitions to work, you need an appropriate amount of head and tail frames on both segments.

	Go to previous/next segment. This pair of controls takes you to the first frame of the clip in question.
Insert	Places a transition at the current time using the current transition settings.
Disabled	Leaves a transition in place, but temporarily turns it off.
Type	Three choices of transition are Dissolve, Splice and Wipe. In the case of the Wipe a choice of Left/Right/Up/Down is available.
Position	This setting determines where the transition will be placed relative to the two clips in question. Choices are start, middle, end and custom.
Length	This determines the duration of a transition.

1. To create a simple transition and experiment with editing, begin by reverting back to (or reopening) *ch11_EditingABC.cws*.
2. Make sure you are in Ripple mode.
3. Trim segment A's tail 20 frames and segment B's head 20 frames by dragging the head and tail durations of each corresponding segment.
4. Go to the first frame and then click the Next Segment button (→|). This will jump the Timeline indicator to the exact point between segments A and B. Figure 11.15 shows the resulting Timeline.

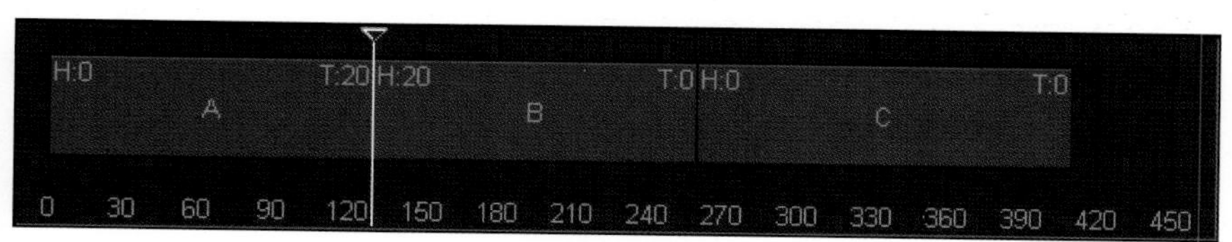

Figure 11.15

5. Change the Transition type to Dissolve, the Position to Middle and the Length to 40.
6. Click the Transition Insert button and you will end up with this:

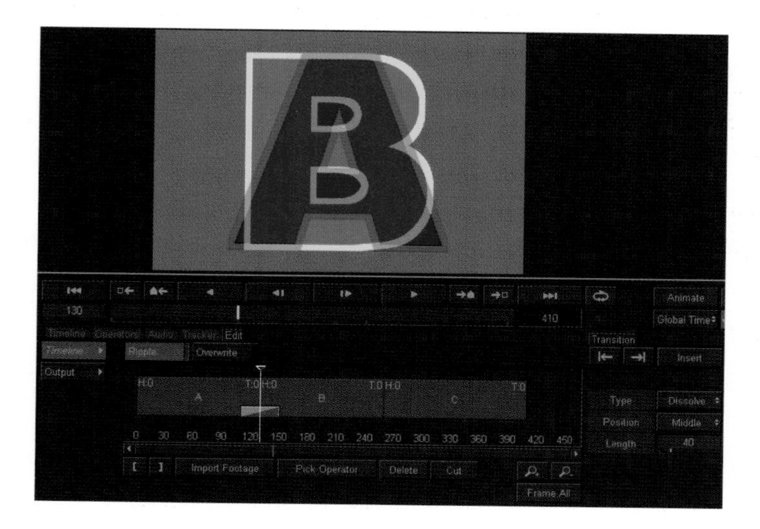

Notice that the current frame is halfway between the two segments and the viewport shows this transition in progress. You can play the series from the beginning and you will see the 40-frame dissolve take place.

7 Select this transition in the Timeline by clicking on it. It will become highlighted yellow when selected.

8 To the right of the Edit Timeline, change the transition type to Wipe (Right) and play the clip. Notice that the duration is still the same, but the effect and icon for the transition are both changed to a Dissolve.

One- and Two-Point Editing

In one-point editing, you set an in point *or* an out point and add a clip to the Timeline. This point will be used to 'forward fill' or 'back fill' the incoming segment in its entirety.

In two-point editing, you set both in *and* out points ([ ]) in the Edit Timeline. Then when you insert a new segment, it gets trimmed to accommodate these limits (set by the in/out markers).

Note: Ripple and Overwrite perform as usual with one- and two-point editing.

To perform a simple, two-point edit:

1 Revert to the project *ch11_EditingABC.cws* from the File menu.

2 Go to frame 50 and set an Edit Timeline IN point by clicking on the in point button ([) under the Timeline.

3 Go to frame 175 and set an Edit Timeline OUT point by clicking on the out point button (]).

4 Click the Import Footage button below the Edit Timeline.

5 Browse to the . . . _footage\sequences\digital juice\ directory and double click on any of the clips.

6 The clip will be inserted and the tail trimmed to accommodate the duration you dictated. Notice that the new segment has a head of zero frames.

7 Select this new segment in the Edit Timeline.

8 While holding down the Control key, click and drag on this new segment. This will 'slip' the in and out points of the segment at the same time, but will leave the overall duration of the segment the same. While dragging the cursor left and right, you will notice a representation of the entire segment's duration below the Timeline. Figure 11.16 shows this procedure at the midway point.

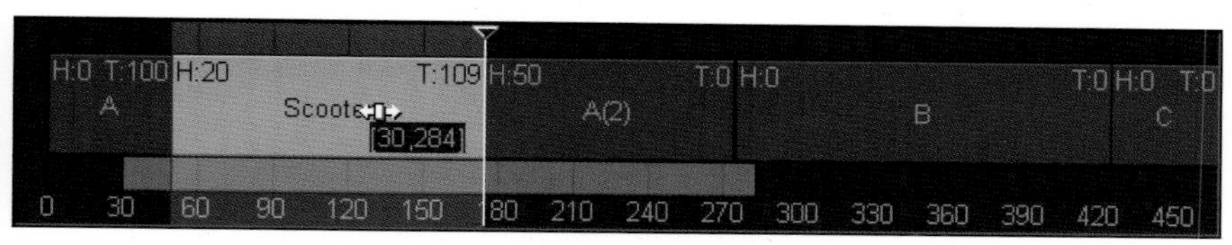

Figure 11.16

Edit Markers

When you are in either the Timeline or Output Controls of an Edit operator, you can tap the M key on the keyboard to create a marker at the current frame. These markers are identical in function and features to the layer markers detailed in Chapter 10. Like the layer markers, these are provided in the Edit operator's Timeline for your convenience and notation of any point in time. Figure 11.17 shows the Edit operator markers.

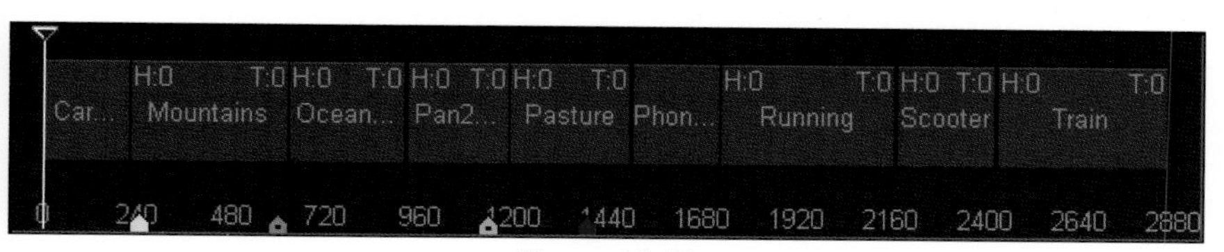

Figure 11.17

Remember that you can edit the markers by right clicking on them. Also, the Playback Controls have quick buttons to jump through your markers.

Split Layer

This feature is actually a function in the Composite operator, but it is detailed here because of the editing capabilities of this new feature to combustion 3.

This performs several tasks at once. It duplicates the layer and all the keyframes, operators, etc. and also takes the out point of one of the created layers to the in point of the other layer.

To split a layer, you do not even need to be in the Timeline. You simply select a layer, go to the frame where you wish to split the layer, right click on the layer name and select Split Layer. The Timeline does, however, show the effects of the Split Layer function quite well, as can be seen here.

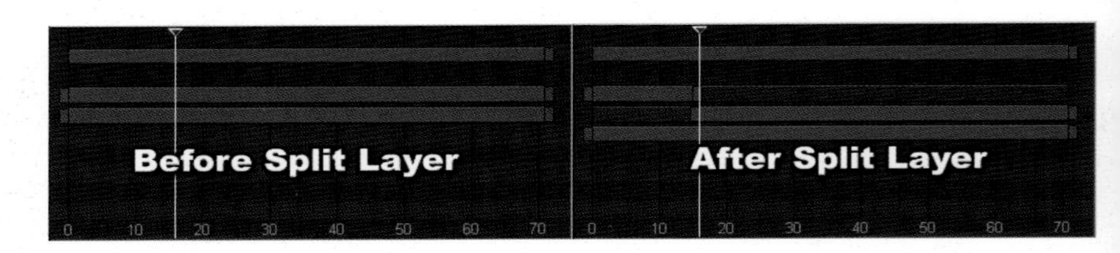

There are many reasons why you might want to split a layer. One example is if you want a new operator to seemingly affect a layer midway through an animation. Instead of animating the operator or setting in and out points for it, you can easily split a layer and add an operator to the second, resulting layer. Playing back this sequence will result in the two layers playing back end to end, but the new operator (a blur, for example) will only affect the second of the split layers.

The project named *ch11_Editing.cws* is provided as a starting point for experimentation with the Edit operator. This project is over 2000 frames long and should allow for numerous experiments. You can alternatively start a new Edit project by opening several clips with the Thumbnail Browser directly into an Edit operator. The order that the footage clips are selected in the Thumbnail Browser will be the starting segment order in the resulting Edit operator. Lastly, keep in mind that the Edit operator is just another operator. You can take the output of an Edit operator and make it the input to other operators, composites, or even other Edit operators.

CHAPTER 12
EXPRESSIONS

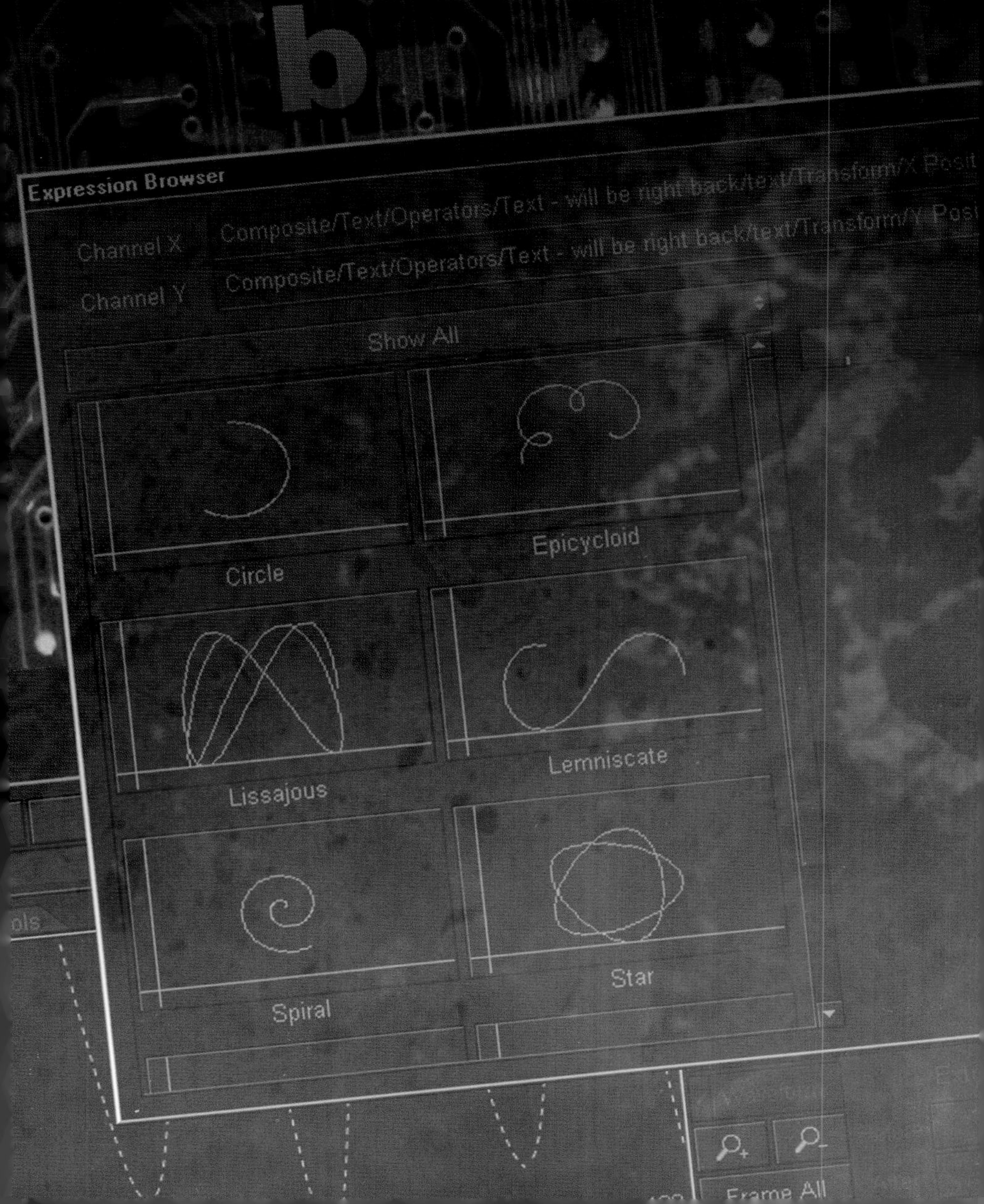

Expressions in combustion are a means of introducing an embedded programming environment into the application. The sound of this (argh, math!) sometimes turns people (artists) off and yet it excites others (coders). Working with expressions can be taken as deep as you want to go, yet they should not intimidate you because of their programming nature. With a few simple tips as background, you can be well on your way to customizing animation controls to your specific needs.

The good news about this whole inclusion of the JavaScript programming language is that there are two means of creating expressions that allow non-programmers access to its power right away. The first is the **Quick Pick** feature and the second is the **Expressions Browser**. Using either of these tools allows anyone to either wire parameters together (i.e. this controls that) or see visual representations of the expressions.

The programming language that Discreet has chosen to incorporate expressions in combustion is JavaScript. This is a programming environment with deep roots in the Internet, but it can also be used for mathematical formulation to drive parameters and variables in software applications like Discreet combustion. This chapter will introduce you to the basics of programming expressions with JavaScript, but I encourage you to pick up JavaScript resources if this is an area that interests you further.

Quick Pick

To see how you can create a simple expression, we will look at the Quick Pick feature introduced in combustion 3. The easiest way to describe how the Quick Pick works is to think 'this controls that'. That is a pretty vague way to put it, but you can also see the power of how easily you can create complex animations.

1. Begin by opening the Workspace named *ch12_QuickPick.cws*. This Workspace contains two layers. The top layer has text with animated tracking values from 199 down to zero. The tracking values can be found in the Paint Controls > Text > Basics section. Cache the clip to see the project and the effect of the animated tracking value.

2 Expand the Workspace panel as seen in Figure 12.1 to reveal the contents of the layer named *Paint – Text.*

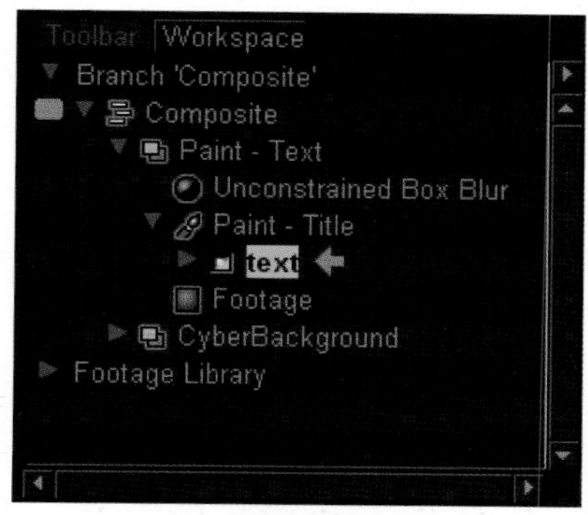

Figure 12.1

Notice that there is an Unconstrained Box Blur operator applied to the Paint Text layer. Select this operator by clicking on its name in the Workspace panel. This will activate the controls for this operator.

3 Scrub the Vertical Radius slider back and forth to see the effects of this operator. When you are finished, reset the value to zero.

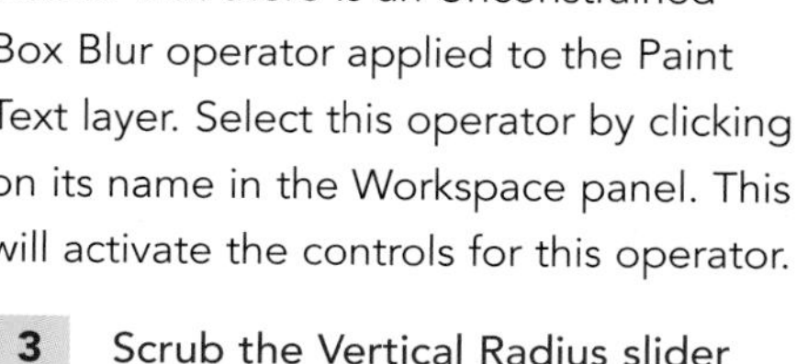

4 With this operator still selected, switch to the Timeline and select the channel named Vertical Radius.

Note: Make sure you have the 'Show Only Animated Channels' option of the Timeline disabled, or you will not see the two empty channels related to the operator controls.

5 To the right of the Timeline, enable the Quick Pick button detailed in Figure 12.2. It is active when it is green.

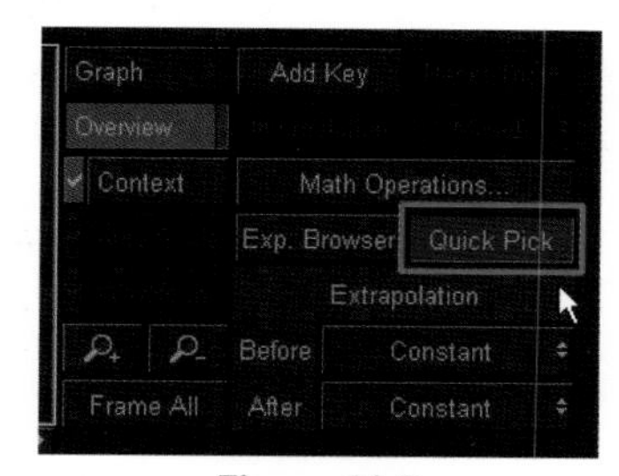

Figure 12.2

While the Quick Pick button is green, combustion is basically waiting for you to pick another animation channel to tie the Vertical

Radius to. You can think of this as a slave to the value you are about to pick, in this case the animated text tracking value.

6 Switch the Timeline to Overview mode if it is in Graph mode.

7 Click once on the small up arrow indicated in Figure 12.3. This will take you up a level from just seeing the channels for the blur operator. Then scroll down, expand the text entry and then expand the 'Basics' entry until you see the animated tracking channel and its keyframes indicated in the Timeline.

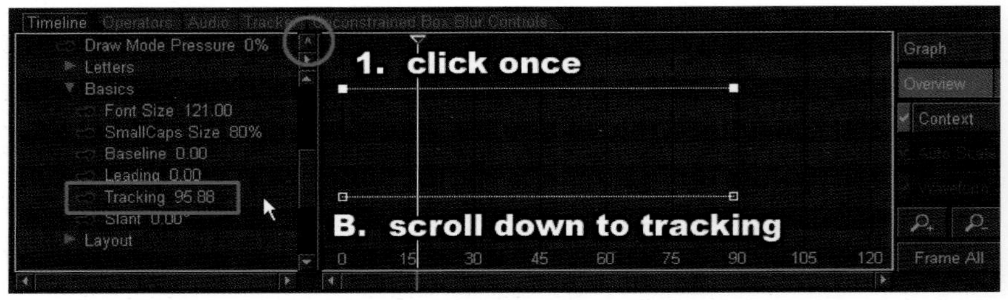

Figure 12.3

8 Click once on the name of the channel called *Tracking*. The Quick Pick is now complete, the button returns to gray and the two channels have been linked. Look at that – you just wrote some pretty nifty JavaScript expression code without knowing it! Cache the clip and notice that the vertical blur is now tied to the animated tracking value. At this point, if you edit the tracking keyframes or their Bezier interpolation (Graph mode), you will see the blur respect this change and follow along blindly. Keep this project open to continue the next lesson.

9 Scroll the Timeline back up until you see the animation channel named Vertical Radius (for the Unconstrained Box Blur operator). You will notice that there is an expression where keyframes typically reside in the Timeline.

> **Note:** This is a one-way connection using this technique. The tracking value is 'unaware' that the Blur operator is tied to it.

Editing an Expression

Ok, so now you are a JavaScript expression-programming fiend. Let's go edit some code!

1 In the Timeline, you can scroll back up to see the Vertical Radius of the Blur operator. Notice the small icon 'E' indicated in Figure 12.4. This means that this channel is being driven by a JavaScript expression.

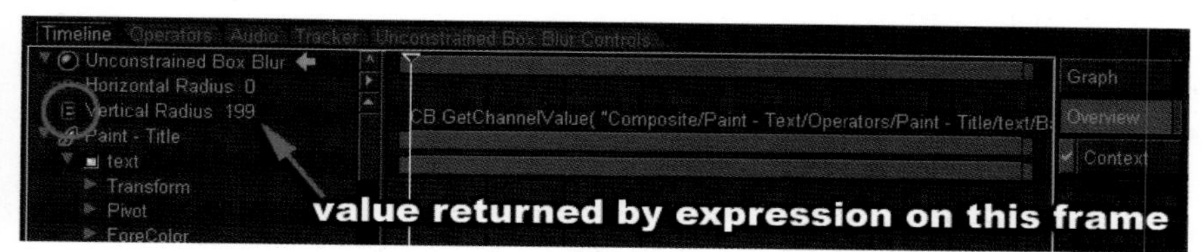

Figure 12.4

2 Right click on this channel to bring up the dialog in Figure 12.5. Here, you are presented several options for editing, copying, deleting and so forth. Select Edit Expression for now.

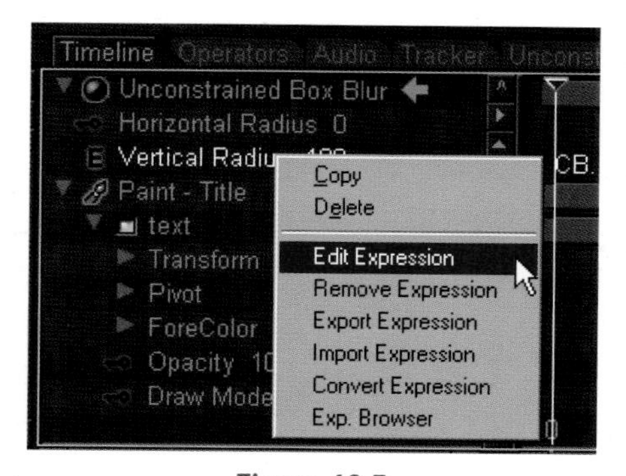

Figure 12.5

> **Note:** This menu allows access to export and import expressions as *.CJS files. These allow you to build libraries and share expressions with other users.

3 The code for the expression will be highlighted and there will be a small button available named 'Multi'. Click this button.

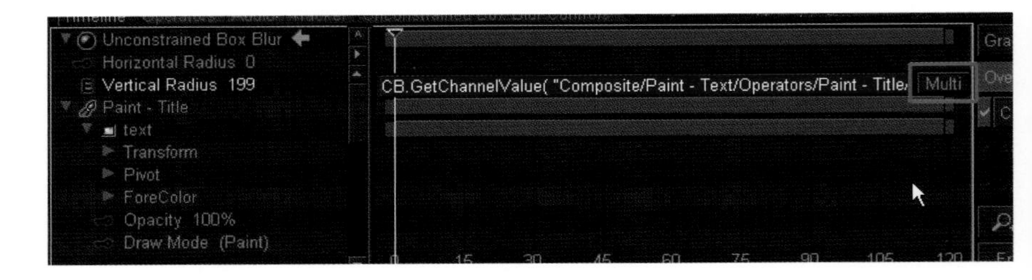

> **Warning:** You will go into a larger editing window but the entire contents of all the characters making up the expression are selected. If you begin typing, you will lose the existing expression. To deselect, click in a blank area of the expression edit window.

This is where a lot of the reverse engineering of the JavaScript language can be done in combustion. Again, the use of expressions is an extremely powerful new feature that can be explored in great depth outside of the scope of this book.

4 For a simple edit, at the very end of the expression is the text

```
CB.GetCurrentFrame() );
```

Change this to:

```
CB.GetCurrentFrame() )/2;
```

> **Note:** To accept the change of code, you can click elsewhere in the UI of combustion. The expression edit window has no 'OK' button and you should therefore be careful not to hit the return key on your keyboard (unless you want to add that to the expression).

This simple addition of '/2' at the end of the line will halve the value of the previous expression. This means that the vertical blur amount will be half of the animated tracking value of the text driving it. Using this simple methodology, you can easily achieve things such as Layer01 controls rotation. Layer02 rotates 9/10ths as much; Layer03 rotates 8/10ths as much, and so on.

Expression Browser

The second automated means of accessing the expression controls in combustion is by utilizing the Expression Browser. Like the Quick Pick, this feature can be easily used by anyone to generate JavaScript code that can be reverse-engineered, examined, and edited by the user. This workflow is an excellent way to become familiar with the power that lies in the use of expressions.

The Expression Browser is a dialog of presets with adjustable variables that you, the user, input to control the resulting animation keyframes of an element in the Workspace.

Camera Shake – The following exercise introduces the Expression Browser for a simple camera shake effect.

1. Load the Workspace named *ch12_Camera Shake.cws*. This is a simple 3D composite with a still image as a layer. This layer is 800 × 600 so its edges are slightly outside the visible viewport.
2. In the Workspace panel, select the camera.
3. Bring up the Timeline controls by hitting F4.
4. Navigate to and expand the Transformation category for the camera.
5. The first transformation is named *X Position*. Click and drag the mouse up and down directly on the name of the channel. You will notice that the layer seems to move in the viewport. What is actually occurring is that you are slipping the camera laterally back and forth so that the edges of the layer can be seen, as in Figure 12.6.

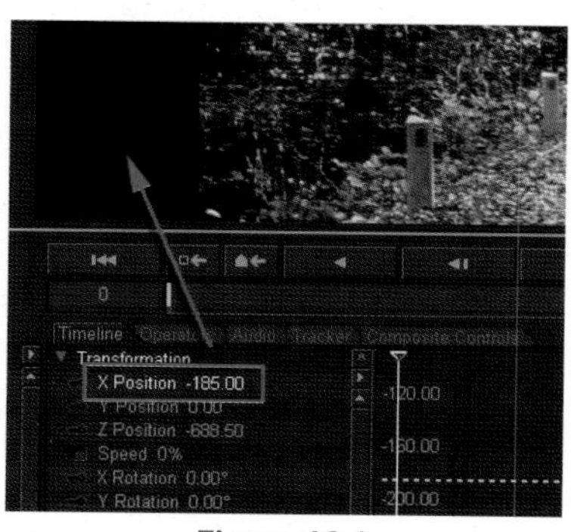

Figure 12.6

If you slowly scrub the value back and forth, you will see that at values around −70 to +70, the layer is visible without a transparent edge. Make a mental note of this.

6 Undo any position changes or manually return the camera to the zero X position. Also, verify you have only the X Position channel of the camera selected in the Timeline before continuing.

7 To the right of the animation channels, there is a button (Figure 12.7) for evoking the Expression Browser. Click it.

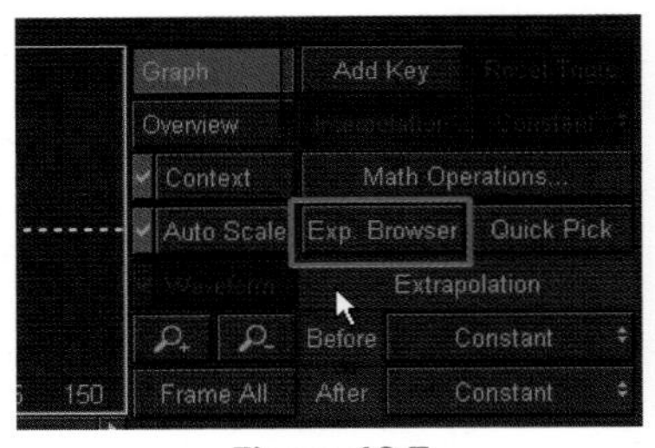

Figure 12.7

8 You will be presented with the menu seen in Figure 12.8. Click on the Picon named *Random*. To the right, you will notice there is a Picon Frame Range indicator slider that can be used to see how the different expressions look over time with the current values.

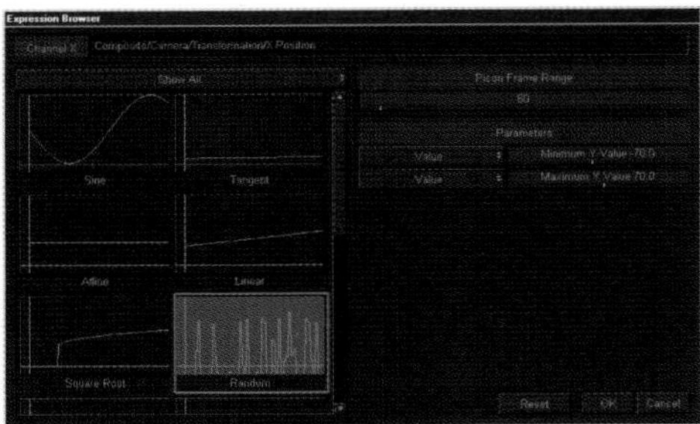

Figure 12.8

The Expression Browser is where you can generate many starting point values for your JavaScript controls in combustion, and you can edit them after they are applied. If you do not like the results of a particular setting, you can also come right back into this dialog and edit the values accordingly. This becomes a lot of trial and error at first, but it is a very fun way to spend your time when on hold with an insurance or credit card company.

9 Change the minimum and maximum values to −70 and 70 respectively. This represents the range we determined that would keep the layer in frame. Click OK when you have set these values.

10 Cache the clip and you will notice sporadic horizontal movement of the camera in the viewport. While the camera does, indeed, jump about randomly on its horizontal axis, the image stays in frame because of the range we provided with the expression controls.

11 Using these same techniques, make a camera shake for Y position information and use a *Random Growing* expression as a starting point. You will have to begin by selecting the camera's Y Position channel in the Timeline and then activate the Expression Browser again. For this example, you can use the default values of the *Random Growing* preset.

> **Tip:** To apply a motion blur to this camera shake effect, select the composite itself and apply a Blur/Sharpen > Motion Blur operator. You will have to double click this applied operator to view it in the active viewport. When you cache the clip, the effects of the motion blur will be visible. At that point, you can experiment with motion blur settings should you so desire.

Two-Point Expressions

In the previous example, the Expression Browser was used to create animation on one channel and therefore singular expression presets were made available. If you have more than one animation channel selected in the Timeline when you enable the Expression Browser, different options will be made available.

1 Open the file named *ch12_Spiral.cws* and select the layer.

2 Expand the Timeline (F4) and select both the X and Y Position channels under the Transformation category for the soccer ball layer.

> **Tip:** As in the Workspace panel, you can hold down the Control key to select multiple items in the Timeline.

3 Open the Expression Browser. Notice in Figure 12.9 that there are new expression presets available. This is because you are creating an expression for two values in the Timeline. Choose Spiral and, with default values, click OK to accept.

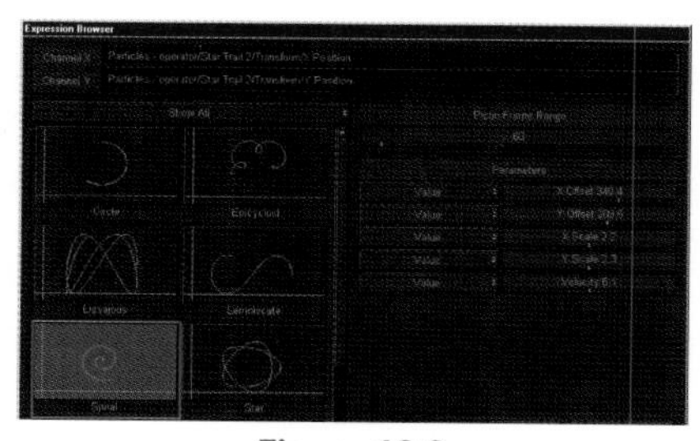

Figure 12.9

4 Play the animation. Notice that the expression forces the soccer ball to start nearly off frame and loop back into frame. This starting point was set by the expression *offset* values.

5 Instead of redoing the expression over again, try changing these offset values with the editor. Simply select the X Position channel and right click to access the edit expression flyout.

6 Notice that the expression is largely in plain English. Even if you do not know a great deal about expressions or JavaScript programming, the resulting expressions created by the Expression Browser are very easy to edit and manipulate because of this. Change both the XOffset and YOffset values to 0.0.

7 Repeat this editing for the Y Position channels. Since you created expressions for both X and Y positions of the layer, two expressions must be edited. The resulting clip is a soccer ball starting in the center of frame and spiraling outward as time progresses.

8 Leave this project open for the next lesson.

Converting Expressions to Keyframes

At the end of the previous exercise, you may have noticed that the animation of the soccer ball is centered and moving out of frame in a growing spiral. Let us assume that we want to edit this animation as actual keyframes.

1 In the active viewport, select the layer and attempt to move it. You will not be able to move the layer by clicking and dragging on it as is the norm. This is due to the expression having total control of the position in X and Y. You can still rotate, for example, but the X and Y positions have been tied to your JavaScript code.

2 In the Timeline, select just the X position and switch to Graph mode. You will see a dotted line that represents the resulting animation curve; however, notice in Figure 12.10 that there are no keyframes. This is a virtual curve like the extrapolation curves seen in Chapter 10.

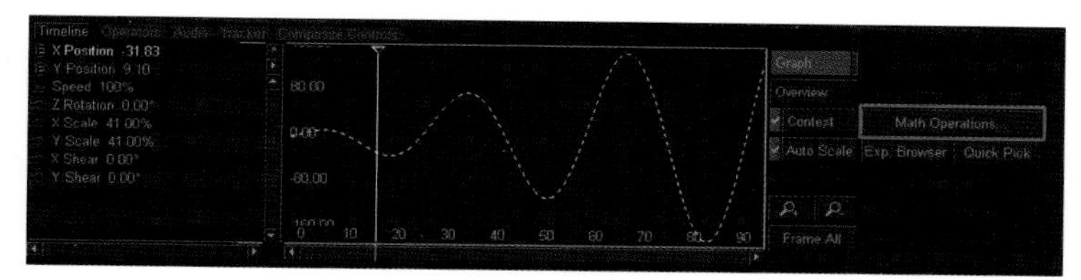

Figure 12.10

3 To convert this curve to actual, editable keyframes, you can right click on the channel name or select Math Operations as indicated in Figure 12.11. This will bring up a dialog with options for the conversion accuracy. Lower values will result in a curve that closely resembles the virtual curves generated by the expression.

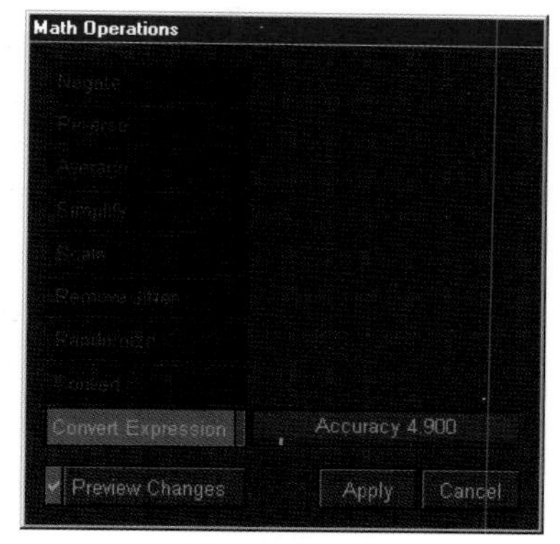

Figure 12.11

4 After you click Apply, the keyframes for the X position will be made actual keyframes that you are free to edit normally.

Note: The Y Position channel is still being driven by an expression at this point. It did not get converted because this is an independent animation channel. In Figure 12.12, both channels have been selected and you can see that one is still being driven by the expression controls. You can also see that there have been manual edits in the keyframed channel.

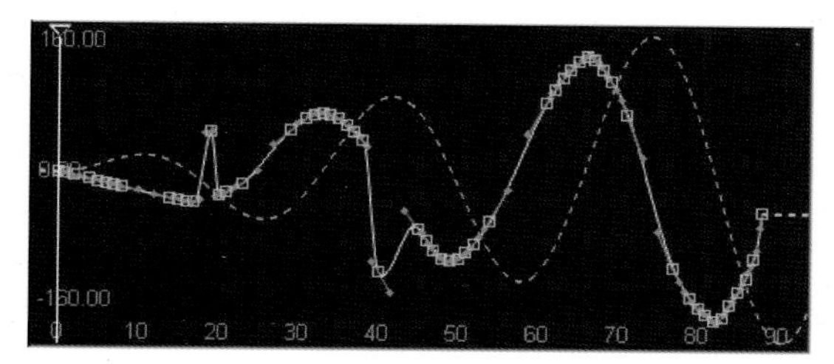

Figure 12.12

Ideas for Further Exploration

Set up an empty composite with several null objects. These can be renamed quickly and made into slider controls for things like puppeteering lights. Use the X position of a null to control one value and the Y position to control another. This can be like having a virtual joystick. You can also have these 'sliders' in one viewport and the elements that they control in another viewport.

In a 3D composite, have several layers all with a Blur operator applied to each of them individually. The further they recede in Z space, the more blurred they should become. This is a way to emulate and automate a depth of field effect on 2D elements.

It should now be evident that, with just a few mouse clicks, you can have ties between nearly any parameter using combustion's JavaScript expressions.

CHAPTER 13

INTEGRATED PARTICLE SYSTEM

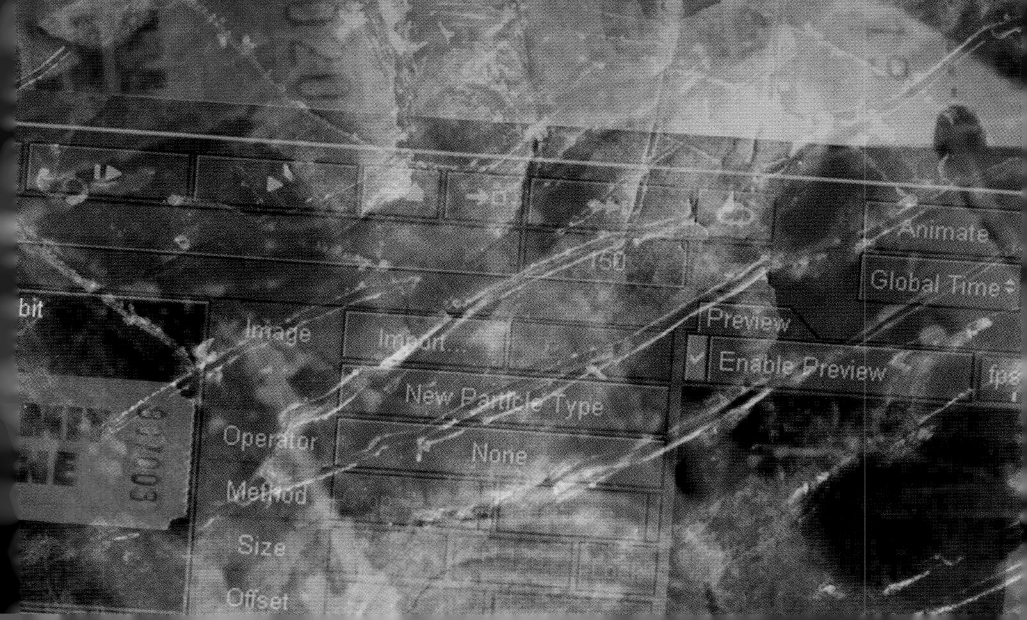

When combustion reached version 2, a very robust particle system was integrated into the application as an operator. This particle operator is, however, different from all the other operators in one unique way – it uses the OpenGL programming language to create all the particle effects created within the operator. OpenGL is a programming language or application-programming interface (API) originally developed back in 1992 for simulations and real-time graphics applications.

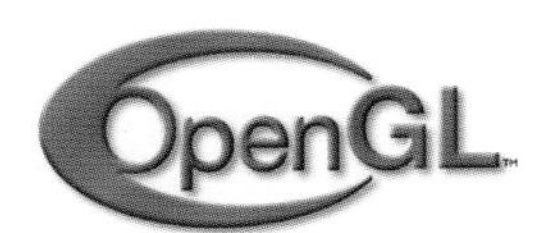

At its core, OpenGL allows software programmers to write code that can utilize special graphics hardware (read: graphics cards). This hardware allows images to be very quickly drawn to the computer screen without first being calculated/rendered on the host computer's main processor.

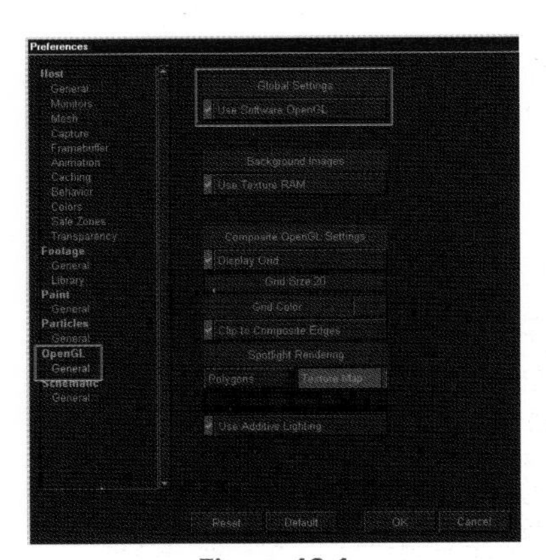

Figure 13.1

In the user preferences of combustion there is a section specifically for OpenGL. Figure 13.1 highlights the primary concern for these options, which is the choice of whether or not to use software OpenGL. Since there are so many different graphics cards on the market, different settings will invariably produce different results. It is well worth the time to test these settings on a saved particle project to see the difference in performance on your particular computer hardware.

To put it simply, you will only want to enable this option for using software OpenGL on computer systems exhibiting problems or poor playback of particles. Enabling this option (as seen here) will bypass the hardware on the graphics card and, instead, draw the particles using the computer's CPU. This is often more reliable, but can be much slower. On my beat-up, two-year-old laptop, particles actually run much faster with this option enabled. On my newer workstations, it would be a mistake to enable this option because of the powerful graphics cards in these systems. I can, however, still achieve real-time playback on a slower system via RAM caching.

Like any other operator, the particle system in combustion can be applied to images off the hard drive, to a solid (usually transparent), to a composite, or added into a series of operators in a long branch. Like a Paint operator, particles only work in 2D space, but they can be applied to a layer that can, in turn, be transformed within a 3D composite.

Another similarity to Paint is the fact that you may have a lot going on within the operator, but the Schematic View only shows the operator itself. The Workspace panel is, therefore, where you will do most of the selections, renaming, and so on when working in a Particle operator.

Components of the Particle Operator

Underlying all the wonderful pixie dust, smoke, water and fire is a single particle engine that is easy to understand and control once you break it down into its primary components. Within this operator are three types of elements. At the most basic level, you have emitters, particles, and deflectors.

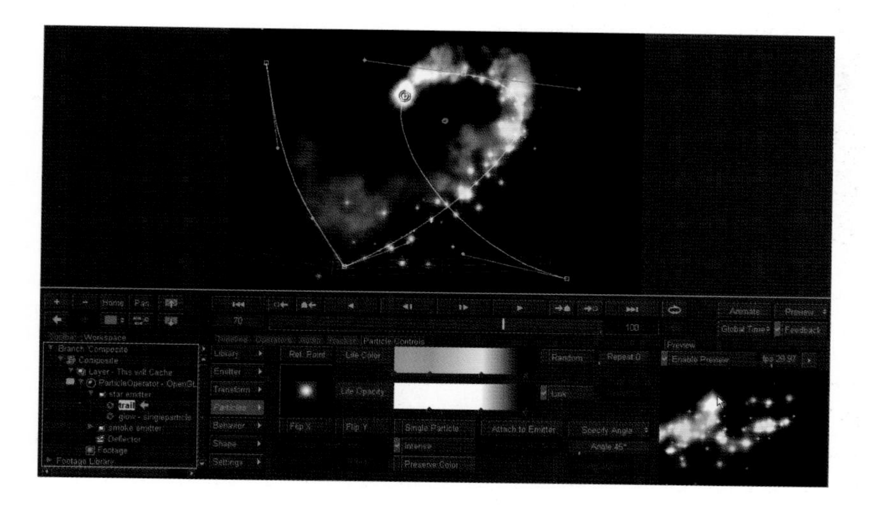

Emitters – These are non-rendering elements from which the actual particles spawn. The emitter objects are what you can manually position and keyframe in the viewports with precision. One emitter can have several different types of particle types coming out of it. For example, sparks and smoke can come out of the same emitter. There are four types of emitters. You can use several different types all within the same particle operator and Workspace.

Point Emitter ( )	This is a single source of particles. Point emitters have position, direction and angle of emission but are merely a single point in space (that can be tracked or animated).
Line Emitter ( )	The name can be slightly misleading, for these can be irregularly shaped and can have Bezier handles to create any shape of the emission. Only a line emitter allows you to edit control points of the emitter shape; therefore, it can be considered the most versatile choice of the four.
Circle Emitter ( )	This creates a hollow ring of particles. This emitter type does not have to be a perfect circle; it can be elliptical as well. Since you cannot add or edit control points to these, you may optionally want to use an irregularly shaped line emitter instead.
Area Emitter ( )	This type is useful if you need to create a solid region of particles, such as a wall of smoke or fire. Unlike a circle emitter, which is hollow, this emitter fills a rectangular boundary with particles.

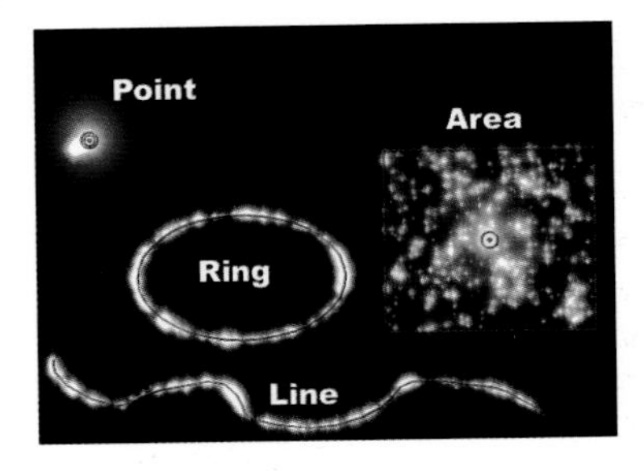

Particles – I like to refer to these as 'spriticles', because of their 2D 'sprite' method of simulating complex shapes and patterns. These are typically bitmap images or even other branches in the Workspace. All the particles in combustion are really just different images mapped onto rectangular shapes (similar to many little layers in a 2D composite). These images, in combination with the characteristics of these rectangles, determine whether the particles look like smoke, disco lights, butterflies, or anything else you dream up.

Deflectors ( ) – Deflectors are used when you want to create particles that appear to bounce off of something and are redirected. Like emitters, they are non-rendering entities that you can keyframe to create different effects. Deflectors will only affect the particles within the same operator and the different particle Bounce settings determine how different particles will be deflected.

The Preview Window

The particle Preview window visible to the right of the particle categories is for testing different particle settings. Depending on the circumstances, this can often be used for much faster viewing than playing back particles in the actual viewports. This window uses the preferences setting for OpenGL and reflects how the particles will render. With a particle selected in either a library or within the Workspace panel, you can drag the cursor around within this window to see their behaviors and appearances. Consider this your particle testing ground.

The button above the window labeled 'Enable Preview' turns this area on and off. You can disable this small OpenGL window to give more processing horsepower to your primary viewports at the top of the UI.

Figure 13.2 shows a flyout button for accessing several options to this Preview window, which are outlined below.

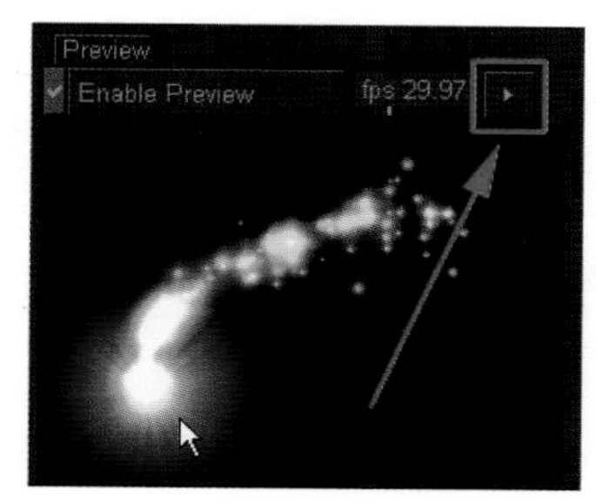

Figure 13.2

Collide with Edges	When enabled, the sides of the Preview window act as deflectors for testing purposes.
Show Motion Blur	When enabled, particles in the Preview window are drawn with the motion blur options in the (last) Settings category of the Particle operator. This option is just for the Preview window and can really slow things down. Use only as needed.
Zoom	This allows you to see what different particles would look like if they were zoomed up or down. Quite often, you can achieve larger particles with an increase in zoom instead of size, and get the same basic results, but much better performance. It is very useful to check this out, but I highly recommend always putting this value back to 100% before you move on.
Repeat	This controls a delay (in seconds) between repetitions of a particle that cycle. To see this delay, try selecting the preset named Simple Explosion from the default particle library.
Color	This allows you to change the Preview window background color. Quite often, particles may look amazing in the Preview window over one color, but when you apply them in the viewport over another color, they appear drastically different (or don't appear at all!). This is to test over black, gray, and white backgrounds.

Show Particle Types	I highly recommend leaving this on at all times. When enabled, it allows you to select a particle *emitter* and see all the various particles coming out of it. However, if you select just one of the particle types coming out of that emitter, only that particle type will be previewed and the rest ignored (but not turned off in the Workspace). This is extremely useful when you have several different particles coming out of the same emitter and you need to fine-tune them.

Note: If the Preview window ever has a red line around it, this means that changes have been made to a particle type that have not been saved to a library.

Categories of the Particle Operator

Library

These are the presets you can use as starting points for nearly any particle situation you will need. Discreet combustion ships with several *.ELC libraries and each contains dozens of particles presets. There is also a special, empty library simple named 'Blank' for a *totally* clean slate – should you want to start from scratch.

You can load either *.ELC or *.IEL library files. IEL files are Illusion Emitter Libraries from the third-party application named Particle Illusion. Upon loading an IEL, it gets converted internally to combustion's native ELC format. In addition, you can only save *.ELC files out of the Particle operator. You can also download additional emitter library files from www.wondertouch.com. These files must, however, be Illusion v.2.0 or prior to load into Discreet combustion.

Add to Current Library	Takes the settings of the selected emitter and adds them as a preset to the current library folder.
Replace from Library	Brings up a dialog for replacing some or all of the characteristics of the selected emitter from a library preset.
Update Emitter	This saves the current emitter settings if they have changed and you wish to save these changes in the library.
Duplicate Emitter	Creates a copy of the current particle emitter and copies all of its settings; you can then edit this and save the settings.
Delete	Deletes the selected preset from the library.
New Folder	Creates a new folder in the current library. This is for organizing your particle presets.

Emitter

All of these settings can be thought of as global 'multiplier' settings for all particles coming out of the selected emitter. You can have several different particles coming out of the same emitter, yet changes made here will affect them all. The Emitter category is the place where you can make the most dramatic changes to an emitter's global particle settings. To work in the Emitter category, you can have an emitter or a particle type selected in the Workspace panel.

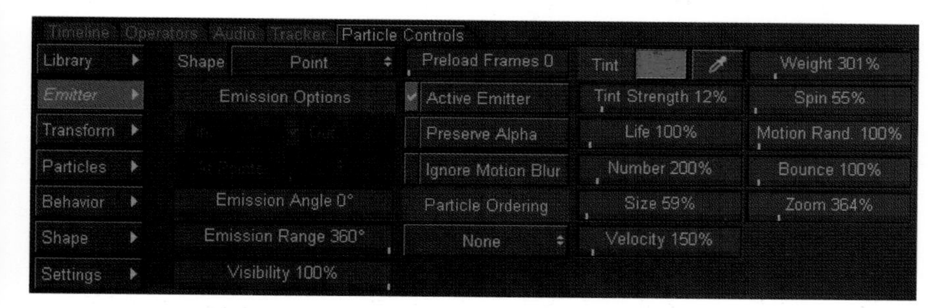

Emission Options:

In/Out	These options control from which side of a line or circle emitter particles will originate.
At Points	When disabled, the entire emitter shape will spawn particles, when enabled, so you can control the spacing of particle emission along any emitter shape. This is disabled for point emitters.
Angle	This controls the angle of emission the particles leave an emitter. 0 degrees points right, 90 degrees is up, 180 is left and 360 is back to the right. You can go past 360 here to loop.
Range	This is primarily for Point emitters. A value of 360 means particles spawn in all directions; values less than this will have direction when they leave the emitter.
Visibility	This is detailed in the 'Scaling Factors' section below.

Miscellaneous Emitter Values:

Preload Frames	This causes an emitter to begin 'already on' by a certain number of frames when it is first seen.
Active Emitter	This is an on/off switch for an emitter. You can also turn an emitter on and off in the Workspace panel by toggling the icon to the left of its name.
Preserve Alpha	This option forces particles to use the alpha channel of elements behind them.

Ignore Motion Blur	When enabled, the selected emitter will not calculate particle motion blur set in the Settings category of this Particle operator.
Particle Ordering	Oldest in Back simulates particles coming at the viewer and Oldest in Front simulates particles going away. If you do not need to use this, leave it to None as this calculation adds processing time.

Tint

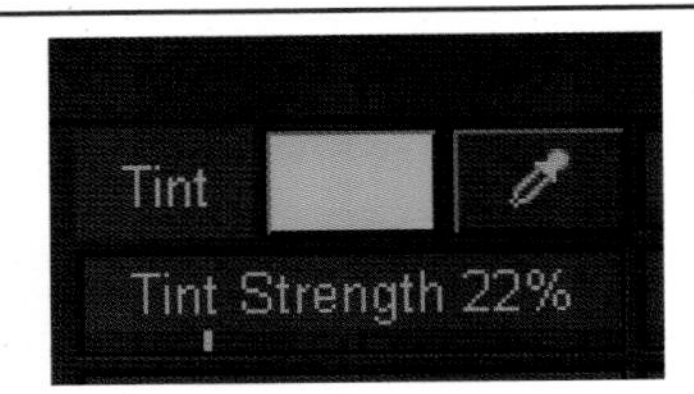

The color swatch and picker seen here provide a basic/quick way to color correct all the particles coming out of the selected emitter.

Scaling Factors	There are several parameters in the Emitter category of a Particle operator that are percentage multipliers that affect *all* the particles coming out of the selected emitter.
Life	This is actually not a frame count, but a generic unit of time. Higher numbers mean longer lives for particles.
Number	This controls the quantity of the particles.
Size	This is not a measurement in pixels, but a generic unit of size. Larger values equate to bigger particles.
Velocity	This controls the speed at which the particles move away from their emitter.
Weight	These values can be positive or negative. A weight of zero defines a particle with no gravity factor. A positive weight falls and a negative weight rises.
Spin	This controls the rotation of the particles. These values can be positive or negative. A positive value is a clockwise rotation and negative values result in counterclockwise rotations.
Motion Random	Increasing this value causes a natural, organic motion that can slightly override velocity and weight values.
Bounce	This controls how a particle reacts when it hits a deflector object. If a particle has a bounce value of 0, it may pass through a deflector.
Visibility	This controls the percentage of opacity. 0 is invisible and 100 is completely opaque.
Zoom	This last Emitter variable scales both velocity and size settings for all the particles spawning from the selected particle emitter. Animating this value is the easiest way to make particles appear to have perspective due to simulated 3D space.

Transform

This is where you can manually transform the invisible emitter object (but not the particles themselves). Depending on the type of emitter selected, different transformations will be available or disabled. When you have more than one emitter within a single particle operator, it can often be easier to move selected emitters using these controls instead of directly in the viewport.

The next three categories (Particles/Behavior/Shape) are where you edit and fine-tune the appearance and behavior of the actual particles themselves. To access any of these three categories, you must have a particle type (not the emitter or the operator) selected in the Workspace panel. Remember that there are particles coming out of emitters that are within an operator. Each of these entities can all be accessed, renamed and selected via the Workspace panel. If you have an emitter or operator selected, these will be grayed out and unavailable for editing.

Particles

The primary controls here are the Life Color and Life Opacity. These largely set the color and transparency value of each individual particle. Figure 13.3 shows the Particle settings for the particles named 'glow' in the file *ch13_Bridge.cws*.

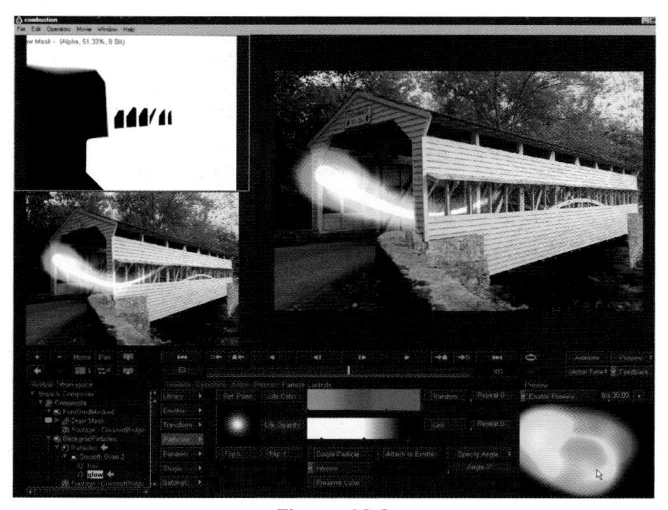

Figure 13.3

Random Start Frame	If a particle sprite image has more than one frame, this will cause it to play back in a random manner instead of sequentially every time. This allows for more natural effects with a sporadic appearance. This will not be available if the particle shape is a single frame.
Life Color	Often, it is actually better to use grayscale particles and let this gradient editor control the color of the particles over their life. This will provide more options for coloration of the different, individual particles coming out of an emitter. On the left is the color of a particle at birth and to the right is the color at the time of its death. The Repeat variable controls how many times a particle will cycle through this gradient over its life. The Random toggle causes the particles to disregard age and instead pick a color at random from this gradient. This is good for sparkle effects.
Life Opacity	Again, birth of particles is on the left and death on the right. The Link option causes the opacity to be obtained from the luminance (grayscale) version of the Life Color gradient above instead of from this gradient editor. Lighter Life Opacity values result in more opaque particles.
Single Particle	This makes the selected particle type one particle that is in the center of the emitter. Instead of many particles coming out of an emitter, only a single particle will be created of this type. This is often used for things like a torch glow that follows the emitter while other particles represent smoke and fire coming out of the same emitter.
Intense and Preserve Color	Intense will make particles brighter by using an Additive Transfer mode. Preserve Color is only available when Intense is enabled and is an option for blending the particles with transparency. When a particle does not appear in the viewport because of the background image 'fighting' the appearance of a particle, these can be used to attempt to make a particle stay visible over different colors.
Attach to Emitter	When enabled, the particles move with the emitter in a user-defined percentage (typically 100%). This option is often used to affect the trails of a moving particle emitter, or on panning footage with a particle operator applied. This is OFF by default.
Particle Angle	The specified angle makes all particles have the same starting angle. Random Angle is for organic effects and Align to Motion forces the particles to spawn at an angle based on the emitter animation.

Behavior

You do not have individual controls over every single particle, but here you can control mannerisms of each particle *type* coming out of an emitter. This simple UI can be broken into three areas, as noted in Figure 13.4.

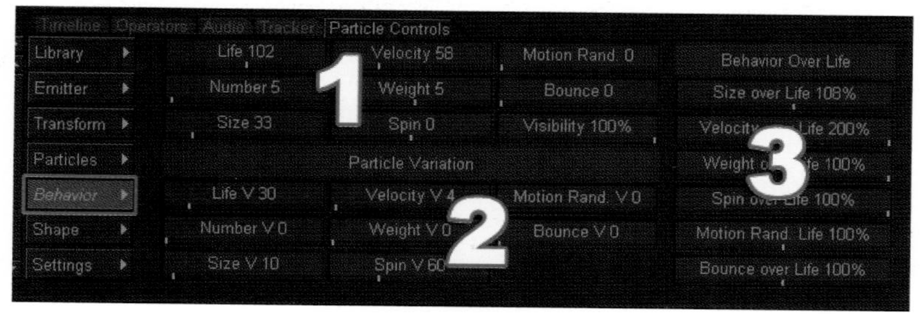

Figure 13.4

1 **Default Behavior** – The top nine fields set the default parameters for the selected particle type. These nine settings have the same characteristics as those previously described in the Emitter settings, but here the controls are local to the selected particle type. You may have several particle types coming off one emitter, and this allows you to control them each independently of one another.

2 **Particle Variation** – You will notice the bottom nine fields have the same labels as those in Area 1. This is because these represent the variation (+/−) of the values above. For example, if you set the default size in Area 1 to be 10 and the variation for size in Area 2 is set to 5, the resulting particles will range in size from 5 to 15.

> **Tip:** If you want particles to rotate clockwise *and* counterclockwise, the Default Spin value should be 0 and the variation for Spin is the value to edit. Again, particle variation is a +/− amount.

3 **Behavior Over Life** – These six fields are presented here but are actually best edited in the Timeline (Graph mode). These six values are the only case in combustion where the horizontal scale of the Timeline does not represent frames or time code. Figure 13.5 shows this special case in combustion.

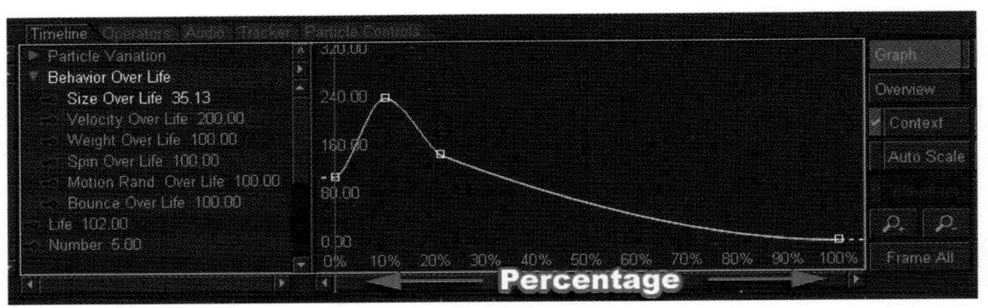

Figure 13.5

In this example, the particle begins its life with a size of approximately 100 and then quickly ramps up in size to 240 after only 10% of its life, then quickly goes down to size 150 at 20% life, and then slowly reduces size to 0 by the time the particle dies. You can see here why editing the six Over Life values is best done in the Timeline.

Regardless of the life value (resulting from the combination of Emitter/Behavior settings), these percentages still represent the entire life of a particle, whether the life is 13, 194, or 1847 . . ., for example.

Remember, the Emitter category of a Particle operator acts like a global multiplier. If you set particle life to 500 in the Behavior (fifth) category but set Emitter life to 25%, then the resulting lifespan is 125.

Shape

This is where you can set what a particle sprite looks like. There are several different types of presets. You can also assign a particle sprite to be an operator elsewhere in your current Workspace or even an image off the hard drive. Again, it is often advantageous to use grayscale images and let the Particle Life color gradient control the hue of particles.

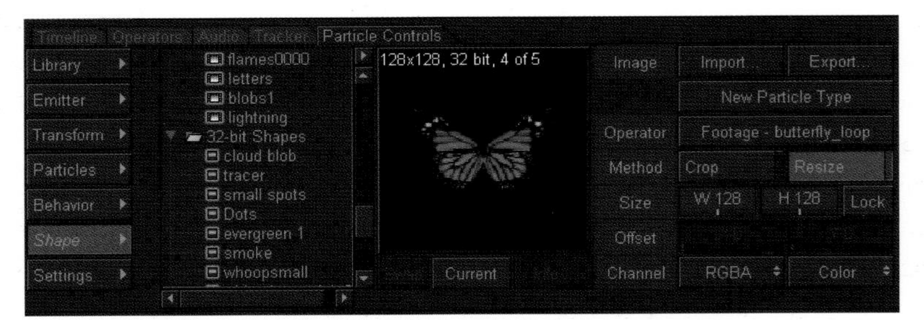

> **Tip:** Because of the nature of the OpenGL programming, it is useful to use particles whose pixel dimensions are 16, 32, 64, 128, 256 or 512 – for example, an image that is 32 × 32 in size. Remember, this is only the size of a *single* particle. The smaller the particle, the faster your system will run. You can use other particle sizes, but combustion will have to resize them to the closest value mentioned here to comply with OpenGL.

Swap	To change the appearance of a selected particle, you can simply pick a new preset sprite image from the list and click the Swap button.
Current	Put the sprite image of the current selected particle in the Shape preview window. This allows you to analyze the sprite in detail.
Info . . .	Provides information as to how and in which emitter a sprite from the shape library is used in the library emitters. It also lists info such as image size and duration.
Import/Export	Brings an image into or out of the particle operator as a sprite image in common formats such as TIF, TGA and JPG.
New Particle Type	Duplicates the selected particle in the Workspace. This new particle will be spawning from the same emitter and have the same starting characteristics as the original. These values can then be edited.
Operator	Allows you to get a sprite from any node in the current Workspace instead of off the hard drive. Useful if you want to create a sprite in a Paint operator, for example.

Settings

Here, you can control particle motion blur settings local to this operator. You can enable motion blur for each Particle operator if you wish to blur particles without blurring the image that the operator is applied to. You can also optionally load a background image into the operator using controls found here. A background image can be useful, for example, if your Particle operator is applied to a transparent solid but you need to keyframe an emitter over footage in another branch in your workspace. This image will not render out of the operator and is only a reference for editing particles over a background plate.

> **Note:** You will not see the background if the solid onto which the Particle operator is applied is not transparent.

Deflector

This category is only available when a deflector object is selected in the Workspace. To edit or animate a deflector, you can transform it as you would any object in combustion. You can also enable control point editing to edit/add/delete control points as you might a mask or vector paint object.

Library Presets as Starting Points

To demonstrate the ability to create custom particles, you will use a Workspace that contains presets which you can tweak, or change the particle appearance, and fine-tune the actions of these particles.

1. Open the file named *ch13_ParticleShapeSwap.cws*. Play the clip and you will see a simple animation created with a point emitter and a preset named Shoot Smoke. This emitter preset has one particle type spawning from it, named 'plumes'.
2. Expand the Workspace panel and select this 'plumes' particle type.
3. Switch the Particle Controls to the Shape category and then tap the Current button. This places the sprite used by the 'plumes' preset in the Shape preview window.
4. Click the Image > Import button seen in Figure 13.6.

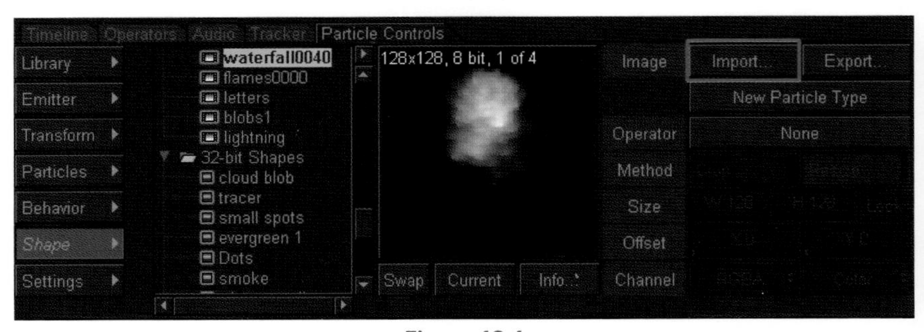

Figure 13.6

5 Navigate to the . . . _footage\sequences\directory and select the file named *butterfly_loop.mov*. You will be presented with a dialog that resembles Figure 13.7. This dialog has a few options for how you wish the incoming footage to be treated as a particle.

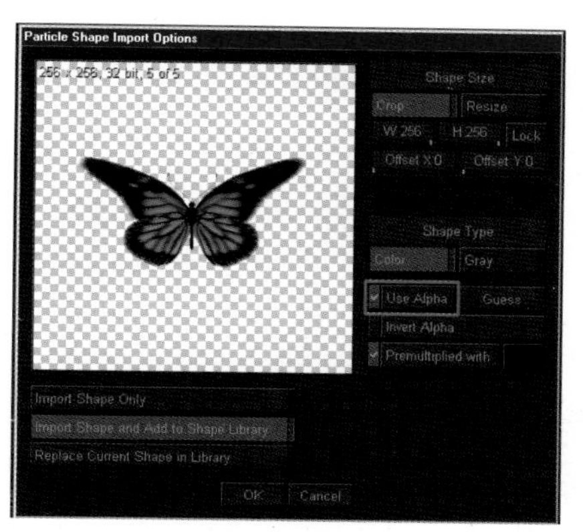

Figure 13.7

> **Tip:** In the case of a multi-frame sequence such as this, you can scrub the viewport to see the frames of the incoming sprite.

6 Select the Use Alpha option and click OK. The result is the butterfly sequence has been added to the shape library and has been put in the Shape preview window.

7 To actually make the switch, simply tap the Swap button under the preview window, and you will have butterflies where you previously had smoke.

8 Experiment with the Emitter, Particles and Behavior settings to tweak the appearance of the butterflies. Also, there are several 'Behavior Over Life' values that can be manipulated in the Graph mode of the Timeline. These affect the different particles over the course of their life in ways such as size, velocity, and so on.

There are a few additional ch13 Workspace files provided for your examination. One recommendation is to expand the Workspace panel of each and go through the settings for the different particle types.

Closing Tips for Particles

If you are not using the preview window, make sure it is disabled. This window uses up a good amount of processing power, whether or not you are using software or hardware OpenGL. If you have lots of particles and emitters in the viewport, this is the place you may end up fine-tuning the particles because you can isolate the different types.

You will often get better response from the OpenGL particles if you use a smaller size particle and zoom the particles up instead. This technically resamples them up, but often this slight loss of resolution is not noticeable and is well worth the trade-off for better performance.

Similarly, you can often have a 'give and take' of size and number of particles to get a very similar appearance, but with much faster playback. For example, size50/number100 might look the same as size100/number 50, but the latter will probably play and cache much faster.

If you have several Particle operators, emitters, and/or particle types in a shot, you can temporarily turn them off to concentrate on one at a time for better playback. Likewise, you can turn off particles while keyframing or tracking emitters to speed up the workflow.

If your OpenGL performance is poor, you can always just double click the layer or composite containing the particles and cache this to RAM like anything else. Instead of attempting to continuously redraw the particle operator in OpenGL, the particles will cache and then have real-time playback on weaker machines without high-quality OpenGL cards.

It is often recommended to use software OpenGL when *network-rendering* particle Workspaces on machines with different graphics cards. This is to ensure the particles bypass the hardware and draw the particles the same on all machines. Experiment with your network and graphics cards to determine what works best for your pipeline.

CHAPTER 14

RENDERING AND OUTPUT

AGH! – this entire process can get confusing pretty quickly. Organization of projects is, obviously, important throughout the entire process. Even so, for delivery to your target audience, all of these considerations would be for nothing if you didn't output your work in some manner or another.

Output Format Considerations

You should actually have a really good idea of your final delivery format prior to starting a project. For example, it would be terrible to do weeks of work at one resolution and the client then says, 'um . . . this was supposed to be a projected feature film, not a DVD'. Knowing your deliverable medium is critical to beginning a project in combustion. If you always work in DV, for example, then the decision is an easy one (or there is no variable whatsoever), but when you have multiple format considerations, and especially when you mix resolutions and frame rates of source material, you need to use caution and think ahead.

There really is no single answer to output considerations. There are so many delivery mediums available today including the Internet, CDROM, DVD, miniDV, BetacamSP, Digibeta, NTSC, PAL, HD (several flavors) and numerous types of film-resolution outputs. The best, brief advice I can give is to look at samples of projects similar to what your target output is going to be. Quite often, the delivery medium(s) will dictate what they 'want' with little room for interpretation. For example, NTSC DVDs are all 720 × 480 resolution at 29.97 fps and lower field dominance – period.

Render Dialog Window

When you are ready to finally output your project, you tell combustion to create or render 'flattened' raster files to the hard drive. These are typically the end result of the entire Process Tree for any given branch. You access the primary render dialog from the File menu, which then brings up the interface (Figure 14.1) for setting output options.

Output Settings

When you bring up the render dialog by selecting File > Render, combustion creates what are called **output nodes**. An output node is automatically placed

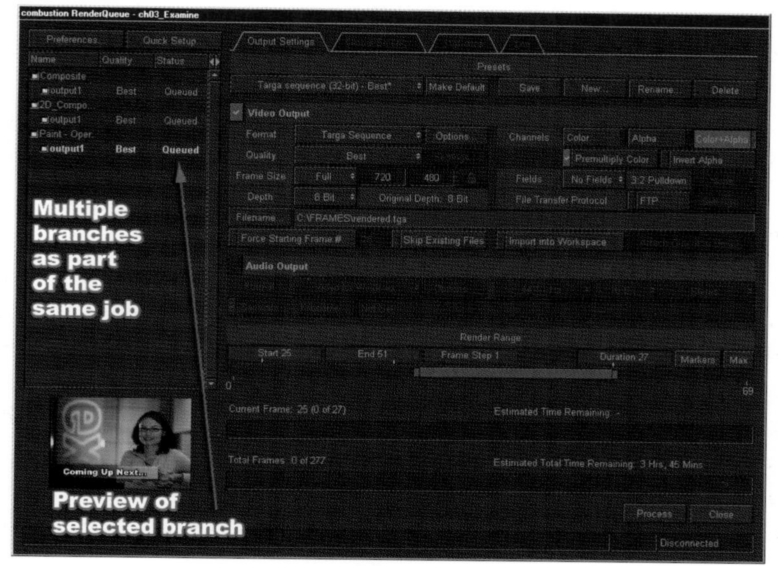

Figure 14.1

at the very end of the Process Tree of each unique branch. If you only have one branch in your Workspace, then there will only be one output node visible in the schematic, and also only one task will appear in the left area of the Render Dialog window.

As you can see on the left side of this example, there are currently three branches in this Workspace that are ready for rendering. These three branches can each have their own output settings and location on the network to store frames. However, this is all considered one render task to combustion (and to network rendering methods detailed in a moment). You can optionally disable render nodes by either turning them off in Schematic or by clicking on the small icon next to its name in the left portion of the Render dialog seen here. The right side of this dialog shows the settings for whichever output node is selected on the left.

Typically you want to render the end result but you can, however, add an output node at any point along the Process Tree. Say, for example, you wanted to render out just the alpha channel of one branch, setting an output node for that point is a simple undertaking. In the left side of the Render Dialog window, you can simply right click and choose to 'Add Operator' for another output node. As an alternative (and a more visual way of working), you can quickly switch to the Schematic View, right click on a node and select *Add Render Output* from the flyout menu. In this case, the choices made available in this flyout menu are pulled from the Preset list detailed below.

Tip: You can always assign any preset as an output node in Schematic, and then change all the output settings in the Render Dialog just prior to rendering.

Note: You can optionally have several outputs off the same node in a Workspace. Say you want to render a full DV version of a clip and also a smaller 320 × 240 version at 12 fps for client review on the Internet.

Presets Area – Along the top of the Output Settings tab is an area labeled 'Presets'. Here, you will find a drop-down list for accessing common output settings such as D1 NTSC, PAL DV, and so on. You can create your own, named custom presets simply by clicking the New . . . (New...) button and then providing a name for this preset. For example, 'Web 320 draft rez'. Then you can set up all the parameters, frame rates, file formats, codecs, etc. and ultimately return here and click the Save (Save) button. Render presets are written to an ASCII text file named *render queue.preset.*

Video Output Area – Here, you select the file format and codec, render quality (typically 'Best' for final work), color channels, field settings and frame size.

Fields – Should you render to fields? Ahh, this question again. Depending on who asked, you will undoubtedly get a different answer every time. For the most part, you should only render to fields if your work is going to be played back on an NTSC or PAL video monitor. Even then, some people prefer to render full frames (no fields) and let their non-linear application such as Avid do the field separation later. You should consult the manuals to the hardware you utilize for input and output to find what suits you best – and render some quick tests (of boxes quickly jumping around in paint) with different settings and look at the results to see which you like best.

Force Start Frame Number – When rendering image sequences, the numbering will be automatic and use the current time settings. For example, frame0001.tga, frame0002.tga, and so on. Setting this to a number will force the numbering of the first frame, for example frame0137.tga, frame0138.tga, etc.

Skip Existing Files – This option can be useful if you have previously rendered part of a segment and do not wish to re-render all the frames. This is also a critical option to check if you plan on using the Watch Folder method of network rendering. This will prevent all rendering computers from processing all frames (each).

Import into Workspace – When enabled, this option will bring the resulting rendered file(s) off the hard drive and into the current Workspace as footage. This footage will then be available both in the Footage Library and in the Schematic View.

Audio Output Area – If your project has an audio scratch track, you can choose to render your project without audio, render the audio to a separate file such as WAV or AIFF, or optionally embed the audio directly into a format such as MOV or AVI.

Render Range Area – This area allows you to specify the duration of a branch to be rendered. You can manually type in a frame range, or you can easily tap the Markers button (Markers) to snap the render range to the markers set back in the primary UI of combustion.

Process – To begin rendering locally on one computer, you simply click the Process button. An estimated time remaining will be provided for you to see how long until the current job is completed.

Tip: While it is obviously an intensive process, after you start a render you can launch another session of combustion on the same machine. This is only recommended if you plan on working on something that does not require intensive processing or caching (such as creating simple text for titles, etc.).

Global Settings

This is primarily used to set up network rendering options. Input and Output folders allow you to specify locations that rendering machines will look to read (input) and write (output) source footage. These can replace the paths set at the footage level of each source clip in the Workspace.

> **Tip:** If you know you are going to take advantage of network rendering, it is a good idea to get source materials from a shared location while building your projects. This will ensure that all computers see the same source material in the same way.

Statistics

This tab is where you can get information about the current render in progress and also all renders that are queued. When a project is actually rendering, the Statistics tab allows you to see information pertaining to the rendering task. Along the bottom of the combustion render window are an updating thumbnail and information about the progress of the current task. When a render is finished, this area will show information pertaining to the last frame rendered.

Log

The Log tab of the Render Dialog window displays information about the rendered jobs in the queue. These logs are only available for render jobs that have completed rendering. They are a summary of the task in question. These logs are also written to a text file that resides in the 'Renders' directory within the combustion installation folder.

Render to RAM

In addition to rendering files to the hard drive from File > Render, you also can access the Render to RAM from the File menu. Render to RAM allows you to cache a 'flattened' version of the contents of the active viewport. This can be especially usefully on longer projects or on systems with less memory than others (i.e. laptops).

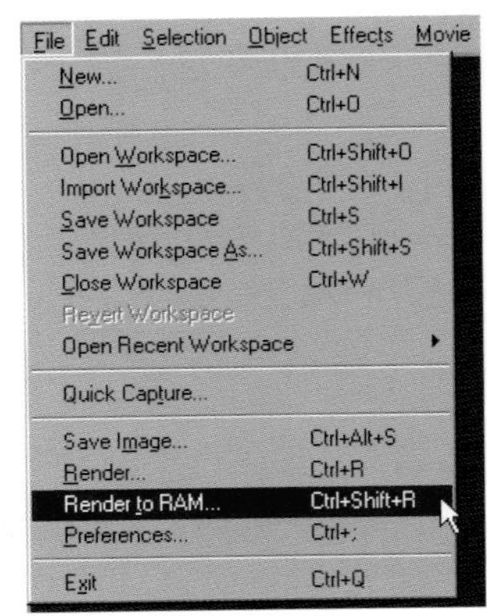

This feature is not actually intended for 'final' renders (but can be used for that purpose as well). It is, in fact, most useful while still in the creation phase of 'heavy' projects that require a lot of memory. Render to RAM allows you to get a feel for certain portions of a project and then, ultimately, render them to disk as actual files using the standard rendering procedure. Render to RAM is something you can do at any time in combustion.

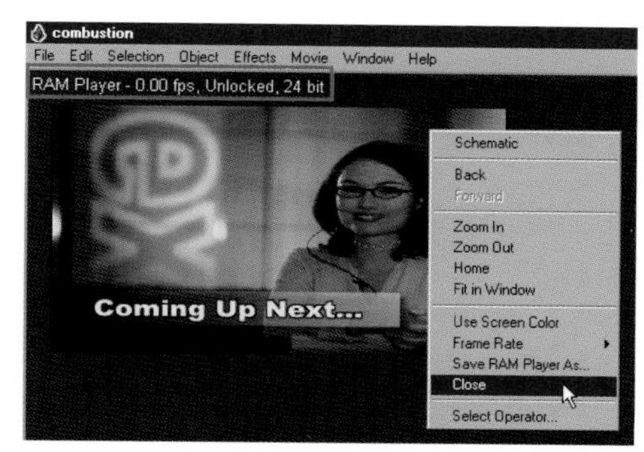

Figure 14.2

When a Render to RAM process is finished, it should be mentioned that the resulting viewport is a special case. This is a cached viewport of the flattened branch. Notice the name of the viewport in Figure 14.2.

Render to RAM created flattened, cached file in memory only. You can, however, save the contents of a Render to RAM viewport by *right* clicking on it and selecting *Save RAM Player As . . .* You can exit a RAM Player window by closing it or merely sending something else to this viewport (in which case the cached RAM player is lost).

Compare – The Compare within the Render to RAM dialog (Figure 14.3) is useful if you want to render the flattened contents of the current viewport to RAM, but also judge this against another node in the Workspace. For example, if you wanted to see a before and after of an image stabilization. This feature is identical in function to the Compare feature outlined in Chapter 7. This is just an option and is not required to use Render to RAM.

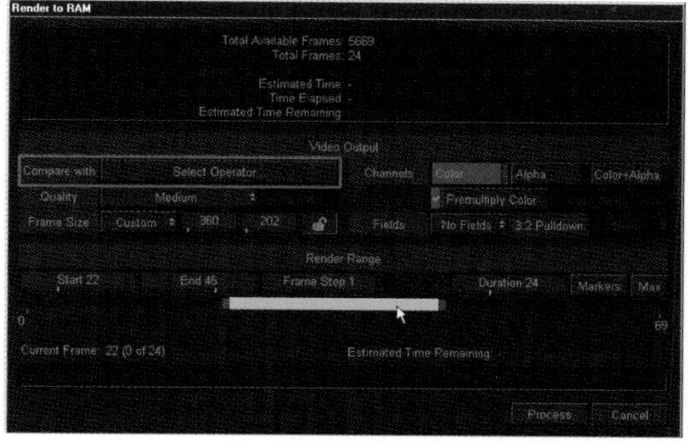

Figure 14.3

Tip: Render Range, Quality and Frame Size settings in the Render to RAM dialog are excellent ways to further optimize this feature. For example, you can be in the middle of building a huge project and, just before leaving for lunch, you can start a Render to RAM of a half-sized version that is limited to frames 128–387 at medium resolution.

Commit to Disk

The Commit to Disk feature of combustion can be accessed by right clicking on any operator in the Workspace. While this can either be done in a Schematic View or the Workspace panel, it is often easier to understand and visualize the process when viewing a Schematic View.

You now know that a non-destructive workflow means we can go back at any time and make changes. Caching was explained previously and you know that combustion caches all the outputs of a Workspace. But what if you feel that you are pretty happy with one part of the Workspace and wanted to cache only the end result of several nodes and not the entire chain of events?

Commit to Disk is an operation that is basically like Photoshop's 'flatten' feature. Instead of caching a series of operator output nodes, you can pick an output in the combustion Process Tree and render images to the hard drive that represent the end results of everything downstream from that output. This process works in conjunction with an operator called **Switcher** (found in the Channel category of operators). The Switcher's role is to flip between the rendered/flattened footage on the hard drive and also keep a wire to the original series of nodes (thus preserving the non-destructive nature of combustion's workflow). At any time, you can switch between the operator's input or the committed footage, if you desire.

1 To perform a Commit to Disk, open the file named *ch14_ComplexComp.cws.*

2 Switch to the Schematic View (F12) and fit the contents to the window by tapping the equals hotkey *twice*. You will end up with Figure 14.4.

As you can see, the node indicated here is a composite with several layers. After this point, several operators are used to 'treat' this composite with more effects.

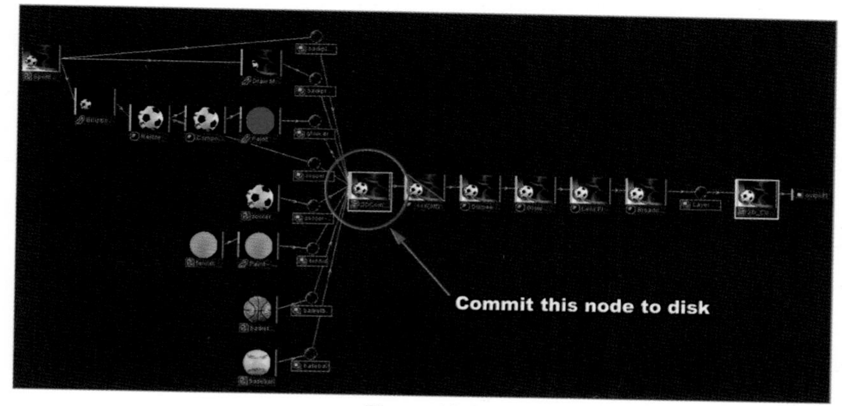

Figure 14.4

3 Right click on the Composite node indicated here and choose Commit to Disk from the flyout menu that appears. You will be presented with a rendering window similar to the primary render dialog. Set an output directory and use settings similar to those seen here:

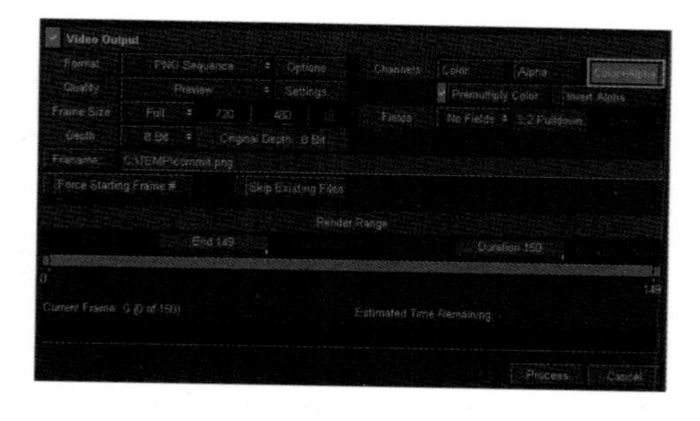

Tip: When you are committing to disk and are in doubt, always render frames as Color + Alpha. This will ensure there is an alpha channel if one is needed. PNG frames are used here because they are a file format that uses lossless compression.

4 Click the Process button and combustion will render all the elements up to that node as files to the hard drive location specified in step 3.

5 Once finished, notice the changes in the Schematic View. There is a **Switcher operator** now in the place of the node that you committed to disk. Figure 14.5 shows how the switcher is tied to both the original branch and also to the footage committed to disk.

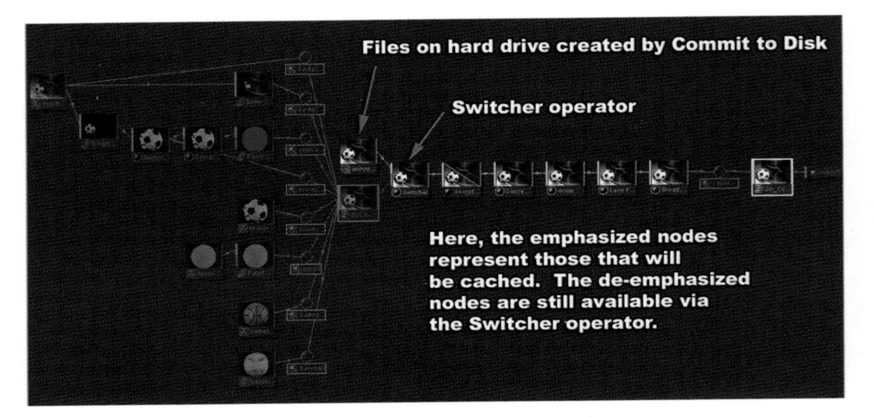

Figure 14.5

6 In the Workspace panel, expand the layer and select the operator named *Switcher*.

7 In the Switcher Controls now visible under the Playback Controls, toggle back and forth repeatedly between input 1 and input 2. Notice in the Schematic the primary and secondary input is getting flipped each time. Only the primary input will be cached, so if you have the new footage as the primary input, then you won't have to cache all the operators and footage still available in the secondary input. In this case, the secondary input does not actually do anything; in effect, it is just 'on standby'. Changes to the long chain of operators can either be recommitted, or you can just switch the longer chain of operators to become the primary input once again. It should be mentioned that switchers can have many secondary inputs on standby in this manner. You can add more by wiring them into the light blue secondary input bar in the Schematic View.

It is often a good idea to render Commit to Disk frames to the same directory for all projects. This is to keep track of the potentially vast number of frames you may generate using this procedure. Also, if you decide to network render, all rendering machines need to be able to access these frames as well. Alternatively just use Commit to Disk as a resource saving tool while building a large project, and then remove any reference to committed footage by deleting it from the Workspace and making the original operators and footage the only input to the Switcher.

Network Rendering with RenderQueue

Network rendering is possible on both Macintosh and Windows platforms through a simple system called the RenderQueue. Essentially, all rendering systems get combustion installed on them and you run an application called **render queue.EXE**. This application looks extremely similar to the render dialog within combustion, but it is a stand-alone application that looks for jobs in a location known as a Watch Folder. The Watch Folder must be a shared location on the network that all computers can 'see'. For each computer, you specify a folder to watch in the Preferences of the RenderQueue application.

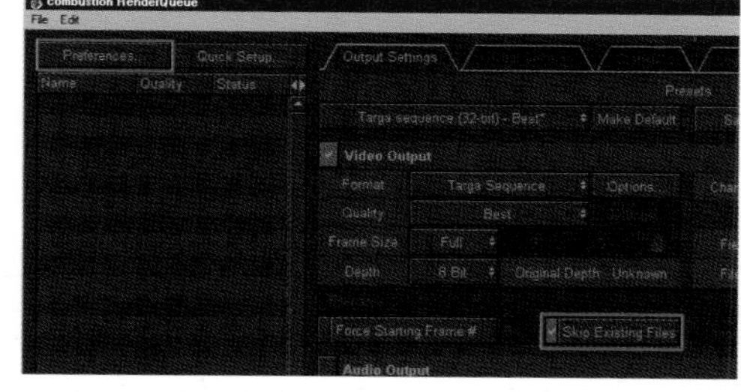

To use the RenderQueue method of network rendering:

1 Build a project as you normally would (or, for now, open one of the completed projects included with this book). You should, however, keep in mind that if you are going to network render on several machines, *all* source footage should be obtained from a location that all computers can access. For example:

Z:\SourceFootage\ClientABC\RawFootage\ . . .

2 Set the output settings in combustion Render Dialog. **For the RenderQueue method of network rendering to work properly, you *must* enable the option for Skip Existing Frames**. If you forget this step, all machines will render the entire job and you will end up wasting valuable network resources (and lose production time). Also, the output location needs to be a location that is shared and accessible to all computers. For example:

Q:\Output\ClientABC\rough_drafts\ . . .

3. Save the finished, unrendered CWS project file somewhere on your computer network.

4. When you want this job to begin network rendering, you simply copy this CWS file into the Watch Folder. Any machine on your network that is running RenderQueue and has this location set as their Watch Folder will begin rendering the jobs, including all active render output nodes within that Workspace.

Discreet Backburner

The Windows version of combustion ships with a powerful, client-server network rendering system called Backburner. On a default installation, Backburner can be found in the 'Discreet' folder of installed applications on your computer. They can be accessed via the Start menu of Windows.

Backburner is, in itself, three small applications that can run on one or several networked computers. All three Backburner applications are stand-alone programs that are task management software. **None of them do the actual rendering themselves**. All Backburner does is talk to other software applications and dish out tasks for them to do. Two graphics software applications that Backburner can control are Discreet 3ds max and combustion. Backburner can also be used by Discreet Burn to process Flame tasks offline on inexpensive Linux computers. You will hear more of Backburner in years to come for sure.

Setting up Backburner is usually a one-time operation and does not require rocket science or any practice of voodoo mumbo jumbo. It's really a snap and the benefits are phenomenal. Do not let the intimidation of dealing with networks stop you from using this incredible tool for productivity. I cannot say enough about Backburner and how it integrates a production pipeline.

Manager.EXE – This is the grand master control of Backburner and the shepherd of the farm. This application only needs to run on a single computer and it controls the entire render farm. This application does not require a lot of memory to run. Remember, Backburner is only task management software. It is combustion that will be doing the actual rendering.

```
backburner Manager
File Edit View Help
INF  Starting Network Manager
INF  Loading plugin: 3ds max 6.0 renderer plugin
INF  Loading plugin: combustion 3.0 render plugin
INF  Successful registration from stable
INF  Successful registration from gmd laptop
INF  Successful registration from bulldog
INF  New client 192.168.1.102 added to client list
INF  Job backplate test added to the queue
INF  Sending backplate test instructions to stable
INF  Sending backplate test instructions to gmd laptop
INF  stable completed 1 task(s)
INF  stable completed 1 task(s)
INF  stable completed 1 task(s)
INF  gmd laptop completed 1 task(s)
INF  gmd laptop completed 1 task(s)
INF  stable completed 32 task(s)
INF  gmd laptop completed 1 task(s)
WRN  Server gmd laptop going down
ERR  Job backplate test (combustion 3.0) failed for gmd laptop
ERR  Error message: Server going down
WRN  Server gmd laptop flagged as failed for job backplate test
Ready                                              Manager  11:54:28
```

Figure 14.6

Figure 14.6 shows the Manager application running. Here, you can see that the Manager application is dishing out frames to render to combustion. You can also see that I have three machines that immediately connected and started rendering. You typically do not need to watch this window, as most of the things you would find of interest here could best be looked at and edited from the Monitor application (described below).

Server.EXE – This is the application that needs to run *on each machine* in the farm that is going to render. This is the application that talks back to the Manager and says, 'Hello there, Manager, I'm ready to render some frames. You have anything for me to do?'

```
backburner Server - backplate_test
File Edit View Help
INF  Starting backburner Server
INF  Loading plugin: 3ds max 6.0 renderer plugin
INF  Loading plugin: combustion 3.0 render plugin
INF  Looking for a manager using 192.168.1.255:3234
INF  Registration to 192.168.1.102 accepted
INF  Receiving new job from 192.168.1.102
INF  Job backplate test received and ready
INF  Launching combustion 3.0
INF  New task assigned: 1
INF  Block of 1 task(s) completed
INF  New task assigned: 2
INF  Block of 1 task(s) completed
INF  New task assigned: 3
INF  Block of 1 task(s) completed
INF  New block of 32 tasks assigned
Ready                                              Server  11:53:35
```

It should be mentioned that combustion will also need to be installed on every computer that is going to be a render server (aka 'render slave'). These installs, however, don't need to be authorized and can be minimal installs.

If you arrive to work, a machine is rendering and someone needs that particular computer to go about his or her regular tasks, just stop Server.EXE from running on that machine. That single computer will stop rendering and you can use it for other things. However, the render queue will still be running and the rest of the rendering computers will pick up the slack. To resume the rendering on that computer, the user merely needs to launch their Server.EXE with a double click, and walk away. The user needs to know nothing about graphics, networks, video or anything else. If someone can check email, they can handle this small task.

Monitor.EXE – This application has several great features. It is basically a front end or GUI to the Manager. However, this application can be run on any machine on the network to monitor the render queue. You don't necessarily have to run Monitor on the same machine as Manager. This means from anywhere in the facility, anyone can launch Monitor on their computer to see the progress of the render farm. Once connected to the Manager application, Monitor can get valuable information pertaining to all the jobs in the render queue. Examples include the speed of each machine, which jobs are done, currently rendering and next in line, and which machines rendered which frames.

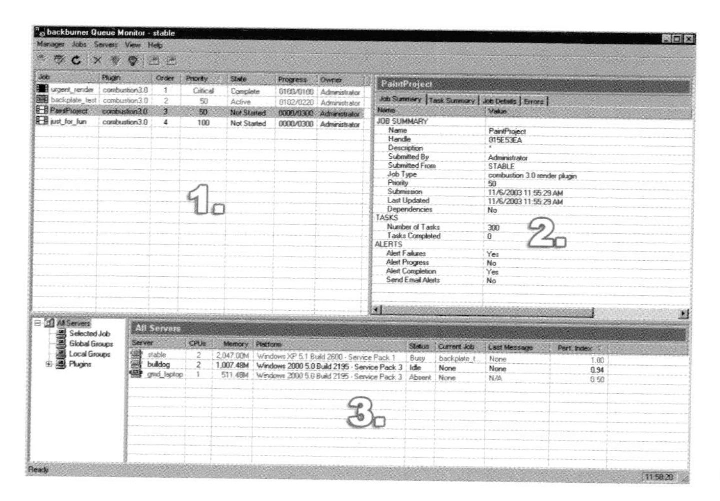

Figure 14.7

Assuming nobody on the network is running Monitor, the first time it is run will create the *controlling* Monitor. From this unique machine, the queue can not only merely be looked at, but you can also do things like stop and start jobs. After one person has launched Monitor and has 'control' of the queue, anyone else that launches Monitor on their computer will only be able to look at this information, but not make changes to the queue. For this reason, it is often wise to have the lead artist or technician be the one running the controlling monitor. Figure 14.7 is the Monitor application interface. You can see that it is broken up into three main areas.

1 The first is the actual queue in all its glory. Here you can see what jobs are rendering, the order they are going to render, etc. If you are in control of the queue on your system, you can also do things like reprioritize jobs, turn jobs on and off, and delete jobs from the queue. When you are in control of the queue, most of the commands to do these tasks are in the *right click* menus. One of the right click menus to investigate is called the Column Chooser. Here, you can determine what specific information will be viewed in area 1.

2 The second area of the UI is where you can see data about the *individual task selected* in area 1. In the above example, the job currently selected is named *PaintProject*. Information about this job is visible in area 2. Examples of information gathered here include which machine is rendering which frames, where the frames are being saved, and how long frames are taking to render. Note that this selected job has not even started rendering. The job actually rendering at the moment is named *backplate_test*.

3 The third and last main part of the UI is where you can see information about each of the machines on the network that can potentially render. The last column called Performance index was added from the right click menu Column Chooser. The Performance index is where you can gauge the speed of your individual systems on the render farm. A Performance index of 1.0 is the fastest machine overall on your network. The rest will be a decimal value that represents a percentage of speed to the fastest. In the above example, my laptop is 50% as fast as my best workstation. It can be good to know which machines are doing how much work, and this is the easiest, single way to check. If two identical hardware configured machines are drastically different in speed, then you should investigate why. The right click menus allow you to access the Column Chooser in this area of the UI as well. Here, you can determine what specific information will be viewed in area 3.

Note: Whether you network render with RenderQueue or Backburner, to use multiple computers for rendering one job requires that you render a sequence of frames and not an MOV or AVI file. This is because multiple computers cannot create an MOV or AVI at the same time.

For more information about the numerous advantages to network rendering and Backburner, check out 'Down on the Farm'. This document details specifics about setting up your network, how to shop for render machines, advantages of network rendering and even presents hypothetical scenarios outlining a few different studio workflows. There are also details about the pros and cons of various file formats when using network rendering. This 23-page white paper can be found at http://www.visualZ.com/free/Down_on_the_Farm.pdf.

Outputting your work is an important last step that should not be an afterthought. When building any project, you should be aware of how it will be presented to the viewer and take the necessary steps to ensure that the delivery format accommodates any and all the artwork you create within Discreet combustion.

APPENDIX I

FILE SIZES AND FORMATS

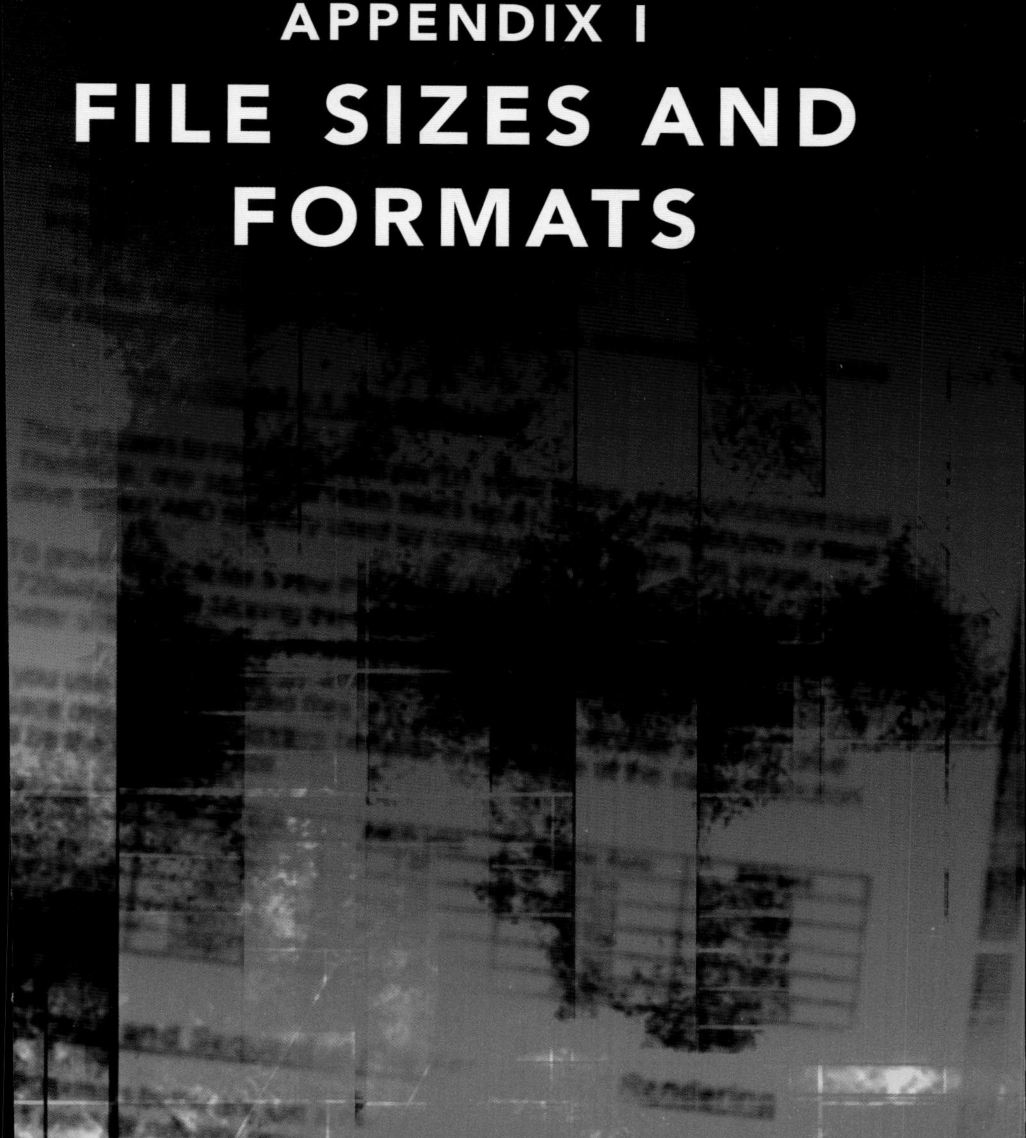

Caching and File Sizes

To calculate the uncompressed file size of an image, you multiply the image height by the width, and then multiply that result by the number of color channels in the image:

$$\text{Uncompressed size} = (\text{image width}) \times (\text{image height}) \times (\text{number of color channels})$$

Note: The last variable (number of color channels) is typically three (RGB) or four (RGBA), depending on if you have an embedded alpha channel in the image or not.

Using the equation on a single D1 NTSC frame, you can see the following result:

$720 \times 486 \times 4 = 1\,399\,680$ bytes.

This equates to roughly 1.4 Mb per frame *when uncompressed*. Therefore, one second of D1 NTSC video takes up 41 990 400 megabytes of hard drive space *and* memory used by combustion to cache this image.

To prove this, create a new Paint branch that is 30 frames, D1 (720 × 486). After tapping the spacebar to begin caching, the cache meter should read 41.1 Mb after playing through once.

If you use uncompressed files, it is very easy to calculate the hard drive space needed to do renders because every frame of the same resolution will be the same file size.

Format	Image size	Mb/frame	Frame rate	Mb/sec
NTSC D1	720 × 486	1.40	30 fps	42.0
PAL D1	720 × 576	1.66	25 fps	41.5
HDTV 720i	1280 × 720	3.69	30 fps	110.7
HDTV 1080p	1920 × 1080	8.29	24 fps	198.9
Film, 2K	2048 × 1556	12.75	24 fps	344.25

Note: Files like Maya IFF and 3ds max RPF can optionally contain extra channels beyond RGBA. These extra channels can be used for numerous effects that are beyond the scope of this introduction to combustion.

Still Image and Sequential File Formats for Rendering

The file formats below are just a few of the more common image file formats used for network rendering. There are certainly more file formats such as IFF, PICT, TIF, SGI and others, but this list provides some information about the more common formats.

TGA – 'Targa'

Pros – This format can most likely be read by any graphics application you will come across. It is extremely cross platform. Targa files can optionally have embedded alpha channels and/or be compressed.

Cons – I have experienced occasional problems when using compressed TGA files in some applications (I do, however, know others who do this all the time without issues). You will need plenty of hard drive space if you use Targa files, especially if you use the feature known as 'Render Elements' in 3ds max.

JPG – (aka JPEG)

This format was made popular by a little thing called the Internet. However, these are widely used in every field of computer graphics. I think far too many people fear JPG compression. JPG at their highest compression look darn good and, to the naked eye (at video resolution), look perfect. I don't care what anybody says about them. If you don't need an alpha channel, JPG files at maximum quality look great if you are hurting for drive space.

Pros – They can be very small because they can be compressed. The user controls the quality of the compression. Nearly every application can read them and they are widely cross platform.

Cons – The compression algorithms used by JPGs, even at 100% quality, are considered a 'lossy' compression. You are technically losing quality and if you later compile to MOV or AVI, you are going through yet another compression stage. JPG cannot contain alpha channels. If you are going to do any blue- or green-screen chroma keying in your project, avoid JPG files on the chroma key footage. In this case avoid JPG compression.

PNG – Portable Network Graphic (aka 'Ping')

This format was created initially as an alternative format for use on the web, but I have been using it recently for almost all my network rendering.

Pros – These files are compressed in file size, but they use a *lossless* compression algorithm. Quite often they are much smaller than JPG files yet lose no quality! They can optionally be up to 16 bits of color per pixel (aka 48-bit color space) for when you might be working with very high-resolution output to film scanners. If you are working with video, you only need 8 bits of color per channel. These would be 24-bit color or 32-bit total color if you include an alpha channel. More and more often, higher color space is used, especially in the motion picture industry.

Cons – Not all applications can read and/or write PNG files. It's a good idea to check your editing system and any film recording facility if you plan on using these files. Make sure your favorite applications can read these.

CIN – 'Cineon'

Pros – Widely recognized as the format for the motion picture industry. Analog film scanners typically output *.CIN files. This format has 10 bits of color per pixel (30-bit color space).

Cons – These files cannot contain an alpha channel. Cineon files are often difficult to deal with due to a color conversion known as Look Up Tables (or 'LUTs'). Most NTSC displays and VGA monitors can't show this much color without applying some form of LUT. Dealing with logarithmic and linear LUTs can be difficult and shall not be discussed here. If you were planning on doing work for a feature film, it would pay to research this and/or discuss it with someone who has used this format for digital postproduction.

RPF and RLA – Rich Pixel Format

Many 3D applications can now write out RLA files. This is a format invented years go by Wavefront that has additional information beyond RGBA. The newer RPF format is a derivative of the RLA and can optionally contain even more great stuff. Discreet 3ds max and combustion currently share a special link, because they are the only two applications that can truly take advantage of every channel contained in an RPF file. Please consult your documentation for additional information regarding the integration of these software products.

Pros – In addition to the typical RGBA information contained in an image, these files can contain metadata such as Z-depth, pixel velocity, material and object effects channels, to name a few. These images can be much higher bit depth than the typical 8 bits of color per channel.

Cons – These individual files are often extremely large. The use of RPF and RLA files often require a deeper understanding of both your 3D software and combustion to fully take advantage of the extra data. A strong coordination between the 3D animator and the compositor is often needed (but when that's the same person, no problem!). RLA files from different 3D applications behave differently.

Single File, Multi-Frame Image Formats

The file types below are just a few file formats that exist today that are a single file on your hard drive, yet they can contain hundreds or even thousands of frames of video or animation. These files are often easier to manage on your system because a single file represents so much information, but quite often they are actually slower than individual, sequential files when used in animation programs such as 3ds max and combustion. This is because, unlike sequential files, these files need to be 'read into' on every frame if you are, for example, using them as a texture map or as a layer in a composite. This is not to say you should never use them as texture maps, etc. – but be aware they are often slowing you down to do so. This is quite often a negligible or even indistinguishable difference, however. Do some tests. Unlike animation software, most non-linear editing systems will, however, work faster with these files *if* they are in the native codec for that particular editing system.

AVI – Audio Video Interleaf (aka Interleave or 'Video for Windows')

Pros – Many different flavors or 'codecs' for different output applications from CDROM playback, web delivery and broadcast. They can also be uncompressed. DivX is a new AVI codec that encodes very fast, creates a small file size and looks real nice. DivX is not intended for broadcast but is great for web, emails, and client reviews – www.divx.com.

> **Note:** This needs to be installed on every machine for files to read. I suggest Cinepak AVI files for playback on any PC worldwide.

Cons – Can only be created by one machine at a time. Cannot have alpha channels. PC only (however, I've heard some Macintosh applications can now read and even write AVI files). Not ideal for network rendering. Must make sure every machine has the same version of different types of codecs installed to access these files.

MOV – QuickTime

Pros – Widely used in the video production field. Cross platform. Many different codecs for different output applications from CDROM playback, web delivery to broadcast. They can also be uncompressed and optionally contain an alpha channel. This is confusingly named 'Millions of Colors +' (note the + character that indicates alpha channels). Many non-linear editing systems can output a software codec MOV file that can be read by any computer for postproduction and FX work. One example is the Avid Meridian Uncompressed format of MOV.

Cons – Can only be created by one machine at a time. Not ideal for network rendering. Must make sure every machine has the same version of different types of QuickTime installed.

MPG – aka MPEG

Pros – Highly compressed files that look very good. There are several basic types of MPEG files. 'Type II' MPEG files can be broadcast quality and are 720 × 480. This is what you need to burn DVDs. Discreet Cleaner is great software for creating these files. MPEG type I files are half as small in each pixel dimension (for a quarter total image size smaller) and are good for client review and web purposes. MPEG 4 is gaining popularity fast.

Cons – You typically don't edit MPEG files. They are often highly compressed and should be considered the 'end result' of your projects. You currently can't render MPEG files out of combustion or 3ds max and you should not want to anyway. Again, they can look good playing back, but are typically very compressed files.

Notes: If you are ever in doubt about what format to use or if another facility can read them into their pipeline, I suggest using uncompressed TGA (Targa) files. They are the 'Fender Stratocaster' of the animation file formats. That is they haven't changed in years and still rock the house no matter what project you are working on. They could be thought of as the Old Faithful of image file formats.

I typically work with PNG files back and forth between 3ds max and combustion, but ultimately output final work as uncompressed Targa files. These files can be given to any non-linear editing system made today. Compiling work to uncompressed MOV or AVI is also good for final work. These are just a few ways of working. Remember, your workflow may be totally different and work well for you.

Different hardware editing systems will allow different file types to play in real time, but you should still consider network rendering individual frames and *then* compiling them to your editing system codec.

For further information on file formats and LUTs, I highly recommend Ron Brinkmann's book titled *The Art and Science of Digital Compositing* from Morgan Kaufman Publishing.

APPENDIX II

GLOSSARY/ INDEX OF COMBUSTION TERMINOLOGY

24p This is the term commonly used to describe a frame rate used in films. This means 24 frames per second in progressive (p) mode.

3:2 Pull Down This is a process that changes frame rates. Typically, one converts the common film rate of 24 frames per second to and from 25 or 30 frames per second of PAL or NTSC video, respectively. This process can also add or remove video fields to images.

Alpha Channel An alpha channel is a grayscale image that represents values of transparency. This information is often embedded in the file along with the red, green and blue color information channels. In combustion, pure black is transparent (0% opacity) and pure white is fully opaque (100% opacity). Any values of gray are somewhere, proportionately, in between. An alpha channel is often called a matte and can easily be created or manipulated using keyers, the Paint operator and/or masking tools.

Anamorphic Has a variety of applications in the film and video world, but in combustion it typically identifies a piece of footage or a composite that is of a wide aspect ratio. This often is accompanied by a non-square pixel aspect ratio. HD is 16 × 9, or 1.77 to 1 aspect, and often referred to as anamorphic. Likewise, many feature films are 1.85 to 1 or even 2.35 to 1 anamorphic wide screen images of different resolution.

Aspect Ratio This is the relationship of width to height in an image. An image that is 640 × 480 is a common 4 × 3, 4:3 or 'four by three'. An aspect ratio can be thought of as a fraction, so that four by three is actually 4/3 = image aspect ratio of 1.3333. Also see Pixel Aspect Ratio.

Bit Depth The amount of color information something contains. Within combustion, you can work in 8, 10, 12, 16 or float bit depths at any given time. In combustion's language, an 8-bit image can use 16.7 million available colors, or (256 reds) × (256 greens) × (256 blues). An 8-bit grayscale image such as an alpha channel can have up to 256 levels of luminance from black to white.

Branches A term that describes the flow of (multiple) operators that are applied to a piece of footage in a certain order of processing. With an empty Workspace, if you select File > New > Paint three different times, you have three branches in your Workspace. These could be joined into one branch by nesting them all into a single composite as layers.

Composites This is where you create complex combinations of images as layers. 2D composites merely stack layers on top of each other, while 3D composites can transform layers in a space. 3D composites can also include lights and a camera.

Compound . . . Several operators begin with the name 'compound'. Examples include Compound Blur and Compound Channel Selection. Very simply put, what a Compound operator does is take information from one source and apply an effect of some kind to another source elsewhere in the Workspace.

CWS combustion workspace. See Workspace.

Fields In the world of PAL and NTSC video hardware, images are often broken down into 'upper' and 'lower' dominant images. Fields are used to help smooth the motion of objects in video and animation intended for playback on video equipment (as opposed to multimedia playback off a computer, for example).

Footage Can either be a solid created within combustion, or images on the hard drive (such as AVI, MOV, TGA, JPG, etc.). Footage can hold a frame rate, duration, pixel size (width × height) and can have field interpolation for use with video equipment.

Footage Library Contains all the 'raw' elements within the CWS. These are not necessarily visible in the currently viewed branch or composite. This area can almost be considered the entire Workspace's 'bin'.

FPS Frames per second. Something that is '24P' is 24 frames per second. Often in NTSC video, 30 fps is the shorthand for a broadcast standard of 29.97 fps. This fractional difference is to accommodate audio synchronization on video hardware. Interlaced video that is shot at 30 fps actually captured 60 *fields* per second due to the two fields for every frame.

Groups Groups of vector objects can only be created within a *paint* branch. To 'group' Layers in a Composite, you use Nesting (below).

HD and HDTV High definition images. There are several different flavors of HD, including 720/30p and 1080/24p. The first number represents the pixel size of an image in height and the second number is the frame rate of the footage. The 'p' indicates progressive, as opposed to interlaced frames. For example, the higher resolution of the two is 1920 × 1080 at 24 progressive frames per second.

HSL Hue, Saturation, Lightness. This is one of the color spaces that combustion can often work.

Instances An instance of something means that it is repeated and used again elsewhere in your Workspace. Instances are like copies but they are not separate. That is, changes made to one will also be made to the other(s). They are 'the same', not just copies. Items with names in italics are instanced.

Interlace/Interleaf The term(s) that can describe footage that contains field separation. You might hear these interchanged depending on the vendor or person. For television, most studios use field separation/acquisition when shooting or generating their clips for broadcast. Opposite = Progressive.

Keyframe This is not only the 'how much', but is also the 'when' of any value that changes over time. There are several different methods of interpolation between keyframes in combustion. Keyframes can be viewed and edited in the Timeline. The easiest way to create keyframes is to enable the Animate button at any time.

Layer An element within a composite. Layers are usually the end result of branches containing operators applied to one piece of footage. Layers hold transformations (move/rotate/scale/etc.) and can have transfer modes applied. By default, in the Schematic View, a layer is represented by a round circle and should look different to composites, operators, and footage. A layer is always rasterized and never a vector.

Luma Keying A process similar to chroma keying, but instead of creating an alpha channel (matte) based on color values, it eliminates pixels based on how dark they are.

Luminance The brightness level of a pixel. In the HSL color space, the L is for luminance.

LUTs/Look Up Tables – Simply put, an LUT is an way of representing one color space in another manner.

Mask Often synonymous with matte. Within combustion, this is a vector object or series of objects that isolate portions and image to show through. They are typically used to generate or edit an alpha channel in some way.

Matte An image that represents the transparency information of another piece of footage. Used loosely, this is often another term for the alpha channel embedded in an image or the result of the keying process.

Nesting Nested composites can have one or multiple layers (at least one of which is a 'group' of independent layers and/or operators to act as one layer). The output of a nested composite can be a single layer within a whole new composite. This is a *very* important concept for complex work in Discreet combustion.

Node/Node Based This is a general term for the iconic method of compositing. The Schematic View is a node-based system of working. Other compositing applications such as Flame and Digital Fusion are also node-based systems. In combustion, items are often called nodes because of the Process Tree.

Non-Destructive Any process or step can be edited at any time. You can 'go back' at any time, make changes and the changes will be reflected 'downstream'.

NTSC National Television Standards Committee. This is the video standard used in North America as well as other parts of the world, depending on broadcast standards acceptance. NTSC is a smaller frame than PAL, but has a higher frame rate of 29.97 frames per second.

Operator An effects process of any kind is applied through the use of operators. Examples include such familiar effects as blurring, painting, masking, chroma keying and color correcting. Third-party plugins to combustion are applied as operators.

Paint combustion has a very special operator simply called Paint. This is arguably half of the power of the entire application. Objects created in Paint can be animated and are always non-destructive (to use a Photoshop term, they are never 'flattened'). You should get to know the Paint operator no matter what you use combustion for. It can be extremely handy to have a built-in, full blown Paint application within a compositing environment.

PAL Phase Alternate by Line. This is a video standard common throughout Europe and in many parts of Asia. This has a larger image than NTSC, but a slower frame rate of 25 frames per second.

Pixel A single element of color information. In combustion, all spatial measurements are made in pixels, never inches, dpi or centimeters.

Pixel Aspect This is a number that represents the aspect of width to height of each pixel in an image. In a 'square pixel' image, the pixel aspect is 1.0 or 'one to one'. Two images might contain the same number of pixels, but the pixel aspect ratio can cause them to be viewed differently by different hardware and monitors. For example, an image that is 720 × 480 with a pixel aspect of 0.9 is a common format for DV. The pixel aspect of 0.9 causes these images to have an aspect ratio of 4 × 3; the same DV image with a 1.2 pixel aspect ratio will be anamorphic and have a 16 × 9 image aspect ratio.

Plate A term often referring to a background. Plate can also describe raw unedited footage as shot by a real-world camera.

Process Tree All the branches in a current Workspace make up the Process Tree.

Progressive The term often used to describe an image that does not contain field separation for video hardware devices. This is a full frame that, if paused on a broadcast video monitor, would not contain the jitter commonly seen in fast-passed clips shot with field separation. Opposite = Interleaved.

Proxy A lower resolution stand-in for a piece of footage. Using proxies makes combustion cache faster and use less memory. Discreet combustion can render proxies within the application at any time, hardly slowing the work process. When roughing out a composite containing numerous and/or extremely high-resolution images, taking advantage of proxies can be a great time saver.

Resolution In combustion, this only refers to raw pixel dimensions of width and height (typically in that order). Nowhere in combustion will you see the measurement of inches, centimeters, or dots per inch (DPI) representing resolution. Since combustion was primarily designed for film and video, the spatial measurements of this type are irrelevant. Think for a moment if you play a video on a small TV or a large one – they both have the same number of pixels, but one is spatially bigger. This might be the case, but they are, however, the same resolution in pixel dimensions.

RGB Red, Green, Blue. This is the primary color space that combustion uses. Depending on the bit depth, the range of each value, when mixed with others, represents the complete digital spectrum.

RGBA Red, green, blue and alpha channels.

Roto or Rotoscope In traditional animation, this is often the name of the process of tracing a live-action plate to create realistic motion in animation. In computer graphics, this is often a generalized term for things done manually frame by frame.

Schematic A 'node' or graphical, icon-based viewer of the entire Workspace. This shows the flow of operators made to footage in the Workspace. The schematic viewer does *not* show hierarchies of layers, vector objects occurring within a Paint operator, or any information about things occurring in 3D space. It tells nothing about animation or keyframes. It only shows the flow of operators applied to footage, and how layers go into composites. You might best think of the Schematic as a river of Effects operations, and the end result is what typically represents that particular branch (layer) of the flow of the project.

Solid A piece of footage that is nothing but a color 'placeholder'. This can hold a few basic statistics for a layer such as duration, frame size/rate and bit depth. A solid is often created (just) to be a source on which operators work their magic.

Sprite A 2D image mapped onto a rectangular shape that, in turn, always 'faces' the viewer. In combustion, the Particle operator uses sprite technology to simulate complex patterns in an extremely efficient manner.

Telecine This is the term often used to describe the process (or the actual machine) that changes film's frame rates to video frame rates. For example, film footage shot at 24 fps might be converted via a telecine to 30 fps so that video equipment can display it at the native frame rate.

Timeline Panel This is where you edit and view keyframes of animation.

Overview Mode – For animation editing, this is 'the big picture'. Here, you typically see and edit *when* (on what frame) something happens, but not how much (value).

Graph Mode – For animation editing, this is the 'nitty-gritty'. Here you typically edit both *when* (on what frame) something happens, and also *how much* (values).

Transfer Modes Different ways of displaying paint objects or layers so that items 'below' show through in different fashions. The default is 'normal' but others exist such as Add, Soft Light, Negative and Screen. A layer's transfer mode cannot be viewed when the viewport is in a Layer view. You must view a composite to see the effects of different layers' transfer modes.

Vector Objects These are mathematically created processes that are resolution independent. Unlike bitmap or raster objects, they will not lose resolution if they are scaled up past 100% size. In combustion, they are typically created within a Paint, Mask, or Selection operator.

Viewport The areas at the top of the UI where you view selections in the Workspace panel. This is also where the Schematic View can be displayed as well as the Footage Library viewer. It is extremely useful to utilize more than one viewport when working in combustion.

Workspace (*.CWS files) Contains all elements in the current session of combustion. Can be considered the current project running in combustion at any time. A combustion Workspace (*.CWS file) contains everything. This can be considered the project at hand. Although you can only have *one* workspace open at a time, this can include any number of branches, composites and operators.

Workspace Panel The tab bar that is docked next to Toolbar by default. This is often where you can build, rename, reorder and edit the elements in your project. In the Workspace panel, the icon that looks like a TV monitor identifies what is being displayed in the current viewport. The icon of an arrow pointing left identifies what parameters are currently being displayed at the bottom of the UI. You select items in the Workspace panel by clicking on the name of the item, not the icon to the left of its name. Clicking on the icons will turn off those items instead of selecting them.

YUV A color space often used by computer graphics and video applications.

Index